INTEGRATION OR SEPARATION?

Integration or Separation?

A STRATEGY FOR RACIAL EQUALITY

Roy L. Brooks

Harvard University Press
Cambridge, Massachusetts
London, England
1996

Library of Congress Cataloging-in-Publication Data
Brooks, Roy L. (Roy Lavon), 1950–
Integration or separation? : a strategy for racial equality /
Roy L. Brooks.
p.   cm.
Includes index.
ISBN 0-674-13295-5
1. Afro-Americans—Civil rights.   2. United States—
Race relations.   3. Black nationalism—United States.   I. Title.
E185.615.B729   1996
323.1′196073—dc20

96–16935
CIP

To George Cole, Joel Kupperman,
Wayne Shannon, and Arnold Taylor

Contents

Preface

Two persons—one white, the other black—are playing a game of poker. The game has been in progress for some 300 years. One player—the white one—has been cheating during much of this time, but now announces: "from this day forward, there will be a new game with new players and no more cheating." Hopeful but suspicious, the black player responds, "that's great. I've been waiting to hear you say that for 300 years. Let me ask you, what are you going to do with all those poker chips that you have stacked up on your side of the table all these years?" "Well," said the white player, somewhat bewildered by the question, "they are going to stay right here, of course." "That's unfair!" snaps the black player. "The new white player will benefit from your past cheating. Where's the equality in that?" "But you can't realistically expect me to redistribute the poker chips along racial lines when we are trying to move away from considerations of race and when the future offers no guarantees to anyone," insists the white player. "And surely," he continues, "redistributing the poker chips would punish individuals for something they did not do. Punish me, not the innocents!" Emotionally exhausted, the black player answers, "but the innocents will reap a racial windfall."

What to do about the American race problem? There is so much right and so much wrong on both sides of this conundrum. Perhaps there is no definitive solution to this, our longest running social and moral dilemma. Perhaps it is time to face such a possibility. As unthinkable as it is, that is the fundamental question raised in this book.

Part I argues that racial integration has failed to work for millions of African Americans, and that well-intended integrationists have got to awaken from their half-century's self-induced hypnotic trance and recognize that they are holding on to a tarnished trophy. Part II maintains that total racial separation, which had been tried in the past both at home and abroad and to which many middle-class African Americans as well as Louis Farrakhan, leader of the Nation of Islam, are looking for salvation, is mere racial romanticism and highly improbable. Finally, Part III advances the theory that cultural and economic integration within African American society—what I call "limited separation"—is the only remaining strategy to try. I believe it, in conjunction with racial integration, can resolve much of the American race problem. If I am wrong, however, then we may have to accept the unhappy fact that the American race problem is without a solution. We would then have to change our whole way of thinking about race relations in American society.

Some people will undoubtedly argue that some things are better left unexplored or unsaid, the unresolvability of the race problem being one of them. But for a scholar, unlike the politician, such evasions are unthinkable. The search for truth is what motivates the scholarly enterprise. I leave it to the reader to judge whether the political approach is more socially wholesome than the scholarly one. But for me, the issue is well settled: looking under rocks beats leaving stones unturned.

My limited support for racial separation may anger, offend, and, preferably, challenge my many liberal friends. I only hope they will suspend judgment long enough to understand the reasoning behind my views, to see the tissue—individual opportunity—that connects them. And I also hope they will answer certain questions: should African American children, whom integrated schools have failed, be denied opportunities for the sake of a policy? Isn't shackling African Americans to racial integration at any cost simply another form of slavery? Why should policy be placed before people?

If liberals are likely to loathe the idea of limited separation, conservatives may take issue with my underlying belief that the problems facing African Americans are not simply internal (that is, behavioral or cultural) but also external (that is, structural). While human capital deficiencies cannot be ignored, we cannot discount the importance of a level playing field. My position, then, is somewhere in the center on race relations, a place in which I am quite comfortable, even though caught in the crossfire.

Undoubtedly, there will be those on the right and the left who will misuse my words to score points in the ongoing racial wars. I can only say that as a scholar, one who searches for objective truths, I cannot always choose my traveling companions. I can only hope to convince a better crowd to come along.

᭜ Writing a book on a complex and controversial topic requires the assistance of a number of individuals. I begin with Kristine Strachan, my dean, who understood the magnitude of my project from the very beginning and stood by me as I consumed three teams of research assistants and extra office space over the five years it took to write this book.

My wonderful research assistants responded with good cheer to my many demands, which often sent them to libraries (some as far away as 150 miles) even on weekends. They are: Julie Vogelzang, Albert Delzeit, William Daniels, Sonia Lee, Esther Kim, Diana Krause-Leemon, Jilana Miller, Erica Jackson, Elizabeth Savage, Jon Bialecki, Leslie Hom, and Jennifer Parker. Students in my civil rights classes at University of San Diego Law School, University of Minnesota Law School, and University of Florida Law School were not afraid to debate the issues discussed in this book with me or among themselves. Their enthusiasm and dedication often carried our discussions well into the night. I am especially grateful to Roanne Shamsky, my secretary, who did an excellent job of typing and sorting out the numerous drafts and managing my research assistants. Finally, my editors at Harvard University Press, Lindsay Waters and Anita Safran, were simply superb.

I

RACIAL INTEGRATION

The nation's official civil rights policy since the Supreme Court's 1954 decision in *Brown v. Board of Education,* racial integration continues to enjoy great moral and political appeal in our society. Nowhere are the reasons for the attractiveness of this ideal expressed more powerfully than in a case decided by a Kansas court in the last century:

> At the common schools, where both sexes and all kinds of children mingle together, we have the great world in miniature; there they may learn human nature in all its phases, with all its emotions, passions and feelings, loves and hates, its hopes and fears, its impulses and sensibilities; there they may learn the secret springs of human actions, and the attractions and repulsions, which lend with irresistible force to particular lines of conduct. But on the other hand, persons by isolation may become strangers even in their own country; and by being strangers, will be of but little benefit either to themselves or to society. As a rule, people cannot afford to be ignorant of their society which surrounds them; and as all kinds of people must live together in the same society, it would seem to be better that all should be taught in the same schools.[1]

The strength of racial integration thus rests on "ideals of the essential dignity of the individual human being, of the fundamental equality of all [people], and of certain inalienable rights to freedom, justice, and fair opportunity."[2]

For all its moral and political appeal, however, racial integration has been an unsuccessful civil rights strategy. It has not helped most African Americans achieve racial equality, by which I mean individual dignity and empowerment in American society. Racial integration has failed to live up to its wonderful billing in numerous ways, starting with elementary and secondary education. For example, scores of public schools remain segregated four decades after *Brown*. The integrated schools, such as they are, have failed to fulfill *Brown*'s expectations of healthier self-esteem and racial esteem, of academic performance among African American students substantially equal to that of white students, and of better racial relations within public schools and in the larger society. In criticizing *Brown* I do not join those who would have us believe the Court's decision was the product of legal skulduggery. I only accuse the Court of inflated expectations. Moving on to higher education, African Americans' experience in predominantly white colleges and universities has been marked by similar disappointment, frustration, and anger. Enrollment by African Americans in predominantly white institutions is low and their attrition dreadfully high compared to white students. Racial tension is an everyday phenomenon.

Housing, employment, and voting come under scrutiny as well. There I argue that, from the "black ghetto" to the "black suburbs," residential segregation largely defines the housing experiences of African Americans under racial integration; this despite a variety of government efforts (such as the Gautreaux Program in Chicago) to create and maintain integrated housing. A great deal of housing segregation is driven by racial discrimination, especially in the home mortgage industry, which, because of fragmentation and specialization, may well be beyond the reach of the civil rights laws. Much of the same can be said about employment. While civil rights laws such as Title VII and affirmative action, along with better education, have substantially improved occupational status, income, and other employment experiences of many African Americans (especially African American women) in the last thirty years, they have not brought about the kind of progress African Americans or the nation as a whole had envisioned. This holds true even for the African American middle class, which faces discrimination and racism despite its socioeconomic success, but it is especially pronounced among the African American poor, many of whom have moved beyond being merely poor to being poverty stricken. Voting problems are perhaps even more formidable. While most African Americans are able to exercise the franchise, their votes still suffer dilution; consequently, they are denied effective political representation.

Having proffered proof of the failure of integration to generate racial equality—in the sense of individual dignity and empowerment—for most African Americans, I attempt to explain why racial integration has been so impotent. In the course of the discussion I primarily rely on the sociological concept of "white racism" crafted by Joe Feagin and Hernán Vera. They define white racism not simply as a state of mind (in other words, a belief system), but also as a state of being. White racism is less an avowed attempt by whites to hurt African Americans than an unconscious, self-perpetuating process of racial subordination. White racism, in short, is a racialized way of feeling, thinking, and behaving that emanates from the American culture at large and that is reinforced by schools, families, friends, and other microsocial entities.

By all accounts, the case against racial integration is quite substantial.

1

Elementary and Secondary Education

The integrationist impulse first came to fruition in our public elementary and secondary schools. Revolutionary in its reach and visionary in its promise, the ideal of integration changed the face of public education in America during the second half of the twentieth century. My discussion of the African American experience under this new order necessarily begins with the act of government that provided the mandate for integrated schools: the Supreme Court's 1954 decision in *Brown v. Board of Education.*[1]

By banning segregation in public schools, *Brown* sought nothing less than to use society's basic outposts of acculturation as the milieu in which African Americans and whites (indeed all races, ethnicities, and cultures) could be brought together for the kind of lateral transmission of values so eloquently articulated in *Ottawa v. Kansas* in 1881. While *Brown* has certainly provided a baseline benefit—it has, in other words, changed the legal status of African Americans from mere supplicants "seeking, pleading, begging to be treated as full-fledged members of the human race" to persons entitled to equal treatment under the law[2]—and while, in that sense, the ruling has delivered more than it has guaranteed, *Brown*'s promise of social transformation brought about by education remains unfulfilled some forty years after its tender. Worse than that, integrated elementary and secondary schools may in fact be doing more harm than good to the very group they intended to help most—African American children.

Historical Context

Public education in America began in schools that were both desegregated and integrated. In the 1640s the Massachusetts and Virginia colonies had no laws segregating African American and white pupils. African American children could attend public schools and were educated alongside white children. For the privilege of attending integrated schools, African American children paid a high price, however. Verbal and physical mistreatment from white teachers and pupils was part of the routine experience throughout colonial America. Under these conditions, the children could not obtain a decent education.[3]

Emboldened by the War of Independence, African Americans began to petition their local governments for separate schools. In 1787 Prince Hall, who had fought in the Revolutionary War, petitioned the Massachusetts legislature for an "African" school in Boston. The legislature rejected the petition, probably for reasons similar to those the Boston School Committee cited years later when it rejected a separation petition filed by Prince Hall's son, Primus Hall: integrated public schools adequately serve the educational needs of African American children; separate public schools are expensive to maintain; and if the government creates separate schools for African American children, German, French, and Irish parents will request separate schools to meet the special needs of their children.[4]

Finding no legislative redress, African American parents pulled their children out of integrated public schools and placed them in newly created separate private schools. These schools were supported financially by white philanthropists, who thought it best that African American children be taught by persons both sympathetic to and knowledgeable about their particular needs. The first African American private school was established in 1798 in Boston; the children were taught by a white teacher in the home of Primus Hall. Separate private schools did in fact provide African American children with a safe and supportive environment in which to learn, which is exactly what their parents had envisioned.[5]

But with private donations running out, African Americans turned once again to their local governments, this time for funds to support their private schools. After a period of time, public financial support for these private schools began to trickle in, eventually becoming quite substantial. The city of Boston, for example, began partial funding of private African American schools in 1818, and provided full funding of its own separate public school in 1820. This was some ten years before the modern system of public education (with state support and compulsory attendance) took shape throughout the nation.[6]

Public funding of African American schools did not, however, provide the type of education parents desired for their children. Students in these schools received a second-class education. The quality of the instruction and the condition of the facilities were poor. Many students were verbally abused, some were physically mistreated, and others were sexually assaulted by teachers and administrators.[7] This grim state of affairs resulted from a kind of Faustian bargain the African Americans parents did not know they had made with the city. In exchange for financial support, the parents ceded control of their schools to the city. The ultimate cost of this exchange was the miseducation of their children.

Another conversion of schools soon took place: they became segregated. African American and white children began to attend separate public schools not by choice but by law. African American schools, which were initially established by parental choice so as to provide a safe and supportive educational environment for their children (what are properly called *separate schools*), turned into African American schools established by law to subordinate and stigmatize these children (that is, *segregated schools*).

In time, African Americans began to believe that if the public schools were integrated, their children would stand a better chance of achieving a good education. The logic of this position was not that an African American child needed to capture a white child in order to obtain a quality education, but rather that educational resources, controlled by whites, were primarily committed to the white schools, and so that was the place to be. Furthermore, the presence of African American and white children in the same classroom would make it difficult even for the most racist whites to deny the former a decent education without also hurting their white classmates. These advocates of integrated schools had obviously forgotten about or perhaps discounted the racial abuse experienced by previous generations in integrated public schools.

Before public schools could be integrated, they had to be desegregated. Governmental constraints on where African American children could attend public schools had to be removed. The first lawsuit to desegregate a public school system was filed in a Massachusetts court under the name of *Roberts v. City of Boston*.[8] In upholding the reasonableness and hence the legality of school segregation in 1850, the state's highest court rejected the plaintiff's arguments that African American schools under a system of racial segregation were inconvenient to African American students, who often had to travel past white schools that were closer to attend a single-race school; unequal to white schools both in facilities and in personnel;

and psychologically harmful to African American and white children alike because they "tend to create a feeling of degradation in the blacks and of prejudice and uncharitableness in the whites."[9]

Following the adoption of the equality amendments to the Constitution between 1865 and 1870, the general issue presented in the Massachusetts case came before the Supreme Court in *Plessy v. Ferguson.*[10] In this 1896 decision, the Court upheld the constitutionality of racial segregation under the doctrine of separate-but-equal. Once again, the argument about lowered African American self-esteem was placed before a court of law and rejected. Responding to the "colored"[11] petitioner's claim that Louisiana's statute requiring the separation of the races in railway coaches within the state "stamps the colored race with a badge of inferiority"[12] and thereby damages its self-esteem, the Supreme Court said: "If this be so, it is not by reason of anything found in the act, but solely because the colored race chooses to put that construction upon it."[13] Like the Massachusetts court, the Supreme Court failed to grasp that, in the absence of mediating institutions (such as family and church), segregation itself was psychologically harmful to African Americans, not because the races were separated but because of the way they were separated. That is, when the government separates the races in a manner that subordinates and stigmatizes a particular race, that race will experience psychological harm in the absence of countervailing community institutions.

More than any other act of the federal government, *Plessy* gave the states a green light to separate African American and white children in the public schools in ways that were ruthless and unforgiving. Racial separation that took place under the guise of separate-but-equal made a mockery of the equality principle. From *Plessy* to *Brown*, public schools in America were clearly separate but definitely not equal.

Academic achievement, or scholastic aptitude, of African American students is perhaps the most telling indicator of the quality of their education in segregated schools. Like the students in the days of Prince Hall, African American children in the days of separate-but-equal had lower academic achievement levels than white children. Because, as Walter Stephan points out, "little or no data existed on the relative achievement levels of Blacks and whites in segregated schools,"[14] social scientists have had to hypothesize the existence of low academic achievement in segregated African American schools by comparing the school facilities and per pupil expenditures of these schools with those of white schools. The assumption here is that inequality in school facilities and per pupil expenditures signifies inequality in academic achievement, that equipment and school spending are among the significant contributors to and hence strong indicators of academic achievement.[15] On the other hand, we know from modern studies of high-expenditure, low-achievement schools in places like Kansas City, Missouri, that school facilities and school expenditures are not always robust determinants of scholastic achievement.[16]

Gross inequality in facilities and per pupil spending for African American and white schools was well documented in school desegregation litigation leading up to *Brown*. Using the research data of such eminent scholars as W. E. B. Du Bois,[17] Horace Mann Bond,[18] and Gunnar Myrdal,[19] NAACP lawyers were able to document substantial racial inequality as it was manifested in school buildings, per pupil expenditures for textbooks and equipment, and teacher salaries throughout the South; this was true even for African American and white schools in the same school district. "The typical black teacher labored in a poorly equipped classroom, taught larger classes for fewer days per year, and earned less doing it than did her white counterpart."[20] Southern states frequently allocated 2 to 5 times more money per pupil to white students.[21] Testifying during the trial phase of *Briggs v. Elliot*[22] as to the condition of the African American schools in Clarendon County, South Carolina, Matthew Whitehead stated:

> The total value of the buildings, grounds, and furnishings of the two white schools that accommodated 276 children was four times as high as the total for the three Negro schools that accommodated a total of 808 students. The white schools were constructed of brick and stucco; there was one teacher for each 28 children; at the colored schools, there was one teacher for each 47 children. At the white high school, there was only one class with an enrollment as high as 24; at the Scott's Branch high school for Negroes, classes ranged from 33 to 47. Besides the courses offered at both schools, the curriculum at the white high school included biology, typing, and bookkeeping; at the black high school, only agriculture and home economics were offered. There was no running water at one of the two outlying colored grade schools and no electricity at the other one. There were indoor flush toilets at both white schools but no flush toilets, indoors

or outdoors, at any of the Negro schools—only outhouses, and not nearly enough of them.[23]

On the basis of such overwhelming evidence, the NAACP in the 1930s and 1940s began winning equal-funding cases against local school boards and public universities.[24] Arguing for equal school funding, as the NAACP did in these cases, is vastly different from arguing for school integration, as the plaintiff did in *Roberts* in 1850. The argument for equal funding tolerates racial separation mandated by the government so long as the money is there; the *Roberts* case does not even if the money is there.

In what turned out to be a pivotal moment in American history, Thurgood Marshall, the lead attorney for the NAACP, changed the NAACP's legal strategy in mid-litigation from equal funding to racial integration. No longer would African Americans, through the NAACP, simply attack implementation of the equality part of the separate-but-equal formula, the effect of which was to concede the policy's legitimacy. Now they would attack the policy on its face, arguing that *de jure* racial segregation is immoral and unconstitutional.[25] With this important modification of litigation strategy, the issue of racial integration broached in the Massachusetts case one hundred years earlier returned to the courts.

The *Brown* Opinion

In discussing the *Brown* opinion, I simply wish to unearth the two or three major principles that have motivated the drive for integration in public schools since 1954. These principles contain *Brown*'s great expectation of what integration of public schools would accomplish, and they provide the basis for assessing the experience of African Americans in this area.

Clearly the most significant civil rights action the government had taken since President Lincoln's signing of the Emancipation Proclamation in 1863,[26] *Brown* began its analysis of the separate-but-equal doctrine with the following question and answer:

> Does segregation of children in public schools solely on the basis of race, even though the physical facilities and other "tangible" factors may be equal, deprive the children of the minority group equal educational opportunities? We believe that it does . . . To separate Negro school children from others of similar age and qualifications solely because of their race generates a feeling of inferiority as to their status

in the community that may affect their hearts and minds in a way unlikely ever to be undone ... [Quoting the Kansas trial judge:] "Segregation of white and colored children in public schools has a detrimental effect upon the colored children. The impact is greater when it has the sanction of the law; for the policy of separating the races is usually interpreted as denoting the inferiority of the negro group. A sense of inferiority affects the motivation of a child to learn" ... We conclude that in the field of public education the doctrine of "separate but equal" has no place. Separate educational facilities are inherently unequal.[27]

This passage indicates that the Supreme Court's invalidation of the separate-but-equal doctrine rested less on a legal principle than on a sociopsychological hypothesis. The Court could not readily overturn the doctrine on the basis of the legal principle that the equal protection clause of the Fourteenth Amendment to the Constitution, which bars every state from denying "any person within its jurisdiction the equal protection of the laws," bans racial separation. The Court was constrained by the fact that the 39th Congress, which proposed that Amendment, supported racial segregation in federal agencies and departments and everywhere else in Washington, D.C., including its public schools. Further complicating the analysis, that Congress also enacted legislation that created many beneficial forms of racial separation—for example, the Freedmen's Bureau Act of 1866, a race-conscious law that mandated food, clothing, legal assistance, special schools, and other services for the freed slaves. The Court in *Brown*—perhaps in part because of the inconclusive legislative history behind the Fourteenth Amendment—felt compelled to search for another peg on which to hang its decision outlawing the separate-but-equal doctrine. It turned to the social sciences.

Yet the 1954 Court did not have to take this turn. It could have stayed within legal boundaries by ruling on the legality of the separate-but-equal doctrine's application rather than on its face. Ample evidence from the NAACP's litigation campaign clearly demonstrated that states were applying the doctrine in a discriminatory manner, denying African American children equal educational opportunity. The Fourteenth Amendment may permit racial separation but it does not permit racial subordination or racial stigmatization. (In Part III, I shall attempt to show how *Brown* might be reread in this light.) So even though the NAACP asked the Court to invalidate the separate-but-equal doctrine on its face, the Court, not having sufficient legal grounds to do so, could have and should have exercised its option to rule on a more limited ground—namely, that the doctrine was unconstitutional as applied. Such a ruling not only would have rested *Brown* on firm legal footing—placing it on more than a decade of Supreme Court precedents—but it also would have paved the way for a more socially beneficial approach to school desegregation.

Eschewing a legal construction of the Fourteenth Amendment in favor of an extra-legal interpretation, the Supreme Court, then, held that separate-but-equal is "inherently unequal." The Amendment, in other words, forbids racial segregation in public schools because racial segregation generates a feeling of racial inferiority in the hearts and minds of African American children that may retard their educational and emotional development, scarring them for life. But what to make of *Plessy*, which ruled that racial segregation as such had no inherent negative sociopsychological impact on these children? "Whatever may have been the extent of psychological knowledge at the time of *Plessy v. Ferguson*," the Court said, the psychological damage racial segregation causes African American children "is amply supported by modern authority," citing in footnote 11 the work of Kenneth Clark and other social scientists on African American identity.[28]

The Court's reasoning is not only based on nonlegal grounds; it is also a *non sequitur*. The Justices rely on an empirical finding—the sociopsychological damage that segregation inflicts on African American children—to conclude that separate-but-equal is "inherently unequal." A thing is "inherently unequal" not because of empirical support but in spite of such support; that is, *a priori* or because of its very nature, which we discern through pure reason. My love of *Brown* does not mean I should ignore its warts.

It is unclear from the text of the opinion in *Brown* whether the Court's conclusion that separate schools generate feelings of inferiority in African American children referred to personal or group feelings (in other words, self-esteem or racial esteem)[29] or both. On the one hand, it could be argued that the Court had in mind only racial esteem, because it cites lower court findings that "the policy of separating the races is usually interpreted as denoting the inferiority of the negro group,"[30] and "State-imposed segregation in education itself results in the Negro Children, as a class, receiving educational opportunities which are substantially inferior to those available to white children otherwise similarly situated."[31] In addition, the dolls test, which contains an explicit reference to an ascriptive characteristic—namely, race or color—was the principal social science study upon which the Court relied in its famous footnote 11.[32]

On the other hand, the general presentation of the case and the state of psychological knowledge at the time would seem to suggest strongly that the Court's findings dealt with both self-esteem and racial pride. There is no doubt that the social scientists who testified during the trial stage of *Brown,* as well as the NAACP lawyers, sought to establish as a legal fact the proposition that African American children suffer from low self-esteem (feelings of inferiority) as a result of racial segregation.[33] Their testimony, which relied on the dolls study made famous by Kenneth and Mamie Clark, was the principal support for this critical "fact." From 1938 to 1960, the dolls test was the established method for evaluating racial identity and, indirectly, personal identity in children.[34]

Because the dolls test forms the basis of several significant arguments advanced in the next section, it may be useful to take a moment here to discuss it in some detail. The test consists of showing African American and white children brown dolls and white dolls, and then asking them to select the doll that they think: (1) they "like best" or "would like to play with," (2) "is nice," (3) "looks bad," (4) has "a nice color," and, skipping questions (5)–(7), (8) looks most like them in appearance. The answers to the first three questions showed an overwhelming preference toward the white doll. Of the 253 three- to seven-year-old African American children attending racially mixed northern schools and racially segregated southern schools, 67% preferred "to play with" the white doll while only 32% chose the brown doll; 59% evaluated the white doll as "nice" but only 38% evaluated the brown doll as "nice"; and, indicating that the preference for the white doll reflected a negative opinion of the brown doll, 59% said that the brown doll "looks bad" while only 17% expressed the same view of the white doll. That the preference for the white doll and the rejection of the brown doll were based at least in part on skin color is strongly suggested by the responses to question 4: 60% of the children thought that the white doll had a "nice color" and only 38% believed that the brown doll had a "nice color." The final question 8, indicating self-identification, showed that 33% of the African American children identified themselves with the white doll while 66% self-identified with the brown doll. When asked to make self-identifications, "some of the children who were free and relaxed in the beginning of the experiment broke down and cried . . . two children ran out of the testing room, inconsolable, convulsed in tears."[35] These results led the Clarks and others to conclude that segregation produced confusion in African American children and proved debilitating to their development of a healthy sense of self-worth.[36]

When the study is examined more closely, however, one sees that the Clarks' conclusions regarding the effects of segregation on African American children (or at least the Supreme Court's understanding of the Clarks' conclusions) were not scientifically compatible with several crucial findings in the study itself. First, the responses to questions 1–4, which indicate racial preference, actually reveal a lesser percentage of out-group preference among southern children who attended segregated schools than among northern children who attended racially mixed schools. Thirty-seven percent of segregated children, compared to 28% of integrated children, preferred to play with the brown doll; 46% of the segregated children, compared to 30% of the integrated children, believed that the brown doll was nice; 49% of the segregated children, compared to 71% of the integrated children, said that the brown doll looked bad; and 40% of the segregated children, compared to 37% of the integrated children, felt that the brown doll had a nice color.[37] Second, although most children in each age group preferred the white doll to the brown doll, this preference *decreased* gradually from ages 4 to 7.[38] Third, the children's "correct" racial identification in response to question 8 was largely based upon "the concrete fact of their own skin color." Thus it is understandable that 80% of the "light"-skinned children (whom the Clarks defined as children who looked "practically white" in physical appearance) self-identified with the white doll. Neither is it too troubling that 26% of the "medium" brown children (those who were "light brown to dark brown" in skin color) and 19% of the "dark" brown children (defined as "dark brown to black" skin color) self-identified with the white doll.[39] Finally, racial anguish in response to question 8, described above (crying and running out of the test room), was more prevalent among integrated than segregated children.[40] These findings tend to contradict the Clarks' and the Supreme Court's conclusion that segregation (certainly more than integration) debilitated the African American child's sense of self-worth.

Why the Clarks or the Court ignored or discounted these findings is open to debate. Perhaps they saw these divergences as statistically insignificant. More likely, they may have recognized that "segregation was one of the most important links in the chains of oppression that maintained blacks in an unequal status," a link they felt needed to be shattered.[41]

The Clarks' hypothesis as to the negative impact of segregation on African American children was supported by other eminent social scientists of the day. For example, psychologist F. H. Allport reported that:

> Segregation, prejudices and discriminations, and their social concomitants potentially damage the personality of all children ... Minority group children learn the inferior status to which they are assigned ... They often react with a feeling of inferiority and a sense of personal humiliation ... Under these conditions, the minority group child is thrown into conflict about himself and his group. He wonders whether his group and he himself are worthy of no more respect than they receive. This conflict and confusion leads to self-hatred.[42]

Likewise, Horace English, under questioning from NAACP attorney Jack Greenberg, testified at trial: "If we din into a person that he is incapable of learning, then he is less likely to be able to learn ... There is a tendency for us to live up to—or perhaps I should say down to—social expectations and to learn what people say we can learn, and legal segregation definitely depresses the Negro's expectancy and is therefore prejudicial to his learning."[43] And finally, sociologist Louisa Holt gave testimony that more than anyone else's "had a detectable impact on the phrasing of the final decision in the case."[44] She argued that "the fact that segregation is enforced ... has more importance than the mere fact of segregation by itself does because this gives legal and official sanction to a policy which is inevitably interpreted both by white people and by black people as denoting the inferiority of the Negro group ... A sense of inferiority must always affect one's motivation for learning since it affects the feeling one has for one's self as a person."[45]

Support for the Clarks' theory was not confined to scholarship or live testimony. Thirty-two prominent social scientists—psychologists, psychiatrists, and sociologists—endorsed a statement testifying that the effects of segregation on personality development left African American children with lower self-esteem than their white contemporaries and with little desire to learn.[46] Consequently, a dual school system was judged to create low self-esteem and group-esteem in African American children. Social scientists argued, and the Supreme Court agreed, that a unitary school system was the best way to create healthy self pride and racial pride.

In light of this discussion of *Brown*, it is possible to discern three major promises, or expectations, about integrated schools the Supreme Court tendered to the nation in 1954. *First,* an integrated academic setting will improve the self-esteem and racial esteem of African American children. *Second,* with a healthier sense of personal and racial identity, along with better facilities and better teachers, African American children will perform as well as whites academically. *Third,* integrated schools will lead to improved racial relations both within schools and the larger society.

More implicit than explicit in *Brown,* the third promise suggests that the Supreme Court saw in *Brown* an opportunity to engineer the beginning of a new social order, one without racial hierarchies. Through society's most basic institutions of acculturation, the public schools, the Court thought that white children would transmit their middle-class values to African American children, including, in the end, a lasting sense of hope and expectation for the future.[47] I believe the Court expected that good racial relations would be nurtured by this shared sense of a brighter future.

The promise of better racial relations is best examined in the context of higher education, where racial relations have been more dynamic in recent years. Accordingly, I shall defer discussion of that promise until the next chapter, and consider only the first two below.

The Failure of School Integration

Well-intended when tendered, the promises that integrated schools would nurture a healthier sense of racial and personal identity in African American children as well as scholastic achievement substantially equal to whites were not promises to keep. The *Brown* Court was naive or foolishly optimistic in underestimating the power of racism and discrimination in public schools. How and why the desired prospect of educational progress and harmony in integrated schools unraveled is the focus of this section.

Any assessment of the integration enterprise in public schools must begin with the unhappy acknowledgment that there has been very little school integration in our country since 1954. While *Brown* has removed segregation by law from our public schools, it has not changed the racial composition of many of these schools. Scores of African American children in grades K-12 attend schools that are segregated in fact, with predominantly minority (that is, more than 50%) student bodies. In 1968, fourteen years after *Brown,* 76.6% of the nation's public schools were *de facto* segregated. That percentage decreased to 63.6% in 1973 and just 62.9% in 1980. But by 1992, it had increased to 66.0%. Racial isolation is even more concentrated in certain school districts. For example, during the 1993–94 academic year, the minority school population was 92.2% in Detroit, 73.5% in Prince George's County, Virginia, and 65% in Little Rock, Arkansas. In Hartford, Connecticut, 94% of the students attending the inner-city public schools during the 1994–95 academic year were African American or Hispanic. As late as 1980, 33.2% of our public schools were 90–100% minority.[48] Thus, although all public schools are desegregated by law, many remain segregated in fact.

Typically, *de facto* segregated schools are burdened by structural decay and besieged by a host of social pathologies associated with urban poverty. These schools are unsafe, underfinanced considering the special problems they face, and provide little in the way of a quality education.[49] The existence of *de facto* segregated schools is by itself evidence of at least the partial failure of *Brown*'s expectations. But even when integrated schools have been established, they have not lived up to their 1954 warranty.

The Promise of Strengthened Identity

Brown's first promise—that integrated public schools will create healthier personal and racial esteem in African American pupils—assumes that their sense of identity suffered under the separate-but-equal doctrine. This assumption, so vital to the Court's reasoning in *Brown,* has come in for a round of bashing from an unlikely source—African Americans of my generation. Whether it is conservatives like Justice Clarence Thomas, who faults *Brown* and its progeny for creating "a jurisprudence based upon a theory of black inferiority,"[50] or liberals like Alex Johnson, who flat out states that "*Brown* was a mistake,"[51] many African Americans who came of age in the 1960s and 1970s have come to reject *Brown*'s assumption regarding African American identity. This is simply one of many parallels in civil rights thinking among African Americans on the political right and political left that the public often misses.[52]

The Supreme Court's assumption about the effect racial segregation had on African American students is only partially correct. This, then, makes *Brown*'s critics only partially (but still largely) correct. In other words, the Court erroneously assumed African American racial pride and self pride in segregated schools were low. The social scientists on whom the Court relied mistakenly thought, on the basis of the information elicited from the dolls test and similar studies, that group pride correlated with individual pride. The evidence of low group pride at the time of *Brown* is inconclusive (the studies go in both directions) but I give the Court's reading of the matter the benefit of the doubt. Although there was little direct testing of individual pride during that period, more recent evidence, including evidence in *de facto* segregated schools, strongly suggests that most African American children had a healthy level of self-esteem. As to *Brown*'s promise itself, I argue that not only have racially integrated schools failed to pump up the supposedly low racial and personal pride of African American students, but worse than that, they have damaged the self-esteem of scores of unprotected African American children, committing the very sin *Brown* sought to wipe away.

De Jure Segregated Schools. The assumption of low racial esteem and self-esteem of children in segregated schools contains three specific sociopsychological subassumptions, which, taken together, are false: (1) racial segregation (the bad form of racial separation) engenders a negative racial perception in African American children; (2) racial segregation produces a negative sense of self (low self-esteem) in these children; and (3) there is a positive correlation between assumptions 1 and 2—that is, racial self-esteem is a reliable indirect indicator of personal self-esteem. Together, these assumptions assert that information on how individuals orient themselves toward their socially ascribed group (which is the type of information the dolls test collected) "can provide accurate information on how they feel about themselves at the personal level."[53] The implicit variable in the equation is the assumption (assumption 3) that there is a correlation between skin color and self-esteem. Based upon this assumption, "self-hatred among Negroes was a well documented trend of empirical studies on black identity by 1954 and an assumed fact by 1960."[54]

My argument is that the social science studies investigating African American self-esteem, upon which the Court in *Brown* so heavily relied, are methodologically flawed. They are flawed procedurally because they failed to distinguish personal identity (PI) from group identity, or, more precisely, "reference group orientation" (RGO).[55] As a consequence of this methodological failure, the social science studies produced the erroneous hypothesis that there is a linear and positive correlation between PI and RGO. Hence assumption 3, which correlates racial pride with personal pride, was as empirically incorrect in 1954 as it is today. This does not necessarily mean, however, that either or both of the constituent parts of the equation are incorrect. Indeed, I contend that while the second part (assumption 2 positing low African American personal pride) was probably incorrect in 1954, the first part (assumption 1 charging low racial pride) was correct in 1954.

A more detailed discussion of PI and RGO studies will clarify these points. PI studies "attempt to investigate how *'universal elements'* of behavior vary in intensity, or are more likely to be present across different racial groups."[56] These studies assume that "one's self-concept, personal identity, or generalized personality consists of certain universal human tendencies, traits, behavioral elements, or capacities."[57] Race is treated as an independent variable. The researcher locates some personality scale, inventory, or questionnaire (such as attitudes toward one's looks, strengths, or capabilities) that purports to tap universal elements of personality and that contains no reference to ascriptive characteristics (such as race, gender, or religion). After this survey is administered to African American and white subjects, the researcher determines whether race, as an independent variable, is statistically significant.[58]

In contrast to PI studies, RGO studies treat race or color as the dependent measure, making it a salient component of the questionnaire. Race or color is a direct measure of one's "racial identity," "racial self-esteem," "racial attitudes," "racial orientation," or "racial group orientation."[59] The subject in such tests must make a preference or relate attitude types toward his or her socially ascribed group in order to achieve a high in-group score. The dolls test, on which *Brown* relied, is an RGO technique.

Although RGO studies adduce direct evidence only on the esteem the subject has for his or her socially ascribed group, these studies "provided almost all of the empirical evidence used to support the negative Black identity notion" between 1939 and 1960.[60] If, however, the assumed PI/RGO correlation exists (assumption 3), then there is nothing wrong with this methodology. Research conducted by William Cross and others strongly suggests that the methodology is flawed in that there is no positive correlation between the two forms of identity studies. Cross examined all the empirical studies on black identity reported between 1938 and 1977, a total of 161 studies. Most of the RGO studies show an out-group orientation (low racial-esteem), while most PI studies document a positive self-image. Thus, to the extent that the PI and RGO trends are significant, they show an inverse relationship between racial pride and personal pride. This certainly questions *Brown*'s faith in using RGO studies as an empirical basis for establishing low African American self-esteem.[61]

Ironically, when each of the RGO studies conducted in the 1938–1960 period is reviewed, the experimenter, as Cross points out, clearly specifies in the methods section that an explicit RGO-related construct was assessed. In the discussion sections, however, "the distinction between PI and RGO information is blurred and the construct self-hatred is injected as if PI and RGO data had been collected or as if it was established that PI and RGO are highly correlated."[62] But "between 1939–1960, in no study was PI and RGO data collected on the same sample in order to test the presumed association."[63]

Studies applying PI and RGO measures on the same sample began to appear in the late 1960s. These studies have, likewise, yielded results that tend to show no correlation. One study found that a larger percentage of African American children than white children felt they were very good-looking or pretty good-looking even though the African American children demonstrated a clear preference for white skin.[64] This would tend to show no correlation between PI (which is positive in this case) and RGO (which is negative). In her study of the personal and group identities of 400 Bostonian preschoolers, Judith Porter found that group identities could be conditioned by socioeconomic class, mitigating an apparent correlation.[65] Another study found no correlation between PI and RGO variables in tests on African American students at various stages in their chronological development.[66] With the exception of one study that shows strong support for a PI/RGO correlation,[67] most studies supporting a PI/RGO correlation were later found to be based on circumstantial data[68] or simply misinterpreted.[69]

There is, on the other hand, support for assumption 1, which holds that African American racial identity suffered under racial segregation. Consistent with the evidence adduced in *Brown,* many RGO studies clearly indicate an out-group preference prior to 1968.[70] Some studies paint a mixed picture, however. W. Curtis Banks, for example, reviewed 32 RGO studies conducted before and after 1968. He found that 69% of these studies reported *no* racial preference and only 6% indicated a pattern of white preference.[71] Thus the evidence concerning the validity of assumption 1 is inconclusive. Perhaps the benefit of the doubt should go to the Supreme Court.

Assumption 2 maintains that African American children suffered low self-esteem under racial segregation. This assumption is highly speculative at best—or simply wrong. Indeed, any assertion as to the negative or positive nature of African American personal identity from 1939–1960 would have to be speculative, once again because of the flawed methodology upon which such conclusions rest. The self-hatred proposition, a PI-related hypothesis, was developed on the accumulation of evidence derived from RGO studies without any correlation between PI and RGO testing. And given that RGO indicators tend not to be indirect measurements of PI, even if all evaluative preference/self-identification studies showed African Americans to have an out-group orientation, such information would have little probative value on the issue of self-esteem.

Because of the modest number of pre-1968 PI studies, there is no way to directly support or refute the validity of assumption 2. It should be noted, however, that although low African American self-esteem was widely assumed prior to 1968,[72] most social scientists now believe that both before and after 1968, African Americans in *de jure* or *de facto* segregated schools have had average to above-average levels of self-esteem, matching or surpassing white comparison groups.[73] The high level of personal self-esteem suggests that African American children in segregated environments derived their self-esteem from comparisons with children in their own group, not with whites.[74] This, in turn, suggests that *Brown's* expectation that integrated schools would increase racial-esteem and self-esteem in African American children was false.

Integrated Schools. The *Brown* decision failed to deliver its first promise. Integrated schools did not increase racial or personal pride. Indeed, the dolls test itself, when carefully examined, contradicts that expectation. As demonstrated earlier in this chapter, that test tends to indicate that racial isolation (even when tied to *de jure* segregation) provides a better environment than does racial integration for the development of a positive African American identity. The dolls test shows that racial self-esteem, although low for all African American students, is regularly higher among those who attend segregated schools rather than integrated schools.

African Americans' racial group preference changed from out-group prior to 1968 to in-group after 1968. This increase in racial pride followed the Black Power Movement (1965–1967) and is likely due to the movement's public celebration of African American pride rather than to racial integration, which predated the movement. Studies consistently confirm a mostly in-group preference after 1968.[75]

Similarly, school integration has not increased African American personal pride, which, as several studies have shown, was probably high already. For example, Walter Stephan concludes that African American students attending *de facto* segregated schools "have self-esteem levels that are similar to or higher than those of white students in more cases than they have lower self esteem."[76] Researchers in three of these studies tested the self-esteem of African American junior high school and senior high school students in segregated and integrated schools in different parts of the country. The results in all three tests showed African American students in segregated schools with *higher* self-esteem than African American students in integrated schools.[77]

Most tellingly, Stephan discovered that African American students who attended integrated schools initially experienced a decrease in self-esteem. Although some studies indicated that their self-esteem returned to normal levels after more than one year in the school, none of the studies Stephan examined reflected an increase in self-esteem as a result of integration.[78] These and other studies indicate that African American self-esteem in fact drops in integrated schools, just the opposite of what *Brown* expected.[79]

A 1994 survey conducted by the *U.S. News & World Report* puts a human face on the statistics:

> Twelve-year-old Nicole Hayman has some special talents, but none allows her to shine where it seems to matter the most—in the classroom. She can jump rope double-dutch style for long stretches without tangling her feet. She is slightly bigger than her mostly white fifth-grade classmates, and occasionally, when angry, she punches or slaps them in the back of the head. They are afraid of her, and that gives her a lot of power in the schoolyard. But for all her strengths, in the classroom Nicole feels powerless. She frequently stumbles over words when reading aloud. When the teacher allows her white classmates to do things, and not her, she feels that the teacher dislikes black people. "Sometimes, I feel like I can't do anything right," Nicole says. "Sometimes, I feel like a failure."

> [Our] survey of those living in some of the communities involved in the *Brown* case found many Nicole Haymans—still haunted by the sense that the world is inherently unequal and views them as worthless.

> Jerome Robinson, 12: "I don't like school. [My white teacher] doesn't

treat me like a student. She acts like I'm not even here." He's a sixth grader at Alexis I. DuPont Middle School in Wilmington, Del.

Dilip Nyala, 12: "I don't show respect if I don't get respect." He's a student at DuPont School.

Stephanie Fells, 11: "I don't really like white people that much. They are just beating black people at everything." She's a student in Farmville.

Chiriga Howie, 10: "A lot of the white girls just look at me and start staring and whispering. Sometimes, they act like I'm not even there."[80]

These comments tear at the soul and ignite anger in the heart. How can any civilized society allow such mental anguish to burden our children? Who or what is to blame? We will return to these questions. It is useful to note here, however, how other commentators have interpreted the emotional damage to African American children in integrated schools.

Two leading scholars, Morris Rosenberg and Roberta Simmons, opine that most African American children live in a "consonant" racial context; a context in which their racial characteristics and those of the surrounding population are congruent. Therefore, when a child who lives in a predominantly African American neighborhood attends an integrated school, this may be her first experience in a "dissonant racial context." Through integration, the child learns firsthand what it feels like to be a member of a minority group. This "dissonant racial context" may lower that child's self-esteem.[81]

Adding to this point, Stephan articulates several more reasons why integration might decrease rather than increase African American self-esteem. "Social comparisons with white students who are academically better prepared than blacks" and "negative evaluations by ethnocentric white students" could cause African American students to evaluate themselves negatively.[82] Stephan further argues that "the loss of status and power that occurs when blacks represent a minority of the student body in desegregated schools could also lower the self-esteem of black students."[83]

Clearly, the homogeneous community rather than the larger white society is the environment in which the personal self-esteem of African Americans develops positively.[84] Hence, contrary to what the Supreme Court thought in 1954, immersing students in integrated schools may do their self-esteem more harm than good.[85] Integration does not by itself nurture self-esteem; it does not make African Americans feel more proud and more self-confident than they would (and did) feel in segregated schools.

Indeed, an integrated context may actually lead to stronger feelings of inferiority. The removal of African American students from their peer groups and immediate social environments, which develop positive self-esteem, may disturb their psychological well-being. African American children may not be able to protect their self-image from the damage received in an integrated school. Young and impressionable students cannot be expected to insulate themselves from racial inequality and racism experienced in integrated environments. We are left, then, with the harrowing thought that *Brown*'s unflinching support for racial integration (and the legal and social regime established to implement racial integration—one-way busing, the closing of African American schools, and the like[86]) may have unwittingly damaged the self-esteem of scores of African American children, creating the very problem *Brown* sought to redress.

The Promise of Improved Scholastic Performance

If *Brown* was naively optimistic about the positive effect integrated schools would have on African American identity, it was similarly pollyannish about the beneficial impact integrated schools would have on academic performance. Scholastic achievement has improved, but not nearly as much as *Brown* anticipated. Under integration, scores of African American children continue to show persistent lags and deficiencies in their education.

By looking at the racial disparities in high school completion rates and dropout rates, we can begin to see how the promise of academic excellence began to unravel. These rates do not, unfortunately, distinguish between integrated and *de facto* segregated (or better, still, private African American) schools, so they have limited probative value in gauging the failure of integrated schools; nonetheless they help to frame the problem of integrated schools. Racial disparity is easily documented. For example, the high school completion rate for African Americans 18 to 24 years of age was 66.7% in 1972, 70.9% in 1982, and 74.6% in 1992, compared to 81.7% in 1972, 82.4% in 1982, and 83.3% in 1992 for white high school students. Although the racial gap has closed from 15% to 11.5% to 8.7% over this period of time, a racial differential still remains as African Americans continue to trail whites.[87]

If one looks at African Americans' high school education from the perspective of the dropout rate, matters look worse. This is especially the case when we focus on our urban centers, where 85% of African Americans reside.[88] In Los Angeles, for example, African American students and white students comprise a roughly equal percentage of the student population, 13.1% and 12.9% respectively, but African American students represent a disproportionate percentage of dropouts. During the 1992–93 academic year, African American students accounted for 18.4% of dropouts while white students accounted for 10%.[89] In urban centers nationwide, the African American dropout rate stands at nearly 50%.[90]

Math and reading scores provide more direct evidence for the case against integrated schools. Assessments of these scores are mixed, but overall they suggest that integration has not made an appreciably favorable impact on the academic achievement of African American students. This statement is more meaningful when we take into account the primary educational deficiency of the schools to which integrated schools are being compared: that is, *de jure* or *de facto* segregated schools are underfunded, considering the special needs of their students.

The Department of Education reports that school integration has not had a salutary impact on African Americans' scholastic achievement. Between 1978 and 1988, African American 13-year-olds attending integrated schools had lower rates of increase in reading and math scores than did children of the same age in *de facto* segregated schools.[91] And as Martin Patchen concludes: "Black students who attended predominantly white classes in grade school ... did not do better academically in high school than those who attended mostly black grade school classes." In fact, the achievement scores of the integrated students were slightly lower.[92]

Other studies, however, show slight improvement in the scholastic performance of African American students attending integrated schools. For example, in his review of several studies of African American scholastic achievement in integrated schools, Thomas Cook found "no effects for math achievement, and ... that reading effects [were] positive but quite small and not educationally significant in all but a few studies."[93] One study showed improvements in the scores of African American students at only three age levels: 9-, 13-, and 17-year-olds.[94] A recent Harvard University study found that African American third graders attending integrated schools in Norfolk, Virginia, scored only 5 points higher on the Iowa Test of Basic Skills, a national-norm assessment exam, than did the third graders attending Norfolk's *de facto* segregated schools.[95] David Armor suggests that any decrease in the gap between African American and white test scores over the years has less to do with racial integration than with the improved socioeconomic status of African Americans.[96]

Still other studies of achievement indicate that even if it is true that African American students learn more in integrated schools than they ever did or could in *de facto* segregated schools, it is also true that they continue to compare poorly to white students there. A study of school integration in Indianapolis during the 1970–71 school year, for example, shows that while African American students attending integrated high schools had higher academic achievement scores than students enrolled in segregated schools during that year, the former received lower grades than their white classmates.[97] Twenty years later, the Harvard study found that in the academic year 1990–91, African American third graders in integrated schools scored 16 points below their white counterparts on the Iowa Test.[98] Clearly, *Brown* contemplated far greater academic improvement than this.

Cook correctly observes that these findings may not reflect true mastery of subject matter, because they are based on standardized tests, the traditional measurement of academic achievement in our schools. African Americans perform much lower than whites on standardized tests. This is true not only in elementary and secondary school but also in college.[99]

Enrollment in college preparatory courses is an important indicator of academic achievement. In the 1975–76 academic year, 66% of all African American 17-year-old students, compared with 42% of their white counterparts, were not enrolled in any or were enrolled in only one algebra or geometry course. And in 1982, African American seniors nationwide were twice as likely as white seniors to have taken no math courses at the level of algebra I or higher, whereas white seniors were twice as likely as their African American classmates to have taken four or more advanced math courses.[100]

When the comparison moves to integrated public schools versus single-sex African American public schools, the failure of *Brown* is even more apparent. Single-sex public schools for African American boys and girls violate *Brown*'s integration mandate twice—by race and by gender. Yet a substantial body of research suggests that some girls and some minorities (particularly minority children from poor, single-parent families) do better academically and emotionally in separate schools or classes than in racially integrated or coed schools or classes.

Much of the research on this subject was presented in testimony before Congress in connection with Senate Bill 1513, the Improving America's Schools Act of 1994.[101] Citing a wide variety of sources, Senator Danforth, the sponsor of the bill (which passed the Senate by a vote of 66 to 33), said that the most recent statistics indicate that nationwide, "African Americans and Hispanic students [attending single-sex schools] scored nearly a grade level above their coeducational counterparts in academic achievement tests."[102] Unfortunately, this finding does not indicate the racial composition of the schools. Other studies do, however, identify single-sex schools by race.

For example, the Ronald Coleman Elementary School in Baltimore draws its students from an area in the northern part of the city in which 85% of the students come from single-parent homes or live with their grandparents. All the classes in this predominantly African American public school are separated by gender. The academic ranking of the school is impressive:

> Coleman Elementary School ranked fifth out of 21 in the north area; 13th out of 115 throughout Baltimore. First grade, first in the area; fifth out of 115 in the system. Second grade, second; in the whole system, they ranked third. Third grade, third; in the whole system, 10th out of 115. Fourth grade, fourth; 21st out of 115 in the entire system. Fifth grade, seventh out of 21; 29th out of 115 in the entire system.[103]

Similar results have been reported in Detroit at the Malcolm X Academy. In 1993 and 1994, seventh-grade math scores were "the highest among the 77 schools in Detroit and second highest in Michigan among 780 schools."[104]

Thus although S.1513 primarily addressed single-sex public schools, the research placed in the record was clearly relevant to single-race public schools. As Anthony Bryk of the University of Chicago stated: "[the] results here strongly suggest that schools specifically designed to educate historically disadvantaged populations—such as women, minority men—may be especially effective in expanding educational opportunities in our society."[105]

Making a conservative estimate, one would have to conclude that integrated schools, when they can be found, have not improved the academic achievement levels of African American students in the way that *Brown* had promised. The lessons we must take from this experience are too clear to miss. As a wiser Supreme Court has stated: "Pupil Assignment alone does not automatically remedy the impact of previous, unlawful educational isolation; consequences linger . . . [and] do not vanish simply by moving the child to a desegregated school."[106] Gerald Jaynes and Robin Williams are even more emphatic—"racial mixing should not be relied upon as a major tool to bring about academic achievement of minorities"[107]—as is Cook: "the studies . . . tell us nothing about whether segregation created the Black-White achievement gap, but they do tell us that [integration] by itself will not close it to any important degree."[108]

Why Integrated Schools Have Failed

Setting forth the details of low self-esteem and disappointing academic achievement in integrated schools may be easier than attempting to explain why they have come about. Why have integrated schools failed to deliver the self-confidence of African Americans students? Why, especially, are these students still not performing as well as their white classmates in integrated schools?

Part of the problem could be internal; that is, it could stem from problems at home that are brought into the classroom. African American students from poor or working-class families may lack sufficient study time, or they may fail to take tests seriously in the face of their teachers' low expectations or because they do not see employment opportunities down the line.[109]

Although part of the problem may be cultural, most of it surely lies within integrated schools themselves. These schools may appear racially mixed to the outside world, but they are not so on the inside. "Second-generation discrimination" and "resegregation" perpetuate racial subordination and seriously affect the quality of education as well as the self-esteem of African American students. Motivated in large part by racism, these practices take a variety of forms.[110]

One form is the tendency of administrators and teachers to automatically place African American students in classes for the educable mentally retarded (EMR) without recognizing that performance may be a result of other, simpler learning or development problems. In 1968, for instance, African Americans in the south were overrepresented in EMR classes by a factor of 330%, which rose to 540% in 1974.[111] Such overrepresentation resegregates integrated schools internally. "At best, such policies associate African American students with slow learning; at worst, they reflect the avowed or unconscious prejudice of those responsible for the placements."[112]

Tracking (grouping students by supposed ability) is another form of second-generation discrimination and resegregation. One study concluded that "about half of all black students are in low-achievement reading groups, compared to one-fifth of whites; over one-quarter of whites but fewer than one-tenth of blacks are in high-achievement reading groups."[113] Another study reported that many teachers in kindergarten and at the early elementary levels stereotype and sort young children according to their demeanor, dress, and other socioeconomic characteristics. These examples of racial disparity in tracking show how tracking can engender low achievement and low self-esteem in impressionable children. Such tracking "isolates students, associates skin color with skill, and leads parents, teachers, and students alike to expect little and demand less from blacks."[114] Effectively socialized toward lower levels of attainment and achievement, African American students respond by misbehaving, losing interest, or eventually withdrawing from school.[115]

Too many white teachers in integrated schools harbor negative attitudes and perceptions about African American students. Some of these teachers prefer not to teach them; others simply do not like them as individuals.[116] The sad experiences of the children discussed above—Brittany Williams, Jerome Robinson, Dilip Nyala, Stephanie Fells, and Chiriga Howie—give painful evidence to the fact that when teachers bring racist attitudes into the classroom, African American children will surely suffer low self-esteem and low scholastic performance.

In his 1933 book *The Mis-Education of the Negro,* Carter G. Woodson, the founder of Negro History Month and a member of several integrated faculties at African American colleges, wrote about "the necessity for . . . teachers who understand and continue in sympathy with those whom they instruct."[117] Today, another legendary African American educator, Marva Collins, admonishes that "if a teacher believes that children cannot achieve very much, then those children will not achieve very much."[118] How little we have learned in nearly seventy-five years.

Racial disparity in the disciplining of students also contributes to low self-esteem and low scholastic achievement. In one integrated elementary school in Minneapolis my daughter attended for one year, a special room was set aside for misbehaving students. It was called the Discipline Room, and this name was written across the door. Students could walk by to see who was in it; most of the time most of the children there were black. Few white students were in the room on any given day. In a school that was predominantly white, all the students, African American and white, were taught a subtle lesson each day; they learned to associate skin color with bad behavior. That the principal of the school was a well-respected African American did not matter; to the white students (and I would say a good number of the white teachers) she was not a "black" person—she did not act "black." The principal confided in me that it anguished her to peer into the room each day only to see a sea of little black faces. But think of the pain that must have accumulated in the African American students, both inside and outside the room.

This is not an isolated episode. Jennifer Hochschild notes that African American students on average are suspended "at a younger age, for a longer time, and more often than whites." In some school districts, African American students are punished five to ten times more often than whites. During the 1994–95 academic year, nearly half of all African American males enrolled in Colorado's middle and high schools were suspended, compared to only one in six white males.[119] Racial disparity in meting out discipline not only leads to the exclusion of African American students from the classroom but also contributes to an overall perception of mistreatment and feelings of alienation. While they, like white students, misbehave and need to be disciplined, too often the standards of discipline are made to serve teacher stereotypes and subjectivity, personal racism, and minority group perceptions.[120]

Other factors contributing to low self-esteem and low academic performance can be found in the techniques and methods used to integrate, or desegregate, public schools. African Americans are often required to shoulder the heavy burden of mandatory student busing. As I pointed out on another occasion:

> Mandatory busing is usually considered "successful" when it is one-way (African Americans are bused to white schools rather than the reverse), when the percentage of African American students in white

schools remains below 33 percent, when whites keep control of the school system, and when mandated decreases in the rate of racial isolation in segregated schools are relatively slight and very gradual. Short of mandatory integration, whites are most inclined to accept integration techniques [particularly beneficial to them, i.e.] magnet schools with programs for gifted or academically successful students [or] that involve tracking. These techniques, in effect, use African American children as stepping-stones for the academic success of white children.[121]

Most of the psychological and scholastic damage is visited upon poor and working-class African American children. Unlike middle-class African American families, especially those in the upper-income brackets, poor and working-class African American families do not have enough control over their lives or enough money to shop around for private schools better suited for their children. Also, middle-class students, regardless of race, carry a definite socioeconomic advantage into the classroom. Research shows that students from "higher socioeconomic status backgrounds are more likely than children from low socioeconomic status backgrounds to score high on achievement tests, to receive persistent encouragement from adults, to form high educational aspirations and receive better grades."[122]

Indeed, in the Minneapolis public school my daughter attended, poor African American children were bused in from the northern part of the city. The socioeconomic mismatch was readily apparent not only in academic readiness and performance, but also in the way teachers treated the students. I stood outside a classroom one day, horrified, as a popular white teacher who had been with the school for many years berated in front of the entire class an unkempt 5-year-old boy from north Minneapolis just because he could not recite his street address. I registered a strong complaint with the principal; the teacher returned to duty the next day.

The experiences of poor African American students in the land of milk and honey strongly suggest that integrated schools are better suited for middle-class African American children. That is, the socioeconomic mismatch between poor African American children and middle-class white children may guarantee the failure of school integration. True, there are not enough middle-class African American children to go around, and some white children will, therefore, miss out on a valuable life experience if socioeconomic integration is thrown into the mix. But, on the other hand, scores of African American children will gain their dignity and perhaps some education.

For all its failures, school integration has had its successes. Most importantly, it has given those African Americans least damaged by the legacy of slavery and *de jure* segregation entry to mainstream society. The personal contacts and social mores these students acquire in integrated schools give them greater entry into the larger integrated world than if they attended a segregated school. This includes better access to higher education—African American students who attend integrated schools matriculate at colleges and universities at a greater rate than African Americans who attend segregated schools[123]—and employment. In this sense, *Brown* has been a success. But the question is, do the pluses of *Brown* (do the pluses of racial integration overall) outweigh its minuses? Is it morally correct to sacrifice the innocents of our society—the children—in the pursuit of a particular public policy, however admirable that policy might be in theory? These are the questions our society must face two generations after *Brown*.

2

Higher Education

In many respects, the experiences of African American students in integrated public elementary and secondary schools mirror those of African Americans in integrated (that is, predominantly white) colleges and universities. Feelings of low self-esteem and low academic achievement are common in higher education.[1] Three other problems also frame the campus experiences of African Americans: low enrollment (which fortunately has begun to pick up), high attrition rates, and racial hostility. These problems are not unrelated.

Low Enrollment and High Attrition Rates

The vast majority of African American students enrolled in institutions of higher education attend predominantly white colleges and universities. Historically black universities or colleges (commonly called HBCUs) educate a small but significant number of African American students. Of the approximately 1.3 million African American college students in 1991, slightly more than 1 million (or 80%) attended predominantly white institutions, and approximately 210,000 (or 20%) matriculated at HBCUs.[2]

While the enrollment rate for African American students at predominantly white institutions of higher education has been rising since the late 1980s (even though the percentage of African American high-school graduates has been erratic), it has still not reached parity with the enrollment rate for white students and has only recently begun to return to the high level of the 1970s. This applies to both undergraduate and graduate students. In addition, the dropout rate for African American undergraduate students is far too high, adversely affecting the attendance rate on the undergraduate and graduate levels alike.

College enrollment rates for African Americans 14 to 24 years old reached their zenith in the 1970s. In 1976, for example, approximately 33.5% of African American high school graduates were enrolled at colleges and universities, slightly *exceeding* the 33% rate for white high school graduates.

By 1985, however, 34.4% of white high school graduates were enrolled in colleges and universities, while the enrollment rate for African American high school graduates dropped to 26.1%. These figures are particularly alarming given the greater number of graduates: at a time when the high school graduation rate for white students remained relatively stable, rising from 82.4% to 83.6% (increasing 1.2%), the rate for African American students rose from 67.5% to 75.6% (increasing 8.1%). Since 1985, when a low of 26.1% of African American high-school graduates attended colleges, the African American enrollment rate has been steadily increasing.[3]

Although this is an improvement, the current higher enrollment rate is no cause for great celebration. First, it has not reached parity with that of white students, as it did for several years in the 1970s. The 1992 enrollment rate for African American students was approximately 33.8% (up from 31.5% in 1991), compared to 42.2% for white students (up from 41.7%).[4] Second, the increase in the enrollment rate was largely pushed up by African American women, who greatly outnumber the men in higher education. In 1965, when figures were first collected, 148,000 African American women versus 126,000 African American men attended college. Today the gender gap has grown substantially. Over 300,000 more African American women than men attended college in 1992, 865,000 versus 537,000. In another way of looking at the gender gap, the percentage of African American high school graduates between the ages of 18 and 24 who enrolled in college increased from 22.5% in 1972 to 37.5% in 1992 for women, and *decreased* from 33.0% in 1972 to 29.7% in 1992 for men. The African American gender gap has grown by 78% since 1980.[5]

A number of explanations can be offered for this gender gap, which is not only evident in college enrollment but in almost every other phase of higher education, as we can see in the percentages of undergraduate, graduate, and professional degrees awarded at predominantly white institutions and HBCUs alike.[6] One very important reason is the absence of mainstream African American role models in the home and in the schools, which is "far more acute for black men than for black women." Also, young male high school graduates may believe that a college or postgraduate degree will not be of much benefit to them, because employment discrimination is more intense against African American men than African American women. This may not be an unrealistic view of employment discrimination. Robert Bruce Slater points to a study that shows "the employment growth for black women in professional positions was double the rate for black men in the 1982-to-1992 period . . . Part of the reason for this is that black females benefit from the corporate mentality that a black woman is a 'twofer' or 'double minority.'" Slater believes that "this in itself encourages black women to pursue higher education. However, black men are seen as more threatening to white male-dominated corporate management. For black men, their dim prospects for advancement in corporate America undoubtedly chill their educational aspirations."[7]

Trying to comprehend the fluctuations in enrollment of African Americans overall may be more complex than attempting to understand the reasons for the African American gender gap in college enrollment. Why did the enrollment rate increase in the 1970s and decrease in the 1980s? And why is it now increasing, at least for African American women? One probable reason is affirmative action. The 1970s was a period of considerable support for affirmative action in contrast to the 1980s. More recently, President Clinton's administration has been an unabashed supporter of affirmative programs, especially with regard to minority scholarships. For example, the Clinton administration reversed the Bush administration's policy prohibiting race-exclusive scholarships. Secretary of Education Richard W. Riley announced the policy reversal on February 17, 1994, stating that "colleges can use financial aid to remedy past discrimination and to promote campus diversity without violating anti-discrimination laws."[8]

Cost is another possible explanation. Cutbacks in federal financial aid and the shift from grants-in-aid to loans in 1980 have hit African American students especially hard. Several organizations and college presidents have noted the devastating effect the shift from federal grants to federal loans has had on African American students. Many students come from families with incomes below the poverty line. These students and even slightly wealthier African American students cannot fathom the idea of borrowing amounts that equal or exceed an entire family's annual income.[9] The logic of such borrowing is especially hard to accept when the median earnings of African American male college graduates are lower than those of their white counterparts ($27,452 versus $36,680 in 1992), while the unemployment rate is higher than the rate for white college graduates (4.4% versus 3.0% in 1992).[10] Because of the special financial problems African American students face, many colleges and universities in the late 1980s began targeting scholarships to these students, a practice which, although controversial, has helped to push up the enrollment rate.[11]

Standardized tests may also help to explain the ups and downs in the enrollment rate of African Americans since the 1970s. Colleges and universities placed far more reliance on standardized admissions tests, such as the SAT, in the 1980s, when African American enrollment was down, than they did in the 1970s, when such enrollment was up. Colleges and universities still seem to be continuing their heavy use of these tests.[12] But it is clear that more *qualified* African American students would be admitted to institutions of higher education today if the use of standardized tests was scaled back.

Statistical studies have established fairly conclusively that African Americans on average score lower than whites on the college entrance exam (SAT). For example, in the freshman class that entered Harvard University in the fall of 1991, the average combined English/math score was 1450 for white students and 1290 for African American students, a difference of 160 points.[13]

Some would argue, however, that standardized tests are useful and even necessary, because they are reliable predictors of academic success. This is simply not true. What the studies tend to show, since at least the 1960s, is that the SAT is a more valid predictor of freshman academic performance than the high-school grade point average (HSGPA), and that the law school entrance exam (LSAT) is a more valid predictor of first-year law school than the undergraduate grade point average (UGPA), but that the correlation between standardized tests and academic performance (as measured by GPAs) is less robust beyond the first year of college or law school. Hence the admissions officer, interested in knowing how well a student will perform during his or her entire college or law school career, cannot rely on standardized tests to separate the qualified from the unqualified.[14]

The relatively high correlation between standardized tests and first-year academic performance may mean that standardized tests measure a student's adaptive ability: how well he or she will confront new situations and problems (personal as well as academic). The first year of college or law school is the adjustment year. Although standardized tests are more predictive of first-year performance than GPA, the combination of such tests and GPA is a better predictor of first-year performance than either factor taken by itself.[15]

Several studies of legal education have shown that the UGPA predicts academic performance beyond the first year, while the predictive validity of the LSAT declines in subsequent years. These studies contradict earlier studies, which have concluded that LSAT scores predict 3-year law school performance.[16] One later study found that although the predictive validity of the LSAT declines over the three years, it still has a higher median correlation with law school grades than the UGPA. This study, which consisted of 23 law schools whose students comprised 15% of all students attending ABA-approved law schools, established that "the median correlations of the LSAT with yearly averages decreased from .44 to .40 to .32 over 3 years, whereas those for UGPA remain constant (.28, .28, .29)."[17] As one can see, neither measure has a particularly high correlation.

LSAT and UGPA are as adequate (or inadequate) in predicting minority law school performance as they are in predicting majority law school performance. The LSAT is a better predictor of first-year performance than the UGPA, but loses its predictive validity at a faster rate than the UGPA over the three years of law school. Another study has concluded that the LSAT is an overpredictor of minority GPA in the first year of law school. While this may undercut somewhat the claim that the LSAT is unfair to minority students, especially African American students, it also calls into serious question the LSAT's predictive value. Finally, some studies reveal "a definite tendency . . . for minority students to improve slightly more than white students from year to year, but the improvement was small relative to the difference between the average grades obtained by minority and nonminority group students."[18]

The studies on the predictive value of standardized tests run like an endless river, leading to no clear destination. They permit both sides of the debate over standardized tests to stake out statistically defensible positions. The literature also shows that legal scholars tend to give less credence to the LSAT than scholars trained in statistics and psychology.[19] This may be because every law professor has many stories to tell of law students who outperformed their LSAT scores. These students, especially if they are African Americans, often have a quality that standardized tests undermeasure—determination. There is an old expression in legal education that goes as follows: the A student becomes a law professor; the B student becomes a judge; and the C student becomes a wealthy practitioner.

Undermining the predictive value of standardized tests, particularly for African Americans, are studies that show that test scores are calibrated to an applicant's income and socioeconomic status. Students from families with incomes of over $50,000 will perform on the average 25% better on the SAT than students from families with incomes of $12,000, a differential of about 200 points in both the math and verbal sections. One-third of all African American families have incomes within the latter range, compared to only 10% of white families. Perhaps the correlation between test scores and family income is one of the reasons the SAT literature carries the caveat that "your high school record is probably the best evidence of your preparation for college."[20]

Cultural background also influences test scores. Test questions assume a certain uniformity in educational experience and lifestyle, which tends to penalize students who have had different educational and life experiences. Thus, while middle-class African American students may be able to overcome the economic hurdle, they may not be able to scale the cultural one. "On average, African American students whose fathers are college-educated score *lower* on standardized entrance exams . . . than white students whose fathers had only an elementary school education."[21]

The widespread use of SAT and LSAT preparation courses further supports the conclusion that standardized tests are a better predictor of personal flexibility (the ability to adjust), family income, and socioeconomic status than academic ability. The material taught in these courses is related less to content or subject matter than to test-taking skills. Emphasis is placed on "clever strategies aimed at raising your score by outwitting the system on which the SAT is based."[22] Students who can afford test-taking courses at fees from $500 to $1,800 do in fact greatly improve their test scores and hence chances for admission. The fact that test scores can be artificially pumped up by a cram course speaks little for the test's ability to predict academic promise or merit. Indeed, the promotional literature of these prep courses coolly declares, "The SAT doesn't measure your intelligence. It simply measures how good you are at taking standardized tests."

In short, standardized tests unfairly depress African American college enrollment. These tests measure not native intelligence or academic ability, but the ability to adjust, family income, and cultural advantage. According to the College Board, "if blacks continue to close the gap in SAT scores with whites at the same rate as they have for the past 17 years, black scores will catch up to white scores some time in the first half of the twenty-first century."[23]

In addition to low enrollment, African American students have an alarmingly high college attrition rate. Nearly 70% of all African American students dropped out of college in 1992, compared to 47% of white students.[24] Some students undoubtedly returned to school at a later time or transferred to other schools. These days it often takes longer to graduate—for example, on University of California campuses, 70% of white students graduated within five years in 1992, compared to 47% of African American students[25]—but the dropout rate is still extremely high for both groups.

The dropout rate has a direct impact on the enrollment rate at the graduate level, where African American students are also grossly underrepresented. They received less than 3% of the doctorates awarded by American universities in 1992, and none in over 20 fields of science, including analytic chemistry, bioengineering, genetics, and marine sciences. Although the number of doctorates awarded to African Americans is increasing (951 were awarded in 1992), the total amount awarded is 16% less than the amount awarded in the peak year of 1977.[26] Moreover, the vast majority of doctorates are going to African American women.[27]

Traditionally, HBCUs have been the primary providers of African Americans' Ph.ds. Today, far fewer HBUCs are awarding Ph.ds than in the past. In 1992, 86% of the doctorates were granted by predominantly white institutions. That year, Berkeley awarded 796 doctoral degrees, more than six times the number awarded by all HBCUs the same year.[28]

The undergraduate dropout rate is clearly a critical factor in the story of higher education, affecting the number of doctoral degrees conferred on African Americans. One possible explanation for the high undergraduate dropout rate is the financial burden of higher education. When federally funded programs decreased in the 1980s, the number of African American undergraduate students dropped precipitously. The United Negro College Fund and other organizations have reported that "the shift in federal financial aid from direct grants to loans since 1980 has hit African Americans especially hard."[29]

Another possible reason for the high attrition rate is the dearth of African American professors on college campuses. The number of African American faculty members has remained stagnant for over a decade. In 1979 they represented 4.3% of all college professors; in 1989, 4.5%. Furthermore, less than half of this group is employed by predominantly white institutions (most being employed by HBCUs), whereas approximately 80% of African American students attend predominantly white institutions.[30]

African American professors are important not just as mentors and role models, but as sherpa guides, leaders who take their students through unknown and treacherous terrain. Drawing on their personal experiences, African American professors are able to mediate racial problems and interpret the often mysterious and arcane rules of campus life. Many African American college students feel the same way about college mores as *Washington Post* columnist Nathan McCall felt about his prior prison experience: "In many ways, adapting to the white mainstream was a lot like learning to survive in prison: You had to go in and check out the lay of the land. You had to identify the vipers and the cutthroats and play the game by rules that are alien to nature and foreign to any civilized society. Prison primed me just for that challenge."[31] Poorly conceived or implemented academic support programs can also affect the dropout rate. Like most minority students, African American students do not seek out academic advisers or tutors as much as white students do. Too many academic support programs fail to recognize and deal with this problem. Other components of an effective academic support program often found missing in colleges and universities include small-group tutorials; an emphasis on study skills, learning strategies, and test-taking techniques; improvement of students' basic organizing skills; and good teaching.[32]

Racial strife on college campuses may also affect the college dropout rate for African American students. The state of racial relations on college campuses belies *Brown*'s promise of racial harmony in integrated schools.

Deterioration of Racial Relations

The surge of racial hostility on college campuses since the mid-1980s has been widely reported by many organizations. For example, the National Institute Against Prejudice and Violence has tabulated more than 250 racial incidents at more than 200 colleges in recent years. The Center for Democratic Renewal has reported that racial incidents on college campuses have increased fourfold since 1985.[33] In another recent survey, 64% of newspaper editors at colleges enrolling more than 10,000 students (and 49% of all respondents) characterized the state of racial relations on their campuses as "fair" or "poor." According to 85% of the respondents, at least one incident on their campus during the past year could be characterized as racial.[34]

A closer look at these racial incidents paints a bleak picture. At the University of Michigan in 1988, students spotted posters in classrooms which stated: "Support the K.K.K. College Fund. A mind is a terrible thing to waste—especially on a nigger."[35] In 1988, at the University of Wisconsin, a fraternity held a fundraising "slave auction" during which white students performed skits in blackface and Afro wigs, and afterward the audience made bids for the performers' services. At Yale Law School, ten African American students received letters reading, "Now do you know why we call you NIGGERS?" A group called the "Yale Students for Racism" signed the letter. At the University of Massachusetts at Amherst, an African American residential adviser was beaten up by a white visitor, and feces were smeared on the door of his room. Enraged, scores of African American students rampaged through a 22-story dormitory. Recently, at Michigan's Olivet College, a racial brawl ignited by a white student's allegations of racial harassment resulted in the hospitalization of two students and the temporary withdrawal of almost all of the school's sixty African American students. And at Chapel Hill, North Carolina, racial tensions erupted over a proposal to build a privately funded, free-standing African American cultural center. Associate Vice Chancellor Edith Wiggins described the effect of the controversy on the school: "It has been brutal . . . There is blood all over this campus."[36]

If institutions of higher education are America's repositories of cultural and intellectual tolerance, then the outlook for racial relations for the twenty-first century looks dangerously inauspicious. If integration cannot work in this protected milieu, where can it work? At the moment, it does not appear that *Brown*'s third promise—a promise of racial harmony within integrated schools and within the larger society—can ever be fulfilled under the current racial climate. Thus it behooves us to try to understand the causes of racial strife in higher education.

It has been said that acts of overt racism are often "the physical manifestations of an accumulation of real or imagined grievances."[37] On college campuses, these grievances usually involve racial separation, affirmative action, or perceptions of special treatment, racial stereotypes, and mistrust and misunderstanding.

Racial Separation

Racial separation is destructive when it subordinates or stigmatizes a racial group either by law (as under *de jure* segregation during Jim Crow) or in fact (such as *de facto* segregation in public schools or housing). But there is a form of separation that neither subordinates nor stigmatizes. It merely creates conditions under which members of a particular racial group can eventually become part of mainstream society. Its long-term goal is individual dignity and empowerment, or racial equality. Much of the current discussion concerning racial separation on college campuses is hopelessly confused by the absence of an appreciation for the distinction between these two forms of racial separation. The discussion is further muddled because African American students occasionally practice both forms of racial separation.

Some college programs employ good forms of racial separation for the purpose of providing educational support for African American students. Such programs seek to build a supportive community for African American students within a hostile environment, giving them an equal opportunity for academic excellence. These programs do not subordinate any racial group, white or African American, either by intent or by effect.

At Cornell University, for example, freshmen are allowed to choose where they want to live from seven "program houses." Over the years, most of the minority and foreign students have chosen program houses on North Campus. This leaves West Campus primarily for white students. In 1991, over 64% of minority students lived on North Campus, and only 21% chose West Campus. One of the program houses on North Campus, called Ujamaa, is devoted to African American culture. African American students and professors strongly support Ujamaa and other program houses because these houses provide an essential space that is free from racial tension.[38] In addition, these houses can serve as learning centers, which may, in reality, be the only places on campus where true interactive learning can take place. They also afford white students an opportunity to learn about African American culture and history in an environment established by African Americans themselves.

Cornell's program houses fall into the category of good racial separation because they serve a legitimate educational purpose and do not, in the process, unnecessarily subordinate or otherwise disadvantage any particular racial group on campus. To the extent that these houses enable African American students to improve their academic performance, they are promoting educational equality in the short run and racial harmony in the long run. Scholastic achievement provides the float for African American students to swim in society's economic mainstream upon graduation.

Unfortunately, bad forms of racial separation also appear on college campuses. Although they usually begin with good intentions, they operate in ways that unnecessarily exclude or stigmatize white students and unnecessarily subordinate individual African American students. African American dorms, dining tables, and social or cultural organizations that ban or discourage white students promote an unhealthy "us against them mentality" on campus. This sort of racially hostile mindset can even spill over into areas in which white students attempt to *support* African American causes. For example, some white students report that they have met open hostility when they appear at functions honoring African American leaders or at rallies protesting university investments in racist regimes. Understandably, many of these students feel misunderstood, wrongly labeled, and judged unfairly. They rightfully complain that African American students convey the attitude that "We're going to do our black thing, and if you don't understand it—and if you can't be with it—then screw you."[39] Conflicts often come down to an inflexible stance.

This form of racial separation is particularly pernicious because it fuels the fiery notion that the institution has given its imprimatur to two enemy camps. This excluding type of racial separation lacks the healthy attitude of "come over to my place and let's share experiences." Consequently, racial misunderstanding, mistrust, and, ultimately, animosity are intensified.

The bad form of racial separation hurts some African American students in an additional way. It puts a tremendous amount of pressure on them, especially on freshmen or transfer students, to choose sides. Students who are independent enough to try crossing racial lines are pressured to back off and "be black." A kind of racial tribalism sets in. One African American student remarked that while he did not see anything wrong with identifying with one's own culture, he resented being told that "You're here, we're going to take care of you and you can separate yourself from all that other stuff."[40] Athletes are the only ones who seem to have the status and capability to defy the mores of racial kinship.[41]

Some degree of racial separation on integrated college campuses is necessary at present. African American college students who attend predominantly white institutions are entitled to equal educational opportunity. Widespread campus racism and insensitive college administrators drive many of them into separate environments where healthy self-esteem and academic success can be nurtured. Racial or ethnic solidarity (and, by implication, group esteem) is a reaction to unpleasant contacts with outside groups. Separate dorms, sororities, fraternities, and cultural centers are important tools to foster academic success.

Moreover, many dorms, sororities, fraternities, and other structures in the larger university community are still effectively off-limits to the majority of African American students because of racism. Until colleges and universities create an environment comfortable and accessible to all racial groups, racial separation will remain a necessity in college life.

Affirmative Action

Although some universities, most notably the University of California, have officially eliminated racial preferences in admissions, affirmative action is another source of racial hostility on college campuses. Half of all editors of campus newspapers at large universities agreed that white students on their campuses feel that "blacks receive special treatment that is not warranted."[42] Many white students deeply resent what they believe is a double standard in both the admissions and academic support of African American students. In their view, colleges and universities admit unqualified students, finance the education of students from wealthy families at the expense of poor white students, and permit African American students to escape certain penalties or course requirements. In effect, "whites worry that blacks want to deconstruct the meritocratic principle of equality of opportunity into a numerical guarantee of equality of reward."[43]

Much of this resentment is misdirected. Too often school administrators fail to disseminate clear statements about the legitimate purposes of their affirmative action programs. Most programs are designed to target promising students. These students carry some risk, but they are not "unqualified." In other places administrators or professors do not fully understand or support the goals of educational diversity. White students then get the message and take it as license to react with indignation against African American students. Finally, many college admissions programs consistently fail to identify truly deserving applicants for special financial consideration. When struggling white students see wealthy African American students taking all the special scholarships based on financial need, they have a right to feel resentful. But their anger should be directed not at the recipients of these awards but at those who dole them out. Otherwise, their legitimate resentment will have the illegitimate effect of stigmatizing the more vulnerable and innocent party.

African American students, on the other hand, discern that the concerns of white students receive preferential treatment and that they are not given the same respect as their white counterparts. Many believe that such inequality compels them to speak up, march out, conduct sit-ins and demonstrations. They take from the Civil Rights Movement the well-tested lesson that without protest, issues and matters of concern to them will fall upon deaf ears. African American students are convinced that they must "turn up the heat" in order to be heard. In many instances, such feelings of powerlessness are justified.[44]

Racial Stereotyping, Mistrust, and Misunderstanding

At Chapel Hill, the University of North Carolina once provided space for a statue showing an African American man twirling a basketball and white students with stacks of books. African American students were, understandably, insulted. Several young men reported that white students often thought they were basketball players simply because they were African American and dressed in sweatpants. In another incident, an African American female student was shocked and dismayed when a white student who answered the door at a fraternity house asked her whether she was applying for the cook's position. Many white students look upon African American culture, from civil rights heroes to rap music, as "less intelligent" than white culture.[45]

Thomas Sowell reminds us that "racism, as such, is not new. What is new are the frequency, the places, and the class of people involved in an unprecedented escalation of overt racial hostility among middle-class young people on predominantly liberal or radical campuses. Painful as these episodes are, they should not be surprising."[46] Although many racial stereotypes are, indeed, the product of racism—an effort to exercise power and control over African Americans by degrading them—others stem from a general lack of exposure and ignorance about African American society, culture, and history. Education is the antidote for ignorance; prayer is the only hope for racism.

College campuses are rife with frustration born of racial mistrust and misunderstanding. Many African American students simply believe that racism is a permanent condition of the white mindset. As one said, "the best efforts of well-meaning whites cannot heal the wounds of racism." Another student echoed this fatalistic point of view, remarking that "because of what's happened in the past, there's always going to be white people who consider black people 'niggers' and there'll be black people who are going to hate white people." A female African American student explained that when she becomes friends with white students, they always expect her to come onto their turf, without any desire to come onto hers. The friendship is never mutual in the sharing of experiences. As a result, many African American students believe it is futile to attempt to educate white people, and they do not see the races ever living together in harmony.[47]

White students, on the other hand, report that even the simplest conversations with African American classmates can be fraught with anxiety. One student reports that she worries constantly about African American students jumping down her throat for failing to use the politically correct terms. "There is just such a huge barrier that it's really hard . . . to have a normal discussion." If a student does not completely agree with an African American stance or position, he or she is immediately "stamped as a racist," white students complain.[48]

Economic differences further widen the communications gap between the races. As a group, white students tend to be in a higher economic bracket than African American students. It is often frustrating for an African American student who is trying to scrape together enough money to buy groceries to see white fraternity brothers in "hot" cars spending money freely on beer and socials. At the same time, white students resent being classified as "spoiled rich kids."

Given this level of racial mistrust and misunderstanding, it is no wonder that racial hostility permeates our college campuses. The mistrust and misunderstanding run so deep that it is hard to believe they are newly minted mindsets on college campuses. It seems more likely that they are part of the baggage students bring to college each year. Coming out of deficient public schools, many African American students come to college already embittered and hardened. And white students, having little or no exposure to African Americans save the negative stories they see on TV or read about in the newspaper, harbor many racial stereotypes by the time they enroll in college.

The solution is easy to conceive in theory: more racial sensitivity is needed. But realistically, I doubt it can be imparted successfully to many students, African American or white, at this late stage of their education. If we are ever going to eliminate or ameliorate racial strife in higher education, it will have to be done primarily in the elementary and secondary schools.

3

Housing

The housing experiences of most African Americans have changed little since the beginning of integration. From the "black ghetto" to the "black suburbs," residential segregation largely defines the housing market despite the passage of the Fair Housing Act in 1968. In this area, as in education, understanding the past is essential to understanding the full dimensions of the contemporary housing problem.

Historical Context

Present-day residential isolation did not happen as the random, chance by-product of normal socioeconomic processes. Prior to mandatory integration, white Americans deliberately set out to deny African Americans access to housing markets and in this way created or reinforced housing segregation. From the end of the Civil War in 1865 and for the next hundred years, white Americans and the government at all levels made conscious efforts to erect or strengthen racial barriers in housing.[1] Today's housing patterns stand as grim reminders of prior systems of housing subordination.

Ironically, there was little housing segregation during slavery. Free African Americans and whites actually lived in closer proximity than do African Americans and whites today. The demand for inexpensive labor along with the primitive state of transportation brought most free African Americans within walking distance of white residential and business areas. During 1845, for example, the average freeman in Louisville lived in a neighborhood that was only 14% African American. Of course, the southern slaves were even less segregated. In Charleston in 1861, the "dissimilarity" (or segregation) index between the slave and white populations was 11.4%.

Studies of African American residential life within northern cities around the time of the Civil War also reveal the absence of systematic exclusion from white neighborhoods on the basis of skin color. Overall, the average rate of dissimilarity or segregation between the free African American and white populations stood at 45.5% in the North and at a low 30% in the South.[2]

Nothing resembling the modern African American ghetto had come into being. The communities that developed in cities like Cleveland, Chicago, Detroit, and Milwaukee were dominated by an elite of educated professionals, business owners, and successful tradespeople, all of whom maintained amicable interracial ties, as far as social intercourse went.[3] Furthermore, African Americans living in these communities were not altogether cut off from whites. They interacted frequently with whites in places of employment and on the streets.

Integrated residential patterns for both poor and wealthy African Americans began to disappear from the big cities toward the end of the last century. In the North, the change was due to racial discrimination, which resulted in part from pressures caused by the massive exodus of African Americans from southern rural communities to northern cities. As America became more industrialized, the demand for African American tenant farmers and day laborers in the South decreased while the need for unskilled workers in the northern cities exploded. Lasting for most of this century, northward migration was fed by urban newspapers and periodicals, widely circulated in the South, which exhorted southern African Americans to move northward to "the promised land." Between 1910 and 1920, some 525,000 African Americans migrated, to take advantage of employment opportunities in the North and to escape racial oppression in the South. During the 1920s the outflow became a tidal wave of 877,000 persons.[4]

Although white employers were generally eager to embrace a new supply of workers to satisfy their labor needs, most northern whites viewed the African American migration with increasing hostility. Working-class whites, in particular, feared economic competition from the newcomers. Many in the white working class were first- or second-generation immigrants who were themselves scorned by other whites. They quickly discovered, however, that they could oppress a group of people positioned even lower than they in society's racial hierarchy. White ethnic groups displayed open racial hostility in a series of racial riots that broke out between 1900 and 1920.[5] Scores of African Americans were attacked by roving mobs of working-class whites. Many individuals who had the misfortune of living beyond recognized African American neighborhoods saw their homes destroyed. Although most rioters were white, most of those arrested for the riots were African Americans. During these particularly violent years, the percentage of African Americans and whites who lived in dissimilar (or segregated) locations grew to 58.5% in the North and 38.3% in the South.[6]

Despite racial hostility, the northern migration continued, but African Americans now preferred to move into increasingly one-race communities. The modern African American ghetto was in the making. Chicago led the way. Its dissimilarity index skyrocketed from only 10% in 1900 to nearly 70% thirty years later.[7] By the beginning of the Great Depression, the typical African American Chicagoan lived in a neighborhood consisting of over two-thirds African Americans.[8]

Housing in other northern cities also became segregated, although not as rapidly as in Chicago. During the first 30 years of the century, Cleveland's isolation index increased from 8% to 51%; New York's index increased from 5% to 42%; St. Louis's index increased from 13% to 47%; and Los Angeles's index increased from 4% to 26%.[9]

The most damaging blow to interracial residential housing was delivered in the 1930s and 1940s. Construction of homes came to a sudden halt during the Great Depression. The supply of available housing was limited even for white Americans who could afford it. Yet the pace of the northern migration picked up considerably, squeezing ever more African Americans into overcrowded neighborhoods, as the demand for labor in northern factories reached unprecedented levels during World War II. The tight housing market together with the massive influx of people delivered the *coup de grace* for integrated residential housing; as a consequence, the modern African American ghetto became firmly established. At that time, the residential dissimilarity index between the African American and white populations stood at about 85.8% in the North and 84.9% in the South.[10]

Four years of full employment during World War II combined with wartime consumer shortages to create a massive surplus of savings and a tremendous demand for housing. The confluence of surplus capital and pent-up demand resulted in an unparalleled postwar boom in residential construction. Most of the homes were built in suburbia to satisfy the desire of middle-class white Americans to leave the crowded inner cities. The percentage of suburban residents increased from about 33% in 1940 to over 50% by 1970.[11] In contrast, African Americans remained trapped in the cities. Thus, by 1960, 90% of all neighborhoods inhabited by African Americans were either completely African American or moving in that direction.[12]

More than family income or anything else, residential discrimination, largely engineered by the federal government, created the peculiar racial patterns that developed in the cities and suburbs. As James Kushner explains, "Early federal efforts in the field of housing accepted and even mandated segregation. Through the Federal Housing Administration mortgage insurance programs—the most effective master plan in American land-use history—the Roosevelt and Truman administrations designed and executed suburban apartheid. These programs called for obligatory racially restrictive covenants in racially separate subdivisions."[13] The Federal Housing Administration (FHA), for example, issued underwriting manuals during the 1930s and 1940s that viewed the restrictive covenant as "a favorable condition" for making a loan. The FHA manuals even provided lenders with a prototype restrictive covenant.[14] "From the close of World War II until 1959 approximately 2% of all the housing covered by FHA mortgage insurance was occupied by blacks."[15] As late as 1950, the National Association of Real Estate Board's (NAREB) Code of Ethics explicitly required that "a realtor should never be instrumental in introducing into a neighborhood . . . members of any race or nationality, or any individuals whose presence will clearly be detrimental to property values in the neighborhood."[16] The NAREB's racism reinforced housing segregation long after 1950.

Douglas Massey and Nancy Denton argue that the historical pattern outlined above has created five geographic traits reflected in current residential segregation.[17] First, African Americans may be overrepresented in some areas and underrepresented in others, leading to degrees of *unevenness.* Second, African Americans may be racially *isolated,* rarely sharing a neighborhood with whites. Third, African Americans may be tightly *clustered* either in large enclaves or in smaller neighborhoods scattered throughout metropolitan areas in a checkerboard fashion. Fourth, African Americans may be overcrowded or *concentrated* within a very small area. Fifth, African Americans may be spatially *centralized* within urban centers or spread out along the periphery. Massey and Denton further argue that, because of past segregation, African Americans today are more segregated than other racial groups within these housing segregation patterns, taken individually and collectively. For example, African Americans are highly segregated within six standard metropolitan statistical areas (SMSAs) on all 5 dimensions, a pattern called "hypersegregation." In another four SMSAs African Americans are segregated on 4 of the 5 dimensions. Together, these 10 SMSAs contain 23% of the nation's African American population, and 29% of all African Americans living within urban areas.[18] No other group within the contemporary United States comes close to this high level of racial isolation in urban society.

Effect of Housing Segregation

Housing segregation during the era of racial integration has injured African Americans in several significant ways. It has certainly had a dramatic effect on school desegregation: segregated housing inevitably leads to segregated schools. This process clearly undermines the integrationist mission initiated in *Brown v. Board of Education.*

Residential segregation is also conducive to poverty in African American communities. It is difficult, however, to explain the exact nature of that effect. Massey and Denton have offered one widely accepted explanation. They argue that housing segregation distributes poverty along racial lines by concentrating it in African American neighborhoods. When class segregation is added—when middle-class African Americans leave inner-city neighborhoods—poverty concentration intensifies. Class segregation, then, "exacerbate[s] the degree of poverty concentration that is imposed on poor blacks because of racial segregation."[19] The main point, however, which Massey first made in a 1990 article, is that residential segregation creates small and isolated African American neighborhoods that are especially vulnerable to economic downturns, such as the industrial restructuring that took place in the 1970s. In this way poverty remains disproportionately confined to these neighborhoods.[20]

To illustrate the effect of segregation on the rate of poverty, Massey in his article and later in his book co-authored with Denton constructs a hypothetical city of 128,000 people, 32,000 (25%) of whom are African American. Each neighborhood within the city contains 8,000 residents. The percentage of African Americans and whites who live in households with incomes below the poverty level is set (city-wide) at 20% and 10%, respectively. These population characteristics approximate those of many American cities in the 1970s, including Chicago and New York. Massey then uses four hypothetical models identical in every respect except for the variable degree of residential segregation. Segregation ranges from zero to 100%. In addition, each model simulates the economic conditions of the 1970s, a decade marked by significant downsizing of smokestack industries and other structural changes in the economy. Thus the only variable in the four models is the degree of residential segregation, or integration. We need only consider the models at either end of the spectrum to understand Massey's point—namely, racial segregation (and later class segregation) concentrates poverty.

Hypothetical City 1 (which can be called the Integrated City) occupies one end of the spectrum. It is characterized by complete residential integration, which Massey defines as an African American-white dissimilarity index equal to zero. After subjecting the Integrated City to the economic conditions of the 1970s, Massey found that the *neighborhood* poverty rate for both African Americans and whites is the same, 12.5%: "The [African American] rate of 20% implies that 400 of the 2,000 are poor, and the white rate of 10% implies that 600 whites fall into this category; together they constitute a total poverty population of 1,000 people, which, divided by the neighborhood size of 8,000, yields a rate of 12.5%."[21] At the other end of the spectrum, Massey hypothesizes a city that has 100% residential segregation (which can be called the Segregated City). Here, the assumed African American *city-wide* poverty rate of 20% implies that 1,600 of the 8,000 African Americans in the segregated neighborhood are poor. This number, divided by the neighborhood size (8,000), yields a neighborhood-wide poverty rate of 20%, which matches the assumed rate; the assumed white city-wide poverty rate of 10% implies 800 of the 8,000 whites within the all-white neighborhood are poor, which, divided by the neighborhood size (8,000), yields a neighborhood-wide poverty rate of 10%, which is the same as the assumed rate.

Under conditions of integration, therefore, both races experience identical geographic concentrations of poverty; but with complete residential segregation, poverty is concentrated in the African American neighborhood at a rate of 2 to 1.[22] Stated differently, although the city-wide racial poverty rate (20% versus 10%) remains constant, the neighborhood racial poverty rate varies according to the level of residential segregation (or integration) within the neighborhoods. Racial integration dilutes the concentration of poverty for African Americans by integrating the poor into mixed neighborhoods, while increasing the poverty index for whites city-wide.

As poverty becomes more concentrated in African American neighborhoods, existing social pathologies become more pronounced. They become even more exacerbated when class segregation is factored in—that is, when middle-class African Americans move out. The rates of crime and violence in the neighborhood increase when racial segregation and class segregation increase. As Massey explains:

> With a black poverty rate of 30% (i.e., after the downward shift in black incomes), the major crime rate in neighborhoods inhabited by poor blacks is predicted to be 50 per thousand in a city without class or racial segregation; but, as racial segregation rises, the rate steadily increases to 60 per thousand. . . . In cities that are segregated by class alone, the major crime rate is similarly about 62 per thousand; but this rate steadily rises as racial segregation is imposed, reaching a high of 84 per thousand under conditions of maximum segregation. Thus, the imposition of racial segregation on a class-segregated city inevitably produces extremely high crime rates in poor black neighborhoods.[23]

In addition to crime and violence, housing deterioration, mortality, the quality of education (as measured by school funding and standardized test scores), welfare dependency, family structure (the percentage of single mothers), and joblessness worsen as poverty rates climb and middle-class residents leave the neighborhood.[24]

Massey's statistical models are not mere abstract musings. They are consistent with empirical findings. For example, housing deterioration is obviously a major problem. Research has shown that abandoned and boarded-up buildings often invite arson, which leads to a high incidence of residential fires and the loss of major commercial institutions in the community. This in fact happened in Chicago's West Side ghetto, which lost 75% of its business establishments between 1960 and 1970. Similarly, a North Lawndale neighborhood decayed to the point where it now contains 48 state lottery agents, 50 currency exchanges, and 99 licensed bars and liquor stores, but only one bank and one supermarket for a population of some 50,000 residents.[25] Finally, poor African American communities usually receive inadequate community services—erratic garbage collection, snow removal, and street or other structural repairs.[26] In short, like Massey's statistical models, empirical data strongly suggest that housing segregation substantially diminishes the social environment of poor African Americans.

Residential segregation and its attendant social ills can only dampen the spirits of even the most optimistic individual. Growing up in "underclass" conditions, poor African American adolescents especially become disenchanted with "the system" and with life itself. A sense of nihilism begins to set in—what Cornel West describes as a "profound sense of psychological depression, personal worthlessness, and social despair."[27] While the structuralists look to "external" forces (the lingering effect of prior racial subordination as well as present-day racism) to explain such nihilism, the behaviorists point to "internal" influence (what Thomas Sowell describes as "human capital": education, attitudes, basic values about thrift and family responsibility, and adaptability to change) for an explanation.[28] As the debate rages on, nihilism continues unabated.

Modest but earnest attempts to break up the concentration of poverty in African American communities have met with stiff resistance. Ordinary white homeowners who do not pretend to think about these issues beyond mere self-interest or racism have opposed efforts to move low-income African Americans into all-white neighborhoods in such diverse places as Chicago, Yonkers, and Valparaiso, Indiana. The federal government has empowered these homeowners by giving them the right to exclude federally subsidized public housing from their neighborhoods. Although the government's Section 8 Program bypasses this right by subsidizing rent in private apartments, federal housing officials report that most Section 8 recipients, preferring the familiar to the unfamiliar, remain in their own communities.[29] As a consequence, very little integration has taken place.

Whites are not alone in opposing integrated housing for the poor. Middle-class African Americans, many of whom have managed to escape from the inner city themselves, have offered resistance, if not to racial integration, to class integration. They have vigorously opposed the movement of poor African Americans into their own neighborhoods.[30] In North Hempstead, Long Island, for example, middle-class African Americans challenged the construction of public housing in their neighborhood, claiming that the poor would rapidly destroy property values and good neighborhood relations.[31] Such opposition may also have resulted from the failure of many middle-class African Americans to identify psychologically with the low-income group. Perhaps, also, the very presence of the poor is an uncomfortable reminder to middle-class African Americans of the fragility of their own achievements. Class integration will be possible when it is based on African American self-interest rather than racial kinship or altruism.

In Chicago, the Gautreaux Program has overcome both white and middle-class African American opposition to housing integration. This program was developed as a result of a 1966 lawsuit filed on behalf of public housing residents in Chicago, who alleged that the Chicago Housing Authority and the United States Department of Housing and Urban Development administered Chicago's low-rent public housing program in a racially discriminatory manner.[32] As of 1993, the program, then in its seventeenth year, had moved over 5,000 low-income families to either predominantly white suburbs or predominantly middle-class African American city neighborhoods.[33] (At only 300 families each year, this can hardly be called successful integration.)

Each year the Gautreaux Program opens its phones for one day to select new participants. (In 1992 alone, 15,000 people placed calls.) The first 2,000 low-income African American callers are placed on the certification list.[34] The applicants must satisfy three criteria. First, they must have families with four or fewer children. Second, they must have an income source (most receive AFDC) and regularly pay their rent. Third, they must satisfy an inspection to determine whether or not their housekeeping is good enough to make them desirable tenants. About 50 to 70% of Chicago's housing project residents, many of whom are second-generation welfare recipients, satisfy these criteria.[35]

Qualified applicants are counseled on how to search for an apartment within the target housing market. They are told to find private apartments on their own, either in predominantly white suburbs or in predominantly middle-class African American city neighborhoods. The suburbs average 96% white, and the urban middle-class neighborhoods average 99% African American. Theoretically, the Gautreaux participants are free to choose, but in practice they are simply sent to look in neighborhoods where there happen to be openings at the time. This approximates a random selection, however. Program participants receive Section 8 housing allowances, which means they pay 30% of their income toward the rent, and the federal government pays the rest.[36]

Random empirical studies were conducted on 230 Gautreaux participants who moved to the white neighborhoods and 112 who moved to the African American neighborhoods. Ninety movers were given in-depth interviews. The studies found that 52% of the newcomers to the white neighborhoods faced initial harassment, while 23%, or less than half, of the newcomers to the African American neighborhoods experienced harassment. The harassment consisted mostly of name-calling, racial insults, and other verbal insults. However, 8 of the 27 questioned newcomers to the white neighborhoods reported more serious problems, such as fighting and police harassment, which many believed were racially motivated. In time, there was a decrease in harassment within the predominantly white areas. After a year, only 25% of the newcomers to the white neighborhoods faced harassment. This suggests that their white neighbors grew more accepting over time.[37]

Twenty-five percent from both groups received support from their neighbors while settling in. This assistance included "neighbors going out of their way" to help; for instance, providing tours of the area or watching the children.[38] Both groups reported the same number of new friends. However, neither group was likely to lend money to its neighbors, let a neighbor use the phone, watch a neighbor's children, or eat with a neighbor.[39] Not surprisingly, the movers to the white neighborhoods had more interracial friendships than the movers to the African American neighborhoods. Moreover, the movers to the white neighborhoods increased their opportunities for better-paying jobs with benefits. They became more likely to enroll in school, college preparatory courses, and four-year colleges. And they did not engage in criminal behavior or contribute to other forms of trouble.[40]

These encouraging reports on the Gautreaux Program have helped to convince the federal government to invest an additional $240 million to implement similar programs nationally.[41] Sociologist Juliet Saltman contends similar programs will succeed if sufficient resources and institutional networks are mobilized. In particular, marketing campaigns should be devised to encourage poor African Americans to migrate to areas in which they would normally be least likely to live and to reduce local opposition to housing integration through seminars and other forms of education.[42]

It may be premature to label the Gautreaux Program a success, however. There are too many unanswered questions, some having been raised by sociologist William Sampson. African American himself, Sampson argues that African Americans lose their identity when placed in predominantly white suburbs. In a 1993 television interview, Sampson argued:

> If we're prepared to look, walk and talk, feel, believe, value the same way middle-class white folks do, then we'll be fine. That's assimilation. I have to be just like you in order to function in this society. I

have to value the same music, wear the same clothes and I integrate well. . . . I shouldn't have to be like you. Why don't you like me. . . . I wonder . . . is the price too high? . . . Disruption from and potential alienation from community and maybe self [are the worst things Gautreaux families face].[43]

Sampson's criticism obviously refers to the white suburban side of the program, not the African American city side.

Some evidence supports Sampson's concerns. In the same television interview, Kiah Morris, a young African American woman who had moved to a predominantly white suburb at age one and one-half, expressed her feelings about growing up there:

I mean, all I'd seen were white faces. I can't recall growing up and seeing any other black faces until sixth grade, and that was a student from Nigeria. [Attending a racially mixed junior high school later on,] I didn't fit in. I had white friends, but I wasn't really accepted by them either. . . . And then the black kids, they basically ignored me. Some of them made fun of me; they called me Oreo. I got all the names. I got a list of them. I could write a book about them. And it did carry through to high school. I still never got a connection. I tried, but it didn't work—they still didn't want me.[44]

Eventually, the woman's entire family moved back to Chicago, to a middle-class African American neighborhood called Hyde Park.[45]

These interviews point to two major problems with the Gautreaux studies. First, the studies do not measure cultural alienation among the program participants, whether they move to the suburbs or another part of the city. Judging from the interviews, I suspect that cultural alienation is a problem in the predominantly white neighborhoods but not in the predominantly middle-class African American neighborhoods. Second, the studies do not reveal the return rate, whether in absolute numbers or based on the number of years in the program. The studies count the movers but not the returners, and they do not tell us whether those who return stayed with the program for one month, one year, or, like Kiah and her family, sixteen years. Until this information is collected, it will be difficult to determine the "success" of the Gautreaux Program.

The Gautreaux Program aside, one thing is clear: the Chicago metropolitan area is still one of the most segregated places in the United States.

As Massey and Denton point out, in 1990, twenty-two years after the passage of the Fair Housing Act, the level of residential dissimilarity between African Americans and whites stood at 86%, which is only within two points of where it had been in 1980 and within five points of its 1970 percentage. At the rate of change observed in the 1980s, Chicago will not reach a residential dissimilarity level of 70% (still a very high level of segregation) until the year 2024.[46]

Discrimination as the Primary Cause of Segregation

Why has residential segregation, with all its attendant ills, persisted under racial integration? To many, the most obvious answer is racial discrimination. But several social scientists reject this answer.

Most notably, William Julius Wilson contends that broad-scale discrimination against African Americans has been virtually eliminated by federal civil rights laws such as the 1964 Civil Rights Act and the Fair Housing Act. For Wilson, the ability of middle-class African Americans to move out of segregated communities, something they simply could not do under Jim Crow laws, is substantial proof that crippling housing discrimination is no longer a critical factor. Poverty and class are more important variants than race in explaining continued residential segregation.[47]

While I have on another occasion recognized that the exodus of middle-class African Americans from inner-city communities has resulted in a degree of class segregation in African American society,[48] I would not go as far as Wilson. Racial discrimination is still a major cause of housing segregation. In the first place, past racial discrimination created patterns of housing segregation from which millions of African Americans, mainly the low-income earners, have not been able to escape. Second, Wilson's claim that middle-class African Americans have completely or mostly pulled out of urban centers is not supported by research conducted by Massey and his associates. This research, postdating Wilson's work, has shown that middle-class African Americans have not left urban communities in large numbers since the end of Jim Crow.[49] To the extent that there has been an outward migration of middle-class African Americans, it has largely been to the suburbs adjacent to the inner city, resulting in what George Galster calls "near-central-city suburbanization." Such suburbanization is not equivalent to desegregation, and it has not led to relief from crime and other burdens of ghetto life.[50] Moreover, class segregation among African Americans is significantly lower than class segregation in other minority groups.[51] Thus, today, the cities and near suburbs are "chocolate," while the far suburbs are "vanilla."[52]

Public opinion supports the idea that housing discrimination continues to exist. One survey, for example, indicated that although 57% of the white respondents felt that whites do not have the right to discriminate against African Americans, only 35% of these respondents would vote in favor of a law that prohibited a homeowner from refusing to sell his or her home to a buyer on the basis of the buyer's racial background. Likewise, while 88% of the white respondents agreed with the opinion that African Americans have a right to live wherever they can afford, only 43% of these respondents said that they would feel comfortable living in a neighborhood that was 33% African American.[53]

Various studies, including some conducted by the Department of Housing and Urban Development (HUD), indicate that face-to-face discrimination by homeowners, landlords, and intermediaries (real estate agents and lenders) is rampant in the housing industry. At one time HUD estimated that "there are 2,000,000 instances of unlawful discrimination each year,"[54] despite federal antidiscrimination laws. (I have discussed these matters in some detail in *Rethinking*.[55])

Considerable housing discrimination also takes place within the context of the government's regulation of the housing and credit markets.[56] In 1994, for example, HUD settled 17 discrimination lawsuits for a total of $75 million, confessing that for almost two decades it had promoted racial segregation by building its housing projects almost exclusively in low-income, minority areas.[57]

Likewise, there is no question that discrimination within the home mortgage lending market has flourished. Despite the elimination of restrictive covenants from federal mortgage insurance programs through laws banning discrimination in the home lending market, the Federal Reserve Bank of Boston Reports that in 1992 minorities were 60% more likely than whites to be rejected for a mortgage loan. Drawing from its findings, which have been defended against a variety of challenges,[58] the bank report concludes that 17% of African American applicants are denied loans even if they possess the same obligation ratios, credit history, loan to value, and property characteristics as white applicants.[59] This is discrimination, pure and simple.

In several discussions with Tom Carter, one of the leading banking executives in the nation, I have come to understand exactly how discrimination in the home mortgage industry can be so prevalent despite so many federal and state antidiscrimination laws on the books. Discrimination in the home mortgage industry, Carter explains, is subtle and, to some extent, may be beyond the reach of antidiscrimination laws. The complexity of the topic leads me to begin with a brief historical overview of the home mortgage industry.

The Home Mortgage Market

The financing of individual home ownership in the United States is an enormous industry. It has one of the largest dollar volumes of annual new loans and is one of the largest categories of existing debt of all types of debt financing, including the financing of corporate inventories or plant and equipment. The providers of home mortgages have changed as the mortgage industry has evolved.

Traditionally, home mortgages were provided primarily by local community banks, especially by savings and loans or savings banks. These institutions took in local savings and earned an "interest spread" on savings deposits by lending them out in the form of home mortgage loans. Both the deposits and the mortgages were usually long term and predictable, and the banks were protected from competition by banking regulation that controlled the issuance of bank charters. Savings banks were limited to offering only savings accounts, on which they could pay slightly more interest than commercial banks, and also mortgage loans. Large commercial banks generally avoided home mortgages because they earned better interest margins on shorter-term business and consumer loans.

The economy and the banking systems were relatively stable from the end of the 1930s to the late 1970s. During this period the institutional structure worked well to provide money to those who were able to realize the American dream of home ownership. In the late 1970s, however, the Federal Reserve Board changed its approach to managing the economy to strengthen its control of the inflation that resulted from the Vietnam War, expanded social programs, and the Arab oil cartel. The Federal Reserve chose to discontinue its practice of maintaining stable interest rates, and instead sought to influence economic activity by more closely controlling the money supply, without regard to what impact this would have on interest rates. The result was that short term interest rates rose to unanticipated levels, the economy slowed down, and banks suffered from "disintermediation." Disintermediation is what happens when savings depositors decide to take advantage of the high interest rates available in government bonds by withdrawing their savings from banks (which were limited by regulation as to how much interest they could pay), and investing the money in government securities. This practice became widespread in the late 1970s, and had the effect of removing money from the savings bank industry that had been established to provide home mortgage loans.

In the early 1980s the legislative response to the problems of the savings banks was to allow the banks to pay higher interest rates for savings deposits and to allow them to diversify their lending activities into commercial real estate, consumer loans, business loans, and other well-publicized riskier asset categories. At the same time as the savings bank industry both struggled and moved a portion of its assets out of home mortgage loans, other competitors entered the home mortgage business. These mortgage lenders were not banks or savings banks, did not offer government insured deposits, and therefore did not come within the same regulatory structure as their insured depository bank competitors. In the face of competition, the mortgage banks relied on more direct access to institutional and Wall Street capital sources to provide funds for mortgage loans.

A more direct access to mortgage capital was aided by FannieMae and FreddieMac. These agencies, backed by the federal government, performed a major role in the expansion of the home mortgage industry by purchasing pools of home mortgages from mortgage originators, which could then be grouped with other mortgages as collateral for bonds issued by FannieMae or FreddieMac, thus making more capital available for home mortgages. The bonds issued by FannieMae and FreddieMac, both inexpensive and desirable because of the government agency status of the issuers, have turned the mortgage loan into a type of financial commodity.

Although the introduction of FannieMae and FreddieMac has led to great standardization in the mortgage business—resulting in market efficiencies and a continuous supply of capital for the home mortgage industry—the industry is no longer predominantly limited to insured depository institutions but has expanded to include more non-bank providers of mortgages. There is also a movement toward specialization within the processing of mortgage loans. Specialization has led to breaking up the mortgage process into disparate segments: the marketing of mortgage loans to potential applicants; the underwriting and approval of mortgage applications; the documentation and funding of the mortgage loan; and the servicing and collection of payments.

This picture of the home mortgage market shows how difficult, if not impossible, it is to eliminate discrimination in the industry. The introduction and subsequent proliferation of non-bank mortgage providers and the segmentation of the mortgage process have made regulation more difficult, and the opportunities for discrimination more plentiful. To reverse this situation, the government would have had to either streamline the industry or strengthen antidiscrimination law. Because the first choice could dry up the industry's source of capital or create market inefficiencies that would surely increase the interest rate on home mortgage loans, the government chose the second course of action.

Antidiscrimination Law and Its Effects

The home mortgage industry is subject to numerous federal and state regulations, many of which are interrelated and complex, and (important to note) not all of which apply to all home mortgage providers.[60]

This section focuses on four of the major statues that regulate mortgage lending and discrimination in home mortgage lending: Equal Credit Opportunity Act (ECOA),[61] Home Mortgage Disclosure Act (HMDA),[62] Fair Housing Act (FHA),[63] and Community Reinvestment Act (CRA).[64]

As originally enacted in 1975, ECOA banned discrimination on the basis of sex or marital status in the extension of credit. The Act was amended in 1976, however, to include discrimination on grounds of race, color, religion, national origin, age, and whether all or part of the applicant's income derives from public assistance. Responding to an ECOA charge to promulgate implementing regulations, the Federal Reserve Board has issued a package collectively called Regulation B.[65] In its most relevant part, Regulation B states that "[a] creditor shall not discriminate against any applicant on a prohibited basis regarding any aspect of a credit transaction."[66] The term "credit transaction" is defined broadly to cover most aspects of an applicant's relationship with a creditor, including the application, the credit decision, and also advertising, preapplication information, and loan collection.[67] In fact, ECOA applies even before a borrower and a lender have formally entered any relationship and continues throughout the financial relationship to protect against discrimination in the collection practices of a lender after a loan is made. For the purposes of ECOA, a creditor is one "who, in the ordinary course of business, regularly participates in the decision of whether or not to extend credit."[68] This definition covers all mortgage providers as well as the many specialists involved in the processing of home mortgages.

The decision to grant credit to one applicant and deny it to another is, by its very nature, discriminatory. In determining whether such discrimination is illegal, it is not necessary to show that a prohibited criterion, such as race, was expressly used in the approval process. If the process has a negative impact on a protected class, that constitutes illegal discrimination. This is an application of the "effects test," as developed in employment discrimination law.[69] The Federal Reserve Board explicitly adopted it in a footnote to Regulation B: "The legislative history of the Act indicates that the Congress intended an 'effects test' concept, as outlined in the employment field by the Supreme Court . . . to be applicable to a creditor's determination of creditworthiness."[70] Under the effects test, if an applicant can show that a lender approves disproportionately fewer loans to members of a protected class, the lender must demonstrate that its approval process serves a business purpose and was not a means to discriminate against a protected class. Individuals can sue for actual or punitive damages, and the Department of Justice can bring a "pattern or practice" suit against lenders who violate ECOA.[71]

In 1976 Congress enacted the Home Mortgage Disclosure Act (HMDA), which was amended in 1980, 1983, and 1989. HMDA requires mortgage lenders to compile in a prescribed manner specific information about their lending activities and to file their reports with the appropriate supervisory agency. The data from an individual lender's HMDA reports are available to the public. HMDA's main purpose was to attack "redlining," a discriminatory lending practice in which a lender chooses to withhold mortgage loans in a particular geographic neighborhood. The lack of mortgage loan availability in such neighborhoods then leads to the deterioration of the housing supply in the neighborhood. HMDA does not require lenders to make specific categories of loans nor does it provide penalties for not making loans in a particular community; it is only a reporting law. Lenders must disclose information regarding the race, sex, income, and census tract of mortgage applications received and processed. In enacting HMDA, Congress, rather naively, hoped that the public disclosure of discriminatory lending patterns would cause public officials and depositors to pressure lenders not to discriminate in making loans. Although only a reporting law, HMDA data has been used as the basis for action taken under other statutes, such as the Fair Housing Act and the Community Reinvestment Act.[72]

The Fair Housing Act (FHA) was enacted as Title VIII of the Civil Rights

Act of 1968. Under the 1988 amendments to FHA, regulations implementing the provisions of FHA are issued by the Department of Housing and Urban Development (HUD). The FHA makes it illegal to discriminate in the sale, rental, or financing of housing because of race, color, religion, sex, disability, family status, or national origin.[73] Furthermore, the 1988 amendments to FHA expanded the prohibition against discrimination in financing beyond the conduct of lending institutions to include "activities relating to the purchase of residential loans." This extends coverage of FHA to the secondary mortgage market, including FannieMaes and FreddieMacs discussed above.[74] Individuals as well as the Attorney General may sue under the FHA in federal court, state court, or through an administrative hearing. Recovery may include damages (actual or punitive), attorneys' fees, and court costs.[75]

The Community Reinvestment Act of 1977 (CRA) became effective on November 6, 1978. The purpose of CRA is "to require each appropriate Federal financial supervisory agency to use its authority when examining financial institutions, to encourage such institutions to help meet the credit needs of the local communities in which they are chartered consistent with the safe and sound operation of such institution."[76] Unlike ECOA and FHA, which seek to reduce discrimination based on a borrower's characteristics, CRA, like HMDA, seeks to reduce discrimination based on a community's characteristics—that is to say, redlining.[77]

Compliance with CRA has received increasing regulatory scrutiny since Congress passed savings and loan legislation in 1989. The Financial Institutions Reform, Recovery and Enforcement Act of 1989 (FIRREA) requires public disclosure of the CRA ratings of financial institutions.[78] This requirement coincides with the HMDA-mandated reporting of completed loan applications by census tract, income level, racial characteristics, and gender.[79]

CRA applies specifically to "regulated financial institutions,"[80] which means insured depository institutions including banks, savings banks, and savings and loans. The Act does not, however, apply to such mortgage lenders as credit unions or the large number of mortgage bankers.[81] Although CRA does not explicitly address racial discrimination, it does so indirectly by focusing regulatory scrutiny on low- and moderate-income communities.

Like HMDA, CRA is essentially a reporting law. It chiefly relies on the public to take action by putting pressure either on institutions with low CRA ratings or on their regulators. The only enforcement action CRA can take is to authorize a bank's supervisory agents to consider its CRA record when evaluating that bank's application for a deposit location in a particular community. This includes applications to merge with or acquire another bank. Banking supervisory agencies, operating through the Federal Financial Institutions Examination Council (FFIEC), issued a joint statement on June 17, 1992, to clarify their CRA expectations: "The agencies base their evaluation of CRA performance primarily on how well an institution helps meet the credit needs of its community or communities, not on the amount of documentation it maintains . . . . [A] lack of documentation is not sufficient basis on which to grant a poor rating if an institution's performance can otherwise be determined to be satisfactory or better."[82]

Under President Clinton, the use of CRA as an enforcement tool to encourage lending in low- and moderate-income communities has increased. In February of 1994, the Office of Thrift Supervision (OTS) rejected applications from four institutions it supervises in New Jersey and in Pennsylvania to convert their federal charters to state charters. OTS denied the charter conversion applications on the ground that the thrifts had not met the CRA requirements that they lend in all communities from which they take deposits.[83] As Jonathan Macey and Geoffrey Miller point out, the CRA "allows groups to bring pressure against depository institutions at a point of maximum vulnerability—when the institution has applied for permission to consummate a transaction and stands to lose both the costs of negotiating the transaction and the expected profits from the deal if the application is not approved. To avoid these losses, institutions are usually willing to remit some of their wealth to the community groups that mount the most vociferous challenges to the applicant's performance."[84]

Bank supervisory agencies have encouraged lenders to code their activities geographically to assist the agencies in analyzing how well the lenders can demonstrate the progress they are making in addressing whatever problems are disclosed in the lending data. This policy "gives significant direction concerning the data to be collected and the manner in which that data must be presented. However, it provides almost no useful guidance about the specific lending patterns which will be deemed acceptable or unacceptable."[85] The CRA's inherent subjectivity and lack of specific guidance for lenders have led to frequent criticisms of the legislation by the banking industry and consumer groups.

The combination of increased use of CRA ratings by banking supervisors, expanded HMDA data reporting, and the public nature of both CRA and HMDA have brought new attention to insured depository institutions and their mortgage lending activity. As a result of this new interest, the Comptroller of the Currency issued a pamphlet to lending institutions on March 31, 1992, entitled "Home Mortgage Lending and Equal Treatment." Intended to "make home mortgage lenders aware of the possible unintended consequences of [their] policies and practices,"[86] the pamphlet addresses "possible sources of unintended discrimination," as follows:

> Policies, procedures, and underwriting standards that are assumed, without justification, to be necessary and that have disproportionate effects along racial lines.

> Ambiguous and subjective lending criteria.

> Waiving standards, granting exceptions to standards, and adjusting standards. Interpreting certain secondary market standards as inflexible. (The Federal Home Loan Mortgage Corporation's Seller-Servicer Bulletin 92–2, issued in January 1992, clarifies a number of Freddie Mac's underwriting standards to remove the potential for such misinterpretation.)

> Dealings with appraisers, realtors, and private mortgage insurance companies.[87]

Using HMDA data, the Federal Reserve Bank of Boston released in 1992 the study (mentioned above) of Boston mortgage lenders. It controlled for 38 relevant variables in order to isolate the effect of the race factor on the lending decision. The report concluded that minorities were discriminated against because the approval ratio was 1.6 white loan application to 1 minority loan application. In the words of the report:

> A black or Hispanic applicant in the Boston area is roughly 60 percent more likely to be denied a mortgage loan than a similarly situated white applicant. This means that 17 percent of black or Hispanic applicants instead of 11 percent would be denied loans even if they had the same obligation ratios, credit history, loan to value, and property characteristics as white applicants. In short, the results indicate that a serious problem exists in the market for mortgage loans, and lenders, community groups, and regulators must work together to ensure that minorities are treated fairly.[88]

Clearly, antidiscrimination law has not ended racial discrimination in the home mortgage industry. Although part of the problem lies in the sheer number of loan providers and the segmentation of the mortgage industry—making regulation difficult at best—some discrimination is evident in the way credit decisions are traditionally made by banks.

Banks traditionally follow "the three c's of credit": credit, collateral, and character. Credit means the applicant's credit history, typically reviewed on the basis of credit reports showing a history of repayment of other credit obligations and a record of employment. Applicants may be rejected simply because they have held numerous jobs or had no credit history at all. These requirements may be unfair to African Americans if they have held several full-time or part-time jobs for a number of years (demonstrating steady employment) or have had no occasion to borrow. As for the collateral for the loan, it is the home the loan will finance. Regulatory agencies have alerted banks to be aware of the potential for discrimination in their appraisal reports. The Justice Department, in preparing a Fair Housing Act suit in 1976 against several housing industry organizations, documented examples of subtle discriminatory wording in appraisal reports. Comments as to the "desirability" of a neighborhood and of the "pride of ownership" shown by residents should not appear in appraisal reports. Specifically, lenders have been alerted to two potential loan collateral appraisal problems:

> In the cost approach to value, racial bias may be reflected in unsupported adjustments for "functional and economic obsolescence." Lenders should not assume that, because a home or neighborhood is over a certain age, large adjustments are appropriate.
> In the comparable sales approach, racial bias may cause the appraiser to select comparables or make adjustments that are inappropriate.[89]

Lenders are encouraged to incorporate "nondiscrimination considerations into their regular appraisal quality control process."[90]

Character as a criterion for extending credit is the most subjective one of all. If the person making the character determination, a loan officer or the branch manager, is insensitive to the cultural differences of minorities and women, the loan will likely be denied. Each of the "three c's," in short, is traditionally assessed under the implicit assumption, made from the lender's perspective, that all loan applicants ought to have the same economic background. In addition, the assessment of each criterion is largely subjective.

To curb their discriminatory traditions, banks and other mortgage lenders must change the process by which they grant credit. They must modify their loan approval criteria, and work to bring minorities into the mainstream of lending opportunities. Loan underwriting criteria must also be expanded to allow frequent job changes to constitute evidence of employment and to permit utility, phone, or other payments to substitute for more extensive loan histories. Lenders must serve low income communities and develop additional lending opportunities in these communities by establishing special educational programs and loan programs tailored to meet the particular needs of these communities. Finally, lenders must explore ways to stimulate lending and economic activity in low income areas through the establishment of new institutions such as the community development banks proposed by the Clinton administration. To what extent these or other initiatives can alleviate clearly demonstrated bias built into the home mortgage industry remains an open question.

4

Employment

The experiences of African Americans in the employment sector must be viewed against the backdrop of the two most important legal events in this area since the demise of Jim Crow: antidiscrimination law and racial preference (or affirmative action) law. Although these laws, along with better education, have substantially improved the employment experiences of African Americans, they have not brought about the employment progress African Americans or the nation envisioned. Not only does equal employment opportunity still elude scores of African Americans some thirty years after the passage of the first comprehensive employment discrimination law, but the rate of racial progress is also disappointing. "Look how far we still have to go" is a much more accurate assessment of African Americans' employment experiences under integration than "look how far we've come."

Even more disturbing than the slow rate of economic progress in African American society is the distress talented middle-class African Americans suffer at work in white institutions. Pathbreaking research by Joe Feagin, Melvin Sikes, Andrew Hacker, Ellis Cose, and others demonstrates that racism in high-level jobs impedes the socioeconomic progress of society's most successful African Americans, and kills their spirit. "One step from suicide" is how one "successful" middle-class African American summed up the experience of his class.

Antidiscrimination Law

Title VII

Title VII of the Civil Rights Act of 1964 is the nation's major antidiscrimination law in the employment sector. Its key section provides as follows:

It shall be an unlawful practice for an employer—

(1) to fail or refuse to hire or to discharge any individual, or otherwise discriminate against any individual with respect to his compensation, terms, conditions, or privileges of employment, because of such individual's race, color, religion, sex, or national origin; or

(2) to limit, segregate, or classify his employees or applicants for employment in any way which would deprive or tend to deprive any individual of employment opportunities or otherwise adversely affect his status as an employee, because of such individual's race, color, religion, sex, or national origin.[1]

Senator Hubert Humphrey explained the central meaning of this section: "[Title VII] make[s] it an illegal practice to use race as a factor in denying employment. It provides that men and women shall be employed on the basis of their qualifications, not as Catholic citizens, not as Protestant citizens, not as Jewish citizens, not as colored citizens, but as citizens of the United States."[2]

Title VII's political birth can be traced to the 1960 presidential election. Democratic candidate John F. Kennedy promised African Americans civil rights legislation, a promise that helped him capture 68% of the African American vote in a presidential election decided by the narrowest margin ever recorded. Despite Kennedy's promise, Congress was slow to act on civil rights legislation. Leaders of the Civil Rights Movement once again took to the streets to bring their cause into the homes and consciences of white America. Such media images as those of peaceful African American demonstrators in Birmingham, Alabama, brutally attacked by dogs and pummeled by fire hoses, highlighted the need for change. President Kennedy's assassination gave new impetus to the legislation. President Johnson signed the long-awaited Civil Rights Act into law on July 2, 1964. The Act has been amended several times since then.[3]

Looking at several indicators of equal employment opportunity, it is clear that Title VII, despite its lofty goals, has not engendered employment parity between African Americans and whites. Indeed, the economic condition of African Americans has actually worsened in some respects. Paul Krugman paints a dismal picture of employment progress among African Americans under racial integration:

BLACKS ARE STILL STRUGGLING. The dismal experience of blacks stands in contrast to the qualified success recently enjoyed by women. While some blacks have achieved success, the overall figures are grim. In 1970, the median income of black families was 60 percent of white family income; by 1990, the ratio had actually fallen to 58 percent. Over the past 20 years, unemployment among blacks has risen higher in each successive recession and fallen less with each recovery. In 1970, black unemployment was 8.2 percent; by 1990, it had reached 11.3 percent. Black impoverishment hasn't fallen either. In 1990, almost 32 percent of blacks lived in poverty, up from about 30 percent in 1974. And black men who work full time earn 30 percent less than white male counterparts, a gap that has grown since the 1970s. Working women are an exception. Black women who hold full-time jobs earn just 10 percent less than white women.[4]

Other studies support Krugman's analysis of the employment progress of African Americans under integration.[5]

One important study is the Equal Employment Opportunity Commission's (EEOC) annual Employer Information Report, called EEO-1 Report. This study is the only nationwide source of employment data on minorities and women in the private sector. Each private employer with 100 or more employees must file such a report with the federal government's EEOC annually. Companies with 50 or more employees who contract with the federal government must also file EEO-1 reports. It is estimated that about 50% of all private sector "payroll employment" (which excludes the self-employed) is covered by EEO-1 Reports. The EEOC also collects data on state and local governmental employment and on the unemployment rate in the Civil Labor Force (CLF).[6]

According to the EEO-1 reports, African Americans remain underrepresented in the best occupations.[7] There has been progress in this area, to be sure, but it has been painfully slow, which, to African Americans, does not spell success. The percentage of jobs in the top two employment categories—professionals and business managers—held by African Americans increased from 0.9% in 1966 to 3.7% and 5.3% in 1978 and 1992, respectively, compared to 98.2%, 93.1%, and 89.4% for whites in each of these years, respectively. At this rate, it will take several generations for African Americans to catch up. This is especially the case for men because women account for most of the African American gains in the best paying jobs.[8]

Adjusting the racial wage gap for education and experience adds further support to Krugman's dismal conclusions. A Rand Corporation study found that African Americans earned 20 to 30% less than comparably educated whites in 1980. According to another study published in 1989, this gap shrank to 10 to 26% by the end of the decade. One important lesson to be taken from this data is that *"simply equalizing the number of years of schooling alone would [still] leave a sizable racial wage gap."*[9]

Although the incidence of social pathology, such as family disintegration, helps to explain the slow progress toward equal employment opportunity under integration, such issues do not account for all the racial disparity, especially when the data are adjusted for education and experience. Indeed, there is a strong body of evidence (Farley and Allen, Jaynes and Williams, Neckerman and Kirschenman, Feagin and Sikes) that racism remains the key factor.[10] For example, one study concluded that senior executives at 185 firms in the Chicago area engage in gratuitous racism, freely using racial stereotypes in evaluating the quality of applicants.[11] Another study concluded that a "capable minority attorney might not be hired by some Los Angeles law firms, if the firms' partners believe their clients would not work with a nonwhite lawyer—or that a minority attorney would not fit in at the firm."[12]

Nor can the breakdown of family structure and poor education explain the psychological pressures African Americans face on the job, pressures that can inhibit effective job performance and cause health problems. In *Living with Racism: The Black Middle-Class Experience,* Joe Feagin and Melvin Sikes recount the story of a talented young journalist, Leanita McClain, who committed suicide in 1984 at the age of 32. Ms. McClain was the first African American to serve on the *Chicago Tribune*'s editorial board. Shortly before her suicide, *Glamour* magazine named her as one of the outstanding women in corporate America. Feagin and Sikes point to "the culture shock blacks face having to cope with a culturally different, often discriminatory white world" as the reason for McClain's suicide. (In a videotaped interview in the early 1980s, McClain talked about these pressures.) Quoting one African American respondent to their hypothesis, Feagin and Sikes elaborate: "In the white-normed corporate environment, 'Black women consciously choose their speech, their laughter, their walk, their mode of dress and car. They trim and straighten their hair. . . . They learn to wear a mask.' "[13]

It is important to understand that Feagin and Sikes are not referring to the normal pressures of adapting to the discipline of the workplace, which includes showing up to work on time every day, following instructions, and doing a good job. The inability or unwillingness to submit to such discipline prevents many poor and working-class African Americans from being employed even by minorities (such as Chinese or Korean restaurant owners) who create the kind of low-wage, entry-level jobs they need to get started.[14] Feagin and Sikes have in mind a much more devastating and racialized pressure that targets up-and-coming African Americans and subjects them to humiliation and marginalization. This is not to say that other African Americans do not face employment discrimination. But, as the authors state, "it is possible that in the workplace middle-class black employees face an even greater range of instances of everyday discrimination than working class black employees because they are pioneers in many formerly all-white settings."[15]

Other commentators agree with Feagin and Sikes. Ellis Cose, for example, captured many of the job-related problems middle-class African Americans encounter in his book *The Rage of a Privileged Class*.[16] There and in a magazine article he discusses a dozen recurring pressures middle-class African Americans face in white companies (what Cose calls "The Dozen Demons"):[17] inability to fit in; lack of respect; low expectations; shattered hopes; faint praise; coping fatigue; pigeonholing; identity troubles; self-censorship and silence; mendacity; collective guilt; and exclusion from the club.

Problems such as these add unnecessary pressures to the job. They exact on African Americans a special tax—"the black tax." White employees are simply not called upon to pay such a levy. But the nation as a whole does have to pay. According to a former member of the Federal Reserve Board, the estimated cost of employment discrimination on the gross domestic product was $215 billion in 1991 and $241 billion in 1993.[18]

Affirmative Action Law

Affirmative action attempts to compensate for the inability of the existing antidiscrimination law to redress employment discrimination effectively. Given its limited purpose, affirmative action, whether "voluntary" or "involuntary," can only be used in the context of a discriminatory predicate. I shall elaborate on this important point as I proceed to discuss the history, purpose, and basic structure of affirmative action law.

In the employment field, affirmative action can be defined as "actions appropriate to overcome the effects of past or present practices, policies, or other barriers to equal employment opportunity."[19] This definition, promulgated by the EEOC in the early years of affirmative action, can be viewed as the official definition of the national doctrine.

Affirmative action is remedial by nature. Contrary to common opinion, the policy cannot be implemented arbitrarily but comes into play only when there is evidence of employment discrimination. In this way, it complements antidiscrimination law, providing a second-line defense against employment discrimination. Race-conscious employment practices (from racial preferences to racial quotas) are implicit in the definition of the policy. Affirmative action can and often does mean that qualified African Americans should receive preferential treatment at all levels—hiring, promotion, and retention—to ensure their equal treatment by an employer who has treated them, or is suspected of treating them, in a discriminatory manner. Furthermore, the government's definition of affirmative action is broad. It encompasses all "barriers to equal employment opportunity." A liberal definition is justified, because the inertia of discriminatory traditions and the growing subtleties in personal attitudes about race have made the quest for equal employment opportunity by African Americans in an *integrated* workplace a needlessly burdensome task.

While affirmative action for African Americans may ultimately rest upon theories of equality of opportunity and equality of results,[20] I find George Schatzki's explanation, which underscores the doctrine's antidiscrimination focus, to be the most compelling:

> Racial discrimination is not random. Most of us do not suffer the burdens and barbs of ethnic discrimination; more importantly, whether or not we do suffer this irrationality sometimes, most of us have been treated most of the time by dominant persons or institutions without our race being a handicap. Saying that about blacks or chicanos, for example, would be an outright lie. These are people in our society—as a whole—who suffer in a vastly disproportionate way because of their ethnicity. The degree of suffering and disparity are probably immeasurable, but few—if any—would deny their existence.[21]

The federal mandate for affirmative action is primarily formulated through judicial, congressional, and executive rules that put antidiscrimination policy into effect; there is no separate set of rules for affirmative action. The first formal mandate for the establishment of affirmative action programs was an Executive Order issued by President Kennedy in 1961.[22]

It required recipients of government contracts to take "affirmative steps" to guarantee that employment decisions were free of discrimination based on race, color, creed, or national origin. Like most executive orders, this one was accorded the force and effect of law.[23] It did not, however, create a private right of action; individuals could not use the Executive Order as a basis for a lawsuit and sue a private employer for failing to abide by its terms. A plaintiff could, however, sue federal officials to compel them to enforce the order.[24]

Led by the Fifth Circuit Court of Appeals in the South, the federal judiciary also provided an early mandate for affirmative action programs. In giving shape and substance to the Supreme Court's school desegregation decree announced in *Brown v. Board of Education*,[25] the court developed the doctrine of "affirmative duties." This doctrine "shifted the burden from black plaintiffs to school boards to disestablish a dual school system."[26]

Today there are several expressed mandates for the establishment of affirmative action programs, of which the most prominent are Title VII and Executive Order 11246.[27] In Section 706(g) of Title VII, Congress has given the courts a clear mandate to impose affirmative action programs on employers who violate Title VII: "If the court finds that the respondent had intentionally engaged in or is intentionally engaging in an unlawful employment practice charged in the complaint, the court may enjoin the respondent from engaging in such unlawful employment practice, and order such affirmative action as may be appropriate, . . . or any other equitable relief as the court deems appropriate."[28] The affirmative action mandate under § 706(g) is neither race- nor gender-specific. It applies to all Title VII plaintiffs, whether white or African American, male or female. However, some governmental mandates for affirmative action at both the federal and state levels do favor particular groups, such as the disabled and veterans.[29] None favors a particular gender or racial group.

Promulgated in 1965, Executive Order 11246 provides that all federal contractors with contracts exceeding $50,000 and with more than 50 employees must "take affirmative action to ensure that applicants are employed, and that employees are treated during employment, without regard to their race, color, religion, sex or national origin."[30] The Office of Federal Contract Compliance Programs (OFCCP) was established to monitor compliance with Executive Order 11246. Race-conscious employment practices imposed on employers under this order have been repeatedly upheld by the courts. Like other orders, Executive Order 11246 does not create a private cause of action, but OFCCP officials can be compelled by court order to perform their duties under the Executive Order.[31]

The basic technical requirements for acceptable Executive Order compliance programs are set forth in Revised Order No. 4, as amended. Each written compliance program must include a work force analysis that looks at the racial and gender composition of the contractor's job titles. This analysis helps to determine whether African Americans, for example, are underutilized in particular employment categories. ("Underutilized" simply means that there are fewer minorities or females than would be expected within a particular job, given their availability in the relevant labor market.) Revised Order No. 4 lists at least eight factors that can be used to determine the "availability" of minorities for each job category. If underutilization is found, goals and timetables are established to correct the deficiencies.[32]

Goals and timetables are usually distinguishable from quotas. The latter are rigid standards, hard and fast commands that must be satisfied before any white male can be selected. Quotas can also act as ceilings on the number of qualified minority or female candidates selected. In contrast, goals and timetables are flexible milestones, or benchmarks, that take into account many factors, among which race or sex is simply a "plus" factor. Goals and timetables are dependent on the good-faith efforts of white male decisionmakers. Although they are not as rigid as quotas, goals and timetables under the Executive Order must be specific, attainable, and "should consider the anticipated expansion, contraction and turnover in the work force."[33]

A distinction must also be drawn between voluntary and involuntary employer affirmative action programs. The former are not imposed on an employer by executive order, court order, or as a remedy for a proven violation of constitutional or statutory law. Voluntary affirmative action programs may, however, arise in anticipation of a threat of litigation. Like the Supreme Court, I would include consent decrees in the category of voluntary affirmative action.[34]

Effect on Employment

There are at least three ways to assess the effect of affirmative action on African American employment. One can determine whether more African Americans have been hired; whether and to what extent they have shifted from low-status to high-status jobs; and, finally, whether their earnings have increased. The evidence will show that while affirmative action has had a positive impact on the growth of African American employment and occupational status, it has had little impact on African American wages. The data on employment and occupational status are, however, somewhat problematic.

Most of the studies that have attempted to gauge the success or failure of affirmative action on the African American employment rate have focused on male workers, both in firms not covered by the OFCCP and in firms covered by, and hence subject to, the OFCCP's affirmative action requirements. One of the first and most important of these studies came out of the Labor Department in the early 1980s. This study was never published and likely would have gone unnoticed if reporters had not picked it up for articles in the *Washington Post* and *New York Times* in 1983. There was speculation that the study was pushed aside because of the Reagan administration's disdain for affirmative action. Indeed, the Labor Department's results challenged opponents of affirmative action. The study, which evaluated the practices of 77,098 businesses between 1974 and 1980, found that minority employment grew during this period by 20.1% at companies governed by the OFCCP, compared to only a 12.3% increase at companies not required to engage in affirmative action.[35]

Several studies conducted by Jonathan Leonard have also concluded that affirmative action—more specifically, the Executive Order and compliance reviews by the OFCCP—has expanded the employment of both minorities and females.[36] In one of these studies, Leonard compared employment rates at 68,000 firms with more than 16 million employees between 1974 to 1980. He found that the employment rate of African Americans grew faster in contractor firms than in noncontractor firms during this period. The annual employment rate, or growth rate, for African American males in the contractor sector was 3.8% greater than in the noncontractor sector, yielding an annual growth rate (if we take the 6th root) that was 0.62% higher in the contractor sector. In contrast, the annual employment rate for white males in contractor firms was 0.2% lower than in noncontractor firms. Hence the annual growth rate for African American males relative to white males was 0.82%—"contract status appears to shift the demand for black males relative to white males by 0.82% per year."[37] Leonard's findings are consistent with those of other scholars using different specifications, who have reported an annual relative growth rate of 0.86% for African American males during the period 1966–1970.[38]

When direct pressure is placed on contractor firms through OFCCP compliance reviews, the employment rate for African American males is even more pronounced. Compliance reviews have had a positive impact on the employment of African Americans over and above that of mere contractor status. One study, for example, found that compliance reviews advanced "black males by 7.9%, other minority males by 15.2%, and black females by 6.1% among reviewed establishments" in the years studied.[39]

In short, the general consensus among researchers is that "while generating tremendous public criticism and resistance . . ., affirmative action has actually been successful in promoting . . . [African American] employment."[40] Furthermore, "all the studies agree that the added effect of an OFCCP compliance review on black male employment is positive and greater in magnitude than the effect of merely being a government contractor."[41]

James Smith and Finis Welch found similar advances in a study they conducted for the Rand Corporation. However, they view the affirmative action effects as a "reshuffling" of African Americans from noncovered firms to covered firms, rather than as a net increase in the African American employment rate. They point out that the percentage of African American male employees working in covered firms increased from 48% in 1966, when the Executive Order became operational, to 60% by 1980.[42]

In addition to looking at employment rates, researchers have also attempted to assess the effects of affirmative action on the occupational gains of African Americans. While prior to 1974 African Americans made occupational advances mainly in the low-paying blue-collar jobs, between 1974 and 1980 their presence was significantly increased in the higher-paying professional and managerial occupations. In fact, African American male managers and professionals went from half as likely as white male managers and professionals to work in covered firms in 1966, to equally as likely to work in such firms by 1980.[43] Smith and Welch claim, however, that a substantial part of the growth in occupational status may have been due to title changes of jobs in response to affirmative action requirements.[44] But, clearly, most of the occupational growth is not just due to an eraser and pencil.

Other problems with the data used to evaluate the impact of affirmative action on African American employment and occupational status should also be noted. First, most studies deal only with the Executive Order and hence only with involuntary affirmative action programs. Voluntary affirmative action programs have not been reviewed. It is quite possible that additional data would show a much greater expansion of hiring or occupational status. For example, law schools have established voluntary affirmative action programs for faculty and administrative hirings. The percentage of minority law professors increased from 6.2% in the 1990–91 academic year to 7.4% in the 1993–94 academic year. In addition, the percentage of minority law deans increased from 6.8% to 9.8% during the same period.[45] Without the impetus of affirmative action, it is doubtful so many minorities would have been hired in such a short period of time.

According to Smith and Welch, most of the employment growth took place between 1966 and 1970; the pace slowed down but continued at a diminished rate until 1974, when it stabilized.[46] Dave and June O'Neill accepted and expanded this observation, concluding that federal affirmative action programs have had no significant or lasting effect on the employment status of African American men. They based this conclusion on the fact that although the OFCCP's maximum enforcement effort took place between 1974 and 1980, "the relative movement of black men to federal contractors [had] slowed markedly between 1970 and 1980."[47] But, as the O'Neills themselves noted, the employment patterns for African American women "more closely coincided with the timing of changes in [the OFCCP's] enforcement strength,"[48] so it is possible that the higher hiring rate for African American women may have had a negative impact on the hiring rate for African American men. Employers will often attempt to comply with affirmative action goals by double-counting African American women, in effect "killing two birds with one stone." Such hiring strategy may be beneficial to African American women but harmful to African American men.

Smith and Welch found two positive wage effects attributable to affirmative action. One was the short-term improvement in the wages of young African American workers from 1967 to 1972. The second was the increase in the wages of young African American college graduates.[49] Beyond these areas, the general consensus among researchers is that affirmative action has had no significant long-term impact on African American wages.

The failure of affirmative action in this area highlights the importance of education in generating high income. No amount of affirmative action can increase the wage rate the market sets for high-school graduates or dropouts. That rate will always be lower than the rate for lawyers and doctors. For this reason it can be said that "the sharp rise in the income returns to schooling . . . favors the more highly educated white worker over the average African American worker in terms of wages."[50] Moreover, structural changes in the economy since the 1960s have exacerbated the educational deficiencies of African Americans. As Dan Farber has noted, "relatively few African Americans have obtained the educational background needed to function effectively in technical fields. Even more seriously, although some aspects of African American education have improved, African American workers are apparently chasing a moving target, because the level of skills and training needed in the global economy is rising even more rapidly."[51]

The fact that both schooling and wages of African American women have been rising relative to those of African American men may illustrate the importance of education with regard to wages.[52] But it is also true that African American women have been the main beneficiaries of affirmative action. Their percentage in covered firms rose from 48% of all African American women workers in 1966 to 75% in 1980. In contrast, the percentage of African American male employees working in covered firms increased from 48% in 1966 to 60% in 1980.[53]

Minority Criticism of Affirmative Action

Notwithstanding its apparent successes, affirmative action has come under fire in recent years from some of its own beneficiaries. Proceeding from the political left, the right, or the middle, their criticisms of affirmative action vary, ranging from the argument that affirmative action stigmatizes African Americans by implying that they cannot compete on an equal basis with whites, to the argument that preferential treatment entrenches racial divisiveness and exacerbates racial resentment. Although most minority commentators on the left are in favor of affirmative action, some, notably Derrick Bell and Richard Delgado, have voiced some specific concerns. Bell and Delgado contend that affirmative action serves to promote white self-interest far more than it aids African Americans.[54] As we shall see, this argument is, however, less an attack on the concept of affirmative action than on the way in which it has been implemented. Bell supports affirmative action in theory, but is skeptical about its effectiveness, because it has been applied in a way that adopts rather than challenges traditional standards of evaluation. In particular, he rejects evaluating college or graduate school applicants based on grades and test scores alone. These standards, he argues, are not predictive of minority success in such fields as the practice of law and medicine. One example of his point is Judge Harry Edwards, a graduate of Michigan Law School and a former professor of law at both Michigan and Harvard law schools. The judge in turn names many "affirmative action admittees" of the Michigan Law School (that is, students admitted on the basis of average test scores) who, like himself, have gone on to achieve great distinction in the legal profession.[55]

Bell, in short, believes that the current approach to affirmative action—simply recognizing minority exceptions to traditional admissions standards based on grades and test scores—"has served to validate and reinforce traditional policies while enveloping minority applicants in a cloud of suspected incompetency."[56] Affirmative action, in his words, is the "latest contrivance the society has created to give blacks the sense of equality while withholding its substance."[57] In the end, the policy "furthers the interest of the relative few at the cost of growing hostility borne by many."[58]

Like Derrick Bell, Richard Delgado raises doubts about traditional standards of evaluation that inform affirmative action decisionmaking. "Affirmative action enables members of the dominant group to ask, 'Is it fair to hire a less-qualified Chicano or black over a qualified white?' . . . Our acquiescence in treating [affirmative action] as a 'question of standards' is absurd and self-defeating when you consider that we took no part in creating those standards and their fairness is one of the very things we want to call into question."[59] His assessment of affirmative action is actually more pessimistic than that of Derrick Bell. Delgado believes that affirmative action is "psychologically and materially injurious to populations of color" and can cause its beneficiaries to "feel guilty, undeserving, and stigmatized."[60] It is "something no self-respecting attorney of color ought to support."[61]

One of the strongest arguments in support of affirmative action—the role-model hypothesis—has also come under Delgado's sharp criticism. This argument, he contends, stands affirmative action on its head. It has come to mean that African Americans are to be hired not because of talents and accomplishment, but in order to stand as role models for future generations of minorities who will hopefully follow in their footsteps. "Being a role model is a tough job," Delgado points out, because "you are expected to uplift your entire people."[62] Because these role models are supposedly assimilationists, Delgado compares good African American role models to high fashion models, "expected to conform to prevailing ideas of beauty, politeness, grooming, and above all responsibility."[63]

Like Bell and Delgado on the left, Stephen Carter, a more moderate critic, has doubts about the consequences of affirmative action. He calls it a mixed blessing at best, because while it may have benefited middle-class African Americans, it has worsened the position of those in the lower class.[64] In addition, affirmative action reinforces stigmas and perpetuates stereotypes. It may call into question the legitimate achievements of highly qualified African Americans—did they get that far solely on their merit? Likewise, affirmative action based on diversity fosters "stereotypes about different ways in which people who are white and people who are black supposedly think."[65]

Along with Delgado, Carter criticizes the role-model hypothesis. He rejects the notion that African American role models are expected to advance a particular viewpoint and be "black people of the right kind" in order to fill their "representational slots" in society. Quoting Derrick Bell, Carter explains, somewhat curiously, that the "ends of diversity are not served by people who look black and think white."[66] Finally, affirmative action perpetuates the belief that African Americans are unable to compete intellectually with whites. The concept he calls the "best black syndrome" captures this criticism. In the perspective of the syndrome, an African American candidate is not the best-qualified candidate for the job, but only the best-qualified black candidate for the job.[67]

On the right, Thomas Sowell and Shelby Steele have articulated the African American conservative criticism of affirmative action quite well. Like Stephen Carter, Sowell argues that under affirmative action *the advantaged have benefited in the name of the disadvantaged.*[68] Women who head households and individuals with little education and job experience are among the disadvantaged who suffer most from affirmative action, Sowell claims.[69] Neither Sowell nor Carter, however, deals with the fact that affirmative action, as we have seen, was established to aid *qualified* minorities—people who could take advantage of opportunities created by antidiscrimination law, if it were working properly—and was never viewed as a full employment program for minorities or as a substitute for education. In the end, Sowell rejects affirmative action as a concept on the ground that it builds up resentment against all African Americans.[70]

Shelby Steele also believes that affirmative action has done more bad than good. He argues that the idea reinforces a self-defeating sense of victimization among African Americans and enlarges self-doubt. "Under affirmative action the quality that earns blacks preferential treatment is an implied inferiority,"[71]

Steele maintains. Affirmative action nurtures a "victim-focused identity in blacks" by "indirectly encourag[ing] blacks to exploit their own past victimization as a source of power and privilege."[72] It also creates the false impression that preferential treatment is something owed to African Americans, when in fact it is impossible to compensate for the "historic suffering of the race."[73]

Clearly, affirmative action has exacted a heavy psychological toll on its beneficiaries, even if it has provided them with employment opportunities. What this tells us is that affirmative action is an imperfect response to employment inequality, which our antidiscrimination laws were supposed to resolve in the first instance. If antidiscrimination laws and affirmative action are African Americans' best hopes of achieving equal employment opportunities under integration, it would be absurd for them not to try something else.

5

Voting

The right to vote is not just an important right; it is a fundamental right. Its inviolability is grounded in the principle of representative government on which our nation was founded. Voting is a sacred right as well because, according to the Supreme Court, it is "preservative of all rights."[1]

Yet precious as it is, the right to vote has been denied to African Americans for most of the nation's life. Indeed, it was not until the Voting Rights Act was passed in 1965[2] that the right to vote, granted to all citizens by the Fifteenth Amendment to the Constitution, finally became a reality for millions of African Americans in the South. In bringing the franchise to them and "thereby fulfilling the promise of the Fifteenth Amendment ninety-five years late,"[3] the Voting Rights Act has brought important positive changes in the lives of African Americans.

Granting this, however, is far from concluding that the Act has been a complete success. A minority of African Americans still have not been able to exercise the right to vote freely or at all since the passage of the Voting Rights Act. And those who do vote question the efficacy of their voting power. Problems such as vote dilution and, ultimately, effective political representation have replaced the simple right-to-vote issue as the most significant challenge facing African Americans since 1965. Many African Americans believe that the dilution problem, a problem whites do not experience, does not allow them to judge their experience in the political process under integration as wholly positive. Yes, it has clearly been the best political experience African Americans have ever had, and, more particularly, the number of African American elected officials at all levels of government has increased from about 300 in 1965 to 4,912 in 1980 and 7,370 in 1990[4]; yet this means little if the political interests of African American constituencies are not met, or, worse, cannot be met.

What African Americans fear most these days is that Justice Oliver Wendell Holmes's dismal observation at the beginning of this century may hold true at its close—namely, that legal rights alone will not protect African Americans if the "great mass of the white population intends to keep . . . blacks from voting."[5] Substitute "voting power" for "voting," and there can be no better way to express the concerns of African Americans at the threshold of the twenty-first century. They have not been able to wield political influence in a racially integrated society, and fear that perhaps they never will.

Worsening the situation, the Supreme Court in recent years has made it more difficult for African Americans to exert political power. The Court's rulings place in jeopardy the use of racial redistricting, a favorite antidilution device the Supreme Court itself had championed as late as the 1980s. Racial redistricting, or minority-majority districts as it is sometimes called, may, however, be overrated (see Chapter 18).

In looking at the African American political experience since 1965, we should not overlook the right-to-vote problems that have lingered long after the enactment of the Voting Rights Act. The difficulty of casting the ballot defines the political scene under integration even if the problem is not quite as severe as those related to mustering political strength.

Thwarting the Right to Vote

Congress enacted the Voting Rights Act in 1965 to end the myriad of tactics employed by southern states to disfranchise African Americans after the passage of the Fifteenth Amendment. There has been much resistance to the Act. From the time immediately following its passage until the present, government officials and private citizens alike have tried various ways of subverting this important law. In the early years of the Voting Rights Act, opposition to enfranchising African Americans was blatant. Today, some thirty years later, the resistance has become more subtle.[6]

Shortly after the passage of the Act in 1965, the Mississippi Attorney General instructed city clerks to continue to use a recently adopted voting registration procedure. The official stated that the new procedure did not violate the Voting Rights Act's ban on the use of literacy exams, even though it required a registrant to fill out a form stating his or her name, address, and date of birth. Mississippi was not alone; other southern states also continued to use literacy tests in one form or another despite the ban. In Alabama, for example, three counties continued to use a simple literacy test based on a local court order that predated the Act. Federal examiners were subsequently sent in to prevent further violations.[7]

An attempt to reinstate a literacy test in Gaston County, North Carolina, was turned back by the Supreme Court in an early case brought under the Voting Rights Act. Gaston County's request to reinstate its literacy test appeared neutral, but the Supreme Court invalidated it anyway because the test denied or weakened the ability of African Americans to cast votes. In its opinion the Court noted that North Carolina's public schools had been segregated and had provided African Americans with an inferior education, making it difficult for them to pass a literacy test.[8]

Violence was also a factor. For example, in Lowndes County, Alabama, Jonathan Daniels was killed on August 20, 1965, as he attempted to register to vote. His alleged killer was tried but acquitted on September 30, 1965. Other forms of threat—for example, a pick-up truck with a rifle displayed out the window parked in front of the examiner's office—also interfered with the right to vote. Violence and the threat of violence intimidated African Americans so much that they were afraid even to register, never mind actually vote.[9]

In *Toney v. White*,[10] several African American candidates and their supporters filed suit in Louisiana to protest an election the candidates lost because registered voters were struck off the rolls barely a month before the primary election. On the closing date of registration, the registrar published a list of 141 voters to be removed from the rolls for failing to vote in the previous four years. All but 11 of the people on the list were African Americans. The registrar failed to state that those removed from the rolls had the right to reregister by going to the registrar's office and providing proof of their right to register as required by law. The registrar notified an additional 29 African Americans that their registration status was challenged on grounds of failure to report address changes. This particular notification also failed to comply with Louisiana law, but, more importantly, the registrar did not notify any white registrants of challenges to their registration for unreported address changes. The trial court found that there were far more whites than African Americans who should have been challenged on these grounds.[11] It was also discovered at trial that

Louisiana's registrar failed to challenge absentee voters absent for more than two years. This failure did violate Louisiana law. All but one of the absentees who should have been challenged were white.[12]

The court concluded that the registrar's actions violated the Voting Rights Act in that they had a discriminatory effect on African American voters. Notwithstanding this ruling, the defeated candidates and their supporters failed to have the election results set aside, in part because the discriminatory acts were not, in the court's view, "completely indefensible." The court also found that there was no attempt on plaintiffs' part to obtain pre-election relief.[13]

Problems continued to fester, long after the enactment of the Voting Rights Act, with respect to the times and places set for voter registration. Registration in one South Carolina county, for example, took place at the county seat, which was 20 miles from the county's largest city. The registration hours were 8:30 A.M. to 12:00 P.M. and 1:00 P.M. to 5:00 P.M. Monday through Friday. It was difficult for African Americans to reach the registration office before closing, because they lacked transportation and could not leave work early. Similar handicaps were reported in Alabama, Louisiana, and Mississippi. The registrars in those states either had no set hours or closed early. In Mississippi, the registrar would often close the office early whenever he noticed a large group of African Americans standing in line to register.[14]

Suggestions to remedy these registration problems went for nought. Recommendations that registrars visit areas heavily populated by African Americans were either rejected outright, or mobile units failed to give timely notice of times and places for registration. Requests for appointment of deputy registrars to register potential voters at any time were also refused.[15] Some states required registering twice: with the county for county, state, and national elections and with the municipality for municipal elections. The problems of inconvenient hours and inadequate location for registration were doubled when African Americans had to register twice at two separate locations.[16]

Registration personnel also made it difficult for African Americans to exercise their right to vote. Some of the registrars were the same people who had refused to register African Americans before the Act, in violation of the Fifteenth Amendment. For example, a Mississippi registrar who had openly opposed registration of African Americans prior to the 1965 Act was discourteous and unhelpful toward the registrants. There were also accounts of registrars requiring more information from African Americans than from whites, which included asking unnecessary or embarrassing questions of a personal nature. Others assigned people to the wrong polling sites. Such intimidating, humiliating, and frustrating behavior prevented scores of African Americans from registering.[17]

Difficulties similar to those cited in the *Toney* case persisted. Even after that case, several states maintained similar penalties for failure to vote during a specified number of years or for nonresidency. The registrars were not, however, diligent in informing voters that they had been dropped from the rolls or that they needed to reregister. In one Georgia town, for example, the African Americans who had been removed from the lists did not find out until the day of the election that they were not registered.[18]

Several southern counties had reregistration requirements regardless of how often one had voted previously. These requirements were especially burdensome for the African Americans who had had a difficult and unpleasant enough experience registering the first time and did not want to repeat the episode. As a result, many African Americans did not reregister and hence were not able to vote.[19]

Obstacles to the enfranchisement of African Americans also appeared at polling sites. In a Mississippi election, the white election officials were "hostile and uncooperative" when checking the identity or registration of African Americans. White officials sometimes stated that they were unable to find the names of the voters when in fact the names were on the list.[20]

Absentee ballots presented another set of problems. Too often requested ballots were received too late or not at all, more so if it was known that the voter was sympathetic to African American candidates. In Lowndes County, Alabama, African Americans had difficulty getting required doctor's certificates confirming their reasons for requesting absentee ballots—all the doctors were white. In contrast, white absentee voters were not required to verify their reasons for absentee ballots. Indeed, many absentee ballots were issued to whites who were ineligible.[21]

Economic dependence was a powerful tool in the hands of those who wished to deny African Americans the right to vote. Most African Americans in the South relied on whites for their jobs. Many feared the registration rolls would be checked and they would be fired for registering to vote. Some agricultural workers were actually told they would be fired if they registered. Others were told to vote for a specific candidate.[22]

African Americans were also concerned that if they exercised their right to vote, they would not be able to buy food for themselves and their families. Some who relied on credit from white stores believed they would be denied this essential source of funds if they voted for the wrong candidate. People receiving government aid feared that whites had the power to discontinue it. The reluctance to vote was understandable.[23] In Georgia and North Carolina some white employers discharged their African American employees who ran for office or who were politically active. The message to potential African American voters was: vote for the white candidates or not at all.[24]

By the late 1970s and early 1980s, the obstructive tactics had become more subtle. In Georgia, for example, some whites pretended to assist African American voters with their absentee ballots by taking the ballots directly to the voters' homes. Whites "helped" these voters, many of whom were illiterate, to fill out their ballots. Whenever possible, these assistants filled out the ballots themselves.[25] Louisiana politician Bobby Dupre had another scheme: he bribed many African Americans into voting for him for the local school board by having his drivers take them to the polls and providing them with assistance, whether they requested it or not. The drivers would then give the African American voters tokens that were later redeemed for money. A federal court determined that this scheme abridged the voting rights of the African Americans.[26]

In 1982 Congress enacted an important amendment to the Voting Rights Act that was designed to make the Act more effective. During the mid-1980s, however, several court decisions demonstrated without question that the schemes used to prevent African Americans from exercising the right to vote during the first two decades of the Act were still in use. Some of the tactics were new, but the old ones were still quite effective.

An unlikely problem involving the Reagan administration resulted in a court ruling in 1984. Nine African American voters from Alabama filed a lawsuit against the Attorney General and several U.S. attorneys. The plaintiffs alleged that their complaints of voting fraud and intimidation to federal officials were ignored, while complaints of African Americans' unlawful conduct made by whites were investigated vigorously. The investigators "abusively interrogated" poor African Americans and misinformed them as to their eligibility to vote by absentee ballot. As a result, the turnout of African American voters declined in the 1984 Alabama general election. In ruling for the plaintiffs, a federal court held that the Department of Justice's discriminatory policy of investigation denied African Americans their right to vote.[27]

Another case revealed several of the more familiar tactics. The suit, brought on behalf of all African Americans in Alabama, described numerous instances of harassment and intimidation at the polls, all designed to discourage African American voters. Illiterate voters requesting assistance were required to swear under oath that they were unable to read or write English. Voters were limited to five minutes in voting booths. In its opinion the court also described instances in which white polling officials refused to help illiterate African Americans or did not allow them to vote at all.[28]

In the late 1980s and early 1990s, African American voters in Mississippi were still challenging the state's dual voter registration system. They were also pushing to establish satellite registration, that is, registration in places other than the registrar's office, located in the courthouse downtown. Such procedures, which were prohibited under Mississippi law, help to facilitate registration by bringing the process closer to the voters' homes.[29]

In a 1987 case, African American residents of Perry County, Alabama, challenged a resolution adopted by one of the cities within the county, the City of Merion, transferring supervision and control of the city's public schools from the Perry County Board of Education to the newly created Merion Board of Education. At the time of the resolution, the county was 65% African American and the city was 52% white. Equally important, membership to the Perry County Board of Education was by election whereas membership to the Merion Board of Education was by appointment. The resolution effectively reduced the voting power of African Americans by wresting control of the city public schools from African American voters and then denying voters within the city the right to elect members to their own school board. Given racial polarization within the city, it was unlikely that African Americans would be appointed to the school board any time soon. Although white residents of the city were also no longer able to vote on those in control of their schools, they had gained a more effective voice by cornering the appointments process.[30]

The North was not without its own set of problems. In 1988 a suit was filed in New York City alleging that the negligence of the board of election resulted in the disfranchisement of African Americans. The board had failed to train staff properly, provide voting machines in working order, and register voters.[31] In another incident in the North, an illegal scheme to deny African Americans the right to vote was carried out in the fall of 1993. In a Pennsylvania special election for a state senate seat, the Stinson campaign workers conspired to deny African Americans the right to vote.

Once the campaigners learned that Stinson was trailing in the polls, they targeted African Americans (and Latinos), using "fraud, intimidation, and deception in order to obtain illegal absentee ballots for Stinson."[32] African Americans were approached in their homes to cast absentee ballots for Stinson even though some were not eligible, and the deadline for voting by absentee ballot had passed. In addition, the ballots were neither obtained nor returned in a lawful manner. Stinson's workers chose African Americans to further their scheme because they felt it would be easy to deprive them of their right to vote and, apparently, it was.[33]

Registering to vote and the act of voting are demanding enough without constant harassment and chicanery, and without having to run to court each time to seek legal redress. Although the Voting Rights Act provides an effective array of responses to attempts to deny the right to vote, the average person simply does not have the time, money, and flexibility to engage in the kind of protracted litigation that is needed to vindicate the right to vote.

The Dilution Problem

Although denial of the right to vote has been a persistent problem, the most serious concern for African Americans since the 1970s has been the use of discriminatory schemes that prevent them from using their votes to gain any significant political power. One technique widely used to effect such discrimination is vote dilution. This is "a process whereby election laws or practices, either singly or in concert, combine with systematic bloc voting among an identifiable group to diminish the voting strength of at least one other group."[34] Dilution schemes may take shape in several ways.

At-Large Elections

Picture a city consisting of three ethnically or racially distinct electoral districts. Each district, or ward, is represented by a single member of the city council. The council members can be elected to office under two different systems: at-large and district-by-district. Under the latter voting system, commonly called single-member-district voting, voters elect a representative only from the district in which they live. This system greatly increases the opportunities for African Americans to elect a person especially attentive to their interests. At-large voting, in contrast, allows cross-district voting—that is, residents of each ward may vote on all the elective positions. Because African Americans are usually outnumbered by whites citywide, the winner-take-all feature of citywide voting discriminates against them in effect, if not intentionally. Empirical studies have found a direct causal relationship between at-large elections and under-representation of minorities.[35]

Taylor, Texas, a farming town of 10,000 people located near Austin, illustrates this problem clearly. Twenty percent of Taylor's population is African American, and seventeen percent is Mexican American. These two minority groups are mostly concentrated in a few neighborhoods. Racial bloc voting is common. If Taylor used a ward-based or single-member-district system, African Americans and Mexican Americans would be able to elect candidates of their choice. They would have a fair chance to realize the full potential of their voting strength. Because Taylor uses an at-large election system, however, it is practically impossible for minorities to choose a representative answerable to them. From 1967 to 1981, for example, none of the eight minority candidates who ran for city commissioner won.[36]

When used with an at-large system, the runoff requirement adds to its dilutionary impact. In many places, a runoff election must take place if no candidate gets an absolute majority of the votes (50 percent plus one). Although it seems democratic on its face, the runoff requirement means that if the white vote splits among several candidates, a minority candidate will not be able to win with a mere plurality. Instead, the minority candidate must participate in a runoff against a white candidate and the white voters can unite to produce a majority.[37] In some cases, Houston for example, white officials have changed the rules to require a runoff after a minority candidate came close to winning under a plurality rule.[38]

Opposing the Single-Shot Vote

So-called single-shot voting occurs in the context of an at-large system without a majority requirement. This happens when a group of voters decides before the election to vote for only one or a few candidates and to withhold their remaining votes. Each voter can cast the number of votes equal to the number of seats to be filled. For example, if there are five candidates, including one African American, competing for three seats, African Americans can get together before the election and agree to use only one of their three votes. This allows the African American candidate to be elected, as the white votes will be split among the four white candidates.[39]

Responding to this tactic, white lawmakers have passed various ordinances against single-shot voting. One, the "full slate" device, requires voters to cast all their votes. Another forces candidates to declare for a "place" on the ballot. The place system essentially gives the voter only one vote to cast per candidate per place. This defeats the essence of single-shot voting: the ability to withhold votes from white candidates. Staggering the elections is a third method of preventing the effect of single-shot voting. This is a variant of the place system. Elections are staggered over a two or three year period so that fewer positions per year are filled and voters cannot, therefore, affect the election by withholding votes.[40]

Decreasing the Size of the Governing Body

Manipulating the number of seats on a body, such as a school board, can affect African American electoral success. Decreasing the number of seats in a body of single-member district officials decreases the number of districts from which minority groups can elect candidates. This also discourages cross-over voting. White voters are more likely to vote for an African American candidate when he or she will be one representative among many rather than one among a few or the sole office holder. Decreasing the size of the governmental body is, therefore, another subtle form of vote dilution.[41]

Exclusive Slating Groups

When a dominant nominating or slating group operates in a system that dilutes the votes of African Americans, it may play a role in perpetuating dilution by hand-picking an African American candidate as part of its slate. This robs minority voters of a fair chance to participate in the choice. The slated African American candidate is usually not popular in the community and is chosen for his or her race rather than ability to represent African American voters. Once the white slating group has put this person in office, he or she is pointed out as evidence that African Americans are represented and are able to elect candidates of their choice. In some cases, this scheme has been used to discourage vote dilution lawsuits.[42]

Gerrymandering

Gerrymandering is a redistricting practice that maximizes the political advantage or votes of one group and minimizes the political advantage or votes of another group. In legislative reapportionment there are three categories of racial gerrymandering: "cracking," "stacking," and "packing."[43]

Cracking dilutes political strength by breaking up a minority population large enough for separate representation and dispersing it throughout two or more districts with white voting majorities.[44] Consequently, African Americans who no longer constitute a majority in any one district are unable to elect a representative of their choice. In stacking, a large minority population is combined with a larger white population with the purpose or effect of depriving minority voters of a voting majority.[45] This type of gerrymandering is effective in both at-large and single-member districts. Packing occurs "when minority populations are over concentrated in a single district . . . in excess of the percentage needed for [African American] voters to elect candidates of their choice."[46] The purpose and effect of packing is to deprive African American voters of the opportunity to obtain a voting majority in adjoining districts. Each vote over the number needed to elect a minority candidate is essentially wasted.[47]

Gerrymandering can be crafted to be a complicated means of diluting the vote of African Americans. But because many factors are involved in gerrymandering, it is very difficult to pinpoint the schemes that are designed with the goal of reducing African American political power. For example, Republicans have favored the drawing of minority-majority districts for the politically legitimate purpose of dissipating Democratic strength.[48] Given that African Americans tend to support the Democratic party, heavy majorities of these voters in Democratic districts will decrease the number of seats held by white Democrats. The Republicans, in helping to elect a few more African American representatives, are acting out of self-interest rather than out of a sense of purpose in eliminating racism and inequality in representational politics.

The Benefits of Political Power

Vote dilution has had a great negative impact on African Americans in the social, occupational, educational, and, to a lesser extent, economic aspects of life. This conclusion is drawn from the few situations in which African Americans have in fact exercised political power. The benefits of such power are too obvious to ignore.

An increase in the number of African American representatives, such as that created by shifting from at-large to single-member districts, makes government more responsive to minority interests. A 1984 study of ten cities in California found that minority political participation was "associated with important changes in urban policy—the creation of police review boards, the appointment . . . of more minorities to commissions, the increasing use of minority contractors, and a general increase in the number of programs oriented to minorities."[49] This study also found that the presence of African American council members tended to break down racial polarization and stereotyping.[50]

Other studies support the view that an increase in African American representation leads to greater responsiveness to that community's interests. A study of Newark revealed that under an African American mayor "there was a strengthening of the city human rights commission and the implementation of affirmative action policies."[51] Tom McCain, the first African American county administrator in Edgefield County, South Carolina, reported that "before blacks held elected office, the county always picked up white folks' garbage and sometimes it picked up black folks' garbage. Now, we just pick up the garbage."[52] Carl Eggleston, the first African American elected to the Farmville, Virginia, city council, stated that African American officeholders make it possible for the community at large to know what is going on and to become a part of what is taking place.[53]

The influence of increased African American political participation may also be seen in the passage of the 1975 amendments to the Voting Rights Act, the 1982 amendments to the Voting Rights Act, the Civil Rights Restoration Act of 1987, and the Fair Housing Act of 1988. These great political changes may be traced directly to the increased participation of African Americans in the South's electoral process.[54]

In her 1985 study Margaret Edds argues that political power can produce at least two economic benefits for African Americans: more public sector jobs and an increase in minority contracting. For example, in Richmond, Virginia, African Americans held 12 of the 30 highest-ranking city jobs in 1985 (versus only 4 in 1977) after a majority of African Americans were elected to the city council. In Atlanta, city contracts that went to minority firms totalled $41,000 in 1973, the year Maynard Jackson became the city's first African American mayor. This amount reached $27.9 million in 1985, at the end of Mayor Jackson's last term.[55] Further evidence suggests, however, that the economic problems African Americans face require more than merely electing African Americans to political office. Counties in which they have achieved political control tend to rank at the lowest end of the economic scale.[56] For example, in Lowndes County, Alabama, a county run by African Americans, economic disparity between the races remained as great in the 1980s as it was in the 1960s. Despite decreases in

vote dilution from 1965 to 1985 and increases in African Americans' involvement in politics, "life for many remained almost as segregated in 1985
as in 1965."[57]

The combination of white bloc voting, still a serious problem today,[58]
and at-large voting systems means that an extremely large minority population is usually necessary for African American candidates to be elected.
For example, in 1981, 20 Alabama municipalities had African American
mayors. These were all small localities ranging in population from 95 to
11,028, except for Birmingham and Prichard. In 19 of these districts, the
average proportion of African Americans was 82 percent.[59]

Dilution of their voting strength tends to discourage African Americans
from voting. Their voter turnout and candidacy rates usually drop as they
are excluded from political participation and deprived of alternative means
of exerting influence. One example is Abilene, Texas, where minority candidates first ran for municipal office in 1970. Although they continued to
run throughout the decade, none was able to win an election without the
endorsement of a slating group dominated by a powerful white business
group. The minority communities became so disillusioned with the electoral process that they essentially stopped participating. In the city council
elections of 1979, only 76 Mexican Americans and 31 African Americans
voted out of a minority population of eligible voters of approximately
19,000.[60]

In the problem-filled lives of many African Americans, the hard-fought
right to register and vote has a very low priority. Past experience or poverty
or inadequate education or long-term unemployment teach that voting is
a waste of time.[61] Paradoxically, one of the negative consequences of dilution may be that it fosters the illusion that a dilution problem does not
exist. Low African American voter turnout may lead some white leaders
to argue that the primary reason African Americans are not being elected
to public office is because their supporters are too lazy to bother to vote,
not because there is any dilution problem.

The Legal Response

To understand why the dilution problem has been persistent under integration requires some knowledge of law applicable to voting rights. The
Voting Rights Act is the most important instrument of this law.

When the Act was passed in 1965, Congress realized that even if certain
types of discrimination were made illegal, other forms of discrimination

might develop to replace them. Congress therefore promulgated § 5 of the Act (called the "preclearance provision"), which provides that any change in a voting law or procedure in certain states or localities (called "covered jurisdictions") must be precleared either by a three-judge United States District Court or the Attorney General. The proposed change is precleared if it is "not discriminatory in purpose and not discriminatory in effect."[62] As control over the voting process is "taken out of the arbitrary hands of local clerks and [politicians],"[63] § 5 preclearance remains the cheapest and easiest way to attack vote dilution.

Although § 5 applies to claims of vote dilution as well as to more direct methods of denying the right to vote,[64] its scope is limited in several ways. First, § 5 does not apply to the entire country, but only to "covered jurisdictions," mostly in southern states. Second, voting methods adopted prior to the Act, or prior to a covered jurisdiction's inclusion under § 5, are not subject to challenge unless they were changed after the provision went into effect. Thus if a voting scheme from 1964 or earlier dilutes votes in some way, African Americans cannot use § 5 to challenge the scheme.[65] The third limitation on § 5 derives from a 1976 Supreme Court decision concerning redistricting in New Orleans, Louisiana. In this case, *Beer v. United States*,[66] the Supreme Court held that a redistricting plan that is not actually "regressive" in its effect on minority voting strength does not violate § 5. Accordingly, a jurisdiction may redraw electoral boundaries established in 1960, and such new boundaries can have a dilutionary effect, provided that they do not cause greater dilution than the 1960 boundaries.

The Supreme Court further limited the scope of § 5 in *Presley v. Etowah County Commission*[67] by holding that it only applies to cases that directly involve voting. *Presley* dealt with a situation in which an African American commissioner was elected to the county commission for the first time in "modern times." His election was made possible by a redistricting scheme that produced a majority African American district. Less than nine months after he took office, the commissioners passed two resolutions that diminished his decisionmaking authority. Notwithstanding the obvious relationship to voting and the apparent racial discrimination, the Supreme Court ruled that "changes which affect only the distribution of power among officials are not subject to § 5 because such changes have no direct relation to, or impact on, voting."[68] By restricting the scope of § 5, *Presley* makes it more difficult to challenge racially discriminatory allocations of power in our systems of government. After *Presley*, racially motivated political schemes that adversely affect African American representation need not be precleared under § 5 of the Voting Rights Act.

A further impediment to the use of § 5 in vote dilution cases arose in a 1973 Supreme Court case. In *White v. Regester*,[69] which involved a Texas legislative redistricting plan, the Supreme Court held that "the plaintiffs' burden is to produce evidence to support findings that the political processes leading to nomination and election were not equally open to participation by the group in question—that its members had less opportunity than did other residents in the district to participate in the political processes and to elect legislators of their choice."[70] Plaintiffs' burden, then, is to prove a demonstrable denial of the right to participate in the voting process. Because evidence for this is not always readily available, the plaintiffs' burden is very difficult and costly, thereby preventing many legitimate claims of vote dilution from being brought before the courts.

The *White* case was modified by a fifth-circuit court opinion later that year. In *Zimmer v. McKeithen*[71] the court held that unconstitutional dilution could be demonstrated by proving lack of access to the process of slating candidates; unresponsiveness of legislators to the particular interests of a group; a tenuous state policy underlying the preference for at-large districting; the existence of past discrimination in general; and evidence of large districts, majority vote requirements, provisions against single-shot voting, and the lack of provisions for at-large candidates running from particular geographical subdistricts.[72] The court concluded that "the fact of dilution is established upon proof of the existence of an aggregate of these factors ... [but] all these factors need not be proved in order to obtain relief."[73] *Zimmer* gave the courts much discretion in deciding dilution cases. It also placed a great burden on plaintiffs: not knowing which factors the court would consider most important, they felt obliged to address each one at length. Plaintiffs' lawyers and experts (sociologists, historians, political scientists, and statisticians) were often forced to spend thousands of hours collecting data. Once again, the burden placed on plaintiffs prevented many legitimate vote dilution claims from ever being prosecuted.

In 1980 the Supreme Court made an already difficult burden for plaintiffs an almost impossible one. A controversial and much criticized case, *City of Mobile v. Bolden*,[74] held that "only if there is purposeful discrimination can there be a violation of [the Fifteenth Amendment or] the Equal Protection Clause of the Fourteenth Amendment."[75] The Court further held that the language of § 2 of the Voting Rights Act (which prohibits states and municipalities from abridging the right to vote "on account of race or color") "no more than elaborates upon that of the Fifteenth Amendment, and the sparse legislative history of § 2 makes clear that it was intended to have an effect no different from that of the Fifteenth Amendment itself."[76] Since the Fifteenth Amendment requires a showing of intent to discriminate, § 2 of the Voting Rights Act must likewise require such a showing. According to the Supreme Court, then, demonstrating that a voting system has the effect of diluting African Americans' votes is not enough to make the scheme unlawful under either the Constitution or the Voting Rights Act.

To satisfy the intent test, plaintiffs must sometimes go more than a hundred years back to try to discover the intent of the legislators who created the voting system. The huge burden of such research was illustrated by the *Bolden* case when it was remanded to the Mobile court. The new trial alone took 6,000 hours of lawyers' time as well as 7,000 hours for researchers and expert witnesses. It cost $120,000, not counting lawyers' fees, and lasted two and a half weeks. During the trial, the most minute changes in city government from 1819 to the present were explored. Eventually, seven years after the suit was originally heard, the court found for the plaintiffs. The victorious plaintiffs were more fortunate than most other plaintiffs, however, because they received help from the NAACP Legal Defense and Education Fund and the Justice Department. After *Bolden,* many plaintiffs were forced to abandon their vote dilution claims because of the huge burden of proof placed upon them.[77]

Congress was about to review the Voting Rights Act, the transitory features of which were set to expire in 1982, at about the time *Bolden* was decided. Civil rights activists began an intensive campaign to convince Congress to extend § 5 and to amend § 2 to overrule *Bolden.* Over the initial opposition of President Reagan and other politicians, a bill was passed in both Houses of Congress amending the Voting Rights Act to render illegal any electoral device whose intent *or effect* denied or abridged the voting rights of racial minorities. The amendment was passed after the inclusion of the "Dole compromise," which stated that nothing in the bill was intended to establish that a voting right has been violated solely upon demonstrating the absence of proportional representation.[78] The amendment nonetheless strengthened the Voting Rights Act and resolved many of the problems created by *Bolden.* As a consequence of the 1982 amendment, pre-*Bolden* law continues to govern. Plaintiffs in vote dilution cases can now use the results of a voting plan to show racial discrimination and vote dilution.

Problems remained, however, in the years following this amendment. Plaintiffs had to continue to collect vast amounts of data, which required much time and money, in order to satisfy the precedents established by *White* and *Zimmer,* the most important pre-*Bolden* cases. In addition, the courts struggled to apply the nine-factor or "totality of circumstances" test established after the 1982 amendment.[79] A better mousetrap to catch vote dilution was obviously needed.

In 1986 the Supreme Court established a new standard for determining whether vote dilution claims based on the use of at-large, or multi-member, districts violate the Voting Rights Act.[80] In *Gingles* the Court held that the plaintiff must prove two factors to satisfy the effects test under § 2 of the Act. First, the plaintiffs must show that members of their group experience substantial difficulty electing representatives of their choice. Second, they must prove that significant racial bloc voting exists. For this requirement, they must document an ongoing pattern of typically polarized voting in which whites vote as a unit for white candidates (and win), and African Americans vote as a unit for African American candidates.[81] Some scholars define the *Gingles* test as a three-part rather than a two-part test, insofar as the minority group must show that: (1) it is sufficiently large and compact to constitute a majority in a single member district; (2) it is politically cohesive; and (3) the white majority votes sufficiently as a bloc to defeat any minority candidate.[82]

Gingles affirms the central importance of racial bloc voting in § 2 litigation.[83] It also makes it easier for African Americans to bring vote dilution claims by clarifying the requirements for such claims. Moreover, *Gingles* attempts to end two judicial trends that have hindered plaintiffs in dilution cases. First, the Court notes the fallacy of setting arbitrary standards for proving politically consequential racial bloc voting. The Court's new attitude makes it more difficult for defendants to offer explanations for bloc voting that would defeat plaintiffs' dilution claims. Second, the Court stated that it is not necessary to explain why whites and African Americans vote differently in order to show legally significant racial bloc voting.[84] This means that plaintiffs may now place less reliance on expert explanations for voting behavior. Litigation thereby becomes cheaper and, as a consequence, more cases may be brought to trial.

In several post-*Gingles* cases the Supreme Court has expanded the 1982 amendment to § 2 of the Voting Rights Act. For example, in *Houston Lawyers' Association v. Attorney General of Texas,* the Supreme Court held that judicial elections for trial judges in Texas are covered by § 2 of the amendment.[85] In *Clark v. Roemer,* the Court held that judicial elections were also covered by § 5 of the Act.[86] These extensions of §§ 2 and 5 recognize that African American representation is important in all types of elections, and that in order to redress the voting dilution problem it is essential to enforce voting rights in all election arenas, including judicial elections.

Since 1964 the Supreme Court has refused to hold that at-large elections or multi-member districts are per se illegal under the Equal Protection Clause.[87] The Court did note, however, that these districts may "be subject to challenge where the circumstances of a particular case may 'operate to minimize or cancel out the voting strength of racial or political elements of the voting population.' "[88] Nonetheless, the ultimate burden is always on the plaintiffs to prove that the districts "dilute or cancel the voting strength of racial or political elements."[89] This burden, added to the burden placed on the plaintiffs by *White* and *Zimmer,* means that judicial protection against multi-member district dilution is difficult to obtain. So although the Supreme Court has recognized that multi-member districts or at-large elections may have the effect of diluting votes, it has made it something of an ordeal to prove dilution. In recent years, fortunately, a number of successful challenges to at-large local election districts have been made in lower federal courts.[90]

Since *Gingles,* federal courts have struggled with a thorny "conflict between two constitutional criteria of fair representation: majority rule and non-discrimination against racial minorities."[91] This conflict appeared most prominently in a 1993 Supreme Court case, *Shaw v. Reno,*[92] in which the Court ruled for the first time that white voters could challenge the constitutionality of bizarrely shaped voting districts that had black majorities. Two subsequent decisions by the Court reaffirmed *Shaw.*[93]

The facts in *Shaw* are as follows. North Carolina was entitled to an additional congressional seat as the result of the 1990 census. Although African Americans were 20% of the total population in North Carolina, there had been no African American congressional representative from that state in this century.[94] The state apportioned itself originally so that there was only one voting district where African Americans were a majority. The Attorney General objected to this districting under § 5 of the Voting Rights

Act. In response to this objection, North Carolina added another majority-black voting district of "dramatically irregular shape." White citizens of the state challenged this district on grounds that it amounted to unconstitutional racial gerrymander.[95] The Supreme Court held that "a plaintiff challenging a reapportionment statute under the Equal Protection Clause may state a claim by alleging that the legislation, though race-neutral on its face, rationally cannot be understood as anything other than an effort to separate voters into different districts on the basis of race, and that the separation lacks sufficient justification."[96] The Court based its decision on its belief that race-conscious districting may stigmatize African Americans and violate the rights of whites to participate in a color-blind election. When an odd-shaped district, such as the one drawn in North Carolina, is "created solely to effectuate the perceived common interests of one racial group," the Court said, "elected officials will act as though they are only obligated to represent the members of that group instead of their entire constituency."[97] This, the Court concluded, was "altogether antithetical to our system of representative democracy."[98]

Lani Guinier is one of many scholars who have criticized the Court for its advocacy of color-blind districting.[99] In discovering the right to participate in color-blind elections, Guinier argues, the Court seemed to imply that there is some racially neutral way to draw district lines. However, all districts are "drawn by someone to eliminate or disadvantage the political influence of someone else."[100] The Court failed to realize that without some government intervention, political groups like the North Carolina congressional delegation will be racially segregated.[101]

In cases like *Shaw*, the Supreme Court seems to be looking at the voting problem from a theoretical rather than a practical point of view. If our society were totally integrated instead of partially segregated, if it did not have a long history of racial discrimination, and if racially polarized voting was not such a pervasive reality, then perhaps color-blind districting would work. The reality of segregation and the use of techniques to exclude African Americans from fully participating in electoral politics may make some type of government intervention necessary to ensure parity. The Supreme Court in *Shaw* does not offer a solution for resolving the problems African Americans face in electing representatives.

Although vote dilution precludes African Americans from fully participating in electoral politics, it should be considered in the context of other factors that affect the quality of African American lives. "A fact often overlooked by those who stress the importance of voting is that even if blacks are able to take control of some local governments through effective use of the ballot, they still have little if any influence over the economic situations which in the long run profoundly affect their chances of obtaining a just share of social rewards."[102] In searching for solutions to the problem of vote dilution and, ultimately, the problem of effective representation for African Americans, it is important to be cognizant of all the factors that affect voting and all the aspects of life that are affected by voting. If African Americans are to participate in our political system effectively, they must not only be able to cast votes; they must also be able to vote for candidates who will be accountable to them. Figuring out how to accomplish effective political representation and meaningful political participation is a difficult task indeed.

6

Why Integration Has Failed

"White Racism" and Other Theories

When all the probing, postulating, and proselytizing about the American race problem comes to an end, one thing will remain clear beyond peradventure: the traditional liberal solution to the problem—racial integration—is not the right answer for most African Americans. Four decades after *Brown v. Board of Education*, millions of African Americans are still not receiving adequate education and emotional support in our public schools, are still not living in safe and decent neighborhoods, are still not working to their full economic and emotional potential, and are still not able to protect their social and economic interests through the political process. Many whites see African Americans' low performance in school and on the job as hard evidence of their inferiority. When a little freckle-faced white girl tells an ABC News interviewer on national TV that the only thing African Americans do better than whites is "their hair," that is a sure sign that racial integration is not working. This indictment of racial integration cuts across class lines, so that the African American underclass (largely a postintegration phenomenon) spins in an intergenerational cycle of poverty and despair at the bottom of the socioeconomic ladder, while the African American middle class sits angrily at the top of it.[1]

Many whites would argue that racial integration has in fact been successful. African Americans and whites attend the same schools, ride the same buses, and sit at the same lunch counters. But most Americans, certainly African Americans, believed that racial integration would lead to racial equality. There is nothing intrinsically good about racial mixing. Its appeal comes from its social utility.

Why has racial mixing (when it has taken hold) failed to empower African Americans, leaving so many vulnerable and without racial respect? Why, after nearly a half century, has a policy of racial integration not delivered racial equality and harmony to this country?

Perhaps the great historian John Hope Franklin (whom Peter Applebome describes as "the last true integrationist") is right: racial integration has failed because it has barely been tried.[2] Whites have not been willing to share power with African Americans, as they must if integration is to work. I doubt whites were ever willing to make the necessary sacrifices to ensure integration's success. The chances for success are more remote today than they were thirty years ago: low-skilled jobs are being sucked out of the American economy as fast as companies can build factories overseas; low wages are spreading across what remains of the American labor market like a deadly virus; and the middle class continues to shrink. A dark cloud even hangs over the white elite. Passed over for partnership or pushed out after layoffs, Harvard-educated lawyers are as insecure and uncertain about the future as the unskilled wage earner.[3] Whites are not going to voluntarily relinquish the advantages, whether fairly acquired or not, they hold over African Americans in education, housing, employment, and government when even their elites are overwhelmed with feelings of privation and vulnerability. When human behavior is viewed in this way, I can readily understand how in white America today it is easy to be a conservative or a neoconservative ("a one-time liberal who has been mugged by reality and decides to press charges"). The true liberal (also mugged by reality, but refuses to press charges) is, indeed, an endangered American species.

One might ask why, given that whites are so opposed to sharing power, are other minorities doing better than African Americans? Those who *are* doing better are doing so not because of integration (whites still control our major institutions) but in spite of integration. I elaborate on this point in the last part of the book.

White resistance in promoting racial equality through integration (that is, in fostering two-way or mutual integration) is precisely why we have civil rights laws. In other words, racial integration must generally rely on coercion in the form of civil rights laws to bring about equality for African Americans. Such coercion, however, necessarily diminishes the quality of equality. It begets a low-grade or second-class equality for African Americans, because the ensuing racial mixing is nonconsensual on the part of whites. Even moral suasion taints racial equality for African Americans, because altruistic whites are merely feeling charitable rather than indebted. John Edgar Wideman has it about right: "At best integration demeaned, compromised, [and made blacks] eternally dependent."[4]

Furthermore, even as a form of coercion, civil rights laws are often ineffective. They do not always prevent racial discrimination or deliver racial equality. In fact, they may produce just the opposite effect; they sometimes encourage racial discrimination by placing a myriad of procedural or evidentiary roadblocks in the path of legal recourse, thereby giving the right of way to those bent on discriminating.[5]

Racial integration has had some unforeseen negative results that have undercut its goal of racial equality. It has encouraged and facilitated an exodus of talented individuals and stable families from African American communities during the post-1960s, and thereby depleted these communities of human and economic resources. This flight to integration has left millions of African Americans in the nation's inner cities not just poor but poverty stricken. Yet those rich enough to leave never really get out; they are forever affected by the negative public images that come out of the ghetto each day.

High on the list of possible reasons for racial integration's failure is its inability to conquer personal bias, a psychological phenomenon which liberals, with their Rousseauist romanticism, have never been able to fully acknowledge or understand. In the state of nature, people are biased. Cognitive psychologists tell us that bias is tied to the way the brain works. The mind relies on cultural stereotypes, called "default assumptions," to interpret new, complex, and ambiguous situations. The brain calculates a "base rate" (the normal amount of times an event occurs in a given population) to guide thought and behavior.

Bias, then, is part of the brain's "off-the-shelf taxonomies that classify and organize certain features of the social world into a coherent whole."[6] A female college student who assumes that most drunken men at a wild college fraternity party at 2 A.M. are sexually dangerous is more likely to escape sexual assault than a more open-minded female friend. The average person judges rich people to be more intelligent than poor people, powerful people to be taller than less powerful people. The average white person (and a good number of African Americans) could not conceive of the Supreme Court being the Supreme Court if all its justices were African American or women. The mind relies on stereotypes to make sense of reality and to make all sorts of decisions in everyday life.

Liberals have not been able to change the way the mind works. Higher education, our most progressive social tool, has not been able to purify the mind. "On the basis of observable, external features—lips, nose, color, hair, and paradoxically . . . the 'race' of the parents—[an African American's] destiny is assigned. Assumptions about . . . [his] character, intelligence, ability to launch a jump shot, manage a baseball team or a corporation are swiftly, unalterably ascribed. . . . Wealth, position have no bearing on the deep, general levels of resistance he will encounter, except to add a tinge of irony to success, teach the futility of certain compromises, the bitterness of how close to winning losing can be."[7]

If racial integration has failed to undo racial stereotypes or counteract racial bias, it has also failed to do much about "white racism." This is more than racial bias. It is a continuing system of racial subordination that assigns African Americans to a racial caste. "White racism" is defined not simply as a state of mind (that is, a belief system) but also as *a state of being*. As Feagin and Vera explain:

> We conceptualize racism in structural and institutional as well as individual terms. Racism is more than a matter of individual prejudice and scattered episodes of discrimination. There is no black racism because there is no centuries-old system of racialized subordination and discrimination designed by African Americans to exclude white Americans from full participation in the rights, privileges, and benefits of this society. Black (or other minority) racism would require not only a widely accepted racist ideology directed at whites but also the power to systematically exclude whites from opportunities and rewards in major economic, cultural, and political institutions. While there are black Americans with antiwhite prejudices, and there are instances of blacks discriminating against whites, these examples are not central to the core operations of U.S. society and are not part of an entrenched structure of institutionalized racism that can be found in every nook and cranny of this country. Indeed, they are frequently defensive or oppositional responses to pre-existing white racism.

What is often referred to as "black racism" consists of judgments made about whites by some black leaders or commentators to the effect that "no white people can be trusted" or "the white man is the devil." But these critical ideas or negative prejudices are not the equivalent of modern white racism. The latter involves not just individual thoughts but also widely socialized ideologies and omnipresent practices based on entrenched racialized beliefs. The prejudices and myths

used to justify antiblack actions are not invented by individual per-
petrators, nor are they based only on personal experience. These
patterns of highly racialized thought are embedded in the culture and
institutions of a white-centered society.[8]

This concept of racism ("white racism") is more developed than a similar
definition used by other scholars, such as Anthony Downs and a new group
of legal thinkers called "critical race theorists."[9]

Some people may disagree with such expanded usage of the term "racism." Indeed, some scholars have argued that the many different usages
of the concept is reason enough to ban it from sociological or other theoretical discourse.[10] But the Feagin-Vera usage has precedent in legal terminology. In civil litigation, the concept of *res judicata* has two meanings:
one specific (namely, that claims already litigated cannot be relitigated by
the same parties) and one generic, which incorporates both its specific
meaning and the otherwise distinct concept of "collateral estoppel" (which
means that issues already decided cannot be brought up again in a subsequent case between the same parties). Thus the doctrine of *res judicata*
refers to the study of both claim preclusion and issue preclusion—*res judicata* in the specific sense and collateral estoppel. Racism in the generic
sense (the Feagin-Vera sense) encompasses both the specific (or traditional)
meaning (negative attitudes or racial bias, in particular the belief in racial
supremacy), and also racial subordination (structural disadvantage at society's core). African Americans can be racist in the first sense of the word,
but not in the second.

The "white racism" proposition presents a more complex and enlightened view than the converse belief that broad-scale racial disadvantage has
been virtually eliminated from our society by the civil rights laws. This
belief must now be amended in light of "white racism," to bring us to
acknowledge that while state-of-mind white racism (white racism in the
specific sense) has declined appreciably, state-of-being white racism (white
racism in the generic sense) has not. Whites still hold an unfair share of
the poker chips.

Dignity Harms

Although we have looked at many examples of generic white racism already, it may be useful to point to another area of evidence as well. I mean
to focus on the slights to human dignity even middle-class African Amer-

icans, despite all their socioeconomic success, must endure daily.[11] From racial slurs to the battle flag of the old Confederacy flying over several state capitols, from humiliating service in Denny's restaurants to Rodney King-type of police abuse, assaults on the dignity of African Americans may be an inevitability in an integrated society. They certainly are an everyday occurrence that cuts across class lines. Dignity harms are ubiquitous and permanent because they result from racialized ways of feeling, thinking, and behaving toward African Americans (and other minorities) that emanate from the American culture at large. They are macrosystemic. Furthermore, they are reinforced by schools, families, friends, TV, movies, and the media.

In-depth surveys of middle-class African Americans further reveal that racial humiliation remains a continuing problem in integrated settings. Ninety-eight percent of 107 African American graduates from the nation's top business schools indicated in a 1986 study that subtle prejudice permeated their companies, and 90% reported a cooler "climate of support" than that for their white peers. In a 1990 Gallup poll of well-to-do African Americans on Long Island, where the community is wealthier than in most other areas, two-thirds of those interviewed complained of discrimination. A 1991 *Los Angeles Times* poll of affluent African Americans found that 58% of those interviewed experienced discrimination. And a 1992 New York City Bar Association poll discovered that 61% of the African American lawyers surveyed felt that their work experiences were clearly different from those of nonminority lawyers. These surveys indicate that for most middle-class African Americans, regardless of their achievements, comfortable homes, or Ivy League educations, race remains a significant factor in determining the quality of their everyday existence.[12]

When human faces are added to the statistics, the dignity harms are given more content. For example, when an African American lawyer and a white lawyer, both associates at a prestigious law firm, were meeting with a client, the white associate announced he had to leave early. He paused long enough to assure the client that the African American lawyer was capable. The African American lawyer was devastated because her associate felt it necessary to confirm her competence.[13]

Similarly, an African American partner in a prestigious law firm suffered humiliation when he arrived at the office an hour or so earlier than usual. While he was fishing in his pockets for his key card, a young white associate blocked his way and asked "May I help you?" When the partner shook his head and attempted to bypass the associate, the associate stepped in front of him and again demanded "May I help you?" The partner identified himself, and then the associate stepped aside. Although the partner was dressed better than the associate and paid the associate's salary, he still had to justify his presence, to a subordinate no less.[14] Another African American partner, this time in a New York law firm, was informed by his real estate broker that the purchase of a Westchester home had collapsed because of the partner's race. Although he successfully sued to get the home, the partner says that the experience "still makes me angry. At some level that particularly grates." Similarly, another African American lawyer is constantly hounded by the perception of being "a *Black* litigator" rather than "a litigator." Whenever he goes to court and does a mediocre job, he receives rave reviews from both judges and colleagues. They are impressed because he exceeded their low expectation of his abilities.[15]

Racial humiliation is not limited to lawyers. An African American physician asserts that his practice would be "a lot, lot better" if he were white.[16] Another African American physician believes that "a lot of white people think that Blacks are just here to serve them, and [that] we have not risen above the servient position."[17] Similarly, an African American business executive complains about his exclusion from all-white private clubs. He argues that "the best I can offer my client is a hamburger and a beer in a plastic cup. My competitor takes his client . . . where they can have a great lunch and drinks, the use of the locker room and showers. Then they get their shoes shined."[18] A retired African American schoolteacher characterizes daily assaults on her dignity as "little murders" that make her middle-class lifestyle difficult.[19]

Some African American professionals pursue a course of racial neutrality or racial denial in an attempt to avoid racial humiliation. For example, a personnel vice president dissociates himself from any hint of a racial agenda. Although he thrives financially, he feels distressed because he feels he was not being true to his racial identity and was labeled an Uncle Tom by other African Americans.

Isabel Wilkerson, Chicago bureau chief for the *New York Times,* states that dignity harms reduce successful African Americans to third-class citizenship. In her own case, she once had to race through an airport terminal to make an appointment and was followed by white Drug Enforcement Administration agents. She told the agents that she could not afford to miss the airport bus, and the agents climbed onto the bus with her. Wilkerson was then subjected to an interrogation aboard the bus. When the other passengers on the bus began to stare, she tried to reduce the humiliation and retain her presence of mind, so she took out her notepad and began to ask her own questions. Nonetheless, Wilkerson felt intensely embarrassed. A dignity harm had reduced her from a respected journalist to a suspected criminal. She wonders whether rape could be worse.[20]

Humiliation also occurs when African Americans receive faint praise from their white colleagues. For example, an African American public relations official was shocked when a white colleague tried to compliment him by remarking, "You don't speak ghettoese." The public relations official felt an overwhelming sense that what the remark really meant was "You're almost like us, but not enough like us to be acceptable."[21] Likewise, an African American cringes whenever she is held up as a departure from her race. In addition to worrying about white perceptions, she worries about "what it does to my relationships with other blacks."[22]

Painful recollections of past discrimination can also ruin the infrequent occasions when middle-class African Americans are actually judged according to their talents rather than their color. Racial slights are seen where none were intended. For example, when a high-ranking African American corporate lawyer was invited to spend a weekend at the chief executive officer's home, he panicked because he assumed that his boss did not socialize with African Americans unless something important was about to occur. He spent days dreading the weekend. When he arrived at the house, he realized that his fears were unfounded. The CEO was impressed with the lawyer's presentation a few months earlier and wanted to get to know him better.[23] Similarly, sales clerks who refuse to touch African American hands when giving change may not be touching anyone's hands, regardless of race, because they may fear contracting diseases from the public.[24] And sales clerks who ask "Who's next?" when an African American customer arrives at the counter slightly ahead of a white customer may be engaged in conflict avoidance.[25] Rather than choosing one customer over the other, and possibly losing the other customer's business, sales clerks are sometimes instructed by management to let the customers decide for themselves who was first in the line.

Erroneous perceptions by some middle-class African Americans, however, fail to change the fact that they as a group suffer dignity harms on a daily basis within a variety of settings. Feagin's research makes this point most powerfully. In a 1991 article, later expanded into a book,[26] Feagin analyzed the character and meaning of modern discrimination through 37 interviews from a larger study of 135 middle-class African Americans in Boston, Buffalo, Baltimore, Washington, D.C., Detroit, Houston, Dallas, Austin, San Antonio, Marshall, Las Vegas, and Los Angeles. The interviews were conducted by African Americans to ensure the uninhibited disclosure of detailed information that the respondents might have been hesitant to convey to whites. Knowledgeable consultants within key cities verified the respondents' middle-class status. For purposes of the survey, middle class was defined as professionals, college students preparing for professions, and successful business owners.[27]

The thirty-seven-member subsample accurately represented the demographic character of the larger 135-member sample. The subsample consisted of nine corporate managers and executives, nine healthcare or other professionals, eight government officials, four college students, three journalists or broadcasters, two clerical or sales workers, one entrepreneur, and one retired person. Sixteen members of the subsample earned over $56,000 annually. More than 90% of the subsample had completed some college work.[28]

Within the subsample, the probability of experiencing dignity harms varied according to the site. The survey found that dignity harms in the form of overt discrimination is the most prevalent form on unprotected public streets. Fifteen respondents out of the subsample reported 37 incidents involving street discrimination. The survey found that middle-class African Americans must endure recurring dignity harms from strangers who react primarily on the basis of an ascribed characteristic, color. Middle-class symbols (dress, for example) are ignored. "It's fairly consistently unpleasant at those sites where there's nothing that mediates between my race and what I have to do," an African American professor said.[29] An African American college student recounted that when he walks home at night through a predominantly white area, he is followed by the police and avoided by white pedestrians, although in fact the area is terrorized by an unknown white rapist. Some whites even dart in front of traffic to avoid being on the same side of the street as an African American.[30]

Feagin found that the most common responses to dignity harms on the street were withdrawal, resigned acceptance, or a quick verbal retort. For example, an African American professor angrily drove away without replying when whites, who were laughing at her car because they thought she was Hispanic, exclaimed "Oh, it's just a nigger."[31] But one African

American businesswoman physically attacked a white woman who commented that the businesswoman's new car must have been bought on welfare. She felt incensed that her middle-class symbol had failed to shield her from an unexpected dignity harm.[32]

More often, middle-class African Americans tend to assess dignity harms on the street with a great deal of circumspection, giving whites the benefit of the doubt. This is especially true of middle-class African American children who have been sheltered from racism. A young college student, for example, refused to believe that the hate stares and racial comments on the street were actually being directed toward her. Likewise, another young college student reflexively failed to respond to hate stares on her way to school and was upset for some days thereafter at her own passiveness.[33]

When it is possible, middle-class African Americans try to draw upon their own resources for protection from or retaliation against dignity harms. For example, one man (who worked for a media survey firm) threatened to bring television crews to expose racial slurs that had been visited upon him. In another case, an African American parole officer exercised his discretionary authority and charged his verbal assailant with the often overlooked crime of jaywalking.[34]

Middle-class African Americans are more likely to counterattack verbally, in writing, or through the courts when the dignity harms occur in public accommodations. For example, when an African American retired schoolteacher overheard a clerk refer to her as "that nigger woman," she sarcastically told another clerk who was serving her that she did not know that people were still using that sort of language. When an African American bank executive consistently received poor service at a prestigious restaurant, he exposed the discrimination by publishing letters in several newspapers. The restaurant owners urged him to come again and write a retraction if he was treated fairly. He refused to do that and instead wrote a truthful statement on how he was subsequently treated in that restaurant. Although the executive eventually received hospitable service, he had to expend considerable time and energy to receive service equivalent to whites in the same position.[35]

Because the confrontational response can be time-consuming, many middle-class African Americans will simply reject the poor service and leave the public accommodation, especially if the service is not important. When a utility company executive was told by a store owner to use a side window for services, she just left the store. She decided not to confront the owner because she was just passing through the town.[36] Likewise, a news anchorman avoids time-consuming confrontations by "sounding white" on the telephone whenever he rents a car. However, he does make a point to lecture sales representatives if they are openly surprised to see that he is an African American.[37] When an African American news director for a major television station was denied service at a restaurant, she showed the restaurant manager her credit cards to legitimate her middle-class status. She then threatened to use her middle-class resources and bring a TV news team to the restaurant. But first she had to convince her boyfriend that confronting the restaurant manager was a better way to respond to the dignity harm than withdrawing.[38]

Eliminating White Racism and the Black Tax

Dignity harms are inevitable in an integrated American society. They are as permanent as taxes. But unlike other forms of taxation, dignity harms discriminate on the basis of race. They constitute a badge of slavery pinned to the souls of African Americans in a manner that abases the entire race to the level of chattel. So long as "white racism" exists, dignity harms will always afflict African Americans.

Feagin and Vera believe that white racism can be surgically removed from the body politic without killing the patient. They offer an elaborate set of proposals designed to create "a new socio-racial rationality," a mutually agreeable social contract that ensures full racial justice and harmony. To reconstruct society along these egalitarian lines, the authors propose that we educate or re-educate the majority of whites in U.S. racial and ethnic history, a task to which Feagin has committed his entire professional life. This educational process must also include an understanding that eliminating white racism is not a zero-sum game. Whites as well as African Americans stand to gain from its elimination, because white racism also exacts heavy costs on whites. Whites must expend a tremendous amount of time, energy, and resources just to maintain a system of racial domination. Vigorous enforcement of our civil rights laws is also needed, but so are more radical measures—namely, "substantial governmental reparations" to African Americans and "a new constitutional convention" in which, for the first time, all Americans would participate.[39]

If American society could be reconstructed along these lines, white racism and its attendant evils—dignity harms, racial violence, and racial inequity in education, housing, employment, and political power—would be eliminated. But I do not believe Feagin and Vera's prescription has much chance of succeeding. A new constitutional convention would open debate and reconsideration of the existing document, and the consequences could be dire. I shudder to think what might emerge from a society that grows more intolerant each year—a constitutional ban on free speech and reproductive rights; mandatory prayer in public schools; a balanced budget amendment (rather than a legislative enactment), which most economists say is bad economic policy even if politically popular. And we must also speculate about what happens if, say, the Second Amendmenters (those who believe not only in the right to carry a gun in pocket or purse but also in the right to form citizen militias) or the abortion activists on either side do not get their way. Are we not inviting a second civil war by renegotiating the social contract? I doubt that either Feagin or Vera would want a constitutional convention dominated by the electorate responsible for the Republican stampede in the 1994 congressional and gubernatorial elections. But that's probably what they would get, even though they envision a more enlightened electorate.

Moreover, I am not so sure that white racism is not a zero-sum game. Whites can accrue a net benefit from white racism. Sometimes it makes economic sense to discriminate. For example, a mortgage lender can reduce the costs of analysis when it uses general categories (such as race or gender) in deciding whether to extend credit to an individual. This is similar to a law school admissions officer who finds it easier and hence less costly to base her decision on the numbers rather than on the particular characteristics of each applicant. Complying with customer preferences, let us say a client who does not want to work with an African American lawyer, is another example of market-driven discrimination. The existence of market-driven and other forms of "rational" discrimination is precisely why economists and law-and-economics scholars, led by Nobel-prize-winning Gary Becker, are wrong in their belief that there is no need for civil rights laws because competitive markets punish those who would relinquish profits just to cater to prejudice. In fact bigots do not make bad competitors when discrimination is market-driven. Where discrimination is economically irrational, some business persons are of course willing to indulge their taste for discrimination at the cost of profits.[40]

I suppose I agree with Derrick Bell and Richard Delgado: whites have not, in 400 years of trying, found it to be within their interest to pursue a strategy of full racial equality, and there is no reason to believe that they will in the future.[41] While a few enlightened whites would be willing to submit to re-education or pay reparations, most whites (who have less control and more fear in their lives) would not. The fundamental flaw in Feagin and Vera's prescription is that it is predicated on a belief in what constitutional scholars and judicial activists call "the evolving standards of decency in a maturing society." But why should we assume that societies only mature and never rot?

Whether racial integration can be saved without killing the patient is an important civil rights question. I believe it can survive with less invasive procedures; that is, with the assistance of "limited separation." Before discussing this solution, let us consider why total separation, which so many mainstream African Americans and whites now advocate, is not the answer.

II

TOTAL SEPARATION

More than at any time since *Brown v. Board of Education,*[1] mainstream Americans on both sides of the color line are openly considering a total separation of the races as the only satisfactory solution to the race problem. Disillusioned by racial integration, many African Americans, including ministers, lawyers, and other members of the middle class, now believe that racial integration is a dead letter. Convinced that total separation is the only real solution to the race problem, many frustrated and exasperated whites, especially former liberals, hold back from fully committing themselves to strategies and programs that bolster racial integration. It is an example of mainstream America's dwindling commitment to racial integration and its supporting institutions (such as affirmative action) that no national civil rights leader came forth to criticize Sam Donaldson of ABC News for wondering aloud on national TV whether racial integration made sense anymore.[2]

It is important to make the point that racial segregation and racial separation (either as total separation or limited separation) are different concepts. Racial segregation is an official policy of government-sanctioned limitations on a racial group that subordinate and stigmatize it (*de jure* segregation); it can also consist of racial patterns that linger from former limitations (*de facto* segregation). In contrast, racial separation is voluntary racial isolation that serves to support and nurture individuals within the group. Consequently, *de jure* and *de facto* segregation can be distinguished from African American separatism, which is a form of racial isolation that results from a conscious choice or strategy of self-support. Malcolm X made a similar distinction between racial segregation and racial separation.

"When you are segregated," he said, "that is done to you by someone else; when you are separated you do that to yourself."[3]

Logic dictates that African Americans and society in general should question the wisdom of pursuing racial integration into the next century. Indeed, nearly 150 years ago, Alexis de Tocqueville observed that in any society "a natural prejudice . . . prompts men to despise whoever has been their inferior long after he has become his equal"; and that, in the United States, "the abstract and transient fact of slavery is fatally united with the physical and permanent fact of color. The tradition of slavery dishonors the race, and the peculiarity of the race perpetuates the tradition of slavery. . . . You may set the Negro free, but you cannot make him otherwise than an alien to the European."[4] Thomas Jefferson was equally pessimistic about racial integration:

Deep rooted prejudices entertained by the whites; ten thousand recollections, by the blacks, of the injuries they have sustained; new provocations; the real distinctions which nature has made; and many other circumstances, will divide us into parties, and produce convulsions which will probably never end but in the extermination of the one or the other race.—To these objections, which are political, may be added others, which are physical and moral. The first difference which strikes us is that of colour. Whether the black of the negro resides in the reticular membrane between the skin and scarf-skin, or in the scarf-skin itself; whether it proceeds from the colour of the blood, the colour of the bile, or from that of some other secretion, the difference is fixed in nature, and is as real as if its seat and cause were better known to us. And is this difference of no importance? Is it not the foundation of a greater or less share of beauty in the two races? Are not the fine mixtures of red and white, the expressions of every passion by greater or lesser suffusions of colour in the one, preferable to that eternal monotony, which reigns in the countenances, that immoveable veil of black which covers all the emotions of the other race? Add to these, flowing hair, a more elegant symmetry of form, their own judgment in favour of the whites, declared by their preference for them, as uniformly as is the preference of the Oranootan for the black woman over those of his own species. The circumstance of superior beauty is thought worthy of attention in the propagation of our horses, dogs, and other domestic animals; why not in that of man?[5]

But is total separation of the races the answer? This is the question explored in this part of the book. After examining several separatist theories to clarify our understanding of racial separation, I turn to the African American experience under racial separation. That experience is skewed for the researcher because African Americans who sought racial isolation in the past were constrained by Jim Crow. In other words, racial isolation (and its formulations) took place within a larger regime of racial segregation; the races were *legally* separated in a fashion meant to subordinate and stigmatize African Americans. No amount of racial isolation can engender feelings or conditions of racial equality—individual dignity and empowerment—for African Americans when they are universally limited and permanently disadvantaged by law.

Six separatist theorists, all black or African American, are examined in the chapters that follow. I begin with the first significant theorist, Booker T. Washington (1856–1915), and his bitter enemy who in later years would switch sides, W. E. B. Du Bois (1868–1963). After discussing the best known separatist, Marcus Garvey, I then consider the Nation of Islam and delineate the views of Elijah Muhammad, Malcolm X, and Louis Farrakhan, the Nation's current leader.

Washington saw separation as a necessary step toward eventual racial integration. But his brand of separatism lacked social, economic, and political ambition and ultimately demeaned African Americans. Washington stressed an independent economy built around agriculture and manual labor. He favored vocational education and preached racial accommodation—acceptance of political and social subordination—in exchange for economic independence. Although he publicly acquiesced in white racism, he believed in racial dignity and empowerment, the kind found in self-sufficiency.

In contrast, Du Bois' style of separatism was more interesting to the African American elite. For Du Bois, economic independence meant that African American consumers should support African American merchants. Racial pride required higher education as well as vocational education, an appreciation of one's heritage, and political and social rights to protect "self-segregated" communities. Du Bois was willing to accept "an increase in . . . prejudice" against whites to accomplish this goal.[6] Together, Washington and Du Bois teach that community, identity, and culture are integral to the struggle for racial equality.

Known as the father of black nationalism, Marcus Garvey (1887–1940) influenced all the separatists who came after him. Washington had died by the time Garvey came on the scene, and Du Bois, at that time still an integrationist, opposed Garvey's advocacy of total separation of the races, self-reliance, African American institutions, African pride and nationalism, capitalism, and, for as many African Americans as possible, a "return to Africa." Although at its height in the 1920s Garvey's movement mobilized millions of African Americans and blacks worldwide, it ultimately failed, leading to Garvey's controversial imprisonment for fraud and his eventual deportation. Some of the problems Garvey encountered were internal: major business failures, ideological conflict, disorganization, mismanagement, the refusal to reach out for white assistance when needed. Others were external: dishonest white businesspersons, hostile domestic and foreign governments, and the enmity of integrationists (such as W. E. B. Du Bois and the NAACP), who capitalized on Garvey's affiliation with the Ku Klux Klan, a white segregationist group with a penchant for lynching African Americans.

In the decade following Garvey's departure from the American scene, another African American group, heavily influenced by Garveyism, began to take shape. Founded in the 1930s, the Nation of Islam (or Black Muslims) presented a comprehensive program of total separation as a logical and preordained solution to the race problem. Drawing from Islamic religious orthodoxy as well as from Garvey, W. Fard Muhammad and Elijah Muhammad, the creators of the Nation, preached African heritage, racial unity under a racist Muslim theology (the War of Armageddon, for example, "will destroy the evil white race" and "restore the black people to their rightful place as rulers of the universe"), disciplined behavior under a strict moral code (no tobacco, alcohol, or criminal activity), and a separatist strategy that took three alternative forms. Territorial separation (four or five southern states constituting a separate Black Muslim nation) was the first alternative. In the second alternative, separate African American communities would operate collectively as a "nation within a nation," from which whites would be legally excluded and in which African American residents would obey Muslim laws (among them laws forbidding racial mixing) and be exempted from many federal and state laws (such as the income and property tax laws). The third alternative would be the creation of African American educational and economic institutions within African American communities. These institutions, although operating within federal and state laws as private enterprises, could engender racial self-reliance. In the early 1960s, Malcolm X, at the time the most recognized Black

Muslim in America, broke with Elijah Muhammad (Fard had disappeared in the 1930s) to form his own secular organization, which rejected the Nation's theological racism and stressed racial unity and movement toward a largely undefined "independent black nationhood."

Today Louis Farrakhan heads the Nation, and its ideology remains the same as that of the original Black Muslims with a few exceptions (emigration to Africa is now an acceptable alternative to other forms of separation previously proposed). Internal ideological conflict, the inherent limitations of theological racism, African Americans' appetite for racial integration since the 1960s, lack of economic independence, and passive political leadership are among the factors that have contributed to the Nation's substantially diminished influence in the African American community today, and to its inability to mobilize its separatist strategies.

At this juncture, racial separation looks about as problematic as racial integration. This assessment comes into sharper focus when we look at actual experiments in racial separation; that is, separatist theories that were fully implemented. Two separatist theories that have received relatively extensive application are emigration to Africa or another foreign country and migration within the United States.

Foreign emigration is perhaps the oldest form of racial separation. Marcus Garvey and, currently, the Nation of Islam under Louis Farrakhan advocate a "return to Africa." In 1822 a small group of free African Americans, assisted by prominent whites, returned to Africa and founded the Republic of Liberia. Unfortunately, these freedom-loving African Americans transplanted the antebellum southern culture of subordination, a culture they knew quite well, to their new homeland. The American-Liberians, as they were called, extended their rule over the regional tribes and denied them democratic government and basic freedoms—freedom of speech, press, and religion. This colonial or caste-like social and political structure continued until 1980, when a bloody military coup engineered by Samuel K. Doe brought the First Republic to an end. After another military coup and an ongoing civil war fought along tribal lines, Liberia has sunk into shambles. Half of its 2.5 million citizens have been displaced, the economy and social structure have collapsed, and, at last count, seven factions have claimed the territory and allegiance of the remaining citizens. Even if foreign emigration were a practical form of racial separation, it would not be an attractive alternative to racial integration unless democratic traditions, ideals, and institutions were transported to the new country. Liberia teaches us that the American way of life—with its modern liberal thinking about the individual, society, and politics—is difficult to perfect at home and more difficult to replicate in a foreign land.

Domestic migration, or territorial separation, has also been a failure. The vast majority of African Americans who engaged in this form of racial separation did not find individual dignity or empowerment. This conclusion is well illustrated by the historical record of "black towns," the most prevalent form of separation within the United States. A "black town" is defined as "a separate community containing a population of at least 90 percent [African Americans] in which the residents attempt to determine their own political destiny."[7] Most black towns sprang up during Jim Crow, which made surviving, let alone thriving, all too difficult. Despite the dearth of data on most black towns, there is some recorded history from which to draw generalized conclusions about such towns. First, most African Americans who moved to black towns were primarily motivated by expectations of economic prosperity, political freedom, and racial pride. Most of all, they wanted to escape racial oppression in the South, which intensified after federal troops pulled out at the end of Reconstruction, a period sometimes mislabeled "Redemption." In contrast, the motivation of the town promoters, both African American and white, is more complex and the subject of much debate. Unlike some scholars, I come to the conclusion that although many promoters used black towns to increase their personal fortunes, often through false or misleading advertisements, there is no reliable way to determine whether the ultimate purpose of all or most promoters was to gain riches at the expense of other African Americans or to aid those less fortunate than themselves.

The black towns were small agrarian communities which were not self-sufficient, and life was hard for most of their residents. Some of them died of starvation, others succumbed to the elements—harsh winters, coyotes, rattlesnakes, and flea-infested sod homes on the Great Plains; heat, humidity, and mosquito-infested swamp land in the Mississippi delta. Jim Crow prevented the residents from totally insulating themselves from white oppression, which made life even more difficult. Finally, most black towns faded away because their economies were hopelessly dependent upon outside capital, lacked diversification (most depended upon a single crop such as cotton), and, like hundreds of other small towns across America, they fell victim to industrialization—structural changes in the larger economy that moved jobs from the farms to the factories. Many black towns suffered from greedy promoters who placed profits over people. Still others were destroyed by the lure of employment opportunities for African Americans in northern cities.

In the final chapter in Part II, I highlight a point that separatists are loath to recognize: no amount of racial separation will solve all the problems of African Americans. Internal conflicts based on color, gender, politics, class, religion, geography—in short, all the conflicts that plague *homo sapiens*—will make antidiscrimination laws necessary in any black town, state, or nation. Just look at Liberia, and just look at many of the black towns.

This observation leads to an even larger point. If we look objectively at the separatist theories and emigration (foreign and domestic) as a whole, we must honestly conclude that the failure of total separation has had less to do with whites than with what I call "racial romanticism." By this I mean the tendency, prevalent today especially on college campuses, to romanticize "blackness," to believe that anything authentically black (none more so than Africa or black towns) is, *ipso facto,* better for African Americans than anything white or European. More than that, racial romanticism carries an essentialist claim of epistemic advantage—that African Americans and other oppressed people or outsider groups have not only different ways of knowing but better ways of knowing, that African Americans, other people of color, and women make better leaders and citizens than white males. It hardly needs saying that this is no more than wishful thinking. African Americans are *human beings;* no more or less moral, wise, altruistic, self-interested, or dishonest than whites.

7

Booker T. Washington and W. E. B. Du Bois

Often portrayed as arch rivals, Booker T. Washington and W. E. B. Du Bois at times converged in their approaches to the race problem. Both men espoused the need for racial empowerment. They differed, however, in their strategies for achieving racial advancement.

Washington focused on the economic plight of African Americans. He believed that African Americans would benefit most from building an agrarian base and a matching educational system that emphasized vocational training. While this approach is separatist in nature, Washington's ultimate goal was integration. But racial separation was a necessary prerequisite for it. Before achieving political and social equality in an integrated society, African Americans should create a separate economic and educational system.

An unwavering integrationist and civil rights champion during his early years, Du Bois rejected Washington's call for a separatist, agrarian-based economic and educational system. To Du Bois, political, social, and educational opportunities in an integrated society were the means by which African Americans must seek racial empowerment. Preferring legal reform to economic separation, Du Bois argued that it was impossible for workers and property owners to protect their economic rights without legal support. But, in a remarkable turnaround, Du Bois changed his civil rights strategy in later years, leaning toward a more Washingtonian position that favored separation with an eye toward integration.

Booker T. Washington

Booker T. Washington's childhood greatly influenced his approach to civil rights. Unlike the other separatists—Du Bois, Garvey, Muhammad, Malcolm X, and Farrakhan—Washington experienced white racism in its most oppressive manifestation—slavery. He grew up as a slave in the South until freed by the Emancipation Proclamation. During his years as a slave, Washington's sole purpose in life was to educate himself. Early on, he came to the conviction that without an education African Americans had no chance of achieving racial equality in white America. Washington's reputation as a self-starter with a tremendous work ethic was confirmed in everything he did. He was much admired by African Americans and whites alike.[1]

Washington strongly believed African Americans must establish an independent economic base as a prerequisite to political and social advancement in an integrated society. The way to build such an economy was, literally, from the ground up. Equal in importance to the agrarian economy was the establishment of a complementary educational system, designed to study and teach manual labor. This was consistent with Washington's belief that knowledge without application would be useless in the struggle for racial empowerment. He thoroughly rejected the argument made by Du Bois and other African American leaders at that time that higher education was a necessary path to racial equality.[2] Not surprisingly, Washington also rejected the notion that all African Americans should move into the cities to look for jobs. Washington was adamant: most African Americans should work the land with their hands.[3] He poignantly summarized his beliefs in the following speech:

> Our greatest danger is that in the great leap from slavery to freedom we may overlook the fact that the masses of us are to live by the production of our hands, and fail to keep in mind that we shall prosper in proportion as we learn to dignify and glorify common labour and put brains and skill into the common occupations of life; shall prosper in proportion as we learn to draw the line between superficial and the substantial, the ornamental gewgaws of life and the useful. No race can prosper till it learns that there is as much dignity in tilling a field as in writing a poem.[4]

For Washington, then, a separate agrarian economy and educational system were the *first steps* toward African American empowerment, not the last step.

Washington's master plan was to educate African Americans at schools like the Tuskegee Institute, which he founded in 1881. Tuskegee taught the skills needed for farming and developing small businesses. Following its early success, the Institute received much acclaim and funding from northern industrialists such as Andrew Carnegie. Indeed, Washington was a master negotiator and market strategist. As one scholar writes, "he showed patience and mastery of detail in the untying of Gordian knots, diplomatic skill and agility developed in a lifetime of interracial negotiation, and ability to play several roles simultaneously in dealing with various groups."[5]

Washington's focus on economic empowerment eclipsed any interest he had in civil rights laws. While he undoubtedly believed that such laws were important and privately supported them, he felt that African Americans needed economic power first and foremost: "I tried to emphasize the fact that while the Negro should not be deprived by unfair means of the franchise, political agitation alone would not save him, and that back of the ballot he must have property, industry, skill, economy, intelligence, and character, and that no race without these elements could permanently succeed."[6]

On another occasion he said: "Brains, property, and the character for the Negro will settle the question of civil rights. The best course to pursue in regards to a civil rights bill in the South is to let it alone; let it alone and it will settle itself. Good school teachers and plenty of money to pay them will be more potent in settling the race question than many civil rights bills and investigation committees."[7] Accordingly, Washington preached political and social passivity to his followers. He emphasized self-help rather than protest against racist laws. African Americans, Washington believed, must educate themselves in ways that will enable them to fend for themselves and eventually gain equality in American society.

A disturbing yet underlying theme of Washington's civil rights philosophy is its assumption that African Americans must earn the respect of whites by prospering economically. To what degree Washington not only argued this tenet but also believed it is unknown. Nonetheless, whether by way of strategy or otherwise, he taught that African Americans must earn whites' respect before they can fully participate in society as equals. In his famous "Atlanta Compromise" speech, directed at a white audience in 1895, he stated: "As we have proved our loyalty to you in the past . . . so in the future . . . we shall stand by you with a devotion that no foreigner can approach, ready to lay down our lives, if need be, in defence of yours, interlacing our industrial, commercial, civil, and religious life with yours in a way that shall make the interests of both races one."[8] Becoming self-sufficient was the path to independence and respect that would result in racial equality.

Many commentators have criticized Washington for his willingness to defer to whites and to paint African Americans in an inferior light. Although this view of Washington is well supported by his record, the record also shows that Washington put pressure on whites through his behind-the-scenes participation in the National Negro Business League. The League presented "a case for a segregated black economy and the exaltation of black businessmen to a high place parallel to that of white business-men."[9] Thus, notwithstanding his appalling deference to whites in public, Washington worked for equal treatment in private. Taking this bifurcated approach was necessary, he believed, in order to cultivate white support. Washington took his cue from whites who contributed to the Tuskegee Institute anonymously.

In short, Washington hoped that racial justice could be won without a frontal assault on white racism. He was willing to forego a direct attack on segregation in order to pursue economic independence which, he believed, would bring African Americans the kind of racial dignity and empower-ment found in self-sufficiency. Possibly, to the extent that integration was his ultimate goal, he simply espoused racial separation as a means to that end. Yet, despite any integrationist bent Washington might have had, he clearly understood the problems integration presented, as the following quote illustrates: "When a white boy undertakes a task, it is taken for granted that he will succeed. On the other hand, people are usually sur-prised if the Negro boy does not fail. In a word, the Negro youth starts out with the presumption against him."[10] Many commentators have labeled Washington an accommodationist who "sold out" to whites. That might be too simplistic a view; behind his accommodationist stance rested a more complex strategy. As Smock has observed, "mediating diplomacy with whites was only half of Washington's strategy; the other half was black solidarity, mutual aid, and institution building."[11]

We shall continue to debate whether, given the prevailing racial climate, Washington's quest for African American economic independence out-weighed his public promotion of a racial caste system—African American political, educational, and social subordination. Washington may well emerge from such a debate as a committed believer in African American progress and as a skilled politician able to market himself and his program to achieve his goals—a view that seems too revisionist to me.

W. E. B. Du Bois

As was true for Washington, the upbringing of W. E. B. Du Bois signifi-cantly influenced his civil rights philosophy.[12] His experiences as a child were remarkably different from those of Washington. Du Bois had a fairly privileged upbringing compared to other African Americans in the final quarter of the nineteenth century. He was born in New England, where his family owned land. Educated at a public school (the only African American student in the school), he later attended Fisk University, then Harvard and Berlin universities. Throughout his life, Du Bois's contributions were primarily in scholarship. He was uncomfortable in the role of leader of social change[13] and drew his ideas from sociological studies rather than personal experience. Indeed, Du Bois had little personal knowledge of the African American masses. He had to depend on his academic research to gain insights into the race problem.[14]

While Washington pushed industrial education, Du Bois vigorously promoted all education—higher education, as well as industrial or vocational education. He believed education was essential to secure racial dignity and empowerment. He thus agreed with Washington that industrial education was desirable and necessary for some African Americans, but went on to argue that higher education was equally if not more important. Teach all African Americans to read and write, send the majority through vocational training, and allow the remaining 10% (the "Talented Tenth") to go on to higher education and eventual leadership in the community.[15] This elite group would guide the rest of the race.

During most of his career Du Bois presented himself as a staunch integrationist and demanded freedom of speech, education, "manhood suffrage," and "the abolition of all caste distinctions based simply on race and color."[16] These tenets would become the foundation of the Niagara Movement, founded by a small group of African American intellectuals critical of Washington; it would in turn spawn the NAACP in 1910.

Later in his life Du Bois rejected integration, a position that was largely responsible for his break with the NAACP in 1934. In his book *Dusk of Dawn: An Essay Toward an Autobiography of a Race Concept,* Du Bois sets forth a program of racial separation ("not . . . as the final solution of the race problem") in which he admonishes African Americans to take responsibility for their own lives:

> This low social condition of the majority of Negroes is not solely a problem of the whites; a question of historic guilt in slavery and labor exploitation and of present discrimination; it is not merely a matter of the social uplifting of an alien group within their midst; a problem

of social contact and political power . . . It must be . . . primarily an inner problem of the Negro group itself, a condition from which they themselves are prime sufferers, and a problem with which this group is forced itself to grapple.[17]

African Americans must make choices that are beneficial to their community, such as supporting African American merchants.[18] Some form of economic self-help is espoused by each separatist discussed in Part II.

In his embrace of racial separation, Du Bois shifted away from the "Talented Tenth" concept. Writing in 1935, he denied "that the problem of twelve million Negro people, mostly poor, ignorant workers, is going to be settled by having their more educated and wealthy classes gradually and continually escape from their race into the mass of American people, leaving the rest to sink, suffer and die."[19] African Americans should band together for the benefit of the whole group and create a "cooperative state within their own group."[20] To those who continued clinging to integration as the salvation of African Americans, Du Bois wrote:

> Any planning for the benefit of American Negroes on the part of the Negro intelligentsia is going to involve organized and deliberate self-segregation . . . If the economic and cultural salvation of the American Negro calls for an increase in segregation and prejudice, then that must come. American Negroes must plan for their economic future and the social survival of their fellows in the firm belief that this means in a real sense the survival of colored folk in the world and the building of a full humanity instead of petty white tyranny.[21]

It is of no small moment that this great scholar, at the forefront of the integrationist movement for over thirty years, chose racial separation in the end. Washington must have been smiling in his grave.

Conclusion

Booker T. Washington and W. E. B. Du Bois each offered a unique civil rights strategy. Though they may have been bitter enemies, they were identical in one important respect throughout their lives—both men were deeply committed to making life better for African Americans. They simply disagreed on which avenue should be taken to reach that goal. Washington's focus on economic independence as the way for African Americans to attain equality made sense; for economic success is fundamental to individual well-being. Du Bois's critique of Washington's "equality through a back door" also scores points, because Washington made no attempt to publicly confront the claim of African American inferiority and, in fact, acquiesced in antiblack racism. Beyond that, both strategies were flawed: Washington's because it did not explicitly encompass legal reform and higher education; and Du Bois's because it focused solely on education and civil rights laws and hence offered no immediate and concrete prescription for improving the day-to-day living conditions of most African Americans.

Nonetheless, both men succeeded to various degrees. Washington's "accommodationist" stance portrayed a realism of sorts. Washington imitated white behavior by guarding against alienating the powerful while secretly aiding African American causes. Whatever one thinks about his "selling out" to whites, Washington did secure a school for African Americans and in this way offered them an empowering concept of self-help. On the other hand, Du Bois's ardent defense of equal treatment under the law spurred later movements that eliminated many racial barriers. The NAACP's protracted struggle against school segregation is the most obvious example.

What is perhaps most remarkable about Washington and Du Bois is that the lessons they offer are not confined to the particular times and circumstances of their lives. Washington's economic focus is as relevant today as it was a hundred years ago, and Du Bois's early concern about legal rights is likewise relevant. Furthermore, taken together, Washington and Du Bois later in his life teach us that community, identity, and culture are integral to the struggle for racial equality. Most importantly, both legendary figures (Washington first, Du Bois later) came to embrace separation of the races as a necessary prerequisite to successful integration. Until African Americans can achieve success in their own right, whether through political, economic, or educational means, true integration with whites will be impossible. These two great men who dedicated their entire lives to studying the race problem came to the same truth: African Americans could not truly succeed until they separated from whites and white racism.

8

Marcus Garvey

Marcus Garvey, known to many as the father of black nationalism, successfully mobilized in the 1920s a tremendous economic and social movement on the twin platforms of "return to Africa" and nationalism. His separatist strategy was rooted in "race first," self-help, and nationhood. By appealing to black pride and dignity and promoting a black economic power base, Garvey eventually created a huge international following as well. He profoundly changed the way many African Americans and other black people viewed themselves and their role in predominantly white societies. "Garveyism," as his separatism came to be known, introduced to many oppressed blacks the possibility of independence and free choice under a separate racial regime.[1]

The Early Years

Born in Jamaica in 1887, Marcus Garvey grew up in a racially stratified society. Descendants of African slaves were held at the bottom of the social structure, descendants of white slaveowners at the top. The social classes were divided by rigid walls of racism, and the dark-skinned Garvey ran up against them at an early age. Most African West Indians, like most African Americans at the time, were also extremely poor. Garvey, whose early years were marked by an acute awareness of racial oppression, at sixteen became a strike leader and advocate for the rights of the poor. In his twenties he traveled to Latin America, where he observed the social and working conditions of other oppressed people. Later he went to England and helped publish a Pan-African and Pan-Oriental magazine.[2]

When he returned to Jamaica in 1914, Garvey arrived with a specific goal in mind: he wanted to uplift his race and unite blacks worldwide. To achieve this goal, he founded the Universal Negro Improvement and Conservation Association and African Communities League, later called the Universal Negro Improvement Association (UNIA). Years later, another UNIA was established in the United States. The general objectives of the Jamaican UNIA were as follows:

> To establish a Universal Confraternity among the race; To promote the spirit of race pride and love; To reclaim the fallen of the race; To administer to and assist the needy; To assist in civilizing the backward tribes of Africa; To strengthen the Imperialism of independent African States; To establish Commissionaries or Agencies in the principal countries of the world for the protection of all Negroes, irrespective of Nationality; To promote a conscientious spiritual worship among the native tribes of Africa; To establish Universities, Colleges and Secondary Schools for the further education and culture of the boys and girls of the race; To conduct a worldwide commercial and industrial intercourse.[3]

Initially, Garvey stated that he did not wish "to belabour any race question in this country as some may be inclined to believe. . . . What concerns us here is the development of our people and country . . . The negro people of Jamaica need a great deal of improvement."[4] Garvey wanted to raise black Jamaicans to a standard of which whites would approve. He did not at that time address racial conflict per se; indeed, Garvey's principal supporters at this time were white people, including members of the clergy and the business sector, and colonial officials.[5] The majority of black Jamaicans were indifferent to his plan to "raise them to the standards of civilized approval."[6]

In 1916 Garvey moved to the United States and spent a year traveling across the country, speaking publicly and meeting with many prominent African Americans. Inspired by Booker T. Washington's autobiography, *Up from Slavery,* Garvey originally hoped to solicit funds in the United States to build a school in Jamaica modeled after Tuskegee Institute, but was not able to raise much money. Eventually, black business development replaced black educational development as Garvey's primary strategy for improving the position of blacks worldwide.[7]

Great changes were taking place in the United States at this time that made African Americans particularly receptive to Garvey's ideas. World War I left African Americans less tolerant of racial inequality. Many agreed with the Texas Grand Mason of the Negro Masons when he stated, "we believe that our second emancipation will be the outcome of this war."[8] Approximately 370,000 African American soldiers served in the U.S. armed forces during World War I. But instead of gaining the respect of whites, they were segregated and subjected to gross indignities in training camps and were usually assigned to labor battalions. When they returned from the war, African American troops were degraded, assaulted, and lynched. One Negro Masonic leader claimed, "we have been fighting the wrong fellow. The low American, and not the German, is the brute who has ravished our women, lynched, flayed, burned and massacred our men and women."[9] Finally, to escape relentless racism and to seek new job opportunities, thousands of African Americans migrated from the South to the North. This led to fierce competition for limited jobs and housing in overcrowded northern cities, and the economic pressure further increased racial clashes in postwar America. In the summer of 1919, race riots and lynchings injured and killed many African Americans. "The riots of 1919 convinced Marcus Garvey more than ever that the Black man [and woman] had no secure place in America."[10] Garvey cried out against white people's hypocrisy: "during the world war, nations were vying with each other in proclaiming lofty concepts of humanity. . . . Now that the war is over we find these same nations making every effort by word and deed to convince us that their blatant professions were meaningless platitudes never intended to apply to Earth's darker millions."[11] These sentiments proclaimed the feelings of many African Americans after the war.

Garvey's Separatist Theory

Garvey's strategy of racial separation was predicated on a fairly simple theory: people of different races will never treat each other as equals until they are on the same economic level. In order to reach economic parity with whites, African Americans must have their own institutions, including their own businesses and educational facilities, and, ultimately, a homeland, which for Garvey meant an independent state in Africa.[12] In an essay titled "Let the Negro Accumulate Wealth—It Will Bring Him Power," Garvey wrote that in modern society people are judged solely by wealth. Because African Americans have no wealth, they are mistreated. Hence "economic independence or wealth is the recommendation of a people in order to gain full consideration of others . . . wealth is strength, wealth is power, wealth is influence, wealth is justice, is liberty, is real human rights."[13]

Garvey believed that in order to attain and maintain their own wealth, African Americans must separate from white Americans.

Economic parity was to be achieved through capitalism. Garvey was an unabashed capitalist. He had a healthy respect for white society's economic success under capitalism and argued that African Americans must imitate the economic endeavors of whites. He wanted, in addition, to copy European culture because he believed that future socioeconomic success rested on the cultural underpinnings of European civilization. He also believed that European society was a duplicate of the Africa of the past. So, in studying European culture, blacks worldwide would be studying their own heritage.[14]

A cherished concept of Garvey's was that of color solidarity. Within his own Jamaican society, light-skinned blacks received better opportunities. These blacks often distinguished themselves from dark-skinned blacks, reinforcing a color-coded pecking order to improve their social position. He saw this happening in American society as well. To avoid such internal conflict, Garvey stressed communal self-help. Blacks who rose within society, whether in America or Great Britain or elsewhere, must be responsible for less fortunate blacks who were denied the opportunity. Or else, "how can the Negro ever hope to rise when the very men who should have been our props and leaders draw themselves away and try to create an impossible and foolish atmosphere of their own, which is untenable and never recognized?"[15] African Americans must, in short, take care of their own. Racial uplift goes hand-in-hand with personal success.[16]

Finally, Garvey promoted the idea of "race first" to solidify African American pride and unification. The race-first theory states that black people worldwide must put their self-interest as blacks before any other interests. This meant that African Americans must patronize their own businesses, see beauty in their own race, worship a God created in their own image, learn African history, and marry within their own race.[17] Not just black people but each race should be governed by the race-first criterion. Favoring his own race, he therefore cooperated or at least sympathized with white groups engaged in anticolonial or antiracist struggles and with the Russian revolutionaries Lenin and Trotsky. He was also sympathetic to white segregationists in the United States. However, unlike many white segregationists, such as the Ku Klux Klan, who preached racial superiority, Garvey did not preach black superiority. He believed instead in black equality.[18]

The race-first theory was consistent with Garvey's belief that African Americans and other blacks would never be truly respected in this world until a strong black nation, preferably on the African continent, was created.[19] Whether Garvey truly intended a mass emigration of blacks or even African Americans to Africa to be the mainstay of his separatist strategy remains unclear.

Garvey's Separatist Strategy

In 1917 Garvey set up an organization in the United States to implement his theories. Organization was very important to him. He often said, "the greatest weapon used against the Negro is disorganization."[20] This new organization, the United Negro Improvement Association, had essentially the same goals as his original UNIA established in Jamaica a few years earlier. The new UNIA, like the old one, sought to unite blacks worldwide and establish a country and government absolutely their own.[21] Garvey intended to accomplish these goals by creating African American institutions, businesses, and schools in this country in preparation for a black takeover of colonized Africa in the future.

His new slogan—"up you mighty race, you can accomplish what you will"[22]—accompanied the first major step toward implementing the UNIA's goals in 1919. In that year Garvey purchased an auditorium in Harlem, renamed it Liberty Hall, and held nightly meetings attracting as many as 6,000 listeners at a time. In the next few years, liberty halls were established in UNIA centers in several other cities across America. Those who could not hear Garvey in person received his message through *The Negro World*, a publication he launched in 1918, with a weekly circulation reaching 200,000 by the early 1920s. *The Negro World* carried columns in Spanish and French, which enabled it to communicate with its international audience. Garvey also created a variety of African American groups and organizations: the African Legion, whose members dressed in blue military garb; the Black Cross Nurses; uniformed marching bands, choristers, and various auxiliaries. These groups marched in the streets of Harlem during the UNIA's First International Convention in 1920.[23]

Garvey's separatist strategy included a religious element. In 1921 he founded the African Orthodox Church in America, a church that would be true to the teachings of Christ and reject the hypocrisy of the white churches. Garvey urged his followers to conceive of a multiracial heaven and to think of Christ as embodying all races, black no less than white. In 1924, the church advised Garveyites to replace their portraits of a white Madonna and Child with black figures. Garvey noted wryly that henceforth, "only the Negro's devil would be white, instead of the traditional black."[24]

Garvey also made plans for separate schools. African American children must learn black pride and history—a black way of looking at the world. "The education that will enable the Negro to see through his own spectacles, that will enable him to take on his own vision, must be promulgated."[25] He clearly intended black institutions to embody his race-first ideology, an ideology that tolerates no permanent alliances with other racial groups. Racial purity was to be paramount: Garveyites were instructed that blacks and whites absolutely may never marry or produce children. Black families should not even have pictures of whites in their homes. As Garvey stated: "I am conscious of the fact that slavery brought upon us the curse of many colors within the Negro race, but that is no reason . . . [to] perpetuate the evil . . . we should now set out to create a race type and standard of our own which . . . could be recognized and respected as the true race type anteceding even our own time."[26]

Garvey compared his strategy of total separation to the Jewish yearning for a Palestinian homeland and the Irish desire for an independent Eire. In 1920 the UNIA moved closer toward its goal of establishing "a central nation for the race" by adopting a national anthem and creating a red, black, and green flag for the planned African republic. Garvey publicly agreed with Senator Joseph France, who wanted the United States to trade all of the World War I war debts for the white colonizers' African lands— enough to set up an independent nation for African Americans. In addition, he asked the League of Nations to place the ex-German colonies in Africa in UNIA's custody and made plans with Liberia for a UNIA settlement in southern Liberia. It is important to stress here that Garvey was less a cultural nationalist than a multiculturalist. His opposition to the West was political. "Those of us who lead are well versed in Western civilization and are determined that the Black man shall not be a creature of the past, but a full-fledged man of the present."[27]

In reality, Garvey's "back-to-Africa" movement was not a call for a mass emigration of blacks worldwide or even of all African Americans. His intention was probably to settle a limited number of skilled African Americans in Liberia. However, the notion of mass emigration proved appealing to many of Garvey's disillusioned working-class followers, and he did little to discourage this popular misinterpretation of his strategy. By 1924 he had finished the plans for the Liberian settlement and fully intended to make it the new headquarters of the UNIA. His idea was to restore Africa to Africans by building Liberia into an industrial power that would penetrate greater Africa and conquer the whole continent.[28]

The Liberia negotiations ultimately failed, for a variety of reasons. The power of the European nations, the fears of the Liberian government, and disarray within the UNIA (weakened by financial struggles and internal and external enemies) all contributed to the collapse of the negotiations. For example, the European powers put pressure on Liberia to reject the proposed UNIA settlement because they believed that Garvey's propagation of the African nationalist spirit would spread throughout Africa and put an end to colonial rule.[29] Liberian government officials also began to fear his political power, thinking that it might overwhelm them, especially when Garvey began to refer to himself as the "Provisional President of Africa."[30]

There was no possibility that Garvey would have attempted to turn Liberia or any other African nation into a communist regime. Garvey condemned communism; he felt communists were lazy; and he especially disliked white working-class racism. Yet Garvey also recognized that capitalism could get out of control. To prevent that from happening, he planned to limit individual fortunes to one million dollars and corporate assets to five million dollars. Capitalism, Garvey said, is "necessary to the progress of the world."[31]

In 1919 Garvey formed the Negro Factories Corporation, which offered 200,000 shares of common stock to African Americans and other blacks at a par value of $5.00 per share. The corporation was formed to establish and operate factories throughout the Western Hemisphere and Africa that would manufacture any marketable commodity. The corporation's New York division ran three grocery stores, a printing plant, two restaurants, a laundry, and a men's and women's clothing factory, which made the uniforms, hats, and shirts worn by members of the UNIA. In addition, the New York division operated several buildings, trucks, and the UNIA publication, *The Negro World*. In the 1920s, the UNIA and its allied corporations occasionally employed more than 1,000 African Americans in the United States alone.[32]

Garvey's efforts to set up African American enterprises were severely hampered by the difficulty of raising sufficient capital from impoverished

African Americans during an economically depressed era, and by dealings with unscrupulous white businesspersons. Such problems were graphically illustrated by the failure of Garvey's most significant economic endeavor, the Black Star Line (BSL). Formed in 1919 to operate an international network of steamships, the BSL had only black stockowners and officers. Some whites helped to get the line started, however. Within one year, the BSL owned three ships and had raised $610,000 by selling five-dollar stock certificates exclusively to African Americans.[33]

The BSL was launched as much for public relations (that is, to show what self-reliance could produce) as to make a profit. Indeed, the ships toured the Caribbean as symbols of black success and glory. In time, however, the shipping line became a financial disaster, losing an estimated $47 million.[34] By 1922, the BSL was forced into bankruptcy, a casualty, in part, of white businesspersons who sold Garvey malfunctioning vessels at exorbitant prices. For example, the UNIA bought an old ship for twice the amount it was worth. The ship made three trips to the West Indies in three years. Finally, it was sold for $1,625 at an auction.[35] Inexperience (including the lack of shipping experience) and carelessness on the part of Garvey and his chief associates, plus the dishonesty of some of Garvey's officers, also contributed to the bankruptcy.[36]

The Downfall

In June 1923, Garvey announced that six million blacks worldwide were UNIA members. The UNIA had established more than 700 branches in thirty-eight states in this country. More than 200 branches were organized outside the United States, principally in the West Indies, Central America, and northern South America.[37] Yet the association soon began to fall apart, as a result of discrimination, ideological controversy, poor organization, and financial problems. The failure of the BSL, of course, was a critical factor in the UNIA's ultimate downfall. Without the revitalization of the BSL or the creation of another, more successful economic enterprise, the association could not survive. Indeed, the UNIA went into a decline even before the Great Depression eventually crushed it.

Garvey's inability to unite with other African American leaders also contributed to the failure of his civil rights strategy. Profound disagreements between Garvey and the integrationists, particularly the NAACP and W. E. B. Du Bois, were especially detrimental to Garvey's movement. Du Bois argued that African Americans could not strive for separatism and equality at the same time. Du Bois also wrote letters to various individuals to verify allegations of fraud in Garvey's various business ventures. Garvey baited Du Bois by challenging him to public debates and accusing this "near white" or "colored" man and the NAACP of "advocat[ing] racial amalgamation or general miscegenation with the hope of creating a new type of colored race by wiping out both black and white."[38] At the height of their rivalry in 1924, Garvey and Du Bois "took the irreconcilability of their views to mean that total black unity was not only an impossibility, but a goal not even worth striving for."[39]

In addition, Garvey lost much support when he engaged in a number of flirtations with the Ku Klux Klan, the Anglo-Saxon Clubs of America, and other white supremacy groups. In a speech he gave in New York in 1922, Garvey explained this strange relationship: "I interviewed the Imperial Wizard . . . to find out the Klan's attitude toward the race. . . . He said this: 'That the Klan is not organized for the absolute purpose of interfering with Negroes . . . but . . . of protecting the interests of the white race in America.' "[40] To Garvey the Klan was a purely racial organization whose goal was to make America a white persons' country, while the UNIA wanted Africa to be a black persons' country. He maintained that it was futile to try to fight the Klan and other white supremacy groups because they not only represented the white majority in the United States, but also shared the UNIA's desire for African Americans to make something of themselves apart from white people. Garvey also argued that white supremacy groups were less hypocritical than white supporters of integrationist groups, such as the NAACP, who professed to believe in racial equality.[41] Despite this reasoning, his support of white supremacy organizations alienated many African Americans.

Garvey's real difficulties began in 1922, when he was charged with several counts of mail fraud. Culminating in a highly complex and controversial case, a federal appellate court in New York affirmed Garvey's original conviction on one count of mail fraud. Garvey was jailed in 1925 for five years, fined $1,000, and ordered to pay the court costs. During Garvey's imprisonment, Liberia canceled an agreement for the UNIA to set up a small embassy in Monrovia, its capital. In addition, power struggles within the UNIA helped to destroy the organization. While still in jail, Garvey himself was sued by the UNIA on charges that he "exhibited an intention to use the Association as a means of acquiring an income for himself."[42]

Responding to a campaign to release Garvey from jail, President Calvin

Coolidge pardoned him. Garvey was deported to Jamaica in December 1927 and died in London on June 10, 1940.[43]

Conclusion

The continuing oppression of African Americans provided fertile ground for Garvey's brand of racial separation. African Americans were targets of racism and lynchings and were unable to rise economically, politically, or socially. Emancipation, northern migration and industrialization, and the First World War did little to improve the plight of African Americans. They were still viewed and treated as second-class citizens. For many African Americans, Garvey's civil rights theories and strategy were a welcome response to racial subordination.

"Race first," African (or black) nationalism, and economic prosperity were the cornerstones of Garvey's philosophy. His message of black unity and pride was effectively conveyed through such instruments as the UNIA's international publication, *The Negro World.* Blacks around the world were touched and moved by Garvey's ideas. His attempts to implement them— the UNIA, with its many African American institutions, and the BSL— were valiant efforts to create an independent African American economic base.[44]

Garvey's endeavors failed in the end, however. Conflicting ideologies emerged within his movement, and outside it, organizations (such as the NAACP), powerful African Americans (Du Bois), and foreign governments perceived Garvey as a threat. The UNIA became increasingly disorganized and dysfunctional. Finally, Garvey refused to reach out to whites for assistance and in fact scared away otherwise sympathetic whites with his "race first" ideology.

For me, the main cause of Garvey's failure was a myopia that continues to afflict many African Americans (and whites) today, especially black nationalists. It is the belief or expectation that a change of venue will bring out the best in African Americans or blacks in general; that African Americans are in principle better than they actually are or better than whites. In terms of such racial romanticism, African Americans are no longer individuals but soldiers in a protracted racial war. Racial romanticism often blinds us to the failure of character, such as that exhibited by key persons in Garvey's organizations. We do not always see that a snake, as the late Justice Marshall once said, comes in different colors.

Looking at the other side of the story, Garvey's greatest success was his ability to mobilize so many African Americans. He was able to do this by instilling racial pride and dignity in African Americans, and by implementing at least a few elements of his separatist strategy. Other separatists were greatly influenced by his brand of racial separation, as we shall see.

9

The Nation of Islam

During the tumultuous 1960s, when racial tensions and political unrest shook the United States, the Nation of Islam (or Black Muslims) offered a solution to the American race problem that focused on African American pride and unity but also incorporated a strong religious element and strict moral code. Largely perceived as militant yet law-abiding, the Black Muslims demonstrated an extraordinary ability to communicate with poor and working-class African Americans. The Nation, as it was also called, appealed to this group by publicly, repeatedly, and angrily articulating what many of them wanted and needed to hear most—namely, that their lowly socioeconomic status was deliberately created by whites. Black Muslims formulated and presented a comprehensive strategy of total separation as a logical and preordained solution to the American race problem.

Historical Background

The Nation of Islam is essentially a religious sect, a variant of Islam. Although its present leaders teach that its religious origins are shrouded in mystery and that its first leader was an incarnation of Allah, the Nation of Islam was actually founded in a Detroit ghetto in the summer of 1930.[1] A street peddler named W. D. Fard (later called W. Fard Muhammad) began preaching among African Americans as he walked door-to-door, selling garments said to be worn by their ancestors in their African homeland.[2] Once he gained access into people's homes, Fard would discuss his religious beliefs and the basic concepts of the Nation of Islam. His teachings soon attracted the young son of a Baptist minister from Georgia, Elijah Poole. Poole had attended elementary school before he was forced to leave and find employment to help support his family (he was the youngest of twelve children). While working, he met and married Clara Evans, and in 1923 they moved to Detroit. But Poole lost his automotive factory job and sought welfare relief for two years. At some point during that period he attended one of Fard's sermons.[3] The preacher told Poole that he (Fard) was actually Allah and had come to help African Americans follow the "right path."[4] He claimed to have a "cure [for the] problems in the African American Community: ... social problems, lack of economic development, undisciplined family life and alcoholism."[5] Thereafter Poole studied Fard's teachings and eventually became his partner in the creation of the Nation of Islam.

Fard believed that freedom and justice for African Americans could never be achieved until they regained their true religion: Islam. At first he taught from the Bible, using it to show African Americans how "white" Christianity was geared toward enslaving the mind. Gradually, he introduced the Koran to his membership. He also drew from orthodox Islam in such areas as dietary law, and took some ideas from Marcus Garvey's Universal Negro Improvement Association.[6]

By 1934 the Nation was headquartered in Chicago, and membership had grown to almost 8,000. Fard was now perceived as a prophet among his followers, but a fraud among police officers. After a series of arrests and confrontations with the police, Fard disappeared without a trace. Poole, who changed his name to the holy name of Elijah Muhammad, took over as the leader of the Nation. He then began teaching his followers that Fard was Allah personified. Elijah Muhammad was almost "singlehandedly responsible for the deification of Fard and for the perpetuation of his teachings in the early years after Fard disappeared."[7] This depiction of Fard would become a source of great conflict among the Nation's leaders in later years. It led to internal strife that contributed to the movement's decline.[8]

After its founder's disappearance, the Nation went into an extended period of stagnation. In the decade following Fard's departure, Elijah Muhammad did not expand or elaborate upon Fard's teachings. As a result of such unimaginative leadership, the movement sagged in the 1940s and dramatically plummeted in both size and influence when Elijah Muhammad was jailed for draft evasion during World War II. At the time he was paroled, there were only a few functioning Muslim temples in the United States.[9]

During the 1950s, a more committed Muhammad took steps to expand the Nation of Islam. He utilized aggressive recruiting techniques and sent ministers into the streets of America's inner cities. The movement began to grow, owing to these efforts and to a more secular emphasis. To the original teachings the movement's leaders added a Garvey-inspired sense of racial identity and unity.[10]

Membership in the Nation of Islam really began to expand, however, when Malcolm X, a.k.a. Malcolm Little, became a devoted follower of Elijah Muhammad. Malcolm X had been serving time in prison when he learned about the Nation; from there he began writing daily letters to Elijah Muhammad and joined the Nation upon his release. Devoted and dynamic, Malcolm X soon rose to leadership within the Nation and during the early 1960s was its most influential member. By reaching out to the masses and stressing the importance of unity, Muhammad and his ministers, particularly Malcolm X, were able to transform the Nation from an insignificant religious sect to an influential civil rights organization. To understand how that happened, it is necessary to understand the Nation's religious tenets and moral code.

Religious Tenets and Moral Code

The Black Muslim movement is founded upon a unique set of religious tenets. The most significant are: Allah is God; the white person is the devil; and "the So-Called Negroes are the Asiatic Black people, the cream of the planet earth."[11] Note that while Black Muslim writings and speeches refer to white people exclusively as white "men" or "man," such references were probably intended to include white women as well, although Black Muslims primarily blame white men for African American oppression. Here I shall refer to "people" or "persons" rather than "men" or "man," unless a direct quote is given. Note also that Muhammad referred to "So-Called Negroes" because "Negro" is a term created by white people to name black people. American blacks are not Negroes, Elijah Muhammad maintained, and they are not Colored. Once the "So-Called Negro" has come to know the truth, his or her "slavemaster name" is rejected and replaced with a holy name given by Allah. The last name becomes X to show all the world that the individual is now a member of the "Lost-Found" people of the world.[12]

For Black Muslims it is a religious dogma that the "original people" were black and that they will be the last people as well. Blacks are the creators of all other races. White people were set upon earth about six thousand years ago by Allah, to rule until the War of Armageddon is waged to destroy the evil white race and "restore the black people to their rightful place as rulers of the universe."[13] Muslim leaders further teach that it was the will of Allah that some blacks should be brought as slaves to North America so that they could understand and know themselves better.[14] According to Elijah Muhammad, this group of slaves was descended from the Tribe of Shabazz, the original "man."[15]

Underlying each aspect of the Nation of Islam's religious doctrine is a vehement rejection of Christianity. As Muhammad stated, "we believe in the truth of the Bible, but we believe that it has been tampered with and must be reinterpreted so that mankind will not be snared by the falsehoods that have been added to it."[16] Muslims contend that whites promoted Christianity to hide the true faith, Islam, from African Americans, and continue to use its teachings to oppress them. As a result, to a Black Muslim, any practicing Christian, black or white, is immoral and doomed to damnation.[17]

A major tenet of the Black Muslim faith is that of black goodness and white evil. By adamantly rejecting white people's religion and by teaching that whites manipulate the Bible and Christianity for their own wicked purposes (namely, to keep the black person down), the Nation invites African Americans to embrace a separate religion of their own, with their own belief system, their own convictions that cannot be touched or desecrated by whites.

Elijah Muhammad used his religious convictions—particularly the tenet that blacks were God's chosen people—to instill pride in his followers:

> It is important that my people learn the true knowledge of self, as it is their salvation. . . . We are not Negroes, because God . . . has taught me who we are. We are not "colored" people because God has taught me who the colored people are. The American Negro is without knowledge of self. You are a so-called Negro because you are "not" a Negro. . . . Allah has taught me and today I do not fear to tell you, that you can discard the name "Negro."[18]

Like Marcus Garvey, Elijah Muhammad encouraged converts to redefine themselves in terms of religious dogma and racial self-identification and to reject white values. The Nation taught that only through such a process can blacks achieve unity. Malcolm X stressed the unity theme in a speech at a freedom rally: "Mr. Muhammad says that disunity is our number one stumbling block, and this disunity exists only because we lack knowledge of *self* (our own kind)."[19] More than anything else, the unity theme helped to transform the Nation from a religious sect into a social movement. As one commentator notes: "The characteristic feature of a mass movement is its unique capacity for united action without consideration for the individual sacrifices of its members. The personal self is lost in the corporate whole and is expendable in the interests of the whole."[20]

Followers of the Nation, then, developed a "groundwork of racial self-consciousness, a black self-conception as well as a black identity."[21] Muslims rejected white society and called for brotherhood of African Americans under the Black Muslim faith. In fact, the "brotherhood" concept fostered unity not only because of its focus on family, but also because of its simultaneous rejection of the hostile white world outside. In joining the Nation, "the individual became part of a community of proud black people, whose trust in and loyalty to each other contrasted markedly with the hostility and paranoia of the hustling society and of the ghetto way of life in general."[22]

Black Muslims constantly and consistently claim that black "self-conception" does not mean hatred for white people. Rather, it is "a negation of the symbols of [white] culture, [white] power and [white] status."[23] This rejection is not "anti-white, just pro-Black."[24] The aim is to enhance racial pride and to create strong feelings of adequacy among the members of the Nation. Obviously, such contentions are open to question, given the Black Muslims' teachings that white people are the devil and will be destroyed in the War of Armageddon.

Black Muslims are required to observe a strict moral code. It regulates nearly every aspect of personal behavior and helps build racial pride and solidarity. For example, "the rank-and-file Muslim is expected to evince general character traits that can only benefit society as a whole. Men are expected to live soberly and with dignity, to work hard, to devote themselves to their families' welfare, and to deal honestly with all men . . . Women are especially enjoined not to imitate 'the silly and often immoral habits of the white woman,' which can only wreck their marriages and their children." Interestingly, Muslim ideology claims that while women are "equal in every way" to the men, they must nonetheless "obey them." Women's chief goals are to be modest, thrifty, and offer service. Sexual morality is adamantly enforced. Premarital and extramarital liaisons are forbidden, and those who conduct interracial liaisons are subject to particularly severe punishment. In addition, Muslims must adhere to all laws, even the laws of the oppressors. Convicts and criminals joining the movement had to repudiate their past activities and live a moral existence. In fact, the Nation developed a reputation for successfully reforming unrepentant criminals whom the "system" had failed. The Black Muslims also stress dietary laws, personal hygiene and a dress code, while the use of tobacco, alcohol, or other drugs is forbidden. On the whole, the Black Muslims' pervasive strictness was apparently quite successful with the general membership, and in their efforts to reform hardened criminals. Authorities in the criminal justice field acknowledged that they have encountered virtually no problems with the Black Muslim community.[25]

Any violation of the moral code is dealt with through the quasi-military arm of the movement, the Fruit of Islam. The purpose of this branch of the organization is threefold: to protect officials and property; to enforce the doctrines and objectives of the organization; and to prepare for Armageddon.[26] The group operates in a paramilitary fashion. All of its members are schooled in self-defense techniques and hand-to-hand combat. They are very visible and constitute an intimidating force at public events.[27]

The Muslims' emphasis on race pride and unity created a theme with which many African Americans could identify. Its code of moral conduct, while strict, showed the Muslims to be an organized and efficient group which, despite its radical notions, was committed to abiding by the law and respecting traditional notions of proper behavior.

The 1950s and Separatism

Religious faith and stringent private and public codes of morality served as a foundation for launching the Black Muslims' social reform movement in the late 1950s. Significantly, the change in emphasis coincided with Malcolm X's ascendancy within the Nation. Elijah Muhammad seemingly recognized the appeal of the handsome, articulate Malcolm X. As he told his older ministers, "You are teaching the same thing we taught in the thirties. Malcolm X is modern times: he knows how to help me."[28] And soon enough Malcolm X emerged as the most influential voice of the Nation of Islam.

Malcolm X was born Malcolm Little in 1925 in Omaha, Nebraska. His father was a freelance Baptist minister and an organizer for the UNIA. His mother, like Garvey, was of Caribbean origin. During Malcolm's adolescence his father was murdered, and his mother was later institutionalized; the children were then raised in various foster homes. Once, Malcolm recalls, he was reprimanded by a teacher for wanting to become a lawyer (the teacher remarked that carpentry would be a better choice, a realistic occupation for a "nigger"). As he became ever more alienated from school and white America, he started a life on the streets and finally turned to crime. He was arrested at age 21 for burglary and sent to prison for six years. There he converted to Islam and wrote daily to Elijah Muhammad. During his years in prison he educated himself in history, philosophy, languages, writing, and public speaking. Upon his release he devoted himself to the Nation of Islam.[29]

In the 1950s Malcolm X started a newspaper, *Muhammad Speaks,* to help disseminate the Muslim message. By 1959 the Muslims were able to tap into the mainstream American media. The charismatic Malcolm X appeared on a nationally televised special news program in that year, "The Hate That Hate Produced."[30] The appearance led to many speaking engagements and considerable coverage in popular periodicals. As one commentator writes, "the white press ... made [Malcolm X] famous, and notoriety sharply enhanced his attraction to the masses."[31]

While the teachings of Fard Muhammad laid the blueprint for political and social change, Elijah Muhammad and Malcolm X formulated the particulars of the program. At the heart of the plan rested the decision that Black Muslims would not patiently and passively wait for Armageddon. Malcolm X, in particular, with a fiery rhetoric and a confrontational style, urged immediate and sweeping changes for African Americans. Given that whites are inherently evil, African Americans must "get away from the devil as soon and as fast as [they] can."[32] Simply put, the program they devised called for African Americans to reject every aspect of white America—in essence, to isolate themselves from whites, so that they could remain pure.

Elijah Muhammad and Malcolm X believed total separation was the simplest way to repudiate white society in its entirety. They viewed integration as a scheme by white people to save themselves from damnation.[33] Furthermore, they argued, white people did not propose integration when they were the undisputed rulers of the world. It was only after they saw the impending destruction of their empire and the loosening of their hold over the African Americans that they began to consider integration. Muhammad also maintained that African Americans would not improve their lives through integration, because whites would not allow integration to advance to the point where it would disadvantage them. Through it all, the "So-Called Negro" would continue to remain at the bottom of American society. Hence the solution for African Americans is total separation.

Elijah outlined the essential requirements for total separation in speeches across the country as well as in two documents entitled "What Do Muslims Want" and "Message to the Blackman in America." The simplistic "What Do Muslims Want" sets forth ten points:[34]

1. Full, complete freedom
2. Equal justice under the law, regardless of creed, class, or color
3. Equality of opportunity
4. A separate state or territory—either on this continent or elsewhere
5. Release of all believers of Islam held in federal prisons
6. An immediate end to police brutality and mob attacks against African Americans
7. Equal employment opportunities
8. Exemption from all taxation
9. Equal education, including separate schools
10. Intermarriage or race mixing should be prohibited. The religion of Islam should be taught without hindrance or suppression

In "Message to the Blackman in America," Muhammad declares that African Americans must separate themselves from whites in all ways—mentally, economically, and physically. Mental separation occurs when African Americans repudiate the heritage and culture of the "slavemaster" and adopt their own, that of a racially superior tribe of Shabazz. Economic separation includes living frugally, as debt is bondage to whites, and supporting only African American (that is, Muslim-owned) businesses. Physical separation, of course, is the ultimate goal, which will occur when African Americans settle in their own territory in North America or elsewhere. All of Elijah Muhammad's major writings express similar ideas, and the gist of his thinking is that a successful program of liberation must touch every aspect of the African American's life.

The Black Muslim program appears to contain three alternative scenarios. The first and least complex is complete separation of the races. Black Muslims claim that because black identity is unique and integration is hypocritical,[35] African Americans have no place in the white American system. Malcolm X maintained that the "only solution was complete separation," and Elijah Muhammad declared that "our former slavemasters are obligated to maintain and supply our needs in the separate territory for the next 20 to 25 years—until we are able to produce and supply our own needs."[36] Total separation was also viewed as a form of reparations for the "400 years of free labor" white Americans had taken from African Americans. Muslims demanded separate land in which the Nation could set up its own system, complete with farms, factories, businesses, schools, and its own set of laws. Four or five southern states would suffice for a viable nation that enjoyed total self-reliance and self-sufficiency. Muhammad preferred to remain in the United States rather than return to Africa, because "we have as much right to the soil as the white man. Why should we claim the land of our Black brothers in Africa; our destiny is right here in America."[37]

In the second alternative, if total separation were untenable, the Muslim program called for separation within the confines of white society. Black Muslims accept this imperfect form of racial separation because they believe "separation . . . can . . . take a psychological, a religious and an economic form even if it cannot express itself in the ultimate guise of a national territory."[38] The Nation is willing to settle for a "nation within a nation," but only if whites make certain concessions. First, they must establish separate schools staffed by African Americans, because whites do not teach "the truth." In addition, Muslims want freedom from taxation and a law forbidding racial mixing. Nor do they want to participate in white people's wars or be considered United States citizens. In essence, Black Muslims want to be isolated as much as possible while living within the white society. They want to practice their religion in peace and prosper economically without white interference. In return, Muslims would continue to obey the laws and respect the citizens of the United States.[39]

Because this proposal too was premised on tremendous governmental cooperation, which was not forthcoming, Muhammad fashioned a separatist strategy that required no governmental intervention. It called for the creation of African American educational and economic institutions within the African American community. In response, Black Muslims did establish their own private schools, called the University of Islam, for ages one through nineteen. The Nation also created a five-point economic plan. The plan admonishes African Americans to: (1) recognize the necessity for unity and group operation (activities); (2) pool your resources, physically as well as financially; (3) stop wanton criticism of everything that is black-operated and black-owned; (4) remember, jealousy destroys from within; and (5) work hard in a collective manner.[40] Thus, the movement attempted to build self-reliance through a mixture of economic achievement, black pride, collective thinking, and a strong work ethic.

The Nation of Islam, in short, presented a program of racial separation replete with demands, details, and alternative strategies, in the event that the United States government would not meet its demands. This multilayered program rested on a racial ideology composed of religious tenets, black pride, self-reliance, and vulgar racism. Supporting the program were thousands of followers and strong leaders, working during the most active period of civil rights since Reconstruction—the 1950s and 1960s. Despite these advantages, the Nation eventually weakened and the movement lost its momentum.

The Decline

In the 1960s the Black Muslim movement had an estimated membership of 100,000 to 250,000.[41] James Baldwin hailed it as the "only grass roots Negro movement in the United States."[42] Indeed, the Nation of Islam was widely considered the most powerful and feared black nationalist movement since Marcus Garvey. At the very least, it was a formidable social-religious movement. The Black Muslims seemed to offer thousands of African Americans a solution to racial oppression. From the mid-1960s, however, the Nation's influence steadily declined. It never produced the social reform it had prophesied.[43]

Conflicting ideologies and fractured leadership were significant factors leading to the Nation's decline. Muslim leaders argued about whether Fard was really Allah and about other tenets of Black Muslim ideology. Muhammad's son, Wallace, questioned his father's teachings on Fard. Malcolm X spoke publicly after President Kennedy's assassination, though he had been ordered not to do so, and angered the vast majority of Americans when he said the killing signified the "chickens were coming home to roost." He was then removed as minister from his temple. Perhaps in retaliation, Malcolm questioned Elijah's morality when two secretaries revealed they had ongoing sexual relations with Elijah Muhammad and had borne his children.[44] Malcolm left the organization and, after a visit to Mecca, formed his own group, the Organization of Afro-American Unity (OAAU). Then, in a sudden reversal of belief, he rejected the idea of building a separate black nation in North America based on racial superiority. Many commentators believe that he totally abandoned the concept of separatism, but it is more likely that his views had just grown more nuanced. His goal was to achieve racial autonomy as a first step in a long struggle toward "independent black nationhood."[45]

Malcolm's departure undoubtedly contributed to the Nation's loss of influence. In addition, its strict rules of behavior could not withstand modern mores. In 1974, toward the end of his life, Elijah Muhammad consented to jettison Black Muslim ideology and adopt the changes favored by his son, Wallace Muhammad. When Elijah died in 1975, Wallace was named as his successor. This shocked many in the Nation because the younger man had been suspended many times for refusing to believe that Fard was Allah. Wallace changed the movement from one advocating separatism and racial superiority to one advocating orthodox Islamic practices, and even allowed whites to become members of the Nation. Feeling betrayed and outraged, a group of Muslims, led by Minister Louis Farrakhan (Louis Eugene Walcott, born in 1933), broke away. Farrakhan's group returned to the Nation's original racist theology and separatist program, with a few modifications. For example, whereas Elijah Muhammad rejected Marcus Garvey's return-to-Africa strategy, Farrakhan saw emigration to Africa as a credible option. And while Elijah Muhammad considered territorial separation within the United States as a form of reparations, Farrakhan expanded the notion of reparations to include not only money but also the release of all African Americans from state and federal penitentiaries. Today, Farrakhan's group is generally regarded as the continuation of the Nation of Islam (Farrakhan considers it to be the "true" Nation) but, although more influential than Wallace's group, it is less powerful than Elijah's Nation was at its height.[46]

One scholar suggests that Elijah Muhammad's movement simply peaked as a social force and could not attract additional recruits because most African Americans did not believe that "going somewhere else" was an acceptable solution to the race problem.[47] Perhaps the Muslims' emphasis on racial pride in the end served to further convince African Americans that they should remain a part of America "without apology for [their] blackness"[48]; that they should stay and fight for their rightful place in American society. Moreover, in the 1960s most African Americans were stirred by the new promise of racial integration. Conversely, the antagonistic and racist rhetoric against whites and the black superiority doctrine surely deterred many potential followers.

Economic failure was another contributing factor to the Nation's decline. Although the movement correctly recognized the link between economic self-sufficiency and socioeconomic power, it was never able to achieve economic self-sufficiency. Most Muslims were unskilled or semi-skilled laborers; many were employed by white-owned businesses and were thus dependent on white America. On its own and without resources, the movement was unable to generate the autonomous economic system it had hoped to create. As one commentator has noted: "Membership in the Nation could . . . insulate [individuals] from some of the frustration of living in the white [person's] society; but it could not bring [them] equality, justice, or freedom within the American system."[49]

Finally, despite the Nation's bombastic rhetoric and radical ideas, Elijah Muhammad chose a policy of political nonengagement, a policy that may well have destroyed the momentum the movement had so carefully cultivated.[50] Privately, Malcolm X was convinced that the Black Muslims could have had a significant impact if they engaged in political activism. African Americans in the 1960s were eager to participate in the political process through voting or fielding candidates. In rejecting that path, the Nation cut itself off from a substantial source of potential support.[51] Such passivity created a void that was filled by other black nationalist organizations, such as the Black Panther Party. Similarly, the plans for total separation lay dormant because significant government participation was required to implement them. The leadership knew this, yet it took no action to force the government to consider total separation as a serious alternative to integration. Possibly they refused on principle to strike a deal with the "devil" or to rely upon governmental assistance in any form, but these principles proved self-defeating, as they could not succeed without governmental intervention. Elijah Muhammad chose to wait for the War of Armageddon—a sure sign of procrastination.

In short, internal ideology conflict, the obvious limitations of a "theologically falsified racial doctrine" in a secular age, the African American appetite for racial integration in the 1960s, the lack of an independent economic system, passive political leadership, and the simple fact that territorial separation was "politically unrealizable," all contributed to the decline of the movement.[52]

Conclusion

As much a theological as a social movement, the Nation of Islam offers a few valuable lessons for African Americans. The importance of racial pride and unity in uplifting and mobilizing the masses is one of them. Garvey, however, taught this first and with greater drama. Black Muslims also teach us that religion, traditional moral values, and the work ethic can combine to create an effective program of behavior modification, turning career criminals into law-abiding citizens and allowing the poor and downtrodden to help themselves.

The Black Muslim program also has negative features. A plan of racial separation, regardless of what good it does for African American self-esteem, loses the moral high ground as well as practicality when it is grounded in racist ideology or theology. Without creating and executing a political program and without government cooperation, territorial separatists cannot succeed.

Elijah Muhammad nonetheless symbolized unity and pride for African Americans. Rhetoric and racism aside, he showed a true love for African Americans and a genuine concern for their plight. Elijah Muhammad, later Malcolm X, and now Louis Farrakhan have dared to say what most African Americans wanted to say: "We have had enough." Together, these leaders offered a dignified proposal for African Americans, a potential haven from racial discrimination and oppression. Whether or not one agrees with the Black Muslims' separatist strategy, at least they did something, at least they assessed the situation as they saw it and *acted*, even if they came up short.

10

Emigration to Liberia

The most radical form of racial separation, emigration, is also the oldest idea. From the time they were brought to the New World as slaves, African Americans have thought about returning to Africa or moving to other lands to escape racial oppression in this country. The West African nation of Liberia, founded in 1822 and presently a country of approximately 2.5 million people with a land mass the size of Ohio, is undoubtedly the most famous attempt at emigration.[1]

The Founding of Liberia

Separated from family, friends, and linguistic, religious, and other cultural roots, held in bondage or in racial limbo—neither enslaved nor as free as whites—African Americans, whether free or enslaved, were pariahs in the land of liberty and opportunity. Many African Americans saw emigration as the only way out of a hellish situation. Indeed, as early as 1787, former African American slaves helped to found Freetown, located just north of Liberia in what is now Sierra Leone. These slaves were freed by Sir Henry Clinton, the British commanding general in the South during the Revolutionary War. He guaranteed the freedom of all slaves who deserted their rebellious masters. This guarantee is often called the "first emancipation proclamation."[2]

Despite their desire to emigrate, neither free African Americans, a group that included "mulattoes" (most were the issue of illicit unions between white slavemasters and their female slaves), nor, of course, slaves, possessed the economic, political, or military means to organize and fund a successful emigration program. White assistance was needed, and over the years it came from some of the most prominent public figures in American history—Thomas Jefferson, James Monroe, Andrew Jackson, Henry Clay, Daniel Webster, and Abraham Lincoln.[3] But the organization most responsible for emigration and, in particular, the founding of Liberia, was the American Colonization Society (or ACS), founded in 1816.

The society's motives for sponsoring emigration were decidedly mixed. Some of its members saw emigration as an honorable if only symbolic restitution for the abhorrent human trade and bondage. Others saw resettlement as a convenient device for ridding both the North and South of free African Americans, whose ranks had swelled from approximately 59,466 in 1790 (the first census taken in the United States) to approximately 186,466 just two decades later.[4] Free African Americans could not be successfully integrated into the American mainstream. Some of the southern planters who took prominent positions in the resettlement movement were particularly concerned about the threat these "untenable people" posed to the institution of slavery. The very existence of free African Americans within the slave states held open the possibility of freedom and self-reliance for their enslaved brethren. Others saw emigration as part of the "white man's burden." Such a colony in West Africa would establish a beachhead for Protestant Christianity and Western civilization and thereby facilitate the spreading of the Gospel throughout the "dark continent."[5]

Fears of miscegenation also drove the emigration movement. Whites grew fearful of interracial liaisons, which grew more frequent although they were prohibited. In 1640, the Virginia General Court issued a precedent-setting ruling in a case of interracial coitus involving a white man named High Davis. The court ordered that Davis be "soundly whipped, before an assembly of Negroes and others for abusing himself to the dishonor of God and the shame of Christians, by defiling his body by lying with a Negro."[6] Mulatto families were oppressed in the larger society as well. One white man, married to a mulatto woman, petitioned the ACS for permission to emigrate to Liberia.

> "My wife is a Quadroon of New Orleans," he declared. "We have been married five years and have two children, who being only one-eighth African, are blue-eyed, and flaxen haired; and nearly as 'pale faced' as myself. Still they are *coloured* and that is a word with tremendous import in North America!" Although he was established in his community, his neighbors constantly reminded him of his "transgressions against National feeling," and he feared "bequeathing to

(his) children a hopeless degradation! I will go anywhere," he concluded, "to avoid so hateful an alternative."[7]

The mulattos within the free African American population were victimized because they embodied the worst fears of a race-conscious society.[8]

Although the ACS enjoyed substantial support from its members, it needed and obtained the federal government's assistance to translate its emigration plans into reality. President James Monroe, for example, gave official recognition to the ACS's agent in West Africa. More importantly, Congress appropriated $100,000, the first of a series of grants, toward the purchase of land, the construction of homes and forts, the acquisition of farm implements, and the execution of other projects necessary for the care, training, and defense of the settlers.

As part of its aid package, the federal government made the USS *Elizabeth* available for the ACS's use. Accompanied by the *Cyane,* the *Elizabeth* carried settlers who made an ill-fated attempt to establish themselves on Sherbro Island, just off the shore of Sierra Leone. This settlement lasted only a year, ending with the U.S. Navy rescuing the remaining colonists and transporting them together with a new group farther down the coast to Cape Mesurado, near the present city of Monrovia.[9]

At Cape Mesurado, in December of 1821, the ACS began heated and protracted negotiations with African tribal leaders. Using gunboat diplomacy, naval officers attempted to persuade "King Peter" and other minor Bassa and Dei chieftains that the settlers came as benefactors, not as enemies. Some days into 1822 the officers successfully negotiated on behalf of the ACS the purchase of Cape Mesurado for $300 worth of muskets, beads, tobacco, gunpowder, clothing, mirrors, food, and rum.[10] This was the first of an endless string of transactions in which the tribal inhabitants only belatedly realized the full implication of the sale of their land to the aliens from America. Suspicion turned to hostility as the settlers began to press the locals into service as field hands and household domestics and imposed the English language and American forms of justice and commerce in the areas under their control. As the ACS and the settlers extended their control over tribal lands, often at gunpoint, it was sometimes only the timely interventions of American, British, and other naval forces that prevented the colonists from being thrown back into the sea.

Although the federal government provided substantial assistance in the establishment of Liberia, it steadfastly refused to recognize the settlement as an official American colony. This created many international problems for the ACS, the Americo-Liberians (as they eventually came to be called), and the American government itself. Washington's official aloofness was put to the test in the 1840s, when the British government, in support of European traders from Sierra Leone who rejected Liberian land claims and refused to pay custom fees to its southern neighbor, declined to acknowledge the ACS as a sovereign power. Although the United States intervened on their behalf, it was the Americo-Liberians themselves who resolved the impasse. In 1847 the Monrovia settlers issued a Declaration of Independence, severing their ties with the founding ACS and establishing Liberia as the first sovereign and independent black republic in Africa. Similar action was taken by a settlement farther down the coast near Cape Palmas. This colony was established by the Maryland State Colonization Society, which broke away from the ACS in 1831 and started sending African Americans south of Cape Mesurado in 1833. Cape Palmas (or Maryland as it was also called) remained independent until 1857, when the Republic of Liberia annexed it.[11]

The timely recognition of the Liberian republic by Great Britain in 1847 contrasted sharply with the American stance. Despite continued U.S. economic and military support, it was not until President Lincoln's administration, in 1862, that diplomatic recognition was extended. Apparently, the Civil War had silenced those who objected to the presence of an envoy of color in Washington, D.C.

Despite the enthusiasm of ACS's founders and subsequent resettlement efforts made by white organizations in Maryland, Pennsylvania, Mississippi, and other states, emigration to West Africa involved only a small fraction of free African Americans, whose numbers had risen to over half a million by 1867.[12] Fewer than twenty thousand persons were resettled in Liberia, and close to six thousand of these, Africans rescued from slaving vessels on the high seas, had never even been to America.[13]

The limited success of the colonization scheme was partly due to lack of funds. The ACS failed to persuade the federal government to underwrite its operations, while few free African Americans possessed the financial means to pay their own way to Liberia and to survive until the first harvest. The emigrants were thus dependent upon funds provided by former masters, appropriations by Congress or the various state legislatures, or funds from private sources raised by the ACS.

The idea of resettling in Africa was not universally welcomed. Abolitionists and other antislavery groups saw repatriation as a strong counterargument to their cause, because it removed from America smoking-gun evidence that emancipated African Americans could be industrious. Emigration, they felt, also gave support to the idea that the races could not peacefully coexist in our society. This particular objection was voiced by many free African Americans as well. For example, in 1816, the leaders of the Philadelphia Bethel Church characterized emigration to Africa as a slur upon their reputation and little more than a plan to dump free African Americans "into the savage wilds of Africa." It was, they claimed, "a circuitous route" back to bondage.[14] Frederick Douglass spoke for many free African Americans when he thundered:

> For two hundred and twenty-eight years has the colored man toiled over the soil of America, under a burning sun and a driver's lash—plowing, planting, reaping, that white men might roll in ease, their hands unhardened by labor, and their brows unmoistened by the waters of genial toil, and now that the moral sense of mankind is beginning to revolt at this system of foul treachery and cruel wrong, and is demanding its over-throw, the mean and cowardly oppressor is mediating plans to expel the colored man entirely from the country. Shame upon the guilty wretches that dare propose, and all that countenance such a proposition. We live here—have lived here—have a right to live here, and mean to live here.[15]

The Early Years

A form of social stratification emerged almost immediately among the settlers and between them and the indigenous tribal inhabitants. The colonists from the United States were joined during the mid-nineteenth century by a remarkable group of West Indians who had become dissatisfied with British home rule in Barbados, Jamaica, and other Caribbean islands. At the lowest level in the hierarchy of the settler group were the so-called recaptives, Africans who had never seen the New World but had been rescued from slaving vessels by the British and American navies and sent to Liberia to start a new life. Whether they came from present-day Nigeria, Ghana, or elsewhere, this lowest-status group within the Americo-Liberian fold came to be called "Congoes." Curiously, "Congo" later became one of the terms the tribal people used to refer to all persons who claimed descent from the African American founders of Liberia. The social elite consisted of the five thousand African Americans (including mulattoes) who were born free, had been emancipated by their slave owners, or had been sufficiently enterprising in America to purchase their own freedom. This group, whose ambitions paralleled those of the ACS's white founders, provided dynamic leadership during Liberia's formative years.[16] Men like Loft Carey and Colin Teague, who were Baptist preachers, not only tended to the needs of the settlers but carried the Gospel to the tribal villages along the coast. As Carey said: "I am an African. I wish to go to a country where I will be estimated by my merits, not by my complexion; and feel bound to labour for my suffering race."[17] So enterprising were Americo-Liberian and white missionaries that "by 1838 there were over twenty churches along the Liberian coast, representing most of the major Protestant denominations."[18]

Until the end of the First Republic in 1980, the Liberian elite set the political, social, and religious standards for the entire nation. Ironically, their culture was the culture of the antebellum American South. Far from rejecting the institutions, values, speech, and dress of the society that had enslaved them, the free African Americans painstakingly attempted to reproduce their oppressors' culture. They had only rejected their inferior status in American society, not American culture. For them, emigration was not an attempt to rediscover African culture by returning to Africa as her lost children, in the ACS's image. "These were Americans, and their views of Africa and Africans were essentially those of nineteenth-century whites in the United States. The bonds of culture were stronger than the bonds of race, and the resettlers clung tenaciously to the subtle differences that set them apart from the tribal 'savages' in their midst . . . Thus, it was not unusual to hear tribal people refer to the Americo-Liberians as Kwee, or 'white' people, or to have them refer to Monrovia as 'the American place.' "[19]

Through trading with African tribes, serving as representatives of American and European trading firms, investing in the construction of schooners, and even directly participating in the continuing transatlantic slave trade, some Americo-Liberians accumulated great wealth and political privilege.[20] Years later such prosperity would end, and the country would go into a steady economic decline.

The Later Years

In a continent that has experienced famine, civil strife, and severe poverty, Liberia (until recently) has not fared as badly as most. In the 1960s and early 1970s, when the majority of African states were experiencing both the fruits of political independence and the despair of economic privation, Liberia was experiencing economic growth and showing a potential for more prosperity. It seemed to have developed a healthy economy buttressed by strong export markets. According to the World Bank, Liberia was a "middle income oil importing country," and ranked 38th from the bottom of the list of less developed countries (LCDs). The country offered a bright contrast to the majority of new African states.[21] In the view of many economists, during most of the decade from the mid-1960s to the mid-1970s Liberia was one of the few fiscal success stories among the LCDs. It had the ability to generate significant revenue, which exceeded its public expenditures, from a broad base of economic activities.[22]

Much of Liberia's potential mineral wealth is still unknown. Indeed, only in the late 1980s did the Liberian government, with the support of both private and public Western funding, undertake a thorough and systematic geological survey of the country. We do know that it is one of the few African states with adequate rainfall and cultivable land. It is also well known that, between the mid-1960s and the mid-1970s, Liberia's most significant asset was its human capital. As a result of strengthening its institutions of higher education and creating a vast government scholarship program, and as a consequence of efforts by Christian missionaries, international agencies, and foreign donors, Liberia's pool of educated people was one of the highest per capita on the African continent.

By 1986 Liberia's optimistic prospect had dissipated completely. It is not an exaggeration to characterize the Liberian economy after 1986 as chaos in search of disaster. The once healthy economic growth rate plummeted during the decade following the 1973 oil crisis. Sharp declines were recorded in agriculture, transportation, and manufacturing. The population growth rate was well over the global average, climbing from 2.8 percent in the 1965–1973 period to 3.3 percent by 1983.[23] Many Liberians living in the depressed areas of Monrovia and the rural hinterland had a standard of living approximating that of people living in the poorest countries of the world—the roughly forty nations around the globe popularly called the "Fourth World."

In the mid-1990s the situation is even worse. A sizable portion of educated Liberians lives in exile. Various tropical and temperate zone diseases are endemic to the country, and the roughly 54-year life expectancy of Liberians is only slightly better than that of other West African nations.

While its potential for industrialization remains great, Liberia is one of the least industrialized nations in Africa. Further complicating economic development is the flood of migrants from the countryside into the city, which has created food shortages that have had political as well as economic and health consequences.

Liberia's economy has been described as "growth without development."[24] That is, although the country has enjoyed a significant physical facelift and has taken on a variety of new economic activities, the basic institutions and infrastructures needed to sustain economic development are either lacking or deficient. Instead of contributing to national prosperity, members of the political elite—who provide little real economic entrepreneurship—and the expatriate investors, bankers, and advisers have turned out to be the primary beneficiaries of economic growth in Liberia.

The Liberian Paradox

On April 12, 1980, Samuel K. Doe, a 28-year-old master sergeant who dropped out of school in the 11th grade, seized power from President William Tolbert by shooting and bayoneting him to death at the Executive Mansion. Two weeks later, former senior government officials were marched nearly naked through the streets of Monrovia, tied to posts at the seaside, and executed at point-blank range.[25] For most Liberians, political independence did not come with Liberia's formal declaration of independence in 1847, which severed the country's ties with the ACS Founding Fathers, but in that bloody month of April.

Prior to Sergeant Doe's overthrow of the First Republic, most Liberian members of the Krahn, Gio, and other African tribes were relegated to low-caste life in a quasi-colonial country. From the very beginning of the nation the Americo-Liberian minority annexed and then subordinated the regional tribes politically, economically, socially, and religiously. The tribes soon became "dependent" on the settlers and their descendants.

Liberia's political paradox is too clear to ignore. A country founded on a dream of racial equality begets racial oppression. Having secured the blessings of liberty for themselves on their ancestors' continent, African Americans forcibly denied full freedom to their racial kin, not only during the tutelary period under the ACS (1822–1847) but also during the tenure of the First Republic (1847–1980). It was not until the Unification Program of President William Tubman (1944–1971) that a concerted effort was made to remove many of the more odious distinctions between the descendants of the American settlers and the indigenous population. Improvements in education, health care, and other aspects of Liberian life that resulted from economic growth under both Tubman and his successor unleashed political and cultural expectations among the tribes that could not easily be controlled or contained by the settler minority. Nation-building in Africa has always been difficult in the face of poverty, tribal diversity, and a tradition of military coups. Tribal subordination made matters worse.[26]

Despite the violence associated with the overthrow of the First Republic, there was a broad spectrum of support for Samuel Doe, the new president. The 1980 coup gave Liberia what the tentative starts under Tubman and Tolbert had not—the first real opportunity to fulfill its 160-year quest for democracy. President Doe established a new governing body, the People's Redemption Council (PRC), which would return Liberia to civilian rule at the end of the first year of military governance. Constitutional government and popular suffrage reinforced a sense of optimism among the Liberian people.[27]

But it became clear early on in the Doe regime that Liberia's experiment in democracy would never succeed. The electoral process was irreparably flawed. President Doe placed a moratorium on political speeches and dem-onstrations. Other freedoms that are a vital part of democratic rule—free-dom of the press and freedom of religion—were also smothered. Most tell-ingly, President Doe and the PRC engaged in a level of corruption and brutality far in excess of anything known previously in Liberia, intending to remain in power permanently.[28]

With Doe at the helm, Liberia's Gross National Product shrank by 1.3 percent between 1980 and 1986.[29] But his pro-American policies won him the favor of President Ronald Reagan. In the early 1980s, the Reagan ad-ministration contributed nearly $500 million to the fledgling regime.[30] Doe promised free elections in return. They were held in 1985, but were marked by widespread intimidation, the detention of leading opposition leaders, press office closures, and flagrant vote-counting irregularities. When early returns showed Doe losing heavily, he seized all the ballots and announced two weeks later that he had won 50.5% of the vote.[31]

On November 12, 1985, less than a month after the discredited election, Doe's regime was nearly overthrown by an attempted coup. The coup was led by Thomas Quiwonkpa, a tribal Liberian (of the Gio tribe) and former general then living in exile. After the coup failed, Doe's mostly Krahn soldiers (his own tribe) went on a rampage of vicious reprisals against Gios and the linguistically related Manos. Eyewitnesses to these killings told of bloodcurdling brutality. "Quiwonkpa himself was captured, beaten to death, castrated, and dismembered. A leading television broadcaster, Charles Gbenyon, was stripped naked in public and later bayoneted to death while in custody of Doe's personal militia, the exclusive Krahn Executive Mansion Guard."[32] General Quiwonkpa's fate was particularly gruesome. "He was divided into pieces and the pieces were paraded around town, and then, in order to assume the strength of this bold pretender and in front of reliable eyewitnesses, Doe's men ate him."[33]

President Doe's new government took office on January 6, 1986. Despite the fraudulent election, there was considerable popular support for the Constitution of the Second Republic. Liberians had not abandoned their desire for democracy, even though many had given up on Doe. Krahn soldiers, under his leadership, would continue to terrorize other Liberian tribes for a few more years.

Charles Taylor, a former government official whom Doe had wanted to prosecute for allegedly embezzling nearly $1 million in government funds, led a contingent of 170 guerrillas across the border from the Ivory Coast in December of 1989. Taylor's men eventually advanced to the outskirts of Monrovia and laid siege to the capital. Another rebel group formed under the leadership of Prince Johnson. Johnson, a Gio, accused Taylor of criminality. His forces, numbering a few hundred, were responsible for the capture, torture, and execution of President Doe on September 9, 1990.[34]

Esquire, a prominent African American magazine, has described the situation in Liberia as "the Civil War from Hell."[35] The civil war in Liberia, in which rebel forces led by Charles Taylor and Prince Johnson tried to destroy each other and overthrow the regime of President Doe, made life in Liberia a nightmare. Much of the country has been destroyed. Members of the Gio and Mano tribes were massacred by government troops simply because they were thought to be supporters of the opposition. In return, rebel troops killed members of Doe's Krahn tribe and the Mandingoes, a mercantile tribe considered too accommodating to Doe. While warfare along tribal lines may seem an ordinary feature of the numerous civil conflicts in African nations and elsewhere, it is quite extraordinary in Liberia. Ethnic and tribal violence have not been a significant part of Liberia's recorded history. Until Doe seized power in 1980, the dominant Americo-Liberians had kept intertribal conflict under control.

In August 1990 the Economic Community of West African States (ECOWAS) sent 4,000 ground and naval forces to Liberia in an attempt to stabilize the area and to negotiate peace talks among the rebel factions. The

ECOWAS military force was given a name to reflect its mission, the Economic Community Monitoring Group (ECOMOG). Troops from Nigeria, Guinea, Ghana, Sierra Leone, and Gambia contributed to this peacekeeping force. In September 1990 ECOMOG took control of central Monrovia.[36] But its attempt to separate Charles Taylor's National Patriotic Front of Liberia (NPFL) from the Independent National Patriotic Front of Liberia, led by Taylor's rival, Prince Johnson, stalled, causing one West African magazine to dub its efforts "ECO-BOG."[37] Meanwhile, Brigadier General David Nimley, commander of the late President Doe's bodyguards, announced that he was the legitimate interim President of Liberia.[38] Another contender, a group of exiled civilians in nearby Gambia (self-described as Liberia's government in exile), has emerged under the leadership of lawyer Amos Sawyer. Critics have said that instead of imposing order among these factions, ECOMOG has become just another faction in the fighting.

Since 1990, some 30 peace negotiations sponsored by a variety of entities—ECOWAS, the United Nations, President Jerry Rawlings of neighboring Ghana, and private relief groups—have started, stalled, and unraveled. Bloodshed and factionalism inevitably resumed after each new failed peacekeeping effort. The war has claimed an estimated 150,000 civilian lives, displaced more than half of all Liberians, and pushed approximately 800,000 Liberian refugees into neighboring countries, making Liberia's problems regional in nature. Seven factions now claim territory and the allegiance of some of the country's citizens, now fewer than 2 million.[39]

Among U.S. observers there are some, like Larry Minear and Thomas Weiss, directors of the Humanitarianism and War Project at Brown University's Watson Institute, who see hope for Liberia.[40] But, as one commentator has observed, if the 1990 Civil War "were to end tomorrow, recovery would take years. Monrovia's power plant has been severely damaged. The iron ore mining industry, which earned Liberia more than $200 million a year in peacetime, will never recover, and the cost of processing low-quality ore with out-of-date equipment is prohibitive. The rubber industry, Liberia's other main money earner, can be revived, but because of growing competition from Southeast Asia, it will never be as profitable as it once was."[41]

Conclusion

The Republic of Liberia is in shambles, a victim of civil war caused, paradoxically, by decades of African American oppression and, more recently, by traditional African tribalism. Even if emigration were a practical option for African Americans today, Liberia teaches us that it is not automatically a good response. African Americans could well do worse living in another land without democratic traditions, ideals, and institutions. What Liberia teaches us most is that the American way of life—with its modern liberal thinking about the individual, society, and politics—is an experiment that is difficult to perfect at home and not easy to replicate elsewhere in the world, even by freedom-loving African Americans.

11

Black Towns in the United States

Most African American separatists have always favored the idea of a separate establishment within the United States—whether territories, states, a single state, or towns—over emigration to African or other foreign countries.[1] Because African American settlements within the United States were governed by American law, democracy was never in doubt. Antidemocratic traditions like those that were rife in the Republic of Liberia simply could not and did not take root in domestic settlements.

For many white leaders, internal emigration seemed not only a more pragmatic form of total separation than emigration to Africa, but also the only real solution to the problem of what to do with the slaves should they be given their freedom. Finding an appropriate place on foreign soil and convincing African Americans to leave the only country most of them had ever known greatly limited foreign emigration as a viable option. Something had to be done because, along with Thomas Jefferson and Abraham Lincoln, most whites did not believe "the Negro would eventually become a part of the American democracy."[2]

Black towns became the most prevalent form of domestic resettlement. A "black town" was meant to be "a separate community containing a population of at least 90 percent [African American] in which the residents attempted to determine their own political destiny."[3] Most black towns sprang up across America after the Civil War—approximately 60 between 1865 and 1915.[4] Very little recorded history remains of these towns. Adequate material, at least enough to support research and analysis, is available on only about a half-dozen of these towns—primarily Nicodemus, Kansas; Mound Bayou, Mississippi; Langston City, Oklahoma; Clearview and

Boley, established in the Creek Nation, in what is now Oklahoma; and Allensworth, California. Their records yield several generalizations. First, most African American residents of black towns were primarily motivated by their desire for freedom—economic and political—and by racial pride. More than anything else, African Americans wanted to get away from racial violence and discrimination by whites, especially in the South. Black towns were a way of dealing with the failure of American society to transform the hopes of emancipation into the reality of everyday life.

In comparison, the motives of the town promoters were more complex than those of the residents. Several promoters saw black towns as a show-place for African American skills and abilities, believing that whites would be more accepting of African Americans if they saw that the former slaves could build and operate their own towns. Some scholars, principally Kenneth Marvin Hamilton in his *Black Towns and Profit,* argue that profit was the primary motivation for the establishment of black towns: these towns were marketed to African Americans as business ventures in land rather than as oases from racism. Other scholars, notably Norman L. Crockett, come to a different conclusion, one to which I would subscribe: while it is not clear whether the promoters' "ultimate intention was to gain riches or to aid those less fortunate than themselves,"[5] there is no doubt that many of them used black towns to increase their personal fortunes.

The black towns tended to be small communities based on agriculture. This is not surprising given the time—nineteenth century—and place—rural America—in which they were established. I do not believe it appropriate to view black towns solely or primarily as a product of the westward migration of the late 1800s; to do so would misdescribe the collective motivation behind the towns' establishment—that is, racial separation. Here I do not agree with Hamilton, who attempts "to demonstrate that, when viewed as an integral part of the frontier urban settlement process [black towns] are neither insignificant nor of special importance."[6]

The point Charles Allen Humphrey makes in his *Socio-Economic Study of Six All-Black Towns in Oklahoma* applies to most black towns: although self-sufficient in religious services, the towns were not "self-sufficient in educational services, . . . social services, and economic services."[7] Understandably, then, life was hard for their residents. Also, white prejudice made everything harder than it otherwise had to be; that is, Jim Crow prevented the residents in most towns from totally insulating themselves from white oppression. Black town settlers, likewise, had their share of conflicts with "freedmen," former African American slaves of Indians. But many residents of black towns still enjoyed economic freedom (even though opportunities were scarce) and, especially, political power—something that had been unknown in their previous environments.[8]

Today only a few black towns remain, none of any particular significance. Most towns faded away, for lack of rail service or other sources of economic self-sufficiency, or as a result of the shift in wealth from the countryside to the city. Many black towns suffered at the hands of greedy promoters (African American and white) and others succumbed to racial integration, which created employment and housing opportunities for African Americans in northern cities.

Nicodemus, Kansas

After the Civil War, African Americans in the South faced discrimination, violence, poverty, and competition from whites for jobs. This was especially true during the period that is often misnamed Redemption, the period that followed the political overthrow of Reconstruction, in which "the Southern gentry, ably supported by poor whites, now began to put the [African American] 'back in his place.'"[9] Also, "the federal government's failure to allocate land to the new freedmen relegated most black adult males to the status of 'farmers without land.'"[10] Lacking money to leave and fearful about what life in another place would be like, most African Americans stayed in the South.[11] Some, however, simply had to get away.

Thousands departed for Kansas, intending either to homestead or purchase land there. Kansas had a special appeal to African Americans. "Since the time of John Brown's militant abolitionist activities in that state, many southern blacks perceived it as the freest place for them in the United States."[12] The westward migration of southern African Americans to Kansas and other places took place in two waves. The first, from 1873 to 1878, "was a period of planned colonization" leading to the establishment of five African American colonies, including two in Kansas: Nicodemus and the Singleton Colony. The second wave, known as the "Great Exodust," began in 1879 as "an unorganized flood of destitute, leaderless people who were seeking what they had come to believe was a promised land."[13] By 1880, an estimated 20,000 African Americans had migrated to Kansas alone.[14]

Nicodemus, the first African American town in Kansas, received its first large group of migrants in 1877. Two African American ministers from

Clarksville, Tennessee, William Smith and Thomas Harris, were later joined in the venture by a white Kansas land speculator, W. R. Hill.[15] Hill promoted "the establishment of a black settlement by speaking before the congregations of rural churches."[16] He told "stories of a western paradise filled with abundant game, wild horses, and soil so fertile that a minimum of labor yielded bountiful harvests"[17] and did not dwell on the perils of life on the Great Plains: its winters; its houses dug into the earth and infested with fleas and ants; and the coyotes, rattlesnakes, and tarantulas. Like most promoters, Hill stretched the truth to entice settlers to Nicodemus.[18]

It was certainly tough for the early settlers to survive. Some farmers worked the land with hand tools. Men walked to other towns in search of work from whites, women and children collected bones from the prairie to sell to companies that ground them into fertilizer, and still "there was not enough money for subsistence."[19] Two Nicodemus ministers sought food and clothing for the destitute from nearby white communities, but the resentment of the locals against the African Americans prompted them to seek help elsewhere.[20] Whites owned many of the businesses in Nicodemus. By 1886 town promoters realized that only a small number of African Americans could afford to invest in land or businesses, so the campaign for new residents was broadened to include all races. Eager for growth, the town newspaper "attempted to advertise Nicodemus to a cross-section of Americans, thereby relinquishing the town's unique position as the only place in Kansas that directed its promotional efforts exclusively to blacks."[21]

Between 1886 and 1888 Nicodemus residents tried to convince railroad companies to service the town and help sustain its economy. No railroad ever came, however, and in late 1888 the residents began moving out. Many businesses moved to Bogue, just six miles south of Nicodemus, because it had a railroad depot. Like most new western towns without rail service, "Nicodemus could no longer efficiently perform its primary function of collecting and distributing goods."[22] With businesses gone and life now tougher than ever, even more residents began leaving Nicodemus. Some returned to the South, others moved farther west, and still others joined back-to-Africa movements. By 1910 the town's population had dropped to under 200 people, compared to approximately 600 in 1877. In 1950 Nicodemus had no stores. The government withdrew its post office three years later. Today, Nicodemus is a town of no special importance.[23]

Mound Bayou, Mississippi

Unlike the residents of Nicodemus, the townspeople of Mound Bayou did not have to worry about rail service. Mound Bayou was established by a railroad company and in this way was blessed from birth. Not surprisingly, then, Mound Bayou enjoyed a longer period of prosperity than Nicodemus.[24]

The town was developed in the Mississippi Delta, in a swampy, mosquito-ridden area "where no man had previously been induced to settle."[25] Isaiah T. Montgomery, founder of Mound Bayou and an African American himself, had inspected this wilderness area on two occasions before accepting an offer from the Louisville, New Orleans, and Texas Railroad (the L., N.O., and T.) to develop the land into tracts for African American farmers with the right to cut and sell the timber thereon.

Isaiah Montgomery was born a slave on Mississippi's Hurricane Plantation. His owner, Joseph Davis, was the brother of Jefferson Davis, the President of the Confederacy. Montgomery was taught to read and write by another slave. Eventually he became Joseph Davis's private secretary and office attendant, performing clerical duties for the plantation. During the Civil War he fled the plantation, and subsequently served on a Union gunboat that patrolled the Mississippi River. He returned to the South after the war, and together with his father (Benjamin) and his brother (William) agreed to manage the plantations of Joseph and Jefferson Davis. Montgomery's ultimate goal, however, was to purchase the Davis plantations. In time he became a major cotton producer on the Davis land. "But recurring floods, a fire, falling prices, and the possibility of lengthy court litigations with some of the Davis heirs convinced Montgomery to abandon the project."[26]

The exodus to Kansas also threatened the Montgomery farming operation. In 1879 twenty families suddenly left the Davis plantations for Kansas. Later, some of these "exodusters" sought Isaiah Montgomery's help in returning to the South. Montgomery traveled to Kansas, where he found that "eight or ten had died en route, and the remaining refugees were short of food and living in makeshift shanties, in boxcars, or in tents pitched along the levee. Unaccustomed to the climate, several had contracted pneumonia or suffered from severe cases of diarrhea from drinking the water of the Missouri River. For those who wished to return, Montgomery booked passage on the next steamboat bound for St. Louis."[27]

In Lawrence, Kansas, Montgomery "found nine families from the Davis plantations who wanted to remain in Kansas, and it was there he conceived the idea for the creation of a settlement composed of people coming from the same part of Mississippi."[28] He purchased land west of Topeka for this purpose, and helped the families relocate in what was called the Wabaunsee Colony. Montgomery also purchased land next to the Colony, which, some claim, he intended to use "as a plantation, exploiting colonists as share-croppers and hired labor."[29] This attitude seems consistent with other aspects of his character, as we shall see.

Eventually, Montgomery left the Davis plantations. He opened a mercantile business and later was approached by the land commissioner for the L., N.O. and T. Railroad about the possibility of opening the Mississippi Delta land to African American farmers. The railroad received a grant for the Delta land in the 1880s and now wanted to have settlements built along its line. White farmers were apparently not interested because of the heat, humidity, and malaria that came with the land.[30]

An Indian burial mound in the area of the town site and the existence of many small bayous gave Montgomery the idea for the name of the town. In February of 1888 a group of 47 people, some of whom had been associated with Montgomery and Sons, entered Bolivar County to settle Mound Bayou.[31]

Mound Bayou grew rapidly, housing 400 residents by 1904. Even so, life was hard. "Entire families took to the fields, clearing the trees and heavy undergrowth in order to plant cotton, corn and other crops. Of necessity, house-raisings and work-sharing became common practices. . . . At harvest time, the women and children of the settlement sought work picking cotton [at other Delta towns]. One settler who brought his family to Mound Bayou in 1888 later remembered that 'many times we had only bread to eat and water to drink.' "[32]

Isaiah Montgomery and his cousin, Benjamin Green, "a practical man who disliked whites," disagreed on the future of Mound Bayou. Montgomery "hoped to create the ideal agrarian community free of class conflict or competition for wealth and with a social order based on brotherly love, all revolving around family life, schools, and churches. His plan, he wrote Booker T. Washington in May, 1904, was to teach 'high class farming, improvement of homes, thrift, saving, and abandonment of the mortgage systems; and add to urban life sufficient attractions to hold younger people.' "[33] Green, however, envisioned "little more than a permanent sawmill and gin, commercial houses, and an economic concentration on the sale of cotton and lumber to outside markets."[34] In comparison with his cousin, Montgomery hardly sounds like an exploiter of people here.

But other evidence suggests that description of him might be accurate after all. It appears that Montgomery received Mound Bayou land at discounted prices because of his relationship with the L., N.O., and T. Perhaps the railroad even gave him some land free of charge. Montgomery had ownership interests in a variety of businesses, engaged in land speculation, and harvested cotton. There is nothing wrong with making money, of course, but the town father's financial interests in Mound Bayou certainly affected the way he hawked Mound Bayou lots. Montgomery toured the South selling town lots and neighboring farmland "for a probable commission of 12 percent."[35] He talked of racial pride and economic opportunity, but, as one scholar writes, "in keeping with his own economic interests and motivations, Montgomery hoped to find settlers who could contribute to the financial growth of Mound Bayou and to the profits of the businesses he and his family had established in the town."[36]

Mound Bayou became an incorporated village in February 1898, and Mississippi's governor appointed a village government, with Isaiah Montgomery as mayor. In 1890 Montgomery narrowly won the mayor's seat in the village's first election. The closeness of the race may have been a product of Montgomery's shameful behavior as representative to the 1890 Mississippi State Constitutional Convention. In describing it, Hamilton lets Montgomery off too easily.

> Montgomery's actions at this convention, where he spoke and voted in favor of restrictions on black enfranchisement, did not endear him to more radical Mississippi blacks but might have increased his standing with mainstream and conservative whites, including his financial backers. . . . In the political climate of Mississippi in the 1890's, black disfranchisement was undoubtedly a foregone conclusion, yet Montgomery's acquiescence at the Constitutional Convention linked him in some minds with the severe curtailment of black participation in county, state, and national elections.[37]

Montgomery did more than acquiesce in the process that led to a literacy test provision in Mississippi's new constitution. His extraordinary support for this provision eased the task of those whites who wanted this affront to Mississippi's African American population drafted into the new constitution. To understand how instrumental he was, a more detailed account of his activities at the 1890 convention is needed.

Montgomery, a loyal Republican party worker, was a delegate to both the county and congressional District Conventions in the 1880s. In an 1890 election, he and a white man were chosen to represent Bolivar County at the State Constitutional Convention. They were both "fusion" candidates; that is, in some counties Republicans and Democrats agreed before an election on the number of offices each race would receive.

The Convention was composed of 130 Democrats, one National Republican, one Conservative, one Greenbacker, and Montgomery. Though other reasons were given for calling the Convention, its overriding purpose was to find a legal method to disfranchise African American voters in Mississippi. Montgomery helped to vote a faction into the chair that had announced its intention of barring African Americans from voting.

Montgomery was appointed to the committee that returned a report to the Convention calling for a state literacy test. Voters could be required to offer a "reasonable interpretation" of the Constitution when it was read to them. At one point Montgomery gave an hour-long speech, referring to an earlier time when master and slave worked hand-in-hand, sharing mutual admiration and respect. Deplorably, outsiders had gained the confidence of African Americans and upset the harmony between the two races. In his opinion, African Americans had not attained the "high plane of moral, intellectual, and political excellence" reached by whites. Montgomery then explained his support of a literacy test on the ground that the test did not eliminate the voting privilege, "but only lifted it to a higher plane." As African Americans improved themselves, they could "re-enter the electorate once they had earned the right."[38] As one scholar notes, "the convention loved him. What better endorsement ... than a supportive speech from the lone black delegate whom many considered a leading spokesman for his race? Any opposition to the committee report quickly faded, and by a lop-sided margin the literacy test was incorporated into the draft of the new state constitution."[39]

In 1902, at the urging of Booker T. Washington, President Theodore Roosevelt's administration appointed Montgomery receiver of federal land revenues for Mississippi. He was an unfortunate choice. A subsequent government audit "uncovered financial irregularities, with federal monies seemingly having been deposited in Montgomery's personal account."[40] Montgomery declared his innocence, but Emmett Scott (Washington's assistant) persuaded Montgomery to resign.

After the death of Booker T. Washington in 1915, Montgomery and Charles Banks engaged in a power struggle. It peaked during Mound Bayou's 1917 municipal elections, when Banks's slate of candidates won. Montgomery did not take this lying down:

> Angry and alleging fraud, Montgomery, esteemed among Mississippi whites for being Joe and Jefferson Davis's houseboy, persuaded the racist Governor Theodore G. Bilbo to oust the winners. Such dissension between two of the wealthiest and most experienced community boosters was bound to affect the town's growth.... Banks, more concerned with racial solidarity than Montgomery ever was, continued his efforts to boost the town and to help lead the National Negro Business League into the 1920's.[41]

Mound Bayou faded after Montgomery and Banks died. Greed and mismanagement by the promoters (Montgomery and Banks principally) certainly set the stage for the decline, but the cotton market crashes in 1913 and 1914 supplied the *coup de grace*. Mound Bayou had a one-crop economy, which virtually assured its failure. After suffering its second fire in 1941, one visitor pronounced Mound Bayou more dead than alive.[42] Except for "the race of its citizens," the town is now "almost indistinguishable from any other small Mississippi Delta town."[43]

Langston City, Oklahoma

Langston's early development and promotional activities paralleled those of Mound Bayou and Nicodemus, while its history "is conditioned primarily by the specific history of Oklahoma and its black population."[44] The Oklahoma Territory was officially opened for settlement in April 1889. Charles Robbins, a white land speculator, purchased a townsite in what is now western Oklahoma. He left promotion of Langston to two African Americans, William Eagleson, a newspaper publisher, and Edward McCabe, a prominent politician. McCabe began promoting Langston as a black town in early 1890. The town was originally called Langston City and later became known as Langston. It was named for John Mercer Langston, an African American scholar and congressman from Virginia.[45]

McCabe and Eagleson published the *Langston City Herald* to promote the town. McCabe's agents in the South solicited buyers for Langston property. Many early settlers were misled by the newspaper, which showed illustrations of massive buildings and broad streets—McCabe's vision of the future—when in fact the town consisted of "one general store and a small cluster of wooden shacks surrounded by a tent city whose residents impatiently awaited the construction of houses."[46]

McCabe was a racial visionary. He wrote to President Benjamin Harrison arguing that Oklahoma should be made an African American state. In 1890 he traveled to the nation's capital in an attempt to convince the President "that the Unassigned Lands represented an ideal geographic location for an all-black state and proposed that he be named governor as soon as the new territory was officially organized."[47] Whites were worried, but there never were enough African Americans in the 1890s in Oklahoma to form a separate state; they did not exceed ten percent of Oklahoma's total population.[48]

McCabe, Eagleson, and Robbins may have sought to establish a black town to make "quick profits from the sale of land to black homesteaders."[49] On the other hand, the *Langston City Herald* contained themes of racial identity and pride. But:

> Under McCabe and Eagleson's leadership, . . . the *Herald's* support for overall racial advancement never overrode concern for the promoters' own financial interests and did not extend to all members of the race. The *Herald* directed its appeals explicitly to blacks with money to invest and actively discouraged poor blacks from coming to Langston and to Oklahoma. McCabe realized from his prior experience in Nicodemus that only blacks with capital could stimulate the growth of Langston, which would in turn provide the promoters with increased profits.[50]

There is some evidence that McCabe also used the *Herald* to assure investors that the railroad was coming to Langston and that it would double the value of town land and "increase business volume tenfold."[51] The St. Louis and San Francisco Railroad Company did eventually extend its tracks toward Langston, but only within three miles of the town. As was the case with Nicodemus, Langston's lack of rail service was a "permanent deterrence" to economic growth. Failing to gain rail service, Langston boosters sought to attract wealthy African Americans by highlighting the town's cotton gin and its educational facility, the Colored Agricultural and Normal School. The two attractions did not suffice; neither one could overcome the lack of rail service or provide an economic base of sufficient size and depth to sustain economic growth and development in the twentieth century. Langston's population decreased from approximately 2,000 residents in 1891 to approximately 300 by the end of the Depression. Money spent by students at the school (now a university) and appropriations to the school have kept the town alive.[52]

Clearview, Oklahoma

Clearview was one of a number of black towns established in what was then called "Indian Territory." After Congress dissolved tribal autonomy and opened Indian lands to settlement, three African Americans, Lemuel Jackson, James Roper, and John Grayson, founded Clearview in 1903. Clearview was located near a railroad, midway between Guthrie, Oklahoma Territory, and Fort Smith, Arkansas.[53]

Clearview's wealthiest resident, James E. Thompson, wished to go beyond the concept of a black town. He proposed the creation of a separate state for African Americans. At the 1911 meeting of the Farmers' Conference at Clearview, Thompson outlined his plan, which included a government bond issue to purchase land for African Americans. The acquisition of land and its transfer to African Americans would proceed as follows: (1) the federal government would set aside some territory for "the colonization of the Negroes"; (2) the government would appraise the land and purchase it with government bonds, then sell the land to African Americans in small tracts; and (3) the government would levy an annual "tax" to collect the principal and interest payments on the parcels.[54] Thompson's desire was to secure

> the complete separation of black and white governments in the new territory or state. Any whites currently living in the designated area would be compensated for their immediate relocation into selected cities. All legal matters involving blacks would be handled by a system of federal courts established there. To ensure elimination of legal discrimination, any black charged with a crime in a white-controlled city could receive an automatic change of venue to one of the new federal courts.[55]

Thompson in fact believed that integration was the eventual solution to race problems, "but since white attitudes made this impossible in the foreseeable future," total separation was viewed as the immediate solution.[56] Of course, the "black state" never materialized, in Oklahoma or elsewhere.

Like Mound Bayou and Langston, Clearview was tied to a one-crop agrarian economy—cotton. It was doomed to fail as cotton prices fell below the cost of production after the 1913 and 1914 cotton market crashes. Today, Clearview is "a tiny agricultural service center" that shall "always [stand] in the shadow of Boley."[57]

Boley, Oklahoma

In 1903 the Fort Smith and Western Railroad was laying track west from Fort Smith, Arkansas. The tracks passed through the Oklahoma land of Abigail Barnett. Her father, James Barnett, realized that Abigail's land would be worth more as a townsite than as agricultural land. James Barnett, Lake Moore (an attorney), and W. H. Boley (the F. S. and W. Railroad roadmaster) joined forces to develop a town on Abigail's land and formed a townsite company. The proposed townsite, named after Boley, was approximately twenty miles northwest of Clearview.[58]

Much of the town land had been owned by "freedmen" (African Americans who were former slaves of Creek Indians). In 1904 President Theodore Roosevelt authorized the sale of this land on the open market. Hostility between the freedmen and African Americans from the South at first resulted in violence and later "took the milder form of complete social separation."[59]

Hamilton correctly notes that "almost purely by chance, Boley became the largest predominantly black town in the entire Midwest and Great Plains."[60] Several factors led to the decision to make Boley an all-black town:

> The Boley station was located almost equidistant between the already established, white-populated railway towns of Paden and Castle, which would offer strong competition to Boley for new white settlers. Conditions in the former Confederate states were causing an increasing number of blacks to seek homes in Oklahoma. The nearest black town, Langston City, was more than seventy miles away and had no railroad station. Attracting black buyers for lots . . . could be the

quickest way to populate the town and the surest road to substantial profit from land speculation.[61]

By April of 1905, Boley's promoters attracted over 400 residents. The population more than doubled in the next three years, as did the number of businesses.

The attractions of Boley were several. First, a relatively large African American population already resided nearby, and it provided a ready-made clientele for the town's goods and services. Second, the fact that Boley was located adjacent to an existing railroad line and station meant that the town had an established distribution line for produce, goods, and other needs of area residents. Finally, more than promoters of other black towns, Boley promoters emphasized Booker T. Washington's ideals of racial pride, self-help, and, with the motto "All Men Up—Not Some Men Down," mutual assistance. Unlike Langston's newspaper, the *Boley Progress* did not suggest "that only blacks with money should settle in Boley and other areas of the Oklahoma and Indian territories."[62] On the contrary, the *Boley Progress* assured newcomers that "No colored man need be in financial straits who came to Boley and intends to make it his home. Every industrious colored man who comes receives the moral and financial aid of its citizens, who are able financially to look after him until he is able to get his business in good shape."[63] This same article listed twenty-three residents, "each with assets of over $1,000, who proclaimed willingness to help newcomers."[64] The favorable location of the town and the civic sense of self-help and mutual assistance made Boley one of the few successful black towns, at least in its early years.

Hamilton points out, with a slightly different emphasis, that the key reasons for the early success of Boley and the few other black towns were "the presence or quick acquisition of a rail line," coupled with "the acceptance of a black nationalist ideology by the black upwardly mobile class and those who aspired to become members of that class."[65]

> The railroad connection brought the intrinsic benefit of accessibility to the townspeople and hinterland farmers, and its early presence allowed the town boosters to intensify their efforts at accomplishing other promotional objectives. The black nationalism ideology created widespread acceptance of the black-town's separatist stance and, by encouraging wealthy blacks to assist poor ones, increased the targeted market of blacks willing and able to relocate in a town with only

black citizens. Boley's promoters continued to capitalize on these two phenomena until World War I.[66]

Boley began to decline after World War I. Cotton failed as a cash crop, and peanuts, the substitute crop, did not provide an adequate income for most farmers. Dependent upon local farmers for business, Boley merchants struggled to survive. Their customers, in turn, complained about high prices, the lack of credit, and the poor quality of the merchandise. Many residents began shopping out of town. As the agricultural depression worsened, some residents headed west, and others lost their property. The local tax base shrank, and then came the Great Depression.[67] In 1939 Boley declared bankruptcy. Subsequently, it lost its bank and its railroad, and the young people of the town moved out. Boley declined from approximately 5,000 residents in 1914 to 574 in 1960.[68]

Allensworth, California

Allensworth was founded in 1908 by an organization owned by African Americans, the California Colony and Home Promoting Association. The town was named after Allen Allensworth, who was born a slave in Louisville, Kentucky, in 1842. During the Civil War, he escaped from his third master and joined the U.S. Civilian Hospital Corps and later the U.S. Navy. Afterwards, Allensworth became an ordained Baptist minister and worked as a pastor for nineteen years. In 1896 he joined the Army as a chaplain for an African American regiment. Allensworth served ten years, distinguishing himself by improving educational opportunities for African American soldiers.[69]

After military service, Allensworth moved to Los Angeles and formed the California Colony and Home Promoting Association. Through the Association, Allensworth established the town named after him in the San Joaquin Valley. Because the Association of five African Americans could not afford to purchase land, it entered into an agreement with three white-owned companies that held land in the San Joaquin Valley. The contract apparently provided that the white companies would plan a townsite and pay the Association to secure African American settlers, and that the surrounding land would be reserved for African American farmers.[70]

Allensworth was situated in the center of the San Joaquin Valley near a main line of the Santa Fe Railroad. The Association invoked racial pride and self-help themes to promote the town. By 1910 only a few lots had been sold at little profit. The Association therefore terminated its relationship with the real estate companies and effectively ceased operating. One of the white companies, the Pacific Farming Company, hired Mr. Allensworth as its agent and began promoting the town, which at that time had about eighty residents, a hotel, a general store, and a warehouse. Most adults worked their own small farms on land surrounding the town.[71]

The Pacific Farming Company helped Allensworth residents establish certain civic amenities, in the hope of attracting new settlers to the area. Finally, in May 1912, the real estate company hit upon a novel boosting strategy: it focused its efforts on attracting African American soldiers. The strategy has been described as follows:

> Many of America's black soldiers had served with Allensworth or at least knew who he was. Allensworth wrote a letter to several first sergeants of the predominantly black Tenth Cavalry, Twenty-fourth Infantry, and Twenty-fifth Infantry, advertising the townsite and providing maps and lot prices. He asked the sergeants to give these to other soldiers upon their request. The *Sentiment Maker*, an eight-page, one-issue, promotional newspaper distributed to the men of the three regiments, also targeted its appeal especially to soldiers.[72]

The *Sentiment Maker* used a number of angles in an attempt to convince African American soldiers to purchase property in the area of Allensworth. The paper promised a good return on an investment in land and claimed that the purchase would improve the image of African Americans and provide safe, healthy, and friendly neighborhoods. Overlooked was the fact that soldiers were not much interested in farming and rural life.[73]

Allensworth's death in 1914 brought these promotional efforts to a near standstill. Two Allensworth residents, William Payne and Oscar Overr, had a new idea. To attract African American settlers, they wanted to establish the Allensworth Agriculture and Manual Training School, to be built on land secured from the Pacific Farming Company and financed by private sources as well as by the State of California. Although Payne and Overr convinced their state legislator to seek state funding for the proposed school, many African American leaders opposed this move, fearing that state aid would establish statewide school segregation. Such opposition, as well as California's financial troubles, led to the defeat of the proposed funding bill. Private donations for the school were inadequate, and the proposed school never came to be.[74]

The failure of the school and, more importantly, the desire of most African Americans to live in large northern and western cities rather than in small rural towns ended any further significant attempts to promote and develop Allensworth. Although Allensworth's population grew a little in the 1920s, inadequate water supplies and the depression of the 1930s caused many residents to move elsewhere.[75] Economic exploitation was another reason for Allensworth's failure to develop into a major town. As Hamilton writes, "altruism was overshadowed by profit-seeking"; except for the use of "black racial pride and the novel experience of black soldiers" to promote the town, the actions of Allensworth's promoters "mirrored those of the vast majority of town developers in the Trans-Appalachian West."[76]

Conclusion

Evaluation of both domestic migration to separate settlements and foreign emigration leads me to conclude that both forms of separation fell victim to human failure and circumstances. Human exploitation and antidemocratic practices, followed by tribal fighting, sank the Republic of Liberia. Human exploitation (the failure to place people before profits), mistiming (the failure to recognize the inherent drawbacks of an agrarian-based local economy at the dawn of an urban-based national economy), and, finally, the strong pull of individual opportunity (the northern migration of African Americans fueled by integration) doomed black towns to failure.

This is not to exonerate past history of slavery and Jim Crow, which placed African Americans at a severe initial disadvantage. In addition, the economies of many black towns were weakened by racial discrimination. For example, by withholding tax monies from the black towns—"underestimating the number of pupils, failing to submit reports on time, reducing the length of the school term ... or openly withholding funds [or shifting them to white schools]"—white officials forced the residents of black towns to form private schools or to supplement the public schools from their own pockets.[77] Overt discrimination by private white citizens also limited the economic opportunities of African Americans and thereby weakened the economies of black towns. For example, residents of "Clearview and Boley found it difficult to find work or to rent land outside the immediate vicinity of each town."[78] In 1911, when whites in Oklahoma were afraid that African Americans would take over the state, several white farmers entered into a written covenant to "never rent, lease or sell any land . . . to any person or persons of negro blood, or agent of theirs; unless the land be located more than one mile from a white or Indian resident . . . [and] to avoid the hiring of negro labor."[79]

But even without white discrimination, the black towns' agrarian character—particularly those that concentrated on cotton—ensured their eventual failure. Such towns ran counter to the socioeconomic forces sweeping the country even before emancipation. Their economies were hopelessly dependent upon outside capital and lacked diversification.[80] Norman Crockett puts it well: "For every Dallas, Chicago, Minneapolis, or Tulsa that won out in the race for urban status, a multitude of small towns succumbed to the devastating onslaught of modernization."[81]

12

Intra-Racial Conflicts and Racial Romanticism

As the preceding discussion illustrates, racial separation can highlight internal divisions among African Americans. Removed from the racial prejudices of white society, African Americans are revealed as ordinary human beings, warts and all. This common-sense observation is of sufficient importance, however, to warrant a more focused discussion in this chapter. The point I wish to make—that racial separation does not eliminate the need for antidiscrimination laws, that Title VII will be as needed in an all-black state as it is in today's integrated society—can be exemplified in the phenomenon of color discrimination, the most ancient form of intra-racial discrimination among African Americans. I refer the reader to other writings on other significant forms of intra-racial conflicts: gender;[1] class;[2] and geographic origin.[3]

Color discrimination among African Americans runs both ways: the rejection of dark-skinned African Americans by light-skinned African Americans, and the rejection of light-skinned African Americans by dark-skinned African Americans. Color prejudice of both sorts is rooted in "white racism" and can be more harmful psychologically to African Americans than white prejudice.

Prejudice against dark-skinned individuals is the more prevalent and earlier form of color discrimination, both within and outside the African American community. During slavery, light-skinned African Americans were presumed by whites to be more intelligent, cultured, and "human" than dark-skinned African Americans, because the physical features of the former more closely approximated those of whites. The preference given to this sector of the community was eventually adopted by the African

Americans themselves, both before and after emancipation. Dark-skinned African American males and females showed an unmistakable desire to marry light-skinned African Americans. "Marrying up" gave the dark-skinned spouse easier entry into the African American aristocracy. And, of course, their children inherited this social standing, especially if they also had the right color.[4]

Conversely, dark-skinned African Americans often regarded light-skinned (or "yellow") African Americans as prideful, flighty, and disloyal to their community.[5] The dark-skinned Marcus Garvey went so far as to define an African American as a "person of dark complexion or race."[6]

Color discrimination knows no intellectual boundaries. Even the great scholar and intellectual, W. E. B. Du Bois, was uneasy about his own identity. His writings are full of references to skin tone, the lighter the more becoming. "The subtext of proud hybridization is so prevalent," David Lewis writes, "that the failure to notice it in the literature about him is as remarkable as the complex itself."[7]

Color discrimination was part of the culture in Liberia as well. Liberian society from its inception practiced intra-racial color discrimination. From the very beginning, light-skinned African Americans and mulattos discriminated against dark-skinned African Americans and indigenous Africans. In time, the question of color became less important in Liberia. Intermarriage and procreation soon blurred the color distinctions, which were replaced with class distinctions. Liberian society became stratified in four layers: the Americo-Liberians, the common people, the Congos, and the natives. The colonists and their descendants tenaciously emphasized cultural differences that set them apart from the native Africans.[8]

In some U.S. black towns, the physical characteristics that helped determine the desired social position were the exact opposite of those favored by African Americans living in the larger, predominantly white society. During the years when optimism about the town's future was at its height, citizens rejected light skin color as a status symbol in the community, and individuals with such complexions sometimes suffered.[9] One man reminisced about his childhood in Boley: "I happened to be light-skinned and, boy, did I have a time. Those 'darkies' in Boley don't like light skinned Negroes and they showed it. I was a victim of their prejudice . . . All the boys would refer to each other as 'nigger' . . . but I could never use that word."[10] The man's complexion proved such a disadvantage that he selected a dark-skinned wife so his children "wouldn't have to go through all that mess. . . . It was hell!"[11]

African American leaders in black towns could never totally control those who sought to make skin color a criterion for social position. As each community took shape and as its citizens recognized that the promise of freedom and prosperity was still far from actualization, emphasis on African American pride subsided in some quarters.[12] For example, in 1910 three women in Boley formed a club emphasizing better English, good housekeeping, and social graces, with membership open "only to ladies with light skin."[13] Community reaction was immediate, however. As one resident related, the "crazy bastards tried to organize a 'Blue-Vein Society' ... but we ran them out of town. I helped run them out 'cause we [could not] divide upon the color question."[14]

Color prejudice is not a relic of the past. It is still operative in the African American community. Malcolm X, for example, noted that he "was among the millions of Negroes who were insane enough to feel that it was some kind of status symbol to be light complexioned—that one was actually fortunate to be born thus."[15] Another African American admonishes that "in 1982 color is still a critical issue among our people. We still discriminate against our own. The darker ones against the lighter ones. The light one against the dark."[16] In a 1988 federal case, *Walker v. Secretary of Treasury,* a light-skinned African American woman sued her dark-skinned manager for color discrimination under Title VII.[17]

Aesthetic standards in mainstream society continue to fuel intra-racial color prejudice. The standard in America for feminine beauty is a white woman who is thin, blond, and blue-eyed. Almost every African American girl grows up entertaining at one time or another the fantasy of being white with long, flowing hair or hair that bounces when she walks. Because society places such a high value on a European standard of beauty, many dark-skinned women have suffered psychologically. They feel "ugly" and that they do not have anything to offer society regardless of how intelligent or warm they may be. Skin bleachers may not sell as well as they used to, but they are still advertised in mainstream African American magazines.

The late Supreme Court Justice Thurgood Marshall offered what might be the best explanation for the phenomenon of color discrimination among African Americans:

Social scientists agree that members of minority groups frequently respond to discrimination and prejudice by attempting to disassociate themselves from the group, even to the point of adopting the majority's negative attitudes towards the minority. Such behavior occurs with particular frequency among members of minority groups who have achieved some measure of economic or political success and thereby have gained some acceptability among the dominant group.[18]

Color discrimination and other intra-racial conflicts suggest that there is a continuing need for civil rights laws. The question of color also leads to the related issue of "racial romanticism."

There is a disturbing tendency among many African Americans, desperately seeking to bolster their self-image, to romanticize blackness. Anything authentically black—such as black towns and, of course, Africa—becomes an object of near-worship. But if there is one thing that comes across in Part II, it is that there is no special magic in blackness, here or abroad. African Americans are no more or less moral, altruistic, self-interested, and wise than whites. We are all human, with all our shortcomings.

Racial romanticism has a strong essentialist element. It advances the essentialist claim of epistemic advantage—that the oppressed have not only different ways of knowing but better ways of knowing: "the oppressed may make better biologists, physicists, and philosophers than their oppressors."[19] This claim is highly questionable. As Christina Hoff Sommers has pointed out, "if they were right, the most disadvantaged groups would produce the best scientists. In fact, the oppressed and socially marginalized often have little access to the information and education needed to excel in science, which on the whole puts them at a serious 'epistemic *dis*advantage.' "[20]

III

LIMITED SEPARATION

I don't need to hate white people in order to love myself. But I also don't need white people to tell me what I am or what I can strive to be or tell me if I've made it or not. I don't need to know a white person or know of white people to make a good life for myself or be happy with myself or to love other people whatever color they may be or not be.

—John Edgar Wideman

Throughout the nation's history, African Americans' sentiment has swung back and forth between racial integration and racial separation. The inclination of many African Americans today, even those within the moderate middle class, is in favor of racial separation. Racial integration is not working satisfactorily for the majority of African Americans, as Part I clearly demonstrates. On the other hand, full-blown racial separation, as Part II indicates, is merely a dream that would be problematic even if it could come true. What other solutions are there to the American race problem? In this concluding part I wish to propose a specific policy, limited separation in alliance with racial integration, to advance such a solution.

By "limited separation" I mean African Americans coming together to support each other, but not for the sake of promoting racial kinship, as in some 1960s Black Nationalism replay; the group in this case would seek to promote the welfare of the *individual.* African American public schools, businesses, and communities would be created or redesigned to further self-interest: "It is not from the benevolence of the butcher, the brewer, or the baker that we expect our dinner, but from their regard to their own interest," as Adam Smith wrote in *The Wealth of Nations II.* Each person employs his own felicific calculus; each African American seeks to maximize her own personal happiness. Limited separation, quite simply, is *cultural and economic integration within African American society.*

Like total separation, limited separation is significantly different from racial segregation in that it is voluntary and designed to create a nurturing racial environment. Unlike like total separation, limited separation does not preclude racial mixing. It does not presuppose black nationhood or exclude whites from participating in African American institutions. Furthermore, under limited separation internal exploitation or subordination would not be tolerated. There would be little room for the racial romanticism of total separation, in which it becomes quite acceptable to sacrifice individual rights for the good of the "nation" or the good of the "cause." The individual is king in the realm of limited separation.

Limited separation does not require whites to give up their poker chips; it simply starts another game. In this way, limited separation avoids the Rousseauist type of romanticism that underpins our traditional civil rights policy—racial integration and its crown jewel, affirmative action—in which it is naively expected that whites will act more nobly than African Americans or any other group would act under similar circumstances. It is an extraordinary person who can look beyond her own self-interest when matters of family and financial security are at stake. As luck would have it, the world is made up of mostly ordinary people. Limited separation, then, is a civil rights policy for ordinary people, one that will allow the average white to keep his poker chips.

In sum, limited separation is voluntary racial isolation that serves to support and nurture individuals within the group without unnecessarily trammeling the interests of other individuals or groups. Racial isolation that results from a conscious choice or strategy of self-support by African Americans and that does not unnecessarily subordinate whites individually or collectively is what I mean by limited separation.

This policy is not, however, intended to supersede racial integration. Rather, it is designed to temper racial integration's tendency to place policy before people. Under limited separation, defenseless African American children would not be used for liberal educational experimentation, and there would be no neglecting the special needs of poor and working class African Americans left behind in racially isolated communities after the civil rights movement. Limited separation provides an option to scores of African Americans who do not have the superhuman strength or extraordinary good fortune to make it in racially hostile, predominantly white mainstream institutions. Racial integration and limited separation should be viewed as different paths to racial equality.

Limited separation not only provides a needed option to racial integration, but it can also be a dependable ally. It can lead to two-way racial mixing among whites and African Americans, something the nation has yet to experience. Nurtured in understanding and supportive environments, African American students and professionals will be able to compete toe-to-toe with whites in predominantly white mainstream institutions without the aid and hence the stigma of affirmative action. But the purpose of limited separation is not to keep the races (already significantly separated) separated or to subordinate or stigmatize any race or individual. Rather, it is to create a supportive environment for African Americans in counterpoint to that of debilitating white racism.

True, individual whites may, on occasion, be denied an opportunity. But such denial—what in law we call the use of an exclusionary or restrictive racial classification—could only happen under extraordinary circumstances. For example, a white student could be denied admission to an African American public school located in an inner city if the school has so many white students already in attendance that the enrollment of the additional white student would cause it to lose its institutional identity or focus. Under these circumstances, the use of an exclusionary racial classification is bona fide, and its legality can be argued not only by analogy to current anti-discrimination law (which permits the use of exclusionary classifications based on religion, gender, national origin or age in the workplace), but also on constitutional grounds. But, realistically speaking, most whites will have about as much interest in sending their children to an African American inner city public school as they might have in voting in the dog catcher's election in Sparks County, Alabama.

A more realistic problem is whether limited separation, as an optional civil rights policy, will apply to other minorities, women, and even whites. My response is yes, provided that they observe three conditions equally applicable to African Americans. First, the group seeking limited separation must be able to demonstrate the need for a supportive environment free of debilitating racism or, in the case of gender, sexism. If our mainstream institutions practice the type of racial subordination against other groups that they do against African Americans, if other groups can point to educational, socioeconomic, or political disadvantage due to race or gender, then they satisfy the first condition. White males will have a difficult time meeting this condition because even the "angry" ones are not disadvantaged on account of their race or gender. A distinct white male group must show that its purpose is not to maintain racial or gender domination.

Second, institutions that operate under limited separation must not unnecessarily trammel the interests of other individuals or groups. This means that gratuitous discrimination is prohibited. The institution that chooses limited separation must grant access to individuals from outside the group, so long as these individuals are willing to support the institution's primary objectives. For example, a white student should be allowed to attend a Historically Black College or University (HBCU) so long as he understands that the institution's primary objective is to attend to the special educational needs of African American students. Likewise, an African American lawyer should be allowed to practice law in a small Korean law firm so long as she understands that the law firm's primary objective is to serve the surrounding Korean community, and a Latino graduate of Harvard Business School should not be denied employment with a Wall Street investment banking firm so long as it is understood that the primary objective of the firm is to service large multinational corporations.

Third, the only time an individual can be denied an opportunity on account of his or her race (or gender)—the only time a restrictive classification can be used—is when race (or gender) is a bona fide selection qualification "reasonably necessary to the normal operation of the particular [institution]," to borrow from analogous civil rights law. Race, for example, would constitute a bona fide selection qualification (or "bfsq") if an African American institution were in danger of losing its identity or focus by the admission or hiring of an additional white applicant. Under these very limited circumstances, limited separation remains faithful to its principle of nonsubordination. It does not unnecessarily trammel the interests of others even while it uses racial or gender classifications.

Limited separation is radical yet reasonable. It is the former because it challenges the received tradition—racial integration—as the nation's only legitimate civil rights policy. It is the latter mainly because it is surely needed, given the sad state of racial relations. Not only is it reasonable to ask civil rights organizations to try something new and to invite the Supreme Court to rethink its civil rights stance; it is also time for African Americans to put a constructive policy into action without waiting for a governmental rescue or the goodwill of whites.

After explaining and making the case for limited separation in greater detail, the remaining chapters describe the application of this notion to various areas of American life: elementary and secondary education; higher education; housing; employment; and voting. For those in a hurry, an overview of the application chapters follows.

In the area of education, limited separation gives all parents of all races the option of sending their children to publicly financed integrated or separate schools. The goal is to ensure that all students, especially African American students, will leave public school academically and emotionally prepared to make life better than they find it—that is, "to live more abundantly," as the great African American educator Carter G. Woodson put it. To achieve this objective, public schools will have to change. I ask the reader to visualize education in computer terminology: money is the hardware and academic programming is the software. The academic failure of well-funded public schools in places like Kansas City and Detroit underscores the importance of both hardware and software.

To secure the educational hardware—public financing—of integrated and separate schools, I favor a "revenue" funding system in which schools operating more expensive educational enrichment programs for the poor would receive more public funds on a weighted per pupil basis than other schools.

Regarding educational software, students in both schools will study the best of American culture in addition to the "three Rs." Because we are, as Walt Whitman said, "a nation of nations," the study of American culture is the study of multiculturalism, a reasonable blend of Western civilization, African American heritage, the cultures of other ethnic groups, and women's studies. Tracking and ability grouping will be prohibited. In integrated schools white and African American students will work and play together, and principals and teachers will be taught in ongoing courses how to foster healthy racial relations in the classroom.

Separate schools must observe the three conditions of limited separation discussed earlier. They can only be established if there are no available integrated schools to address the *special* educational needs of a particular racial group: a concern that will reflect the modifications of the software. Separate schools are acceptable only because education is more important than integration. White students or teachers will not be excluded, but they cannot alter the educational software, the mission of such schools, which is to address the special needs of African American children. The software components include parental and community involvement to bridge the gap between home and school; teachers who understand the needs and conflicts African American children face; multiculturalism; a stronger emphasis on African American pride and heritage; and specialized programs for African American boys and teenagers who are most at risk.

Higher education too will be offered in both integrated and separate schools. At predominantly white colleges and universities I would replace affirmative action with the "whole-person theorem" or "public interest affirmative action" (at least until limited separation is firmly in place in the elementary and secondary schools); base financial aid and academic support on need rather than race; require courses in race relations; and encourage multicultural student centers rather than "black houses" or other race-specific centers or dorms. Limited separation certainly embraces the continuation and fostering of Historically Black Colleges and Universities (HBCUs). These institutions of higher education provide opportunities for many African Americans that integrated colleges and universities do not. This is particularly true in the South, where "Blacks and Hispanics still lack equal access to public colleges and universities . . . even though the Supreme Court outlawed segregated schools four decades ago."[1] Justice Thomas's eloquent and effective defense of HBCUs in *United States v. Fordice*[2] merits serious attention.

Limited separation will have its greatest impact on housing and employment. Rather than fighting a frustrating and demeaning battle against housing and employment discrimination, African Americans, like white immigrant groups, should use their residential isolation as a catalyst for individual and group success in America. In the housing context, limited separation means that middle-class African Americans will run toward rather than away from working-class and poor African Americans. The hope is that the human and economic capital withdrawn from African American communities during the civil rights movement, when America's integrationist drive was in high gear, will return to these communities. Separation will establish a physical as well as a cultural and economic basis for worldly success. It will give to African Americans a sense of belonging and with it a foundation on which to build individual and group pride, economic independence, and political strength.

Limited separation will enable poor and underclass African Americans to jettison a self-defeating and dysfunctional culture and adapt to a more middle class, African American culture. Here I disagree with African American conservatives who argue that African Americans as a whole must undertake a cultural adaptation to the white mainstream. I disagree, for example, with Thomas Sowell, who finds a deficiency of human capital among African Americans, and Shelby Steele, who assumes that African American culture is limiting or impoverished. Both writers totally ignore socioeconomic stratification within African American society. Had they taken class stratification into account, I believe they would agree that the solution to the internal problems of African Americans—welfare, crime, drugs, and teenage pregnancy and motherhood—lies in acceptance rather than rejection of African American culture, a culture that is both shared and unique and that I identify as tripartite: a general or shared American culture; a generic African American culture; and a class-based African American culture.

In the economic sector, limited separation will promote economic integration—by which I mean African Americans of all classes coming together as financiers, entrepreneurs, employers, employees, and customers in a complex interchange that is necessary to achieve economic independence. Proceeding from this premise, I will propose a program of African American economic integration and independence centered in small businesses and the Black Church. Small businesses are important because they open employment opportunities for the African American labor force; circulate money within the communities; foster a sense of pride, self-confidence, and optimism, all of which work to reduce crime, welfare dependency, and other social pathologies; provide a new class of positive role models for the African American youth; and promote the entrepreneurial spirit (constructive risk-taking). One instance of the sort of venture I have in mind is the Family Campus Initiative, a joint project run by Yale University and the City of New Haven to turn abandoned buildings (schools, stores, and others) in the poorest communities into "family campuses" housing an array of social services such as health care, child care, and adult education. These campuses could be supported by the city, private businesses, and free services from African American professionals.

Networking, I argue, is the most effective way to obtain the capital and expertise for creating successful small businesses. The Black Church, as a market maker, can bring people with the talent and desire to start or operate a business together with those with funds to invest—entertainers, sports figures, business executives, and professionals. I also propose networking to secure the services of experienced management consultants and to set up educational programs. My proposal will find prototypes in the American immigrant experience and models in the African American past.

Again, limited separation in housing and employment does not necessitate the exclusion of whites from African American communities or businesses: I reject Black Nationalism and its variants. But, as with public schools and HBCUs, African American communities and businesses will attempt to address issues of importance to African Americans. Whites would have to accept that the main purpose of these efforts is to pursue African American institutional objectives.

To be sure, cultural and economic community integration is not for every African American. Some will eschew it altogether, finding integration fulfilling. And others may use it as a stepping stone to racial integration rather than as a permanent way of life, or as a temporary respite from the harrowing experience of racial mixing.

Voting or political power is the final area in which limited separation is applied. The right-to-vote problem is best dealt with by traditional piecemeal litigation under the Voting Rights Act. Unfortunately, this is the only way to enforce compliance with a law that is generally clear and effective. Of course, some of the problems associated with voting may dissipate on their own in African American communities built in the spirit of cultural and economic integration. Presumably, African Americans will be in charge of the election apparatus in such communities.

The voting power problem would be rectified by a two-pronged approach: cumulative voting together with political coalitions buttressed by the Black PAC, or political action committee. My endorsement of cumulative voting—a race-neutral electoral device that allows voters to cast more than one vote for a candidate, depending on the number of contested seats—is conditioned upon its separation from proportionality, which provides that African Americans are entitled to a certain percentage of seats on the governing body. I favor cumulative voting because it favors the success of the individual. In this case, as in the case of all forms of limited separation—separate public schools, HBCUs, and cultural and economic integration—racial kinship is a distant second to individual opportunity; the latter is never to be sacrificed to the former. This puts me at odds not only with Lani Guinier, but also with the Black Nationalists of the 1960s.

Although cumulative voting can increase the ability of African Americans to express their individual political preferences as well as elect the candidates of their choice to office, it cannot completely resolve the voting power problem. Like racial redistricting, cumulative voting only ensures the election of marginalized African American politicians. They are always outnumbered and hence outvoted in their respective deliberative bodies.

To further build African American political power, I propose cross-racial political coalition building and the Black PAC. Admittedly, such coalitions have had limited success, Jesse Jackson's Rainbow Coalition being a prime example. But they will look very different in the context of an overall strategy of limited separation. The probability of success of these coalitions is substantially increased when our most racially divisive issues—such as busing and racial preferences—are taken out of the mix. As an expression of limited separation, the Black PAC is nothing more than a political action committee like the others. With local and national offices, the Black PAC will raise money (in large part from African American businesses and wealthy individuals), refine political ideology beneficial to most African Americans, influence white candidates and office-holders at all levels, and run its own candidates if necessary.

13

The Case for a Policy of Limited Separation

The Essential Features

In proposing limited separation as a legitimate and desirable civil rights policy, I do *not* argue that racial integration should be jettisoned. In a better world I would strongly favor a policy of racial integration over one of limited separation. Even in our imperfect world, I would not personally pursue a course of limited separation, because racial integration has worked well for me and my family. But, as we have seen, it has failed many others. And it just may be that although I have thrived under racial integration thus far, tomorrow may be a different story for me or my children. Hence, notwithstanding my strong personal preference for a policy of racial integration, I think it is necessary to make some form of racial separation available *as an option* for those African Americans or others who need it to legitimately enhance individual opportunity. Limited separation still leaves ample room for many traditional liberal civil rights strategies.

Limited separation, then, promotes racial equality, by which I mean individual dignity and empowerment. It is an aggressive strategy of racial inclusion in mainstream society, providing the best path for many African Americans to achieve worldly success in a racist society without the aid of affirmative action. It leaves African Americans to themselves to create their own "civil rights."

Limited separation can be defined as *any racial or gender classification that promotes individual opportunity but that does not unnecessarily subordinate or trammel the interests of individuals inside or outside the group.* This sort of separation can be established for any racial or gender group. It is not limited to African Americans. To simplify the discussion, my elaboration and application of the concept will, however, focus primarily on African Americans.

Limited separation is allowable only if three conditions are met. The racial classification must have a "good end," a racially compensatory purpose; it must not unnecessarily subordinate individuals within and outside the group; and it may deny an opportunity to a member of another race only if race is established as a bona fide selection qualification (or bfsq). The third condition—the bfsq principle—is obviously an extension of the second condition—the unnecessary subordination principle. I shall elaborate on each condition, or principle, in turn.

Good Ends

A racial classification must have a racially compensatory or worthwhile purpose. This condition is best satisfied when the purpose is to provide a needed supportive environment for individuals within the racial group. In the case of African Americans, this condition is easily met when the purpose of the racial classification is to redress the uneven distribution of poker chips—the socioeconomic and cultural advantages whites have accumulated over African Americans over the years—without attempting a redistribution along racial lines. (Evidence of this unnatural allocation of poker chips is detailed in Part I of the book.)

Any classification designed to ease racial suffering serves a socially worthwhile and even noble end. But it is important to stress that individual opportunity is key to satisfying the good-ends principle. The helping hand must extend to the individual rather than to the group itself. I would therefore disagree with traditional African American separatists like Marcus Garvey and Malcolm X, inasmuch as they saw one form of racial classification—namely, the African American community—as an end in itself. To my mind the community has instrumental rather than intrinsic value; it exists only for the purpose of facilitating opportunities for African Americans individually. Obviously, the group will benefit from the achievements of many individuals, which is quite desirable, but it must be understood that the community exists primarily to serve the individual.

No form of limited separation should sacrifice the individual to the group. I specifically want to avoid the practices of Black Nationalist groups like the Black Panther Party, whose various expressions of racial separatism in the 1960s (school lunch programs, African American heritage events, and community centers) routinely subordinated women, even party members, in the name of some mystical communal purpose. The minute it ceases to serve the individual, limited separation forfeits its legitimacy.

Unnecessary Subordination

The racial classification must help African Americans without unnecessarily hurting whites. An African American institution such as a public school or employer cannot routinely discriminate against whites by barring them from the institution. Even though such preclusion might create opportunities for more African Americans, it would only be acceptable if the admission of whites altered the character and benefits of the institution.

For example, an African American public school established in an African American community must admit white students residing within the school district. There are two conditions for their admission, however. First, they must come with the understanding that this school is set up to deal with the special problems of African American students. Second, they must not tip the school's racial balance from African American to white. This could only happen if the existing white student population is extremely high, which is unlikely. Under these circumstances, race could be considered a bfsq.

Bona Fide Selection Qualification

In civil rights law, some practices otherwise impermissible are deemed permissible under certain circumstances. For example, Title VII of the 1964 Civil Rights Act prohibits employers from making hiring or promotion decisions on the basis of religion, sex, or national origin. An exception is carved out, however, "where religion, sex, or national origin is a bona fide occupational qualification reasonably necessary to the normal operation of that particular business or enterprise."[1] The Supreme Court has interpreted this statement to mean that the employer must have a factual basis for believing that all or substantially all women, for example, would be unable to perform essential job duties safely and efficiently.[2] There is a similar defense for employment decisions based on age under the Age Discrimination in Employment Act,[3] but there is no such defense for race. Congress felt that racial discrimination could never be justified. Of course, this belief has proved to be false, as Congress and the Supreme Court have sustained racial discrimination in the context of affirmative action, at least for now.

I would permit an employer or any other institution to establish a selection qualification in the context of limited separation, to be applied in individual cases rather than systemically. Thus an African American law firm whose essential purpose is to service the legal and social needs of the African American community and to provide positive role models for young African Americans could use the bfsq defense to deny employment to a qualified white attorney if hiring the attorney would impede the firm's ability to fulfill its essential purpose. There would have to be a factual basis to support this belief. Hiring one or a few white lawyers will not satisfy this burden. Hiring enough to change the firm's character from African American to white would. This, of course, is largely a subjective determination, but so are all difficult questions of law.

White law firms may also be able to use the bfsq defense, but it would be harder for them to do so. A large Wall Street law firm, whose essential purpose is to service the legal problems of large corporations, would have a more difficult time establishing the bfsq defense than a small law firm located in Little Italy, there to service the legal and social needs of the Italian community.

If small enough (fewer than 15 employees) the Italian law firm would be exempted from Title VII's prohibition against discrimination anyway. The same holds true for the African American law firm. So my proposal is not as "radical" as it might seem at first glance.

Defense of Limited Separation

Although limited separation does not constitute a "radical" departure from extant civil rights law, I shall endeavor to defend it from two serious charges that might be lodged against it. One is that it may balkanize American society; the other is that it is unconstitutional.

I readily admit that, if not properly managed, any form of group separation can pose a danger to our society even as it promotes individual opportunities. Racial separation in education, housing, employment, and voting can breed a climate of hostility, a pervasive "us-versus-them" attitude. But I believe that limited separation, with constraints on subordination and a wholehearted acceptance of American values (including liberty, individualism, and democracy), provides a way for individuals to mine the benefits of group solidarity without destroying American society.

Indeed, limited separation is likely to result in healthy interracial interaction. In gaining socioeconomic and political strength through limited separation, African Americans will be able to deal with whites and other groups at a more equal level than they do today. Limited separation enables African Americans as a group, and more importantly as individuals, to gain strength and hence the respect of other groups with which they must deal. Through limited separation African Americans become producers rather than mere consumers, victors rather than victims. In this way limited separation is a friend to racial integration.

Balkanization, in the sense of chronic breakout of racial or ethnic violence, is not rooted in U.S. history. Every successful American immigrant group, whether white or minority, has traveled a path similar to limited separation in its quest for respect and empowerment. Most American ethnic groups have been able to reconcile integration with separation, and the integration/separation issue has never been an either/or proposition for them. Some groups, as the Feagins tell us, worked out a degree of cultural adaptation that was necessary to achieve economic success and lessen prejudice and discrimination against them.[4] For example, while some Jewish Americans felt that they must strip off everything that hindered their ability to mix freely with the rest of the population, most Jewish Americans, like other immigrant groups, managed to maintain a distinct cultural identity. If successful American immigrant groups have been partially integrationist and partially separatist, why can't African Americans follow this course?

There are, of course, obvious limitations in the comparison of white or even nonwhite ethnic groups with African Americans. Phenotypical differences have always been, and may continue to be, unassimilable traits in American society. Failure to recognize this important fact can amount to a denial of the pervasiveness and persistence of racial barriers in our society. But what seems applicable is that limited separation—a sense of cultural identity or group solidarity—in education, housing, employment, and politics has provided immigrant groups with a springboard from which to achieve individual success and a certain level of personal satisfaction in American society.

Although there is no dearth of social precedent for limited separation, the most serious challenge to the concept comes from the Supreme Court. In recent years, a majority of the justices have held that all racial classifications in the public sector—for example, in public schools—must pass constitutional muster under the "strict scrutiny test." Initially designed to facilitate close judicial review of Jim Crow legislative enactments, the strict scrutiny test now operates to strike down, as a denial of equal protection of the laws, any government-supported activity or legislation that either is predicated on an explicit racial or other "suspect classification" or violates a "fundamental personal interest."[5]

Surviving strict scrutiny is like climbing Mount Kilimanjaro two times. The strict scrutiny test is " 'strict' in theory and fatal in fact."[6] The Supreme Court has fashioned a standard for applying the strict scrutiny test that is fatal to most acts of government brought under its review. As I explained on another occasion, "an act under scrutiny is saved from judicial strangulation only if the government can meet a twofold burden. First, the classification must be justified by a 'compelling governmental interest.' Second, the means chosen to achieve the classification's purpose must be the least restrictive, most narrowly tailored means available."[7]

Satisfying the first part of the test is extremely difficult. A state or local government's use of racial classifications to remedy its own past intentional discrimination is the only interest that constitutes a "compelling governmental interest," according to the Supreme Court. Unless a public entity admits to practicing discrimination, finding evidence of the governmental body's intentional discrimination is nearly impossible in this era of subtle discrimination.

Furthermore, the Court has ruled that "the level of Fourteenth Amendment 'scrutiny does not change merely because the challenged classification operates against a group that historically has not been subject to governmental discrimination.' "[8] Thus, the strict scrutiny test applies to all racial classifications, whether invidious, as in the days of Jim Crow, or benign, as in the case of limited separation. Both invidious and benign racial classifications are thereby put at equal legal risk under the Constitution.

The color-blind principle is the major justification for applying the strict scrutiny test to benign racial classifications. Justice Stewart, quoting from Justice Harlan's dissenting opinion in *Plessy v. Ferguson,* articulated the principle as follows: " 'Our Constitution is color-blind, and neither knows nor tolerates classes among citizens . . . The law regards man as man, and takes no account of his surroundings or his color.' "[9] Not surprisingly, Justice Stewart viewed all racial classifications as invidious.[10]

Justice Scalia has provided a spirited defense of the color-blind principle in the context of affirmative action:

> The difficulty of overcoming the effects of past discrimination is as
> nothing compared with the difficulty of eradicating from our society

the source of those effects, which is the tendency—fatal to a Nation such as ours—to classify and judge men and women on the basis of their country of origin or the color of their skin. A solution to the first problem that aggravates the second is no solution at all. I share the view expressed by Alexander Bickel that "[t]he lesson of the great decisions of the Supreme Court and the lesson of contemporary history have been the same for at least a generation: discrimination on the basis of race is illegal, immoral, unconstitutional, inherently wrong, and destructive of democratic society."[11]

What Justice Scalia and other proponents of the color-blind principle ignore, however, is that when this principle is examined in terms of its cultural context, its unconscious cultural connotation, it is very much a racially subordinating principle. It denies black identity and favors white identity by making the latter the "default" cultural standard in matters ranging from beauty to intelligence. When Americans think of "color-blind," they see white, not black or even monochrome. This places African Americans in the untenable position of having to shed their cultural trappings if they are to be successful. True, white ethnic groups have had to shed some of theirs to advance in the mainstream culture. But these ethnic groups possess physical traits that have shortened the leap across the cultural divide. Few African Americans are able to jump from chocolate to vanilla. Color matters greatly.

Along with its failure to recognize, let alone redress, the default culture's devaluation of the Negroid phenotype, the color-blind principle discounts the African American world view, particularly when it is in conflict with the white perspective. To understand this point, one need only remember the disbelief, dismay, and derision of whites, only three years after the Rodney King video, when faced with the widespread belief of African Americans in a police conspiracy or code of silence in the O. J. Simpson trial. The subordinating quality of the color-blind principle is precisely why the principle is so myopic, so unfair to African Americans. It is also why we simply cannot measure racial progress, as so many whites do, by the extent to which society transcends race-consciousness.

In addition to the cultural critique, the color-blind principle is subject to two other criticisms. First, it has failed to help African Americans achieve full racial equality. Indeed, Justice Harlan made it clear in *Plessy* that color blindness would not lead to a restructuring of the social order. He believed that whites would retain their social dominance under a color-blind Constitution, and so they have.[12] Second, the color-blind principle cannot be solidly supported by a close reading of the constitutional text or its legislative history. The central constitutional question is whether the original intent of the Fourteenth Amendment's Equal Protection Clause—No state shall . . . deny to any person within its jurisdiction the equal protection of the laws"—permits the states or their political subdivisions to establish classifications that favor minorities or women if they do not subordinate or stigmatize white males. Admittedly, any answer to this question is going to be problematic. As historian Eric Foner states:

> For more than a century, politicians, judges, lawyers, and scholars have debated the meaning of this elusive language. The problem of establishing the Amendment's "original intent" is complicated by the fact that its final wording resulted from a series of extremely narrow votes in the Joint Committee and subsequent alteration on the floor of Congress. To complicate matters further, the broadest statements of the Amendment's purposes originated with opponents, who, in an attempt to discredit the measure, claimed it would destroy the powers of the states, establish equality "in every respect" between black and white, and empower Congress to legislate on any local matter it chose—an interpretation Republicans vehemently denied.
>
> Whether the courts *should* be bound by the "original intent" of a constitutional amendment is a political, not an historical question. But the aims of the Fourteenth Amendment can only be understood within the political and ideological context of 1866: the break with the President, the need to find a measure upon which all Republicans could unite, and the growing consensus within the party around the need for strong federal action to protect the freedmen's rights, short of the suffrage. Despite the many drafts, changes, and deletions, the Amendment's central principle remained constant: a national guarantee of equality before the law.[13]

Taking a broader view of congressional activity during Reconstruction may add insight into the constitutional question. The Thirty-Ninth Congress not only proposed the Fourteenth Amendment but also, in the same year, enacted both the Civil Rights Act of 1866 and the race-conscious law, the Freedmen's Bureau Act of 1866. The Freedmen's Act mandated that newly freed slaves be given food, clothing, legal assistance, special schools, and other services to help them adjust to a new way of life in America. Eric Schnapper explains the significance of this legislative activity:

> The composition of the majority supporting the amendment was nearly identical to that which supported the Act . . .
>
> [T]he supporters of the Act and the amendment regarded them as consistent and complementary, and opponents viewed the two, together with the Civil Rights Act of 1866, as part of a single coherent policy. No member of Congress hinted at any inconsistency between the Fourteenth Amendment and the Freedmen's Bureau Act.[14]

Although clouded, the legislative history makes it clear that the Thirty-Ninth Congress did not view the Fourteenth Amendment as vindicating a color-blind principle: some racial classifications were permissible. This was also the Supreme Court's view of the Fourteenth Amendment at the time. Most of the justices read the Amendment as a prohibition against governmental subordination or stigmatization of identifiable racial groups. As we shall see, this view of the Amendment, which would uphold the constitutionality of limited separation, is evident in many Supreme Court cases decided between the 1880s and the 1980s. This is not to say that the color-blind principle is nowhere to be found in Supreme Court cases prior to the 1980s. My point is simply that it was not until *Croson*, decided in 1989, that a majority of the Supreme Court justices began to consistently interpret the Fourteenth Amendment as a vindication of the color-blind principle, rejecting in the process truly benign racial classifications—those that neither subordinate nor stigmatize.

A brief historical review of the relevant precedents follows.[15] This more technical presentation is necessary because the adoption of limited separation as an official civil rights policy requires the Court to rethink its reading of the Equal Protection Clause in light of its own precedents.

Strauder v. West Virginia[16] was one of the first Supreme Court cases to suggest that the Fourteenth Amendment is not a color-blind provision, that it does not invalidate all racial classifications but only those that promote the sense that one racial group is inferior to another racial group. *Strauder* overturned a statute that prohibited African Americans from serving on juries. Because the statute singled out African Americans and denied them the right to sit on a jury, the Court concluded that there was "practically a brand upon them, affixed by law, an assertion of their inferiority."[17]

Neal v. Delaware[18] also supports the nonsubordination criterion. In this case, Delaware's jury selection process excluded African Americans "solely because in the judgment of those officers . . . the black race in Delaware were utterly disqualified by want of intelligence, experience, or moral integrity, to sit on juries."[19] Because these officials obviously promoted the idea that African Americans were inferior to other races, the Court invalidated Delaware's jury selection process under the Fourteenth Amendment.

In *Yick Wo v. Hopkins*,[20] the Court held unconstitutional a municipal ordinance that prohibited wooden buildings from being used as laundries and denied business licenses to those who sought to run laundries out of such buildings. Although the stated purpose for the ordinance was to regulate businesses in the interest of public safety, the Supreme Court found the ordinance's true purpose was to run the Chinese out of business. Significantly, *all* Chinese applicants were denied business licenses under this ordinance. Although the ordinance appeared neutral, its enforcement effectively prohibited the Chinese alone from running laundry facilities, clearly a form of racial subordination.[21]

Plessy v. Ferguson[22] upheld a statute that separated African American passengers from white passengers in railway cars. The Supreme Court accepted the argument that the statute's racial distinction "has no tendency to destroy the legal equality of the races, or reestablish a state of involuntary servitude."[23] This view of the statute gave birth to the Court's "separate but equal" doctrine. What is so revealing about this opinion is that the Court addressed the contention of the plaintiff that the statute stamped African Americans with a "badge of inferiority."[24] The Court responded that such a suggestion of inferiority did not arise from the statute itself but from its interpretation by African Americans. It is of some moment that the Court found it necessary to rebut the charges of racial subordination. If the Fourteenth Amendment vindicated only the color-blind principle, there would be no need to discuss the issue of racial subordination. Because the Court did not find racial subordination in *Plessy*, it concluded that the statute was constitutional. The Court should have deferred to the African American perspective on the matter.

Popular opinion traces the color-blind principle to Justice Harlan's dissenting opinion in *Plessy*, in which he declared that "our Constitution is color-blind." Alexander Aleinikoff argues that Justice Harlan did not intend this phrase to be taken as a constitutional enshrinement of the color-blind principle. Rather, he saw it as a denunciation of white supremacy, a constitutional rejection of a racial caste system.[25]

In *Williams v. Mississippi*,[26] African Americans were denied the right to serve on grand juries. Here too the Court upheld the constitutionality of this exclusion, at least in part on the ground that the law creating the exclusion had not been proved "evil."[27] Once again, it was important to the Court that the laws themselves did not stigmatize nor subordinate African Americans.

Likewise, in *Cummings v. Richmond County Board of Education*,[28] the board of education's use of tax funds to build a high school for white children without providing a similar school for "colored children" was deemed to be in the best interests of the latter. Hence the Supreme Court saw no need to interfere in this case. Indeed, the Supreme Court stated that it would only intervene in school cases involving a "clear and unmistakable disregard of rights secured by the supreme law of the land."[29] Because the Court deemed the board's use of tax funds to be in the best interests of African American children, the board's decision was left intact.

Another challenge to a grand jury selection process that excluded African Americans from participating was made in *Rogers v. Alabama*.[30] Here, the Court stated that the process would be unconstitutional if it could be shown that the purpose of the exclusion was to "keep [African Americans] from having any part in the administration of the government or of the law."[31] If this was indeed the motivation behind the practice, it would be an outright attempt to exclude African Americans from enjoying full social and political rights, thereby subordinating them as a racial class.

In *Nixon v. Herndon*,[32] a state statute prohibited African Americans from participating and voting in a Democratic primary election. The statute violated the Fourteenth Amendment, the Supreme Court said, because the Amendment was passed specifically to "protect blacks from discrimination against them."[33] Five years later, in *Nixon v. Condon*,[34] a new statute enacted in response to the *Herndon* decision was challenged and also struck down. Although the challenged statute was different from the statute at issue in *Herndon*, the outcome remained the same for the same reasoning. The Court expressly ruled that the Fourteenth Amendment encompassed a "special solicitude for the equal protection of members of the Negro race"[35] and for that reason statutes that *harm* African Americans required close scrutiny by the courts.

Kotch v. Board of River Port Pilot Com'rs for Port of New Orleans[36] is a case in which the analysis appears to support limited separation. Admittedly, the case does not involve a racial classification; however, the New Orleans requirement that river pilots must complete a six-month apprenticeship under an incumbent pilot did result in a form of discrimination, in a broad sense. This requirement placed a burden on one group, potential river pilots, that it did not place on other groups. The classification, the Court reasoned, did not violate the Fourteenth Amendment because it did not "deny a person a right to earn a living or hold any job because of *hostility* to his particular race, religion, beliefs, or because of any other reason having no rational relation to the regulated activities"[37] (emphasis added). Thus the Court in *Kotch* appeared to support the theory that discriminatory laws, by extension those that are based on racial classifications for example, are constitutional so long as they are not based on hostility against any race; that is, involve no racial subordination or stigmatization.

In *McLaurin v. Oklahoma State Regents for Higher Education*,[38] African American graduate students were required to sit in a designated row in classes, sit at a separate table in the library to study, and sit at a separate table in the cafeteria. The Court recognized that such racial separation placed a stigma on African American students. The racial separation in these circumstances promoted the idea that African Americans are inferior to whites.[39] Because of such racial subordination and stigmatization, the Court invalidated the practice under the Fourteenth Amendment.

Sweatt v. Painter[40] dealt with a petition to compel the admission of an African American to a state-supported all-white law school. A new, non-accredited law school for African American students was available to the applicant. In response to the argument that excluding African American students from the white law school "is no different from excluding white students from the new law school,"[41] the Court stated that "this contention overlooks realities"[42]—white students would not want to attend the African American school because it was not accredited and thus inferior to the white school.

Proponents of the color-blind principle invariably cite *Brown v. Board of Education*[43] in support of it. But the opinion does not so much as mention the word "color-blind" or refer to Justice Harlan's dissent in *Plessy*, where the term is used. The Supreme Court in *Brown* ruled that "separate educational facilities are inherently unequal." At the time of *Brown*, that was certainly true, not only in Topeka, Kansas, but in most other Jim Crow school districts across the country. "The policy of separating the races is usually interpreted as denoting the inferiority of the Negro group," the Court noted.[44] That statement and the fact that the plaintiffs would not have had legal standing to bring the case had the segregated schools' funding been *greater* than that of the white schools, indicate that the Court only invalidated those racial classifications that subordinate or stigmatize a racial group. The same must be said of *Bolling v. Sharpe*,[45] in which the Court, on the same day that it decided *Brown*, overturned a school segregation law in Washington, D.C. School segregation in the nation's capital was unconstitutional, the Court said, because it was not "reasonably related to any proper governmental objective, and thus it imposes on Negroes a burden."[46] In short, *Brown* and *Bolling* can be read as vindicating the non-subordination principle rather than the color-blind principle.

In the years following *Brown*, the Supreme Court continued to denounce racial subordination in a number of cases. For example, the Supreme Court invalidated a desegregation plan in *Goss v. Board of Education*[47] because the racial classifications at issue in that case were deemed to be "obviously irrelevant and invidious."[48] A Louisiana statute that required voting ballots to designate the race of each candidate was struck down in *Anderson v. Martin*.[49] The Court reasoned that this requirement had a "repressive effect"[50] on African Americans. Racial subordination was also the key factor in the Court's ruling in *Loving v. Virginia*,[51] which overturned an anti-miscegenation statute forbidding any marriage between whites and African Americans. Although both races were punished equally under the statute, the Fourteenth Amendment, the Court ruled, requires an inquiry into whether the classification based on race is arbitrary and invidious. In this case, the Court concluded that the racial classification was adopted in order to "maintain white supremacy."[52] *Hunter v. Erickson*[53] is similar to *Loving* in that on its face the challenged law, a city charter amendment regulating transfers of real estate on the basis of race, treated all races in an identical manner. As in *Loving*, the Court ruled that the racial classification was unconstitutional because, in reality, it had a detrimental impact on minorities. The Court opted for substance over form.

In *Swann v. Charlotte-Mecklenburg Board of Education*,[54] the Supreme Court reaffirmed the proposition that racially segregated schools are inherently unequal. The Court went on to rule that courts have equitable power to remedy constitutional violations in school desegregation cases. Critical to the ruling was the fact that although a desegregation plan had been in place for three years, a dual school system continued to exist. This moved the Court to rule that all dual systems embrace invidious discrimination. When the persons controlling the school system cannot be trusted, as in cases like *Brown* or *Swann*, then a dual system should be presumed to be unequal. But when equality can clearly be established, the presumption is obviously invalid.

The same principle can be clearly seen in *United Jewish Organizations v. Carey*.[55] In this case, the Supreme Court upheld the constitutionality of a race-conscious redistricting plan that favored African Americans. White Hasidic Jews challenged the plan on grounds that it diminished their voting effectiveness and employed a racial classification. The Court, however, held that the plan "represented no racial slur or stigma with respect to whites or any other race."[56]

Contrary to popular opinion, *Regents of the University of California v. Bakke*[57] does not establish (or re-establish if one assumes that *Brown* established) the color-blind principle in constitutional law. In *Bakke*, a divided Supreme Court ruled five to four that state educational institutions could not set aside a specific number of slots for which only racial minorities could compete. Of the majority, only Justice Powell rested his decision on the Constitution (the Equal Protection Clause). Justice Stevens and the other three justices who joined in his opinion (Burger, Stewart, and Rehnquist) felt that there was no need to reach the constitutional issue because the quota could be invalidated on statutory grounds. They specifically held that the quota violated Title VI of the 1964 Civil Rights Act, which prohibits federal funds from going to programs that discriminate on the basis of race, color, or national origin.[58]

Going the opposite direction, the Court also ruled five to four that the Equal Protection Clause does allow state educational institutions to use race in "a properly devised admissions program." For Justice Powell, race could be used only as one factor in the admissions process and only to achieve a diverse student body. But for Justices Brennan, White, Marshall, and Blackmun, race could be used to counteract the lingering effects of prior racial subordination (including societal discrimination) as well as present-day racial subordination. Unlike Justice Powell, the other four justices would uphold the constitutionality of a racial classification if it did not stigmatize, stereotype, or otherwise burden other groups. Hence, Justice Brennan's group read the Fourteenth Amendment not as a codification of the color-blind principle but as a prohibition against racial classifications that subordinate or stigmatize a racial group. Justice Brennan correctly notes that "no decision of this Court has ever adopted the proposition that the Constitution must be color-blind."[59]

Although not involving a racial classification, *Mississippi University for*

Women v. Hogan[60] is instructive. Here the Court explicitly recognized that "in limited circumstances, a gender-based classification . . . can be justified if it intentionally and directly assists members of the sex that is disproportionately burdened."[61] In *Hogan,* the Mississippi University for Women, a nursing school, refused to admit a male applicant; the Court struck down this gender classification because women were not burdened in the nursing field. Making an analogy to race-based classifications, it could be argued that such classifications are constitutional if they are not meant to stigmatize or subordinate but rather to aid disadvantaged racial groups.

Although the Court decided many racial classification cases in the 1980s, it was not until 1989 in *City of Richmond v. J. A. Croson Company*[62] that a majority of the justices adopted the color-blind principle. Richmond required contractors to subcontract at least 30% of the dollar amount of each contract or more to a "minority business enterprise." This requirement could be waived if there were an insufficient number of qualified minority businesses available. The opinion broadly stated that "classifications based on race carry the danger of stigmatic harm."[63] The Court thereby chose to draw a bright-line rule that doomed all racial classifications. But such a rule reveals judicial laziness. The rule is designed to ease the burden on courts in distinguishing between good and bad racial classifications. Rather than looking closely to determine whether a particular racial classifications does *in fact* burden or stigmatize a racial group, the courts can now presume that they all do. As the Court itself noted, "the standard of review under the Equal Protection Clause is not dependent on the race of those burdened or benefitted by a particular classification."[64] Since *Croson,* a sharply divided Supreme Court has extended the color-blind principle to other affirmative action cases and voting rights cases.[65]

The Supreme Court, in short, did not begin to consistently interpret the Fourteenth Amendment as a color-blind principle rather than as a non-subordination principle until the late 1980s. This was the wrong turn to take, in my judgment, because it treats racial classifications resulting in racial inequality *pari passu* (on an equal footing) with those that promote racial equality. I claim the *Strauder* line of cases and, hence, the weight of precedents as legal support for a socially beneficial policy—that of limited separation.

14

Elementary and Secondary Education

If integration is going to work for African Americans, their children must grow into adults who can cope with racial indignities and discrimination, because these will not go away in an integrated society. Dignity harms in restaurants, shopping malls, and other places of public accommodation, as well as discriminatory episodes within the workplace are the unfortunate byproducts of racial mixing.

Preparing African American children for this challenge necessarily begins in the elementary and secondary schools, which can help students build the academic and emotional strengths they need for succeeding in a culturally diverse society. Integrated (or primarily white) schools do not currently perform these tasks for most African American children. The educational process in these schools will, therefore, have to be reconstructed to ensure academic performance and to nurture self-esteem and racial esteem in African American children.

But some African American children, particularly little boys, may need an even more special educational environment in which to mature into productive citizens. Accordingly, African American parents must be given the *option* of sending their children either to integrated or to separate (or predominantly African American) publicly financed schools. This option must be made available to all parents of all races, provided the conditions for limited separation can be satisfied. African American public schools will have to eliminate the educational deficiencies that encumber today's *de facto* segregated schools.

My call for integrated and separate schools should not be taken as a repudiation of *Brown,* but rather as a reconstruction of *Brown* in light of current social conditions. To make *Brown* work does not necessitate that public schools be racially mixed at every educational level all the time. *Brown*'s promises of solid academic performance and healthy identity for African American children can be achieved if we allow for limited forms of racial separation at strategic points in the educational process. Taken as a whole, my proposal for educational reform is designed to ensure that African American students who attend public schools will leave these institutions academically and emotionally prepared "to live more abundantly," to make life better than they find it, as Carter G. Woodson instructs.[1]

Necessarily, then, the discussion will extend beyond limited separation and include integrated schools. The question of school funding is also quite germane. This rather comprehensive educational proposal touches upon three interrelated topics presented in the following order: (1) adequate educational funding for integrated and separate schools; (2) the integrated school model; and (3) the African American school model.

Adequate Educational Funding

In most states public schools are funded through a combination of local, state, and federal monies. Local funding sources account for about 50% of these monies, while federal funding sources, largely disbursed for special education programs, account for only about 6%. Local property taxes constitute the primary source of local funding. This has been the historical pattern.[2]

With each school district primarily relying upon local tax receipts to fund educational operations, the level of school funding varies. This, of course, results in intrastate funding discrepancies; school districts situated in wealthy communities receive more educational funding than school districts located in poor communities.

Lawsuits have been filed over the years in federal and state courts to challenge such funding schemes. These lawsuits have not been successful at the federal level. For example, in the seminal federal case, *San Antonio Independent School District v. Rodriguez*,[3] a class action was brought on behalf of poor minority children who resided in a low-tax school district. The lawsuit challenged the school funding system as a violation of the Equal Protection Clause of the Constitution. A divided Supreme Court rejected this challenge, holding that there is no fundamental right in our society to receive an education. The Court also held that the state's funding scheme did not deny the plaintiffs the equal protection of the law because it was rationally related to a legitimate state interest, namely, local control of school districts.

Challenges in state courts have been more successful. In addition to an equal protection clause, virtually every state constitution has an education clause, which typically mandates that schools must adequately prepare students to function in society. The following clause is part of the Massachusetts Constitution of 1780:

> Wisdom and knowledge, as well as virtue, diffused generally among the body of the people, being necessary for the preservation of their rights and liberties; and as these depend on spreading the opportunities and advantages of education in the various parts of the country, and among the different orders of the people, it shall be the duty of legislatures and magistrates, in all future periods of this Commonwealth, to cherish the interests of literature and the sciences, and all seminaries of them; especially the university at Cambridge, public schools and grammar schools in the towns.

While some state supreme courts have upheld state educational funding schemes on the basis of the state's equal protection clause alone or in conjunction with the state's education clause,[4] other state supreme courts have struck down such schemes on identical grounds.[5] Significantly, when a state court does find a constitutional violation, it typically does not fashion a remedy but rather leaves it to the legislative and executive branches to devise a remedy that assures equal protection or adequate education.[6]

State legislatures and executive branches use various educational financing schemes to fulfill their constitutional duty. These financing schemes either seek to reduce the differences in school revenues on a per student basis *(revenue equity systems),* or they attempt to reduce variations in taxpayer burden *(taxpayer equity systems).* Combining several different funding sources (local property or sales taxes or state sales or income taxes), a revenue equity system might attempt to achieve parity by having "no more than a 1.5 to 1 ratio between the 95th and the 5th percentile districts in per pupil revenues."[7] On the other hand, a taxpayer equity system might "allow no more than a 1.5 to 1 ratio between the 95th and the 5th percentile districts in operating tax rates per $100 of Equalized Assessed Valuation."[8]

In *Savage Inequalities,* Jonathan Kozol correctly observes that "the various 'formulas' conceived—and reconceived each time there is a legal challenge—to achieve some equity in public education have been almost total failures."[9] In the absence of legal or moral prohibition against wealthy families contributing money and time to their children's schools through PTG, PTA, Boosters, or other private organizations, it is clear that equalized educational funding is an impossible goal. Even Michigan's highly touted state-wide sales tax and fifty-cent cigarette tax, which virtually replaced the property tax funding system,[10] cannot equalize educational funding in the face of this natural loophole. (The Michigan scheme appears to be based on revenue equity rather than taxpayer equity.) Sales taxes are also regressive in that they disproportionately affect low-income consumers, who spend a greater portion of their disposable income on taxable goods. Furthermore, the revenue from sales taxes tends to decline in times of recession.

In light of these considerations, I do not propose a scheme of equalized school funding for integrated and separate schools. Rather, I favor a revenue system based on local property taxes (households and businesses), to be collected into a state educational fund and redistributed in a manner that is similar to a vertical pupil equity system. Schools running relatively expensive special educational programs would receive more public funds on a weighted per pupil basis than other schools because the added funds are needed to adequately meet the educational needs of their students. I would not try to "equalize" educational funding beyond this point.

My rather modest proposal assumes a certain relationship between educational funding and academic programs. Money is the "hardware" of the educational enterprise; academic programming is the "software." Without the latter, all the gold in Fort Knox will not improve academic performance.

This is one of the findings of the Harvard Project on School Desegregation. Studying academic achievement in well-funded *de facto* segregated schools in Kansas City, Detroit, Little Rock, Prince George's County, and Austin, the Harvard Project researchers conclude "that there [is] no evidence that the efforts to target compensatory dollars on segregated inner city schools had produced substantial gains for the minority students."[11] In the case of the Kansas City schools, which were given $1.2 billion between 1987 and 1993, the Project reports that

> educational achievement data, as measured by standardized tests, is [sic] promising but inconclusive ... Preliminary analysis of com-

parative data on nationally normed tests suggests that while there has been an absolute increase in performance, it is unclear how students would compare to current national norms. Meanwhile, statewide criterion-referenced tests provide no evidence that the district's performance is improving compared to the state as a whole. Finally, analysis of attendance and persistence to graduation rates has not revealed any clear positive trends since the [funding began].[12]

Commenting on this report, Gary Orfield, the director of the Harvard Project, writes: "If simply funnelling large amounts of money and choice into a system can produce large educational gains, we should see them in Kansas City. But in her study, Alison Morantz [the project analyst] finds that there have been some apparent educational gains, but that they have basically followed overall national trends and are likely not evidence of an educational breakthrough."[13]

These findings underscore the significance of educational "software"—the instructional component. Below are the educational programs I would load into integrated and African American schools if I were the Education Czar.

Improving Integrated Public Schools

African American students attending integrated public schools typically experience low academic achievement and low self-esteem, both largely attributed to a racially biased educational process. A multicultural curriculum may be the best response to a racially biased educational system. Multiculturalism incorporates Western and American minority cultures without stigmatizing any group. It is neither all white nor only white and African American, leaving out other minorities or women. A reasonable inclusion of the cultures that come together in our diverse society will help African American and other minority students feel less conspicuous, as well as make all students more sensitive to matters of diversity. Students will learn what Walt Whitman, America's greatest poet, meant when he said: "We are a nation of nations."

Even if properly conceived, a multicultural curriculum can be destructive if improperly implemented. One study, for example, found that African American students in a curriculum that included African American history classes came away with negative attitudes toward integration. Their interracial contacts also declined. Researchers attribute these results to the fact that the classes were offered as electives rather than requirements. Few white students enrolled in the classes, which took on a them-versus-us appearance.[14] Likewise, African American history classes and cultural events like Black History Month can harm self-esteem and nurture white racism when they dwell on slavery, the subordination of African Americans in our society, and other negative aspects of their experience to the exclusion of all else. To counter this effect academic exercises like the Black Americans of Achievement board game are important. Learning, for example, that an African American (Garrett Morgan) invented the gas mask helps African American students to love themselves and their race, and white students to respect African Americans as contributing members of our society.

African American history classes at the elementary or secondary level ought to be incorporated into the regular American history courses. These courses can present historical events that portray minorities in a positive and truthful light. Moreover, they would expose all students to multiethnic history and thereby raise awareness of the many contributions minorities have made to our country. Individual and group pride among minorities would be advanced, and all students would gain exposure to aspects of America they might not have otherwise encountered. The payoff, it is hoped, would be better academics and better racial relations.

In implementing an effective multicultural curriculum, tracking and ability groupings should be avoided. Tracking often results in unhealthy racial separation within integrated schools, what Jennifer Hochschild calls "second-generation discrimination" and "resegregation." Integrated schools with one-race classrooms are breeding grounds for racial conflicts and racial stigmatization. If tracking must be used, it should be carefully administered by enlightened staff members who would regulate the number of African American students placed in low-ability groups and encourage African American and white students with similar abilities to work together.

Instead of tracking, schools should adopt a team approach. Teachers should assign white and African American students to work together as in teams. African American students will develop a more positive attitude toward school and their white peers, not to mention themselves. Academic achievement of all students and better racial relations would result in the end. Of course, African American self-esteem could easily decline and white racism just as easily increase if the teams are not properly drawn among students of roughly equal academic ability.[15] The African American team member would have to carry his or her own weight.

Participation in extracurricular activities, from sports to field trips, must be made equally available to all racial groups. Researchers have found that participation in extracurricular activities nurtures a sense of accomplishment and confidence that carries over into the academic arena. However, these extracurricular activities must have strong faculty leadership, encourage all students to participate, promote racial mixing, and involve diverse student interests.[16]

One of the most important variables in providing a good integrated educational program is the attitude of staff toward students. After correlating teachers' and principals' attitudes with students' perceptions of such attitudes and with the overall effectiveness of the school, one study found that teachers' racial attitudes have a tremendous impact upon the students. Teachers with racially progressive attitudes serve as good examples for white students and make African American students feel more comfortable. These teachers also have higher scholastic expectations for African American students, which leads to higher academic performance. Likewise, the principal's attitude toward race and integration is a major factor in the success or failure of school integration. The principal often sets the tone for the entire staff. Similarly, a student's attitude toward her principal is a strong indicator of her attitude toward education in general. A student who likes his principal is likely to have not only a favorable racial attitude but also a sense of belonging to the school and a feeling that the rules governing student conduct are fair.[17]

Accordingly, both teachers and principals must be trained to teach and to interact with heterogeneous groups, including students who are poor and poorly educated. School personnel must be able to identify stereotyping and other kinds of discriminatory behavior in others as well as in themselves. They must have knowledge of different groups' histories, attitudes, behaviors, and learning styles. Furthermore, they must learn techniques for avoiding crises and relieving daily tensions, both in and outside the classroom. Through their expertise and networks, school counselors can strongly affect the integration process. They should be trained not only in race relations but in helping students gain access to higher education, higher status occupations, and higher income. Like all school personnel, counselors must learn how to prevent and cope with racial conflict. Moreover, their ranks must be thoroughly integrated.[18]

With the implementation of these educational components, it may be possible to accomplish high achievement and self-esteem levels in African American students without resorting to separate schools. Studies show that when interracial contact takes place in a supportive environment and when parents get involved in the educational process, relations between the races improve.[19] Multiethnic curricula and frank discussions of racial relations also decrease hostilities between African American and white students.[20]

Unfortunately, these proposals will not occur without opposition and delay. Accepting the idea of multiculturalism, which suffers a bad reputation in many quarters, will not be easy for many teachers and school administrators. In the time that it takes to reeducate teachers, revise texts, establish new administrative procedures and policies, and cultivate public acceptance and support for a nation-wide multicultural public school system, yet another generation of African American children will have fallen victim to the struggle for equal opportunity in education. Even when fully implemented, these proposals may not meet the academic needs of poor and working-class African American students. The need for African American schools seems quite clear.

African American Public Schools

Black people must not resign themselves to the pessimistic view that a non-integrated school cannot provide Black children with an excellent educational setting. Instead, Black people, while working to implement *Brown*, should recognize that integration alone does not provide a quality education, and that much of the substance of quality can be provided to Black children in the interim.[21] . . .

Theoretically, the Negro needs neither segregated schools nor mixed schools. What he needs is Education. What he must remember is that there is no magic, either in mixed schools or in segregated schools. A mixed school with poor and unsympathetic teachers, with hostile public opinion, and no teaching of truth concerning black folk, is bad. A segregated school with ignorant placeholders, inadequate equipment, poor salaries and wretched housing is equally bad. Other things being equal, the mixed school is the broader more natural basis for the education of all youth. It gives wider contacts: it inspires greater self-confidence; and suppresses the inferiority complex. But other things seldom are equal, and in that case, Sympathy, Knowledge, and the Truth outweigh all that the mixed school can offer.[22]

Because "other things seldom are equal," African American parents must be given the option of sending their children to public schools that are designed to meet the special needs of their children. What African American schools will lack in racial integration, they will gain in quality education. Quoting Du Bois again, "we shall get a finer, better balance of spirit; an infinitely more capable and rounded personality by putting children in schools where they are wanted, and where they are happy and inspired, than in thrusting them into hells where they are ridiculed and hated."[23] African American schools, like integrated schools, must seek to raise academic achievement and self-esteem in African American students. But by removing students from the indifference or hostility of integrated schools, African American schools, unlike integrated schools, allow their students to learn and grow in a more natural and stress-free way. To the extent that separate schools can do this, they will have provided young African Americans with the skills needed to thrive in a predominantly white and often racist society.

Derrick Bell correctly points out that in cities such as Milwaukee, where many African American students attend schools that are both "racially isolated and educationally inept, the goal of racial balance is neither feasible nor required by law."[24] Under *Brown* and its progeny, the courts are unable to offer relief to one-race schools that result indirectly from housing patterns rather than directly from intentional discrimination.[25]

I envision African American schools to be separate and equal. They are "separate" rather than "segregated" because they are *chosen* by African Americans for the quality of their educational programs rather than imposed on them by default; because they are controlled by African Americans rather than whites; because they have educational programs tailored to the special needs of African American children rather than to those of children in general; and because they educate and nurture African American children without subordinating or stigmatizing white children. They are "equal" because their academic programs are first-rate and they are funded adequately.

If attending a *de facto* segregated school is the only viable alternative for low income, inner-city African American children, why not turn these schools into African American schools? Judge Robert Carter has admonished us that "quality education is essential to the survival of hundreds of thousands of black children who now seem destined for the dunghill in our society."[26] Education is often the only way out of a community infested with poverty, crime, drug abuse, and broken families.

Some people may be concerned that separate schools might inhibit the ability of students to live or work productively in an integrated society. This used to be a traditional concern about single-sex schools, until it was shown that graduates of schools for women were overrepresented in traditional male jobs, in comparison with their peers from coed schools. For example, "Wellesley women take up far more seats in executive suites and corporate boardrooms than their numbers suggest they should have."[27]

Several African American professional organizations have created excellent academic programs for private (or "community") schools that can be imported, with slight modification, into African American public schools. The concept of community schools was developed by the African-American Teachers Association (AATA) in 1972. That same year the Council of Independent Black Institutions (CIBI) was founded, its 28 members representing 14 community schools across the country. CIBI's purpose was to organize the existing independent schools into a unified pattern of educational achievement dedicated to academic excellence. Some of the goals established by CIBI include: (1) developing and implementing an instructional methodology that ensures maximum academic achievement for African American children; (2) creating and sustaining African American institutions that provide educational, cultural, and social development for African American communities; (3) establishing a network of mutual support and reinforcement of African values in the education of African American families; and (4) providing direction and inspiration for African American people through an example of nation building.[28]

On a national level, CIBI functions as an advocate organization for member schools and conducts a national public relations program. This program promotes broader acceptance and understanding of African American education and the African American separatist movement, to which I do *not* subscribe. Since 1972, the Council has also sponsored annual teacher training workshops.

The Institute for Independent Education is another clearinghouse for independent private African American schools. According to its founder, Joan Ratteray, the northeast has the highest concentration of African American schools, followed by the midwest, especially Chicago, Detroit, and Milwaukee. The west and southeast have about the same number of schools. Most schools within these regions are clustered in Los Angeles, Oakland, and San Diego in the west, and in Atlanta in the southeast.[29]

Whether they are called "community schools" or "independent African American schools," these schools share many features. They can trace their spiritual and intellectual genealogy to the separate schools established in the eighteenth and nineteenth centuries by such African American leaders as Prince Hall and Richard Allen, founder of the African Methodist Episcopal (AME) Church. These early schools were founded as educational havens from racial oppression in integrated schools. Although most of the schools are church-affiliated, they stress academics as well as Scripture. The superintendent of Love Christian Academy, Connie Sims, a 32-year veteran of the New York City public schools, says unabashedly: "I know I want all my students to go to Harvard. And I want them to know the Lord."[30] The schools usually have strict dress codes, often requiring students to wear uniforms. Their Afrocentric and Eurocentric curriculums are taught in small classes (15 to 20 students per class). At most of these schools parents are required to participate in their children's education—for example, by volunteering time at school at least one day a year and attending parent-teacher conferences. Some of the schools are not entirely one-race: 8 of Love Christian Academy's 135 pupils are white. Thus, some schools do not practice racial exclusion even though they could, being private. Finally, while figures are hard to come by, Ratteray reports that most students attending African American private schools outperform their public school counterparts. "About 64 percent of more than 2,300 students in independent neighborhood schools in 1990 tested above the national average in reading; 62 percent had higher math scores."[31] The test scores of students attending Love Christian Academy are quite impressive. For example, at the end of the school year, all 12 kindergartners scored in the 99th percentile in the math and science sections of the 1993 Stanford Achievement Test.[32] Students at Marcus Garvey (Los Angeles), Ivy Leaf (Philadelphia), and Marva Collins (Chicago), all of whom come from "low and moderate income families," perform "significantly higher than . . . their public-school counterparts" on academic tests, according to conservative economist Walter Williams.[33]

African American private schools cannot by themselves meet the educational needs of all the students who should be in one-race schools. The schools educate only about 2,300 students total. And there is tuition to pay. Though it is relatively low (approximately $3,000 per year, which means private schools spend "a fraction of what public schools" spend yet create a better product[34]), many parents whose children are in most need of single-race schools cannot afford them. Some parents may be put off by the religious emphasis of many of these schools. Consequently, it is imperative that public funds be brought in to support African American schools.

African American public schools will look very different from contemporary *de facto* segregated public schools. For the most part, they will be under the total control of African American professional educators, parents, and the community. But, most important, whether run by African Americans or whites, these public schools will, at a minimum, pursue African American institutional objectives—that is, educational programs tailored to the special needs of African American children in their neighborhoods. African Americans' control of their own educational institutions is the one theme that ties together the educational philosophies of integrationists like Prince Hall and W. E. B. Du Bois (during his integrationist stage) and separatists like Marcus Garvey and Malcolm X (in his pre-Mecca years).

Some of the major components of my proposal for African American public schools are essential for any good academic program and hence will be familiar in light of my earlier discussion of integrated schools, but most will be uniquely tailored to the separate schools.

Parental and Community Involvement

Most successful African American private schools depend heavily on parental involvement. Parental involvement is used as a "bridge closing the gap between home and school," and it serves to facilitate greater parental accountability. This is particularly crucial in inner-city schools, where children are often misdirected and misguided because they lack adequate parental supervision and control.[35]

At one successful African American private school, 60% of the parents participate on any given day as teacher's aides or cafeteria workers.[36] At another, the parents of a prospective student go through an intensive interview. The purpose of this interview is to determine what skills parents are able to offer the school and what services the school can provide parents. At this particular school every parent must participate in three yearly parent-teacher meetings, two annual classroom meetings, and report-card conferences held twice a year. At another successful school, parents receive tips on effective teaching methods to ensure positive reinforcement in the home.[37]

An old African proverb says, "It takes the entire village to educate the child." In the context of African American private schools, members of the community are often considered members of the child's extended family and are therefore important to the educational process. It is no wonder, then, that African American schools often serve as focal points of their communities and as "liaisons between social agencies for students and their families in need of assistance."[38]

There is no reason that parental and community control of African American education, which works for private schools, should not be extended to an institution long dominated by white teachers, white administrators, and white institutional objectives. The following statement, which appeared in 1883 in the *New York Globe,* then a leading African American newspaper, makes the point quite well:

> We want absolute equality in the public schools—mixed scholars and mixed teachers—and if we can't have it, we want colored schools taught by colored teachers . . . Show us one black president of a white college in this broad land; show us one black professor in any white college in this country. . . . On the other hand, we have white presidents of black colleges . . . and white professors in black colleges by the hundreds . . . Who has drawn this line? Certainly we have not.[39]

The Principal

To be an effective leader, the principal of any school (whether public or private, integrated or separate) must operate with a high degree of professionalism. She must take the initiative in identifying and articulating goals and priorities; set instruction as the first priority; handpick the staff; supervise and evaluate teacher performance; spend half of the school day in the classrooms and halls; find ways to reward excellent teachers with greater responsibilities; and set a consistent tone of high academic expectations and a nonpatronizing attitude.[40] Principals with such attributes have dramatically improved student performance and reduced problems ranging from absenteeism to low teacher morale in poor inner-city schools.[41]

One of the principal's most important tasks is to enforce standards of student behavior. Discipline is essential to a successful learning process. Control and order in the classroom is the most consistent variable in all successful academic programs.[42] In African American public schools, principals will make sure every classroom remains under the teacher's firm control. Students will also learn self-control through a dress code. This will be an especially important lesson for the many inner-city African American children whose shaky family structures leave little opportunity to learn self-discipline.

The Teachers

Most public school teachers are white females who have never experienced poverty, crime, or drugs. These teachers simply cannot relate to many of the problems facing African American children who live in the inner city. Rather, their inclination is to believe that these students are "slow learners" and to expect less from them.[43] Sensing this attitude, African American students lose their motivation for academic excellence.

In African American public schools, African American children will be taught mostly by African American teachers, as is presently the case in African American private schools. Most of these teachers are able to understand the needs and conflicts the children face. They have the ability to infuse African American children with pride through positive reinforcement and high expectations of academic and personal excellence. In educational institutions where African Americans are in charge of policy-making and all the teachers share the same interests, views, and experiences as the students, the latter will receive the spiritual uplift and self-assurance necessary to succeed. Some commentators have noted that African American teachers have been far more successful than white teachers in imparting to African American students a sense of self-esteem and confidence.[44]

African American teachers may be able to discipline behavior more effectively than white teachers. African American teachers have fewer feelings of "liberal guilt" than many white teachers and consequently will tolerate less trash talk and "acting a fool" in class than their white counterparts. Most important, the teachers can assert what I have called the African American survival maxim: *"You have the right to be angry about centuries of racial exploitation as well as present-day racism and racial discrimination. But you do not have the right to dwell on that anger, to feel guilty about these matters, to suffer low self-esteem, or to react in other self-destructive ways."*[45] Being in a position to state this maxim adds yet another dimension to the role-modeling capabilities of African American teachers.

I would not, however, bar whites from teaching in African American public schools. There have been many, albeit not enough, effective and dedicated white teachers of African American students. The most important requirement of African American schools is that the curricula address the special needs of African American children. As long as those needs are met, there is no reason to exclude white teachers provided the principal and most of the teachers are African American. In reality, the selection of teachers will hardly become a racial issue as most white teachers do not have a burning desire to teach in African American schools, separate or segregated.

Regardless of color, all teachers must attend training sessions periodically to ensure that they maintain the proper attitude toward their work. The first of these workshops, geared toward prospective teachers, could contain the following opening lecture:

> The first thing you should know about [our school] . . . is there are no contracts. We have no tenure. If you don't do your job, you have to leave. . . . We do not believe in many pedagogically approved practices. We don't try to decide what a child's mental capacity is: we just expand it. Your job is to teach, not diagnose.[46]

> We also believe that every child can learn. We do not buy the idea that because we are teaching children from one-parent families and our community is 99–1/2 percent Black that it is hard for our children to learn. We tell the children they are smart enough to do anything. And you can see the pride and dignity build up in them when we tell them that they are smart, that they are good looking.[47]

This type of lecture may have the effect of weeding out a large percentage of the teachers who should not be teaching in African American schools. But it will certainly convey an important message: in a poor, crime-ridden, single-parent environment, an understanding teacher is often the only source of positive reinforcement and nurturing available to the African American child.

The Curriculum

African American public schools will emphasize basic skills—reading, writing, math, and critical thinking—and, recognizing the importance of building self-esteem and developing racial survival skills, will teach personal values, conflict resolution, family issues, and health-related topics. These subjects are uncontroversial. Many educators at African American private schools, however, criticize the kind of history taught in public schools as "Eurocentric" and advocate teaching African history and value systems as well as correcting the untruths in history as taught at present. Those who run these schools point out that children learn best when they see themselves reflected in what they study. Accordingly, the argument continues, "the only history valid for children is the history of their own ethnic and cultural group."[48]

Rather than an Afrocentric curriculum, African American public schools, like integrated schools, will have a multicultural curriculum. No race is an island in our society. Even though many African American students will be educated in separate schools, they will eventually work in integrated institutions. Moreover, our Western society is built on Western thought. (There would be no Critical Race Theory or Critical Feminist Theory without Justice Oliver Wendell Holmes.) Education must therefore include traditional Eurocentric philosophies and ideals, in addition to knowledge about the culture and heritage of all ethnic minorities in this country. But, contrary to what is taught in most integrated schools today, students will learn that the history of African Americans does not begin or end with slavery or Jim Crow.

I do not mean to suggest that these periods of racial subordination should be ignored. To be sure, slavery and Jim Crow should be dealt with directly. But rather than looking at them from the perspective of historical victimology, students should focus on the perseverance of African Americans against incredible odds. The discussion should take place within the larger theme of the triumph of the human spirit. Teachers should link the experiences of African Americans to those of other people who have also overcome evil. Students will take from this discussion not humiliation, indignity, and shame but inspiration, moral courage, and character.

The Students

The majority of students attending African American public schools will, quite naturally, be African Americans. The preference for African American students will, undoubtedly, invite a constitutional challenge. Currently, public funds cannot legally be used to create or sustain separate schools. "Separate educational facilities are inherently unequal," the Supreme Court declared in *Brown*. Indeed, virtually every school system that operated under Jim Crow's regime of racial apartheid was unequal. But that will not be true of African American schools, at least not the ones envisioned in this book. In other words, *Brown* does not really speak to the issue presented by my proposal. Although *Croson* is more applicable to my proposal, the broad adoption of the color-blind principle in *Croson* and its progeny is clearly inconsistent with the legislative history surrounding the Fourteenth Amendment's enactment and the long line of the Court's own precedents, many of which were written by justices who lived at the time the Amendment was debated and passed. In short, the Supreme Court's current position on racial separation is correct only because the Court has the last word on the Constitution; but for that, the Court's interpretation of the Constitution would be wrong. The Constitution is not color-blind—it can see justice.

My proposal for separate public schools satisfies the true and original principle embodied in the Equal Protection Clause: these African American public schools will not subordinate white students. Because the schools will be located, for the most part, in inner-city neighborhoods, few white students will want to attend them. But if children of white families live in the neighborhood and want to attend such a school, they would be welcomed. Thus far, there is no constitutional problem. A problem would arise if the reputation of a school became so great that white parents in the school district decided they wanted to take advantage of schools supported by their tax dollars. A racial classification favoring African American students may then be needed to preserve the original concept of the school. But the exclusion of white students outside the community does not seek to elevate one race over another, nor does it have that effect. Rather, it is to help African American children catch up with white students—to resolve a serious educational problem. Nor does the racial classification deny an equal educational opportunity to the excluded white students. They have access to adequately funded public schools within their own communities.

Although white students outside the community could be excluded on the basis of a neighborhood-school principle, I would not choose to defend my proposal on that ground. My proposal is available to white parents; they can also set up special schools in their own neighborhoods with public funds. When a white community intentionally excludes African American students from its schools in order to preserve the neighborhood quality of such schools, that smacks of bigotry. But if the exclusion is based on grounds of educational necessity—demonstrated poor academic performance and low self-esteem caused by racial integration—there is no subordination of African American students, either intentionally or unintentionally. Whether a case could ever be made for separate white schools within these guidelines is another matter, but the option should be open, as it should for all races. In short, the neighborhood-school concept ought to be avoided, because it can provide a pretext for racial subordination.

The case for separate schools is strongest when applied to African American boys in elementary and middle school. This does not mean, of course, that we ignore the girls. But, clearly, it is the boys who are most at risk in integrated and *de facto* segregated schools, and their plight is the result of various socioeconomic conditions.

Structural changes that turned metropolitan areas from manufacturing to service are one cause of the educational crisis. Wilson, Ascher, Kasarda, Kain, and other scholars have written extensively about how some low-skilled manufacturing jobs have moved to the suburbs while others have just disappeared from the American scene since the 1970s. As these jobs leave the cities, high-skill service jobs move in. A serious mismatch then develops between the demand side and supply side of labor. The skills required for the new high-tech jobs extend far beyond the academic abilities of inner-city youth educated in inferior public schools.[49] With little hope of obtaining gainful employment even with a high-school diploma, many African American boys fail to see the logic of staying in school or taking education seriously.

The exodus of stable, middle-class African American families and business establishments from inner-city communities since the 1960s has also aggravated the problem.[50] This depletion of human and economic resources brought about a high concentration of poverty in the inner city, helped along by a high birth rate among the poor and a high incidence of female-headed households. Between 1960 and 1985, the proportion of African American families headed by women increased from 22 to 44 percent. According to one study, over 85 percent of all African American female-headed families in which the woman was under the age of 25 were poor. Approximately 41 percent of the African American households under the poverty line are headed by women. Sixty-eight percent of all African American babies born in 1991 were born to unmarried women.[51]

In consequence there is a dearth of positive African American male role models in the home. "Black boys have to learn to become men, and unfortunately they can't learn that from black women. . . . Discipline is a key concern. . . . By adolescence many boys toughened by life on the streets are physically intimidating even to their own mothers."[52] The male role models available to African American boys in the inner cities are often jobless, irregularly employed, or involved in dangerous or illegal activities.[53]

Children can strive to become only what they can imagine themselves to be. Their visions are clearly affected by what they see in their home environment. If all the adults around them are chronically unemployed or work in poorly paid jobs with little security, most children may simply accept this as their own fate. But if African American children see African American adults going to a job every morning and bringing home money to pay the bills and support a reasonably comfortable lifestyle, and if they see young adults becoming teachers and other successful professionals, then their understanding of their own potential grows accordingly.

In their book entitled *Black Child Care*, James Comer and Alvin Poussaint make this essential point in connection with the concept of "significant others." These key individuals testify to the importance of community support in the emotional and psychological development of children, especially in teaching African American children how to deal with racial sensibility. Even children raised in the poorest of homes, who may have grown up with strong feelings of unhappiness that their parents were unable to provide for their economic and social well-being, can learn from others how to successfully adapt to today's world as African Americans by developing a work ethic and an "attitude of black pride, self-confidence, and assertiveness" from other people in their communities.[54]

Statistics on young African American men show the odds are against them. "The leading cause of death among black males between the ages of 15 and 24 is homicide. Nationwide, black men represent 46% of state prison inmates but only 6% of the U.S. population. Among black men who are in their 20's, 23% are incarcerated or on probation or parole."[55] Alcohol and drug abuse are certainly behind many of these percentages, but the problem runs deeper than that. The problem is absence of self-respect. And if these kids have no respect for their own lives, imagine how they feel about your life and my life.

At least one thing poor inner-city students have learned is that little is expected of them in our public schools. Eventually, they become only too willing to live down to this expectation. "Their entire encounter with school is a distortion of reality and a clear indication that their society has low expectations for them."[56] But public schools designed especially for African American boys can help to break the cycle of unemployment, poverty, violence, criminal behavior, and psychological despair by changing the ways in which these boys are educated and socialized into manhood.

But what, specifically, can such schools do? Here are a few suggestions. First, boys must be enrolled in African American public schools at a very early age, the most vulnerable period in one's life. Comer believes that children begin their formative racial and ethnic education as early as age one and progress in the cognitive awareness of racial differences until about age ten. African American boys begin to slide academically some time before the third or fourth grade. Margaret Beale Spencer, who specializes in the educational development of minority children, explains that until age seven a child is so bound by his ego that he can successfully ignore what the world thinks of him. When he begins to look at things in a more objective way, "he begins to pick up on prevailing expectations . . . 'Okay,' he thinks, 'I guess I no longer have initiative. I guess I am no longer expected to succeed.' "[57] Second, African American public schools must provide male role modeling and male bonding, to fill a crucial need in the lives of the boys: namely, the absence of positive male role models. African American male teachers will, therefore, be preferred in the hiring process. Third, African American public schools must offer a "consciousness-raising" curriculum that will emphasize the public achievements and contributions of African American men. The curriculum's purpose is to counteract the "pervasive negative images of blacks on the streets, in the schools, and in the media."[58] These perceptions have an extremely negative impact on racial identity and self-esteem of African American male students.

Fourth, in addition to racial pride and self-respect, African American public schools will attempt to develop character in African American boys—personal integrity, respect for authority, and even "gentlemen's graces" (such as asking students to rise when speaking in class). Uniforms will help in this effort, as well as create a sense of discipline and solidarity. Teachers and administrators will counsel students in conflict resolution, respect for members of the opposite sex, and responsible sexual behavior. Consequently, African American boys will acquire a sense of responsibility toward parents, families, and community members, which, in turn, will lead to better relations with adults in school and on the job.[59]

Fifth, African American public schools might want to use some sort of "initiation rites" or "rites of passage" as a way of aiding and dignifying the often difficult transition from boyhood to manhood. These rites would counteract the rituals of gangs, which many psychologists have identified as a form of initiation rite. Since many young African American males grow up in fatherless homes, formal rituals may help facilitate a transition to manhood that might otherwise be particularly precarious. These initiation rites will be staggered over the course of a year, outside school hours.

The boys will be required to acquire new knowledge, learn rules of conduct, keep a journal, create a genealogical chart, provide community service, and participate in a special ceremony at the end.[60]

Finally, most low-income, young African American males need an environment that shelters and protects them. The new public schools will, therefore, need to offer extended school days and perhaps a weekend component. The goal is to protect students from the streets by offering healthy alternatives in the form of tutorials, recreational programs, and fellowship opportunities above and beyond those found in integrated school settings.

These programs will also lay the foundation for higher achievement and better racial integration in high school and college. This can only lead to healthier racial relations throughout society in the future. The only question is whether programs targeting African American boys should be provided in a co-educational setting rather than in a single-sex institution, both of which are permitted under my proposal. This is a call that is best left to the community. They know what will work best for their children, boys and girls.

15

Higher Education

At the college level, African American enrollment is low, attrition is high, and students suffer racial hostility. The solutions to these problems are inextricably tied to the educational reforms proposed for the elementary and secondary schools. To start by reforming the colleges is to start late in the second half of the game, down by too many points. The reconstructive measures presented in this chapter therefore presuppose the acceptance of the changes described in the last chapter. In the same vein, historically black colleges and universities (HBCUs) will exist in tandem with integrated (or predominantly white) colleges and universities. The integrated institutions will need to be restructured; the HBCUs will need to be made more effective.

Integrated Colleges

If integration is going to work at the college level, reform must take place in four areas: admissions, financial aid, academic support, and racial relations. Changes in these areas will increase the presence and the completion rate of African American students on integrated campuses.

Admissions

Once limited separation is firmly in place, African American high school students will acquire the grades and test-taking skills needed to be competitive in the admissions process at integrated colleges. I would like to believe that affirmative action would at that time become a relic of the past. I am experienced enough in graduate school admissions, however, to know that affirmative action will still be needed to provide minorities and women with a measure of protection from individual and institutional discrimination. For all the talk of diversity, professors still prefer students who look, talk, and think like them. But here is the rub: affirmative action punishes individuals—namely, white male candidates—who are not responsible for this discrimination. I am also concerned that racial and gender preferences harm minorities and women (because they marginalize, tokenize, and demean) and that this leads to unhealthy racial mixing on college campuses.

What is needed is an admissions standard applicable to all applicants regardless of race or gender that can achieve the goals of affirmative action without resorting to racial or gender preferences. I shall propose two programs that may move us in this direction: the "whole-person theorem" (a version of which will probably be adopted by the University of California starting in 1997) and "Public Interest Affirmative Action" (article forthcoming).

The whole-person theorem provides as follows: *if X has traditional credentials that are roughly equal to (that is, not substantially less than) those of other top candidates, and if X has demonstrated greater self-determination and character than other top candidates, then let X be preferred.* The theorem is simply a way to evaluate each applicant's scholastic potential by looking at his or her whole record, in life as well as in school. Rather than relying solely on traditional academic criteria—especially standardized test scores—in making this assessment, the admissions officer examines the distance the applicant has traveled to acquire his or her academic record. The academic record may give the admissions committee the precise position of the applicant's standing in relation to others, but it is not the best predictor of potential for academic success and success beyond the academy. In contrast, the primary objective of the whole-person approach is to facilitate the institution's selection of the most qualified individual without subordinating or stigmatizing the applicants, both successful and unsuccessful. The theorem is an attempt to separate the coaster (such as the student with an A average but C+ motivation) from the striver (such as the student with a B+ average and A motivation). It is a way to test the integrity or substance behind the applicant's achievements.

An admissions committee can look at many factors beyond an excellent academic record to separate the striver from the coaster. Cultural or socioeconomic disadvantages (such as starting out in life in a homeless shelter or growing up in a foster home, the Appalachian Mountains, or the inner city) and an extensive record of volunteer activity are perhaps the most important indicators of self-determination and character.

Let us assume, for example, that the admissions committee is considering two candidates to fill a final slot in the freshman class. The first candidate is a white male from an upper-middle-class family who attended a very good suburban public high school. He graduated with a 3.9 GPA, played on the water polo team, and scored 1450 on the SAT (the average combined English/math score for white students in the Harvard class of 1995). The second candidate is an African American male from a single-parent, working-class family who attended an inner-city public high school. He graduated with a 3.7 GPA, was class vice president, a member of the Big Brothers program, worked 20 hours a week, and scored 1290 on the SAT (the average combined English/math score for African American students in the Harvard class of 1995). Let us further assume that the African American student population is only 4 percent. If we apply the whole-person theorem, we should select the candidate who has traveled the greatest distance in life in acquiring an academic record that is roughly equal to that of the other top candidates. In this case, the admissions committee should select the African American applicant. He is the more qualified of the two because he has had to overcome cultural and financial hardships to achieve traditional credentials roughly equal to those of the white applicant. The GPA averages are roughly the same and the SAT scores, to the extent that they count at all, are close enough, given the test's socioeconomic bias. Moreover, the second applicant has demonstrated considerable social responsibility.

Colleges and universities can augment the effectiveness of the whole-person approach at the admissions level if they employ extensive student questionnaires to probe into the circumstances of an applicant's background and ability to overcome difficulties. Each applicant, whether minority or not, should be required to give the details of his or her life story in the context of the traditional student statement, as many already do. The use of such evaluative measures can save the university much time, expense, and effort.

Given the absence of race- and gender-specific admissions criteria, the whole-person theorem will probably result in the admissions of fewer members of minority groups and women. On the other hand, a greater percentage of minorities will graduate, which is, after all, the purpose of encouraging minorities to attend college. If the larger objective of affirmative action is to isolate those pre-professional qualities in a human being that can help us make morally correct and institutionally sound choices, the whole-person theorem will simply do it better.

As an alternative to or in conjunction with the whole-person theorem, affirmative action could be reconfigured in a way that should satisfy both its supporters and opponents. An admissions preference could be given to qualified students committed to working after graduation in socioeconomically depressed areas. These students need not be of a particular race (as is currently required in most affirmative action programs) nor *themselves* come from a poverty-stricken background (as would be required in most alternative admissions programs). Under my proposal—what might be called Public Interest Affirmative Action—race does not matter. From the perspective of poor people, it does not matter whether Thurgood Marshall or Jack Greenberg is attending to their interests; it only matters that a truly committed person is there to help.

My proposal has several components: an admissions component that gives preference to students genuinely committed to a career in the public interest sector; an academic component that requires students to take a special course of study (a Public Interest major) and perform 10 to 15 hours of intern work each week as a precondition for obtaining a degree; a fieldwork component that requires, for each degree obtained, 5 consecutive years of public interest service after successful completion of the academic component (coursework and internship) as a condition subsequent to obtaining a degree; a financial aid component that consists of a loan forgiveness program in which all educational loans are paid in full if the participant remains in the program through the 5-year, postgraduate work component; and drop-out provisions to protect the integrity of the program (see forthcoming article for details).

Public Interest Affirmative Action satisfies the legitimate concerns of white and minority critics of current affirmative action programs. White males cannot complain because the program as envisaged does not discriminate for or against any racial group. Any white male is eligible so long as he demonstrates a genuine, long-term commitment to working in socioeconomically depressed communities. True, some of these affirmative action beneficiaries may have lower academic indicators than white males denied admissions under the regular admissions program. But some will have higher academic indicators as well. More importantly, any white male who would attack Public Interest Affirmative Action on this score would first have to attack college athletic programs, where students with barely acceptable academic indicators are routinely admitted for the special talents they bring not to the classroom but to the field. I would think it more than hypocritical to allow these admissions while criticizing an admissions program designed to improve the quality of classroom discussions, the character of our citizenry, and the conditions of the poor.

Minority critics of affirmative action should also find Public Interest Affirmative Action acceptable. The benefits of affirmative action flow largely to the more disadvantaged members of our society, regardless of race, rather than to the most advantaged members of any particular racial group. Because some of the most academically qualified students will be admitted under the program, standards will become less of an issue than in other college admissions programs—those for athletes and legacies, for example. Students admitted under this affirmative action program will, in any case, be so committed to tending to the needs of the less fortunate in our society (the real beneficiaries of the program) that they will hardly be concerned about what others think of them. They are less likely to suffer the self-doubt and unhappiness so prevalent among today's affirmative action beneficiaries.

Financial Aid and Academic Support

Awarding aid on the basis of race rather than need is likely to foster racial hostility. Special funding for wealthy students who seem to have enjoyed many of life's privileges generates bitterness and a sense of injustice among other students. Accordingly, consideration of an applicant's financial need should be the controlling factor in determining his or her eligibility for university scholarships. This requirement should not hinder the educational opportunities of African Americans and other minority students. Most of these students will qualify for financial assistance on the basis of need.

Even after attending the improved public high schools of the future, some students, regardless of race, will need academic assistance, especially during the freshman year. Support programs designed for academically at-risk students will therefore be needed. These programs should be widely available to a diverse range of students with diverse academic needs. Administrators should take special precautions to prevent the segregation and hence stigmatization by ethnicity, race, or physical disability of eligible students in such programs.

In addition, outreach programs should be available to all students. Students may gain a great deal from a buddy system that links a freshman with an upperclassman. First-year minority students in particular would profit from an opportunity to communicate one-on-one with upperclass students who have experienced university life successfully. Furthermore, the upperclassman could monitor the first-year student's progress and make sure all problems and concerns are being addressed. Such "checking" would take the burden of contact away from the often reluctant and over-whelmed freshman and place it upon the older, more experienced buddy.

Another alternative is to institute special summer programs to help students orient themselves to the level of college classes and to university life in general. These summer institutes, which have been used at many colleges since the 1960s, have proved successful in revealing the academic potential of individuals and easing the participants' assimilation into the demanding college environment.

The list of support programs that could be implemented to help students academically at-risk and those with special needs and concerns is limited only by the imagination. Very little money is required to implement many of them. But the benefits can be enormous—improved completion rates for all racial groups and better racial relations all around.

Racial Relations

Racial preferences are a tremendous source of racial tension and misun-derstanding on college campuses. By removing racial preferences from the admissions process, policies like the whole-person theorem and Public In-terest Affirmative Action will defuse much of the racial hostility that exists among students. To get this beneficial outcome the administration must explain clearly and often how the admissions process works. Public Interest Affirmative Action requires less explanation, I would think, than the whole-person theorem. With respect to the latter, each student must understand that a *single* admissions standard was applied to each member of the class not admitted under the new affirmative action program, that the purpose of the standard is to admit the most *qualified* students, and that the stan-dard acknowledges that there is no cookie-cutter way of demonstrating academic excellence—people in a diverse society learn and achieve in dif-ferent ways.

Racial hostility on college campuses stems also from a lack of under-standing and empathy among the races. This is due, in part, to racial stereotyping, ignorance, lack of experience, and general misconceptions. All colleges and universities should continuously disseminate information to tear down racial walls. Required courses in race relations or multicul-turalism, as well as less formal opportunities for candid but civilized conversation and exploration of controversial race-related issues, can facilitate this endeavor. The only way members of all races will begin to understand the perspective, viewpoints, and even misconceptions of others is through active discussion and education. Although forums for race topics can create even more racial discord on campuses if not properly structured, that is a risk worth taking. But if these excursions into racial awareness are successful, and if the other components of my proposal for integrated colleges are adopted, there would be no need for Black Houses, Black Tables, Black Cultural Centers (as opposed to multicultural centers) or other forms of racial separation on campus. African American students will feel less threatened by whites and more inclined to jump into the integration experience with both feet.

HBCUs

In the second half of the nineteenth century and the early years of the twentieth century, nearly one hundred African American public and private institutions of higher education were established in the southern and border states. Most of these institutions came into existence through the urgings of the newly freed slaves. The freedmen's enthusiasm for higher learning was undeniable. Initial funding for these institutions of higher education came from the Freedman's Bureau and various church and missionary groups.[1]

Notwithstanding such funding, HBCUs have had financial difficulties almost from the beginning, and they continue to struggle to this day. Congress did pass the Second Morril Act in 1890, which provided public funds for all land grant colleges, including those established for African Americans under the separate-but-equal regime. But, as was typical under that regime, funds designated for African American colleges were either not received or were paid out in measly amounts. Paul Barringer of the University of Virginia reflected the prevailing attitude of turn-of-the-century America toward the funding of HBCUs: "It would be folly for any state to enter upon the industrial training of its deficient race while the laboring class of its higher race is equal to any training and any effort. We cannot equip both, and to equip the Negro to the neglect of the poor white would be a grave political error and an economic absurdity."[2] Financially strapped, faculty and administrators of HBCUs were forced to build, from the ground up, their own system of higher education. This was not an easy task. With insufficient funding, some important facilities and equipment, such as science laboratories and maps, were simply left out. Many of the colleges did not even have an adequate supply of blackboards. As late as the mid-1930s, only one of the seventeen African American land grant colleges received any of the millions of dollars in federal research funds promised them, and then "only the paltry sum of $1,800." At white institutions, the average per student expenditure was $234; at African American institutions, the average was only $138 per student. Such funding helped to ensure that African Americans would remain at the lowest educational and economic levels of society.[3]

Despite the shameful history of state-enforced economic discrimination, HBCUs have, as the Supreme Court has noted in *United States v. Fordice*, survived and even flourished.[4] Between 1954 and 1980, enrollment at HBCUs increased from 70,000 to 200,000 students, and degrees awarded increased from 13,000 to 32,000.[5] For many African Americans, HBCUs, with their distinctive histories and traditions, have become the symbol for the highest attainment of African American culture.[6] "The colleges founded for Negroes are both a source of pride to blacks who have attended them and a source of hope to black families who want the benefits of higher learning for their children. They have exercised leadership in developing educational opportunities for young blacks at all levels of instruction, and . . . they are still regarded as key institutions for enhancing the general quality of the lives of black Americans."[7] A study comparing the experiences of African American students in HBCUs and white institutions concludes that African American students attending the latter are more likely to suffer higher attrition rates, alienation, and lower GPAs. In contrast, students attending HBCUs, despite their relative poverty and lower standardized test scores, are better adjusted, receive higher grades, and are more likely to graduate.[8]

Several factors explain these differentials. The emphasis HBCUs place on community service, leadership, and social responsibility contributes enormously to the success of their students.[9] Compared to their white counterparts, HBCUs tend to have smaller classes, which facilitate better student-teacher interaction. In this way college faculty members can serve as much-needed role models and sources of inspiration and support for African American students.[10] Perhaps most important, teachers at HBCUs promote "teaching at the level of student readiness." This teaching philosophy recognizes that many African American students have higher than average intelligence but that they may need about one semester of preparatory help.[11] Finally, HBCUs form close bonds with the African American community by providing family assistance programs, home improvement programs, legal services, and even health services.[12] In short, HBCUs are more nurturing of African American students than white institutions.

In the *Fordice* case, Justice Thomas supported HBCUs and argued that states should be allowed to operate "a diverse assortment of institutions—including historically black institutions—open to all on a race-neutral basis, but with established traditions and programs that might disproportionately appeal to one race or another."[13] Not surprisingly, the accomplishments of HBCUs in the face of extreme discrimination and deprivation have not gone unnoticed.

Despite the advantages of HBCUs, they face an uncertain future. Enrollments have decreased since the 1970s. Today, in fact, far more African American students attend integrated institutions of higher education than HBCUs.[14] In addition, HBCUs continue to flounder financially. Some of the financial problems facing HBCUs could be ameliorated by government grants of need-based scholarships rather than student loans (this would enable administrators to budget less revenues for financial aid), and by "catch-up" funding for HBCUs to remedy years of discrimination and financial deprivation.[15]

An equally serious challenge to the existence of HBCUs is the color-blind principle. State funds cannot legally be used to support a dual system of higher education—one predominantly African American and the other predominantly white. Such a state-supported system violates the color-blind principle the Supreme Court has in recent years consistently found in the Equal Protection Clause of the Constitution. But, as I have argued, that clause is more correctly construed as a prohibition against racial subordination or stigmatization. The description of HBCUs in this chapter clearly demonstrates that these institutions of higher education neither subordinate nor stigmatize any race. They simply provide a supportive learning environment for African American students, which is what limited separation is all about.

16

Cultural Integration within the Community

This and the next chapter contain the heart of my proposal for limited separation. Together, they argue in favor of a commitment to a different form of integration, namely, cultural and economic integration within the African American community. This chapter focuses on the cultural aspect, envisaged as a blend of a shared American culture and a unique middle-class African American culture. An important precedent for this idea is the American immigrant experience.

The Immigrant Experience

Virtually every immigrant group that came to America in the last 170 years clustered together in economically depressed geographical areas or ghettoes. In part, this early cohesion worked to their advantage. For example, many immigrants formed mutual aid organizations to operate within their neighborhoods. These institutions helped to acculturate new arrivals and, in the process, addressed a myriad of interests common to the group—education, housing, business, politics, discrimination, and so on.

More than a neighborhood, the ethnic enclave developed a sense of community. This feeling of belonging and the sense of shared cultural identity provided a refuge from an otherwise alien and hostile world, while at the same time imbuing individuals with an inner strength and direction needed to succeed in that world. From within these communities, immigrant groups acquired abiding hope in the future—a genuine feeling that, although they were poor, life would get better for them or at least for their children. In contrast, many African Americans, especially those living in underclass communities, do not see such prospects to this day, and that influences their behavior.

The Jewish experience is particularly illustrative of the American immigrant experience. Settling in large numbers in New York City's Lower East Side (primarily from 1881 to the mid-1920s), Jewish immigrants established settlement houses and other private welfare organizations to teach English, basic education, and American culture to each new group of Jews arriving from Europe. At the same time, these settlement houses fostered a sense of cohesiveness, cultural life, and heritage that was distinctly Jewish. For example, well-settled German Jews, fearing that the sudden influx of less-tutored Eastern European Jews would ignite latent anti-Semitic sentiments, founded the Educational Alliance, the most famous of the settlement houses, on the Lower East Side in 1891. Working through the Educational Alliance, in many instances as volunteers, Jewish professionals taught English and provided medical care for the poor. Free concerts, lectures, art lessons, and play groups for children were also sponsored through the Alliance. Strong "subcommunity" traditions were nurtured through these activities. Indeed, the very existence of a self-help organization such as the Educational Alliance underscored a sense of common destiny in dramatic fashion. By World War I, the Educational Alliance served more than one million Jewish immigrants.[1]

As Jewish Americans became more established, the Educational Alliance and other settlement houses were scaled down to serve as smaller "community houses." These community houses, also known as federations, were established in every large Jewish community to provide local services for the very young, the elderly, and the disabled. They also addressed national and international political issues important to Jews, and coordinated local and national fundraising to finance their operations. The Jewish federation system is the strongest ethnic self-help structure ever established in America.[2] Many activities sponsored by Jewish federations are open to non-Jews. Practically every teenage African American basketball player in the 1960s remembers playing in "the Jewish basketball league" on Wednesday nights and Sunday mornings. Even today, many of the after-school "enrichment programs" offered by Jewish federations in Minneapolis and other large cities are open to non-Jews. Scholarships are even provided in some instances. But there is no question that serving their own needs remains the primary function of these and other Jewish organizations.

Italian Americans, perhaps the poorest of the European immigrants, also clustered together in the big cities in overcrowded ghettoes, which have come to be known as Little Italies. Although popular culture portrays the Mafia as the strongest institution within all Little Italies, in reality that honnor goes to *la famiglia,* or the extended family. Composed of one's blood relatives, the family was supported by an important custom known as *comparatico,* or godparenthood. Mutual aid societies and social clubs also arose to serve the needs of individuals directly or indirectly by supporting their families. Like Jewish settlement houses and community centers, these self-help organizations were supported with private funds and personal effort.[3]

Miami today may be the home of the wealthiest immigrant enclave in the United States. In the last decade, Cubans have been joined in Miami by Puerto Ricans, Nicaraguans, Salvadorans, Guatemalans, Colombians, Haitians, Brazilians, and Argentinians. "In Miami, there is no pressure to be American," says socialist Lisandra Perez, a Cuban-born head of the Cuban Research Institute at Florida International University. "People can make a living perfectly well in an enclave that speaks Spanish."[4]

Latin American immigrants and investors are lured to Miami by the prevalence of Spanish language and blend of cultures. About a third of the largest Latino-owned firms in the United States are located in Miami. Many international investors call Miami the financial capital of Latin America. The value of maintaining ethnicity, language, and shared elements of culture is clearly demonstrated in that city. But more than that, Miami attests to the idea that socioeconomic success in America can be achieved without abandoning a culture that may differ from the mainstream.

Japanese, Chinese, Korean, and other immigrant groups, white and non-white, have traveled this path to success. What this tells us is that rather than fight a protracted and seemingly losing battle against housing segregation and discrimination, African Americans should use their residential isolation as a catalyst for individual and group success. If middle-class African Americans ran toward rather than away from working-class and poor African Americans, if the human and economic capital withdrawn from African American communities during the years following the Civil Rights Movement, when America's integrationist drive seemed to be in high gear, returned to these communities, then African Americans could establish a physical as well as a cultural basis for socioeconomic and political success. Shifting the focus in housing from racial integration to *cultural and economic integration within the community* will give African Americans what white and nonwhite immigrant groups have always enjoyed—namely, a sense of belonging and hence a foundation from which to build individual and group pride, economic independence, and political strength. These are the ingredients for an American success story.

Cultural Integration

African Americans need to spend less time trying to live next to whites and employ more energy striving to live together. Pushing so hard for integrated housing is not only largely fruitless (neighborhoods are highly segregated a generation after the Fair Housing Act and will continue to be so for generations to come); it is also demeaning. Liberals and liberal organizations fail to appreciate the fact that demeaning experiences of this nature contribute to the very problem they so passionately seek to attack—racial inequality. When African Americans come with hat in hand pleading for civil rights (rather than creating their own civil rights), they reinforce their social status as mere supplicants. Years ago, the late Judge William Hastie, the first African American federal judge, observed in this spirit: "Say what you will, a man does not choose as his boon companion an individual whom he never sees in dress clothes except when [that individual is] carrying a tray at his banquets."[5]

The place for African Americans to begin creating their own civil rights is in their own communities. African Americans must embark upon a campaign of cultural and economic integration. They must pour human and financial capital and bring stable families and businesses into African American communities, and they must harness the resources of a multi-billion-dollar annual economy. This is the *only* way African Americans can create opportunities for themselves; the only way they can establish civil rights that are organic and that no one, not even an unsympathetic Supreme Court, can take away. After studying civil rights law for most of my adult life, I am sure of this.

African Americans of all socioeconomic classes have a vested interest in pursuing such cultural and economic communal integration. The poor and underclass will improve their socioeconomic conditions by adapting to middle-class African American values while drawing from the strengths of a unique African American culture. They will also have access to new employment opportunities within their own communities. The ensuing positive public image of African Americans will benefit members of the middle class in their interactions with whites, especially the individuals who choose to work, study, and play in integrated institutions. The promise of opportunity and better race relations should convince African Americans that it is within their self-interest to focus more on reinvigorating their communities and less on breaking down racial barriers in white communities.

African American communities can nurture and guide the individual directly or indirectly though the family by following a pattern similar to that of immigrant communities. African American communities can, in other words, act as either a resting point or an end point, a way-station to racial integration or a final destination. The scholar in me would like to see both paths pursued, by way of experiment: the only way to resolve the issue, which the white immigrant experience only begs, of whether a racial group must forfeit its uniqueness in order to succeed in the United States. European immigrant groups have tended to shed their language, dress, and other ethnic features to step into the mainstream, although they continued to draw strength from their cultural uniqueness. On the other hand, some Latino immigrant groups, such as the Cubans in Miami, appear to be succeeding today in the mainstream while retaining their "difference." They have literally changed the direction of the mainstream so that it now flows through their communities. Yet none of these immigrant groups possess the most salient racial characteristic of all—skin color. If this phenotypical difference limits opportunities in integrated, mainstream society—in other words, if racism is permanently debilitating, as many African Americans believe—then stable and vibrant African American communities may be the only milieus in which true opportunity for individual African Americans can be created and sustained.

All African American communities will observe this principle of limited separation: they shall neither subordinate nor stigmatize other individuals or groups on the basis of race even as they nurture African Americans. But all racial or social groups that choose to live within the community must observe the social objectives the community seeks to promote; otherwise, they are free to live somewhere else. Frankly, I doubt that many whites will choose to live in an African American community.

Whites, Latinos, Asians, and other racial minorities can also establish separate communities, so long as they strictly observe the limited separation principle. That is, the communities must be wholly voluntary—no racial discrimination or intimidation—and must be designed to improve race relations in our society. Racial inequality is the primary impediment to better race relations in our society. By augmenting racial equality, African American communities will make for healthier race relations. Each racial community must establish a clear nexus between its existence and better race relations.

Cultural Wars

Thomas Sowell has long argued that problems of crime, welfare dependency, and teenage pregnancy and motherhood must be addressed internally rather than externally; that is, by values rather than by government.[6] Even liberals have largely conceded this point. For example, in a book appropriately titled *Tragedies of Our Own Making: How Private Choices Have Created Public Bankruptcy,* Justice Richard Neely of the West Virginia Supreme Court warns about the catastrophic consequences of most divorces and illegitimate births.[7]

While I advocate a degree of cultural adaptation and, I might add, a spiritual renewal within the African American poverty class and underclass, I disagree with the view expressed by some African American conservatives that the cultural adaptation must come from without rather than from within the African American community. I disagree, for example, with Sowell when he finds a deficiency of human capital among African Americans[8] and with Shelby Steele when he assumes that African American culture is limiting or impoverished because it cultivates rather than counteracts an inferiority complex among African Americans.[9] Both writers totally ignore socioeconomic stratification within African American society. Had they taken class stratification into account, I believe they would be persuaded that the solution to the internal problems of African Americans—welfare, crime, drugs, teenage pregnancy and parenthood—lies in the acceptance rather than the rejection of African American culture.

Shelby Steele argues in his influential book, *The Content of Our Character,* that African American identity protects, nurtures, and perpetuates self-doubt among African Americans, making them afraid to compete toe-to-toe with whites. This argument rests on two assumptions: African Americans suffer an inferiority complex; and African American culture provides no antidote for such anxiety and is therefore a limiting or impoverished culture. I shall accept the basic truth of the first assumption for the sake of the argument, in order to focus on the second assumption, which is more relevant to the issue at hand.

Historians have grappled with the question of African American culture for decades. Some, like Stanley Elkins, have argued that the arduous ocean voyage during slavery robbed African Americans of their African culture.[10] Others have claimed that the slaves retained much of their African culture, which in turn developed into a distinct, autonomous African American culture.[11] Still others, such as C. Vann Woodward[12] and Mechal Sobel,[13] have argued that African American culture developed as (and perhaps continues to be) a shared culture—African-English in the eighteenth century and African-southern thereafter. To see our way through the fog, it may be useful to begin with the traditional definition of culture.

Culture is defined as the sum of behaviors, values, and attitudes (in other words, customs) that differentiates one group of people from another. Culture is transmitted from generation to generation through stories, poems, songs, and other forms of written and spoken language; family structure, religious practices and rituals; art, sculpture, architecture, crafts, clothing, and other physical objects; and special occasions such as dance, holidays, and celebrations. Although a group can choose its own culture, many aspects of culture are often thrust upon a group by external conditions, such as poverty and physical isolation from the dominant culture. Culture has "good" and "bad" elements. The work ethic is a positive cultural trait in the American dominant culture; racism and sexism are not.[14]

From this understanding of culture it is reasonable to conclude that African American society contains several cultures, each of which is manifested roughly along class lines. Thus the African American underclass culture is distinctly different from that of the middle class, the working class, and even other groups of poor African Americans (such as the working poor). It goes without saying that some of the behaviors, values, and attitudes of the African American underclass culture—such as crime, drugs, and welfare dependency—are clearly "bad" in the sense that they are antisocial and harmful to individuals in the group and to outsiders. Many of these customs are influenced by the isolation of the underclass from mainstream society and by the paucity of opportunities available to members of the class. They have no choice but to make their own opportunities in order to survive with some degree of happiness.[15]

African American culture is by no means class-bound, however. Certain customs among African Americans transcend socioeconomic boundaries. Some of these cultural phenomena replicate those of the larger, mainstream American society. Others are quite distinctively African American.

Both African Americans and whites value excellence, education, work, and the work ethic. Next to political values fundamental to the American way of life (such as liberty and democratic process), these values may be the most important shared or common cultural beliefs of African Americans and whites. The African Americans' desire for excellence is limited only by the opportunities foreclosed by racial discrimination. In sports and the arts, particularly music, where opportunities have traditionally been most available, the drive toward excellence is most in evidence. African American artists and athletes—from James Brown, the "godfather of soul music," to Michael Jordan on the basketball court—have set high goals for themselves. And, along the way, they have raised the performance level for their crafts. Rightfully, they bristle at the oft-stated remark that they relied on natural ability rather than hard work to succeed.

On any given day, one can see the desire for excellence in the myriad endeavors undertaken by African Americans. Not only on the playgrounds, where youngsters strive to be today's Willie Mayses or Julius Ervings, or indoors where the future Janet and Michael Jacksons are developing their talents, but also in schools and in work places—in short, wherever African Americans begin with high expectations—we may find expressions of the desire for excellence among African Americans. Too often these high expectations are smothered by unnurturing integrated environments (see Part I).

Education has always been highly valued in African American society; indeed, it is one of the most deeply rooted values. During slavery, when it was against the law to educate slaves and, in some states, free persons of color, African Americans risked their lives to educate themselves.[16] The legal struggle for equal educational opportunity that climaxed in *Brown*, and which continues today, goes back to colonial America, to Prince Hall and other African Americans in Boston who complained persistently about the quality of education.

To be sure, some African American teenagers choose not to attend school or to take seriously the education offered in their schools. Some may view education as a white or "Uncle Tom" value, a belief that attests to the degree to which some young African Americans have been miseducated about their heritage. Alternatively, they feel that the education they receive is so inferior to what is provided elsewhere in society that their best chance for succeeding is to use school time to pursue more productive activities (such as drug dealing). Or they may feel that the teaching, curriculum, and atmosphere in their schools are so unsupportive and even hostile to their individual needs that to show up for classes is tantamount to receiving an emotional whipping several times a day.

Along with the pursuit of excellence and education, work (labor and profit), and the work ethic (an appreciation for thrift and industry) are common values. They are not held by whites alone, nor are they exclusively middle-class or working-class (African American or white) values. A study published by the Rand Corporation illustrates the valuation of work even among young drug dealers. This study demonstrates that although society as a whole views drug dealing as a form of criminal activity, adolescent African American males who live in poverty and deal in drugs view drug dealing as "an important career choice and major economic activity."[17] Drug dealing is what they do for a living. It is not simply their job (they view themselves as capitalists, not as laborers), it is their *business*. And despite the extraordinary risks involved in this occupation—jail or even death—these African Americans continue to work seriously at building their businesses. Not unlike entrepreneurs formally educated in Harvard Business School principles of finance, they consciously seek to establish the optimum level of risk and return. As the report states:

> Drug selling was widely perceived by respondents as both profitable and risky. . . . Perceptions of returns from drug selling were reasonably accurate. A high percentage of adolescents believed that earnings of $1000 per week were readily obtainable; in fact, such earnings are available to those who work steadily in the drug trades (though most participants, by working only occasionally, earn much less). Persons who had sold five or more times saw the risks as lower and the returns as higher than did those who were nonsellers or who sold only very rarely. Nonetheless, even among sellers, 38 percent reported that a person selling drugs for a year would very likely be caught by the police, and half thought that such a person was very likely to be injured seriously or killed. Thus, it is not for lack of awareness of risks that so many are going into this criminal business.[18]

Another study, *Drug Abuse in the Inner City,* also underscores the business aspect of drug dealing: "The structure of drug-dealing organizations is complex and contains many roles with approximate equivalents in the legal economy."[19] Drug "selling by inner-city youths has had major effects on low-income communities by offering substantial economic opportunities that undermine the willingness of such youths to work at *low-wage* legal jobs."[20] The Rand Report concurs: "A substantial percentage of those who sell drugs earn much more than they can earn from legitimate activities."[21] Drug dealing, in short, offers economic opportunities to low-income communities that cannot be found anywhere else.

Because they value not just work but the work ethic, most African Americans look askance at drug dealing and other forms of unethical profit-making. An admonition often heard at the dinner table is "there's nothing wrong with an honest day of work." Thus, African American women have held their heads high as they scrubbed floors, washed clothes, and raised the children of whites from dawn to dusk for hundreds of years just to feed, clothe, and shelter their own children. African American men, far from having an inborn aversion to work, have labored long hours at bone-breaking menial jobs. These good, decent men have often had to work under a constant barrage of racial insults that rip away at a man's dignity.[22]

Excellence, education, work, and the work ethic are common values; values that inhere in both the African American and white cultures. These values militate against the anti-self, inferiority anxiety. They speak to the African American individual in positive, uplifting, hopeful voices. Those who imbibe the messages are not likely to suffer inferiority anxiety.

This is not to say that African Americans do not suffer pangs of self-doubt or embrace self-destructive behaviors and attitudes (such as drug dealing or dropping out of high school). But the self-doubt some experience and the self-destructive acts some undertake are not necessarily the products of inferiority anxiety, as Steele suggests. Anything from inadequate preparation for an assigned task to the uncertainty of a new job could produce self-doubt in an African American professional. The absence of opportunities in education, employment, or housing, a generalized anger against whites, or the act of expressing (*not* denying) one's self-importance could throw a young African American male into drug dealing or some other form of self-destructive behavior.

Steele also fails to recognize that many values or customs in African American society provide a powerful antidote to self-destruction, generalized self-doubt, and self-doubt caused by feelings of inferiority. These cultural phenomena are unique to the African American ethos. Among the most prominent are: (1) adherence to certain survival skills for succeeding in a racist society—such as the African American survival maxim; *soyez méfiant;* "masking"; the belief in personal sacrifice and perseverance; and the take on society as "the system" or "the man"; (2) reliance on the church for leadership and direction in both secular and spiritual matters; and (3) self-help.

The African American survival maxim (see discussion of African American teachers in chapter 14) is a psychological device that helps African Americans deal with mixed emotions about "buying into" a racist society.

Some African Americans feel defiance and anger about the inertia of discriminatory and racist traditions in our society and about the vista of grayness they see down the road. But there are also strong feelings that lead to positive actions. Among these are the desire to excel and the sense that to succumb to the negative emotions plays into the hands of the white racists, does dishonor to the sacrifices of African American mothers, fathers, and heroes, and is altogether self-defeating. The survival maxim is a vindication of the positive emotions and a cure for self-doubt, whatever its cause, and self-destructive attitudes.

Mistrust of whites (*soyez méfiant*) is another important survival tactic taken from the African American experience. It keeps African Americans at an arms-length distance from whites and puts into question the possibility of close friendship between the races. Leon Lewis, a prominent African American commentator, reflects on mistrust in the following passage.

> Everything is different when you're black. It's amazing how the quality of one's life can be changed by what might happen, by what you think might happen and by what other people think might happen.
>
> Often I've been invited to cocktail parties, openings and other gatherings of a business or civic nature, and many times I've been the only black person in attendance. I can become very uncomfortable in that setting. My subconscious might start sending up smoke signals, and I think, say, "What if that lady standing near me should suddenly scream? Every eye would be on me, and I could be in a world of trouble." Why should a thought like that enter my mind? The lady doesn't look as if she is about to scream, but it has happened and who is to say it will never happen again?[23]

"Masking" is closely related to *soyez méfiant*. The term comes from Ralph Ellison's book, *Invisible Man*,[24] but the concept goes back to slavery.[25] It asserts that African Americans must mask their true feelings around powerful whites. Showing your true face, your true feelings around whites in positions of authority only invites trouble. It may, for example, incite white racism (whites may get to feel that you are acting uppity, that you are not staying in your place, that you are capable of causing trouble) or induce other forms of white oppression.

Masking is an essential parenting technique in African American society. Two leading African American child psychiatrists, James P. Comer and Alvin Poussaint, state that the African American child must be "trained to cope with white oppression."[26] Parents must, among other things, pass on "to a growing child both the strengths of the old culture and the rules and techniques essential for successful adaptation in the modern world." These techniques include the art of being "practical as well as cunning," learning "how to win some sort of acceptance from belligerent whites," and even acquiring the habit of containing one's "aggression around whites while freely expressing it among blacks."[27]

Another traditional survival value within African American society is the belief in voluntary sacrifice and struggle. Matriarchal sacrifice and struggle for children and family—such as holding down two tiring jobs, one outside and the other inside the home—is the basis for the deep respect in which African American mothers are held in the culture. Often overlooked, African American men also have a tradition of sacrifice and struggle. They have been the fearless leaders of the race. Prince Hall, Nat Turner, Frederick Douglass, E. E. Just, Charles Houston, Paul Robeson, Martin Luther King, and countless other African American men have been the "marines" in the fight against racial injustice in our society—the first to go and the first to die.

There is no mystery attached to understanding why African Americans were more inclined than whites to believe, in the O. J. Simpson case, that the defendant was the victim of a police conspiracy. African Americans tend to have a negative or suspicious view of American society and especially of the police—"the man." Years of racial oppression have conditioned African Americans to compare their relationship to American society with that of an abused child to an abusive parent. The feeling is that society is unfair and even hateful toward African Americans: "When white folks get a cold, black folks get pneumonia." Langston Hughes's famous poem "Mother to Son" reflects on "the system": "Well, son, I'll tell you: / Life for me ain't been no crystal stair. / It's had tacks in it, / . . . But all the time / I'se been a-climbin' on, / . . . So boy, don't you turn back."[28]

"Mother to Son" is inspiring. It provides a powerful and elegant response to African American self-doubt and self-destructive attitudes—and voices a universal experience in a particular idiom and context.

Perhaps no other institution in African American society has provided a more constant countercheck to self-doubt or self-destructive attitudes, especially inferiority anxiety, than the church. It plays a unique role in the culture. African Americans have traditionally relied upon the church for wisdom and direction in the secular world. The church has never been simply a weekend spiritual retreat for African Americans but an important and lasting presence in their lives, supplying a steady stream of well-educated, middle-class intellectuals and activists who were just as interested in reforming society as in reforming the soul. Adam Clayton Powell, Vernon Johns, Martin Luther King, Jesse Jackson and countless other ministers are known more for their social engineering than for their religious crusades, although none of these heroes would endeavor to separate the two.[29]

Surely no one would claim that these African American heroes suffer from inferiority complex, or integration shock. And just as surely, it cannot be denied that these heroes draw strength not only from their spirituality but also from their culture—African American culture.

Some critics' understanding of African American self-help is also inadequate. Steele, for example, fails to recognize the medicinal value of hands-on African American self-help in fighting the diseases of self-doubt and self-destruction and denounces any form of participatory self-help or assistance from middle-class African Americans. He would only support self-help by example, a kind of armchair version of self-help at a safe distance. He argues that it is counterproductive for middle-class African Americans to provide direct personal assistance to their less fortunate brethren because such help undermines individuality and personal responsibility.[30]

Hands-on assistance from the more successful members of the race, however, is a major feature of African American culture. Ever since the founding of this country, African Americans who have "made it" have consistently believed that they should work closely with those who have not in order to support individual achievement, racial development, and a racially just society. "Beneficial societies," the Underground Railroad, and countless other self-help institutions were formed for just this purpose.[31] Likewise, the civil rights movement, in the course of which the African American middle class engineered protest marches and sit-ins supported by new literary voices, fits this mold. And even Steele's book, with its "middle-class" formula for racial development, follows the tradition of middle-class involvement.

I believe African Americans who lead dysfunctional and self-defeating lives must adopt a more constructive and enterprising culture. This view puts me at odds with some of my liberal friends, who continue to rely on a government rescue to deliver African Americans from poverty and despair. I also believe that the cultural adaptation can be made internally in the context of African American communities; it means embracing some values that are common to African Americans and whites and some that are unique to the African American ethos. This view puts me in disagreement with some African American conservatives who set aside class stratification in African American society in arguing for a purely external adaptation. In all likelihood, some poor and working-class African Americans will choose an internal cultural adaptation while others will find success with an external one. Although I believe most will follow the former path, simply because the unique features of African American culture have served the great majority of middle-class African Americans so well, I would certainly encourage individuals to take the latter approach if the fit is there. In other words, my basic objective, once again, is to assist all individual African Americans, and especially the have-nots and have-lesses, by expanding their options rather than restricting them.

17

Economic Integration within the Community

In a parallel to the integration of culture among African Americans, economic integration—African Americans of all socioeconomic classes coming together as financiers, entrepreneurs, employers, employees, and customers—is necessary for economic independence for African Americans as individuals, as families, and as communities. Proceeding from this premise, I shall propose, elaborate, and defend a program of African American economic integration and independence. I begin, once again, with the American immigrant experience.

The Immigrant Experience

Economic self-help has been the *sine qua non* of socioeconomic success among American immigrant groups, each of which eventually established a measure of economic independence. While some immigrant groups achieved such independence through trade unions, most formed small businesses in the manufacturing sector (such as, the garment industry) and in the service sector (such as, the restaurant industry and the professional trades). All stayed close to home, providing employment for families and friends and allowing dollars to circulate within the community or ethnic group. Economic independence gave the members of each group precious freedoms—freedoms for cultural and political expression, higher education, and further occupational advancement.

Jewish Americans illustrate well the process by which immigrant groups have been able to establish beachheads in the American economy. In Eastern Europe Jews were denied the right to own property. The great majority therefore had lived on the economic fringes in tight little communities, relying on one another. In America Jews were able to organize their marketing and artisan skills into moderately profitable businesses, which generated economic resources necessary for educational and occupational advancement in future generations.[1]

Jewish self-employment in America was also motivated by discrimination in this country. Gentile-dominated businesses openly refused to hire skilled Jewish workers, and there were no employment discrimination laws to protect them. Ironically, such discrimination worked to the advantage of Jewish employers, who could then tap into a skilled labor supply bound by a common language and culture. As Jewish businesses grew stronger, gentile businesses had to deal with them on equal terms in spite of anti-Semitism.[2] In short, the economic interaction between Jewish businesses and workers helped to "foster the growth of an ethnic economy in which Jewish Americans provided economic aid to one another in order to maintain their enterprises and communities."[3]

Jewish immigrants also benefited from fortuitous timing. Their arrival coincided with the emergence of an American economy that needed precisely the type of skills they had acquired in Eastern Europe. Occupational restrictions in Eastern Europe pushed Jews into the textile, tobacco, metal works, and other skilled and semi-skilled trades and industries. When Jews began arriving in America in large numbers at the turn of the century, the garment industry was expanding two to three times faster than all other industries. During this time, Jews made up 80% of the hat and cap makers, 75% of the furriers, and 68% of the tailors in New York City.[4] This large involvement in the garment industry made Jews more than mere accidental beneficiaries of economic expansion. They were catalysts in the growth of an important segment of the economy, and of America itself.

Self-help was essential to the economic success of Irish Americans as well. The Irish unabashedly "took care of their own." In response to storefront signs that read NINA (No Irish Need Apply), Irish immigrants developed strong support networks within their communities, helping each other find housing as well as employment. Irish Americans' initial employment was typically in the building trades and other blue-collar fields. Labor unions provided a structure in which Irish workers could organize themselves for collective strength. Social clubs and other community support groups provided financial backing for small businesses, both legal and illegal. These businesses, in turn, propelled later generations of Irish Americans toward greater educational and economic success.[5]

During the height of their immigration, 1880–1920, scores of Italians came to America with the assistance of *padroni*, labor bosses, who found housing, employment, and food for the new immigrants. While some claim this system of limited separation was imported from Italy, others have argued that it was home-grown in the dozens of Little Italies in the United States. The *padroni* system, which often resulted in exploitation (for instance, the labor bosses would charge the new immigrants exorbitant prices for housing and food), was effectively abolished by 1909 with the passage of state legislation that encouraged businesses to contract with legitimate agents of the workers.[6]

In subsequent years Italian Americans used various other forms of self-help—from union rank and file and leadership to small businesses and even organized crime—to establish an ethnic economy, a presence in certain areas of the American economy. As the Feagins point out, "by 1939 Italian Americans had begun to supplant Jewish Americans as the major group in a number of important unions of skilled workers. They had become numerous in the garment industry and in building trades."[7]

Asian immigrants, like African Americans, could easily be discriminated against on the basis of physical appearance or phenotype. They resorted to separation to an even greater degree than Jews, Irish, or Italians. The strategy of Asian newcomers was to get ahead financially without bothering with assimilation.[8] Like Italian Americans, Asian Americans created economic self-help organizations that provided loans for new businesses and financial aid to newcomers. For example, Chinese custom imposed on employers the duty to help the destitute members of the community. Companies often dealt directly with public authorities, interceding on behalf of their needy employees. In return, the employees owed faithful service.[9]

With conventional sources of capital unavailable to them, Asian Americans resorted to self-help to fund their businesses. For example, the *hui* system was widely used by Chinese Americans as a form of venture capital. *Hui* is a generic term that means an association or club. More specifically, it refers to the system of rotating credit associations that began in Canton, China, approximately 800 years ago. There were many types of *hui*. In one type of system, a person who needed money would organize a *hui* by securing an agreement from relatives or friends of relatives to pay a stipulated sum (say $5 or $10) into a fund each month to create the total amount needed. A more common *hui* was an ongoing fund in which the contributors took turns as recipients. Individuals not necessarily related to each other paid amounts into a fund each month. The total amount collected was paid to a *hui* member at the end of each month. Another *hui* consisted of each member submitting a sealed bid indicating the rate of interest he was willing to pay on the amount of money collected. The interest rate was much less than what a conventional creditor would charge.[10] My Asian students tell me that their parents continue to use *hui* systems quite extensively to this day.

Cuban immigrants also combined residential separation and economic self-help to carve out a successful life in American society. Most were exiles and, intent on returning home, did not attempt to assimilate into the American "melting pot." Instead, they learned only the American way of doing business while building Spanish-speaking enclaves, mostly in south Florida.

The early waves of Cuban immigrants were from the elite and business classes of Cuban society. Former government officials, bankers, and industrialists were the first to come, followed in succeeding years by doctors, lawyers, middle-level professionals, managers, and merchants. With the assistance of considerable federal funds from the Eisenhower and Kennedy administrations, these early immigrants utilized their highly developed skills to gain upward economic mobility in the United States.[11]

In contrast to the successful experiences of these immigrant groups, Native Americans have been economic victims rather than economic victors. Prior to the Indian Wars of the late nineteenth century, most Native American groups had self-sufficient, land-based economies. The loss of land to white settlers destroyed these traditional tribal economies. Nomadic and herding economies would have been difficult to maintain in any event, as urban industry began to emerge during this period.

In recent years Native Americans have begun to turn their reservations into resorts centered on casino gambling. High-technology mining ventures, the ancient tradition of bison herding, and the surging growth of tribal colleges are also helping Native Americans establish a business beachhead in the American economy. None of these businesses quite compares to gambling, however. From the rolling hills of Connecticut to the High Plains, from upstate New York to the Rocky Mountain foothills, and from the southwest desert to the Pacific northwest, gambling has become what some Native Americans have called "the new buffalo economy," grossing over one-half billion dollars in revenues in 1992 alone.[12]

It is uncertain, however, whether Native Americans will be able to enjoy the kind of long-term economic independence other ethnic groups have experienced. White-owned businesses manage virtually all the casinos and are paid a percentage of the profits. New competitors are entering the gambling industry each year.[13] Finally, Native Americans on reservations may lack the entrepreneurial spirit that other ethnic groups have demonstrated in their economic rise, and which is so critical in the emerging global economy. Traditional Native American values place the group above the individual. The group is not viewed as a context for individual social success, as in other ethnic groups. As a *Forbes* magazine article noted: "reservations do not seem fertile ground for the seeds of capitalism. Reservation resources are generally the province of the tribe rather than individuals and shared equally among the membership."[14]

Like Native Americans, Mexicans first lost their land during the American westward expansion and then in a war. Unlike Native Americans, Mexican Americans became landless laborers. Historical circumstances and geographic contiguity drove Mexican Americans from land-based economic independence into landless economic subordination. By 1900 that process had been nearly completed. As the cities began to absorb these new laborers, the predominantly skilled Mexican American rural labor force became predominantly unskilled. Some small businesses were formed, chiefly in the food service industry, but they have remained on the fringes of the American economy. The existence of an unskilled labor force—chiefly consisting of field workers, household help, and day laborers—and the failure to establish a business beachhead in the American economy have left Mexican Americans vulnerable to poverty and employment discrimination not only on account of race but on "English-only" rules.[15]

The lesson African Americans must take from the economic experiences of America's ethnic groups is clear: the inability of a group to forge an economic base in the larger American economy—to develop economic independence—can only lead to economic vulnerability. Economic self-help is an effective antidote to poverty and employment discrimination. Women have already learned this lesson. "Women-owned businesses now number 7.7 million, generating nearly 1.4 trillion dollars [annually], and employing 15 million people. In fact, women-owned firms now employ more people in the U.S. alone than the Fortune 500 companies combined employ worldwide."[16] Women entrepreneurs are advancing not only in the United States but also in the world's poorest nations. Government development agencies and banks are funding "women-led small businesses and farming projects because they realize that women are the mainstays of local economies—and the foot soldiers in the fight against poverty."[17]

Like other social groups, African Americans must attempt to establish a measure of economic independence. They ought to embark upon a program of economic integration centered on the widespread creation of small businesses within African American communities. Increasing the number of small businesses will greatly facilitate economic integration and hence economic independence.

Small Businesses

A small business can be defined as an unincorporated or incorporated form of business association, independently owned and operated and not dominant in its industry segment.[18] The Small Business Association (SBA), for purposes of small business investment assistance, defines small business in terms of the number of employees or the amount of annual receipts.[19] These standards vary from industry to industry. For example, in the wholesale trade sector dealing in nondurable goods, the standard, or cap, is only 100 employees.[20]

Regardless of how they are defined, small businesses play a pivotal role in the United States economy. They provide and create more private employment than any other business sector of the economy, as women-owned firms illustrate. As effective producers in such vital industries as construction, services, retailing, and wholesaling, they help to maintain competitive markets.

Small businesses are the ones that must lead the way to economic rejuvenation in African American communities.[21] That route was determined by the structural changes in the U.S. economy that began in the 1970s and will continue into the next century. As large manufacturing firms downsize and modernize, they replace blue-collar workers with skilled laborers and technically advanced equipment.[22] Like other workers, displaced African American workers often turn to the small business sector because it provides the bulk of all new jobs. Indeed, several studies have found that small businesses create 51 to 56 percent of all new jobs annually. According to the SBA data base, small businesses with fewer than 500 employees generated 45% of the new jobs from 1986 to 1988.[23] Furthermore, since 1982, employment in industries dominated by small businesses has increased more rapidly than employment in industries dominated by larger businesses. For example, between December 1988 and December 1989, employment in small-business-dominated industries increased by 3.2% compared to 1.4% growth in employment for large-business-dominated industries.[24] These recent trends indicate that employment growth in the future will occur in the small-business sector of the economy. Hence this is the place African Americans ought to be. More specifically, this is the place African American businesses ought to be.

Just as white businesses predominately hire white employees even when the business is located in an inner-city minority community, African American small businesses tend to hire African Americans whether or not the location for the business is in a minority community.[25] The Bureau of Census found that 60% of African American-owned firms have a work force that is at least 75% minority.[26] One example is Roland & Associates Transport Services, Inc. located in Morrisville, N.C. Amid today's acute shortage of truck drivers, this small African American business keeps its trucks rolling by "looking [for drivers] in places that whites overlook." As Lewis Roland explains: "A lot of my drivers come from the street. I'd rather have someone with the right attitude and no skills than a fully skilled person who thinks he knows every damn thing."[27] Hence one way to open up job opportunities for African Americans is to promote the creation and expansion of African American businesses.[28]

African American-owned small businesses benefit their communities in a number of ways. In addition to jobs and job-training, African American businesses also provide services within the community. Most important, they circulate money in a consumer-producer cycle within the community. Otherwise, African American communities find that their dollars "wake up in the morning in the African American community, but they go to sleep at night in the white community."[29] When these dollars leave the community, they finance the success of other racial or ethnic groups instead of the success of African Americans. The community grows stronger when money flows into it. And as the community's infrastructure expands, so will self-esteem and self-confidence among its residents. In a strong, economically cohesive community of individuals holding positive mental attitudes, social pathologies such as crime and welfare dependency will be reduced, and investors will want to invest in such communities.

Finally, African American-owned businesses make excellent role models for young African Americans. Successful entrepreneurs are living proof that it pays to stay in school and work hard. Whether these role models are parents, relatives, friends, or business persons in fraternal or other community organizations, having these successful self-employed people around has a positive effect on teenagers trying to find their way in an uncertain world.[30]

Increasing African Americans' participation in small-business owner-ship will not be easy. There are two major obstacles: capital formation and managerial expertise, and they will have to be overcome by drawing upon the resources of African Americans. The would-be entrepreneurs must, in other words, network—call upon the help of fellow African Americans for a wide range of assistance. Networking can provide a dependable source of clientele, informal encouragement from family and friends, managerial training, and investment opportunities[31]; it means, in short, individuals working together for mutual benefit.

Capital Formation

African Americans who need funds to start a small business usually turn to private loans guaranteed by the SBA or to private-venture capital funds. The latter typically expect a return of between 45 to 60 percent on their investment.[32] In matching investors to businesses, the Black Church could be an invaluable networking facilitator. Alternatively, church funds could be used directly for investment.

The Black Church could bring together African Americans with funds and those with business ambition. In effect, it would be playing the role of market maker. One of its functions would be to encourage African Americans with funds to form investment syndicates. These financial in-stitutions could be induced to loan money by the promise of a competitive rate of return, or they could simply take an equity interest in the venture as partners. Using the Black Church as a vehicle to bring together invest-ment syndicates and entrepreneurs is rooted in African American tradition. It dates back to the time of slavery, when the Black Church was the "epi-center for spurring social, political and economic self-help among its con-gregants and extending out into the community."[33]

One specific example of church involvement is the story of Reverend James Perkins from the Greater Baptist Church in Detroit. He borrowed money from the congregation credit union to purchase a dilapidated "crack building" across the street from the church. He then leased the land to Burger King, which built a restaurant that hired young people from the neighborhood. In this series of related steps, the church gave young African Americans jobs and kept money circulating within the community.[34]

Another example of the Black Church's spearheading jobs and economic development in the African American community occurred after the Los Angeles riots in 1992. The First African Methodist Episcopal (FAME)

Church of Los Angeles created the nonprofit FAME Renaissance Program to finance community business and economic development through private and public funding sources. Once FAME's program was established, church officials competed for and received a $1 million grant from the Walt Disney Co. With this money, the church set up the Micro Loan Program to supply low-interest loans of $2,000 to $20,000 to minority entrepreneurs in the area. In addition, the church encouraged congregation members to do business with recipients of the loans.[35]

Networking through the Black Church would have to be significantly expanded to meet the demands of my proposal. Most importantly, networking would have to bring in large businesses, stars of the sports and entertainment worlds, and people who save money through something like the *hui* system (discussed earlier) or investment clubs. If African Americans use the Black Church to help pool capital, they can help overturn the traditional barriers to success.

The larger African American businesses might invest in the smaller ventures. Every year *Black Enterprise* magazine compiles a list of the top 100 African American Industrial Service Companies. These companies include TLC, the Philadelphia Coca-Cola Bottling Co. Inc., Black Entertainment Television Holdings, and Essence Communication, Inc.[36] CEOs from these companies make up the business elite and already use networking to help drive economic growth in the African American business community, although not necessarily within the physical African American community. By working together, these African Americans are "forming pools of capital and new opportunities that are helping to overcome traditional barriers to success."[37] More of this capital needs to be specifically targeted to building businesses, small and large, in African American communities.

Another potential group of investors consists of African Americans from the sports and entertainment worlds. In 1993, Oprah Winfrey made $66 million; Michael Jordan made $45 million; and Bill Cosby made $33 million. These figures include income from all sources: salaries, bonuses, royalties, and endorsements.[38] Some of this money could be put to work in the community, not as charity but as investment. Some entertainers have in the past invested in African American small businesses. For example, when the prosperous African American entrepreneur J. Bruce Llewellyn was building the Philadelphia Coca-Cola Bottling Co., Garden State Cable Television, and Queen City Broadcasting, he attracted many entertainment investors, including Bill Cosby, Julius Erving, and O. J. Simpson. He also received help from Oprah Winfrey when his ABC affiliate in Buffalo ran into financial trouble. Oprah Winfrey also provided financial support, along with Michael Jordan and Bill Cosby, when Spike Lee ran out of money filming the movie "Malcolm X."[39] Such networking ought to become the rule rather than the exception, and it ought to be targeted more directly to the African American inner city.

A third way to obtain investment capital is to combine personal assets. Adopting the *hui* system, African Americans could raise money through rotating savings groups. An even better way to raise investment capital is through investment clubs.

An investment club is a group of 10–25 people (friends, co-workers, family members) who place a set amount of money each month into the club fund. These "dues" are invested, and the profits are typically reinvested into the club portfolio until the club reaches its financial goals. In San Diego, several African American lawyers formed an investment club, the proceeds of which were used to open a bakery in the community. Investment clubs are a low-risk, low-cost way for financial novices to learn and profit from investing in stocks, bonds, and mutual funds. Because each member is required to do thorough research and make regular deposits, 69% of investment clubs over the past decade have matched or beaten the Standard & Poor's 500 stock index. This is quite impressive, since only 19% of professional money managers accomplished the same track record.[40] As investment clubs continue to be successful, more individuals will be willing to invest. This in turn will increase the amount of capital available to start small businesses.

Managerial Expertise

Inexperience and a lack of managerial expertise also stand in the way of African American small businesses. There are, however, several successful programs currently in existence to help with that problem: training programs for high school students and courses for older persons interested in learning more about business management. Some of these programs have, in fact, already been tried on a limited scale in African American communities. Among the good programs that help young African Americans acquire essential business skills is the Young Black Scholars group. Under the aegis of this program, African American professionals tutor business workshops for 2,000 African American high-school students.[41] Preparing the young to be future leaders in the business world is also the objective of another networking program called Inroads. This program, based in St. Louis, prepares young African Americans for business internships with Fortune 1000 companies. Many of the participants in the program have already become owners, partners, and presidents of their own companies.[42]

Even before high school, the trend toward teaching younger children how to run and operate a business is gathering momentum. These programs, which try to cultivate an entrepreneurial spirit at an early age, combine academics and hands-on experience in a fun and educational way.[43] The Heartland Institute's Center for Teaching Entrepreneurship in Chicago, for example, runs a program that attempts to infuse pride, ethics, integrity, brother/sister love and family into the teaching of business skills.[44] These programs are so important because, as Steve Mariotti, founder and president of National Foundation of Teaching Entrepreneurship, says, "in a free enterprise economy, not understanding entrepreneurship is like being an economic illiterate. It's a handicap, the equivalent of not being able to read."[45]

Other programs are also available to help educate African American adults who have no prior business experience. For example, the Dade County Entrepreneurial Institute, which was founded in 1983, provides a comprehensive business education program plus technical assistance to African Americans.[46] All these programs contribute to helping African Americans overcome the lack of business and managerial expertise.

Some programs call upon the skills and the managerial expertise of retired business persons and professional management consultants. Such programs are designed for the experienced business person. "Small business owners who supplement their experience and expertise with that of a consultant will find themselves better positioned for success and long-term growth."[47] Consultants can identify new markets, develop cost-cutting measures, provide technical assistance, and challenge old or inefficient procedures. This is exactly what three M.B.A. students from Duke University's Fuqua School of Business did to help Lewis Roland's trucking business become more profitable. The best-known management consultant for small businesses is Service Corps of Retired Executives (SCORE), which contains 13,000 retired executives, mostly whites, who volunteer their services. There is also the Minority Business Development Centers, a nationwide network of minority business centers that consult about business planning, accounting, inventory control, administration, and franchising.[48]

Many African Americans are already working hard to help their brethren manage their businesses successfully. African Americans, working individually or through the Black Church, need to greatly expand existing programs or organize new ones and encourage many more successful business people to teach and guide novice entrepreneurs. This is essential if African Americans individually and collectively ever expect to increase their economic power and employment prospects.

In sum, my proposal for economic integration, which runs in tandem with my proposal for cultural integration discussed in the last chapter, invites African Americans of all socioeconomic classes to come together as financiers, entrepreneurs, workers, and customers to create economically independent individuals, families, and communities. Increasing the number of African American small businesses in African American communities is the best road toward economic independence. Small businesses provide jobs, keep money circulating within the community, and foster a sense of individual and racial pride as well as the entrepreneurial spirit. Networking is the most effective way to achieve capital formation and managerial expertise. The Black Church, as a market maker, can bring together individuals with funds to invest and individuals with the talent and desire to start and operate a business. In addition to financial networking, educational networking will also be needed to support educational programs for the business want-to-be as well as the experienced entrepreneur. African American communities can replicate the immigrant experience by creating a context that will enable more African Americans to succeed as individuals as well as enable African Americans as a group to compete successfully with both whites and other racial minorities.

Defense of Economic Integration

Some will argue that, notwithstanding the immigrant experience, the idea of economic independence is too optimistic. A central condition of the proposal is that a critical mass of middle-class African Americans move its homes and businesses back to the African American community, where they can be the leavening agents they once were prior to racial integration. But this segment of African American society may be too self-absorbed, self-interested, and overwhelmed in their daily lives to take on such a responsibility. I am, however, counting on self-interest to motivate individual members of the middle class to make the move. If the rage of this privileged class of African Americans is as genuine as Joe Feagin, Ellis Cose, and others have claimed, then we should expect not a few stragglers but a stampede of middle-class African Americans heading back to the community. The time has come for African Americans to put up or stop complaining.

Another argument against my proposal might be that it requires African Americans of all classes to do too much. In the cold light of reality, African Americans need the helping hand of government and the guiding hand of whites. But this scenario simply describes our current civil rights strategy, which has not worked for most African Americans in nearly a half-century of operation. Furthermore, I cannot and will not accept a declaration of African American impotence. It is incorrect, demeaning, and, ultimately, it confines African Americans to a permanent victim status. Two examples taken from the African American past will counter that false perspective: the Greenwood section of Tulsa, Oklahoma, and Durham, North Carolina. There were certainly many other Greenwoods and Durhams (see as an example Henry Louis Gates's wonderful memoir, *Colored People*[49]), but my point can be adequately made and illustrated with these two.[50]

African Americans began moving to Tulsa when Oklahoma was still part of Indian territory. Most came to Tulsa in the years following the Civil War to escape racial oppression under the Jim Crow laws in the deep South. In a relatively short period of time, African Americans in Greenwood created one of the richest communities in the country. To quote one of Booker T. Washington's organizers from the National Negro Business League, who visited Tulsa in 1913, Greenwood grew, despite Oklahoma's own brand of racial segregation, to become "a regular Monte Carlo" for African Americans in the southwest.[51]

Greenwood's population was diverse, consisting of business persons and professionals as well as skilled and semi-skilled workers. The service industry represented the largest sector of the district's economy. It is estimated that by 1921 Greenwood boasted 108 business establishments, which included 9 billiard halls, 2 retail stores, 4 confectioneries, 1 feed and grain store, 11 boarding houses, 2 garages, 41 groceries, 5 hotels, 30 restaurants, 2 movie theaters, and 1 funeral parlor.[52] Because of racial segregation, these businesses served primarily African Americans, many of whom earned little and lived in the poor sections of Greenwood or in living quarters above the garage while serving at the households of wealthy whites.[53] Greenwood also had an estimated 33 professionals, including 2 dentists, 4 druggists, 1 jeweler, 3 lawyers, 2 photographers, 10 physicians, and 6 real estate or insurance agents.[54] "Deep Greenwood," which was the name given to the first two blocks of Greenwood Avenue north of Archer, served as the favorite location for the offices of Greenwood's professional class. It became known nationally as the "Negro Wall Street."[55] Greenwood's economy also consisted of an estimated 24 skilled craftspersons, including 5 builders, 2 dressmakers, 1 plumber, 1 printer, 4 shoemakers, 10 tailors, and 1 upholsterer, plus an estimated 26 low-skilled workers, with 12 barbers, 5 cleaners, 3 hairdressers, and 6 shoeshiners.[56]

In 1921 a bloody race riot literally decimated homes and businesses in Greenwood. The intensity of the riot suggests that it was rooted in bitter resentment lower-class whites felt toward a prosperous all-African American community.[57] The riot was sparked on May 30, 1921, when a nineteen-year-old African American, Richard Rowland, entered the elevator at the Drexel Building in downtown Tulsa to deliver a package. He stumbled against a white elevator operator named Sara Page, and she screamed for help. When Rowland ran from the building, Page screamed attempted rape. A crowd of whites grew rapidly in response to the screams, and two African American police officers were dispatched to arrest Rowland on Greenwood Avenue.

Rowland protested his innocence and explained to the authorities that he became frightened and ran when Page screamed, knowing that many African Americans had been lynched on false charges of raping white women. Rowland also argued that his fleeing did not indicate guilt because the incident had taken place in a public elevator where people were constantly coming and going. His hearing was scheduled for June 7 in the Tulsa Municipal Court.[58]

Rumors began to fly when the *Tulsa Tribune* published an outrageously inaccurate article, titled "Nab Negro for Attacking Girl in an Elevator," that reported Rowland tore Page's dress, scratched her face, and touched her hand. A white lynch mob began to gather outside of the jail. News of the lynch mob traveled to the Greenwood district and reminded the citizens there of an incident that took place the previous year, in which a white man named Roy Belton was taken from the jail and lynched while the police directed traffic so everyone could watch.[59]

Fearing for Rowland's safety, a group of some thirty African Americans armed themselves and proceeded to the jail. Many of them were World

War I veterans who had fought in Europe. At the same time, a chapter of the African Blood Brothers was organizing paramilitary operations to protect the Greenwood community.[60] Rowland's African American protectors were confronted by a white crowd as they arrived at the jail. When an African American World War I veteran refused to surrender his weapon, the riot was on. The fighting escalated over several days as more and more people from both races joined in, with the most active battling taking place around the Frisco railroad station, the dividing line between white and African American Tulsa. As the outnumbered African Americans retreated into the Greenwood district, whites began to destroy African American property as well as lives. In the process, they inflicted between $2 to $3 million in property damage as thousands of African American homes and businesses were burned, and another 304 African American homes were looted. When the riot finally subsided, 4,241 African Americans were left homeless and 300 were dead.[61]

Despite severe white opposition to rebuilding Greenwood, the community rebounded in a few years. Rebuilding was not easy, however. White real estate developers attempted to create a real estate boom for themselves out of the misery. They roamed Greenwood offering African Americans ten cents on the dollar for their property. When white bankers refused to lend money to African Americans who declined to deal with the real estate developers, the African Americans established financial arrangements among themselves. The Tulsa city council attempted to block even these efforts by passing an ordinance making it mandatory for all new buildings to be fireproof. This ordinance was quickly struck down by the courts in a lawsuit filed by African American lawyer and Greenwood resident, B. C. Franklin, the father of the great historian John Hope Franklin.[62]

The ingenuity and determination of Greenwood's African American community created an economic boom that surpassed even the pre-riot level. By 1925 Greenwood's economy was so strong that the Negro Business League decided to hold its annual convention there. By 1938 the "Negro Wall Street" had been completely restored. By 1942 Greenwood's professional class included 5 lawyers, 1 librarian, 4 dentists, 9 physicians, 8 pharmacists, 38 ministers, 8 social workers, 12 nurses, and 98 teachers. More impressive, in that year Greenwood boasted an estimated 242 businesses, which included 6 auto repair shops, 2 bakeries, 8 barbecue establishments, 28 beauty salons, 11 barber shops, 34 cafes, 12 chili parlors, 5 coal and ice dealers, 2 confectioneries, 8 drugstores, 1 electrical service, 3 furniture repair shops, 2 florists, 3 funeral parlors, 8 furriers, 38 grocers, 16 hotels, 3 insurance agencies, 1 jeweler, 7 laundries, 5 photographers, 3 printers, 5 radio repair shops, 6 realtors, 7 service shops, 9 shoe repair shops, 6 clothing stores, 15 tailors and drycleaning shops, 2 taxicabs, and 3 theaters. This extensive listing fails to include businesses which were not listed within the Negro Business League's directory.[63] The community supported two excellent public high schools, Washington High and Carver High, which taught African American history and heritage as well as Western civilization. John Hope Franklin is a product of the Greenwood school system.

After *Brown v. Board of Education,* Greenwood began to die. Racial integration did what the race riots of 1921 had failed to accomplish. African Americans stopped patronizing their own businesses, and whites, of course, never shopped in Greenwood. Most devastating, young and middle-class African Americans left Greenwood to take advantage of economic opportunities in other cities and states. In addition, an interstate highway was built right through the heart of the Greenwood community. One lifelong resident of Greenwood summed it up best in a PBS interview a few years ago: "We got integration and suffocation and degradation and all the other 'gations' you would like to add."[64]

My second example, the African American community in Durham, located in the Piedmont region between Raleigh and Greensboro, North Carolina, also exhibited economic independence through economic integration. As W. E. B. Du Bois remarked after a visit, "there is in this city a group of five thousand or more colored people, whose social and economic development is perhaps more striking than that of any similar group in the nation."[65] Durham offers a slightly different, less separatist model of economic integration than Greenwood: African Americans in Durham relied on jobs in the white economy to sustain their own economy to a much greater extent than their counterparts in Greenwood.

After Emancipation, African Americans began to migrate by the hundreds to North Carolina's rich tobacco industry. At that time, the undeveloped land on which they settled was mostly owned by wealthy whites. When the African American population expanded, whites gradually rented land to them, and eventually African Americans began to purchase land as their incomes grew. North Carolina's African American communities did not really begin to grow, however, until St. Joseph's AME Church was established in 1869, White Rock Baptist Church in 1875, and other African American churches at around the same time. These churches served as the area's primary cultural and civic centers.[66]

Initially, the Durham community had to take care of itself. Segregation forced African Americans to conduct business within their own group. Churches and other community institutions benefited from funds donated by successful African American businessmen. By 1930, when the population had reached 18,717, 5,508 African American males and 5,013 females over the age of ten were gainfully employed in Durham.[67] By the late 1940s, more than one hundred and fifty African American business enterprises flourished in Durham, including cafes, movie houses, barber shops, boarding houses, pressing shops, grocery stores, and funeral parlors.[68]

Many African Americans worked for whites. The Durham Hosiery Mill, which employed four hundred people by 1919, became the first factory in America to use an all-African American work force. The town's African American brick masons created and operated a union, which whites refused to join despite the union's invitation. As late as the 1940s, one-third of Durham's African American women engaged in domestic and personal service, mostly for whites.[69]

By far the greatest African American economic success story in Durham was the North Carolina Mutual Life Insurance Company. Founded in 1898, Mutual eventually became the most successful black insurance company in the world. By 1939 it boasted 1,000 employees and served over 250,000 policyholders. In that same year, it paid $18,336,126 to its policyholders and their beneficiaries, a significant amount considering that the company was limited by segregation to doing business only within its own racial group.[70] Many whites attempted to portray Mutual's success as "general proof of the inevitable progress in store for the black man under the benign race policy of the white South. The black success was made over into a white success."[71] African Americans, however, regarded Mutual Life as an example of their own success in spite of racism.

Because of its success, Mutual carried the burden of representing the entire black race. Indeed, financial aid requests came from as far away as Africa. Beyond its business dealings, Mutual also served as a missing persons bureau, a legal and financial clearinghouse, a complaint center, and a federal legislation information center. It even constructed a dormitory next to its headquarters for its single female employees,[72] and had its own song—"Give Me That Good Ol' Mutual Spirit."[73]

If neither racism nor riots could prevent the economic development of Greenwood and Durham, there is nothing today, save victimization mentality, that can stand in the way of economic independence in the African American community. As in the past, economic independence must be founded upon economic integration—African Americans of all socioeconomic classes coming together for the good of the community, the family, and, most importantly, the individual.

18

Political Power

Two major problems confront African Americans in the political arena: discrimination associated with casting the ballot (called the "right-to-vote" problem); and the inability to muster enough political power to protect or promote their interests (called the "voting power" problem or "dilution" problem). Although both problems have lingered long after the enactment of the 1965 Voting Rights Act, the second is perhaps the more serious. It feeds into voter apathy, which in turn aggravates the problem itself and undermines the whole voting process.

The right-to-vote impediments are best dealt with by traditional piecemeal litigation under the Voting Rights Act. Unfortunately, this is the only way to enforce the right to vote when, as here, the laws are otherwise clear and effective. Of course, some of the right-to-vote problem may dissipate on its own when and if African American communities achieve cultural and economic integration. Presumably, African Americans will be in charge of the election apparatus in such communities. To deal with the voting power problem, I propose a two-pronged approach, which, taken separately, is rather familiar: cumulative voting; and political coalitions buttressed by the Black PAC (political action committee).

Cumulative Voting

Cumulative voting is a race-neutral electoral device that allows voters to cast more than one vote for a single candidate depending on the number of seats available. For example, in an election for five city council seats, each voter would have five votes to distribute any way he or she desired. All five votes could be cast for one candidate. As whites split their votes among the white candidates, African Americans could accumulate their votes on the candidate of their choice, usually the lone African American candidate, thereby assuring his or her election.

Racial redistricting—the creation of a "safe" minority district through racial gerrymandering—is another remedy for racial bloc voting, but the cumulative voting alternative is preferable. First, racial redistricting limits the potential political influence of African Americans, because it leaves no political incentive for potential white allies (conservative and liberal alike) outside the voting district to form coalitions with African Americans inside the voting district. Each group must vote on separate slates of candidates. In contrast, cumulative voting creates a political incentive for cross-racial political coalitions. Second, racial redistricting limits the political power of individual African Americans who live outside the minority district. To the extent that they share common political interests with African Americans inside the district, they, along with white political allies, are politically impotent. Finally, given the constitutional constraints placed on racial redistricting, most recently in *Miller v. Johnson* (wherein the Supreme Court held that racial redistricting is proper only if it remedies past intentional discrimination in a narrowly tailored manner),[1] cumulative voting may be the only way African Americans can elect representatives of their choice to political office.

Although it is a reasonable electoral procedure not just in politics but in the corporate law context,[2] cumulative voting has become controversial in public discussions of electoral fairness. This is largely because of the way it was first brought to the public's attention. On April 29, 1993, President Clinton named Lani Guinier as his choice for Assistant Attorney General to head the Civil Rights Division of the U.S. Department of Justice. A professor at the University of Pennsylvania Law School, Guinier had attended Yale Law School with the Clintons. She was well qualified for the position. A civil rights attorney under the Carter administration, as well as an attorney for the NAACP Legal Defense and Education Fund for nine years, Guinier had also worked on the 1982 Amendment to § 2 of the Voting Rights Act.

Guinier's detractors were quick to attack her nomination. A *Wall Street Journal* op-ed piece written by a friend and former EEOC employee of Justice Clarence Thomas, Clint Bolick, led the attack. Entitled "Clinton's Quota Queen," the column accused Guinier of favoring racial quotas and declared that, given the opportunity, she "would graft into the existing system a complex racial spoils system that would polarize an already divided nation."[3] In the weeks that followed, excerpts from her writings appeared in the media, usually in the context of partisan attacks. She was portrayed as an advocate of proportionate representation who "dismisses 'majoritarian' voting as inherently discriminatory."[4] Senator Orrin Hatch was quoted as saying: "She is an architect of a theory of racial preferences that if enacted would push America down the road of racial balkanization."[5] Senator Robert Dole characterized her as "a consistent supporter not only of quotas but of vote rigging schemes that make quotas look mild."[6] Even the *New York Times*, a pillar of eastern liberalism, opposed her nomination.[7]

Throughout the month of May the attack continued largely unchallenged, while the nominee quietly made courtesy calls on Senate Judiciary Committee members. Following White House directions, Guinier did not defend herself in public. Surprisingly, her supporters were slow to respond on her behalf. When they did respond, they mainly assailed her enemies for taking her ideas "out of context."[8] Not until the first days of June, with the nomination already in great peril, did her fellow civil rights advocates wage a counterattack. By then it was too late. The President did not want to force the Senate into a partisan battle over the nomination when he needed to steer the budget-deficit bill through Congress. Despite her last minute appearance on ABC's *Nightline* on June 2, 1993, in which she tried to muster a broader base of support, on June 3 the President withdrew the nomination, before Guinier had a chance to defend herself before the Senate Judiciary Committee.[9]

In the context of these political battles, cumulative voting has acquired a bad reputation. This is unfair and unfortunate. Cumulative voting was only one of several planks in Guinier's bundle of views on voting rights and is certainly not the one that drew the bulk of the political criticism.[10] Rather, it was her advocacy of "proportionality," which she usually uses to spice up cumulative voting, that ignited the criticism. Her argument is as follows:

> To get the full benefits of cumulative voting, however, it would also be necessary to change the process of governmental decision-making itself, away from a majoritarian model toward one of proportional power. In particular, efforts to centralize authority in a single executive would be discouraged in favor of power sharing alternatives that emphasize collective decision-making. Within the legislature, such devices for minority incorporation as rotation in legislative of-

fice could be introduced, and rules could be enacted that require super majorities for the enactment of certain decisions. Minority groups would then have an effective veto, thus forcing the majority to bargain with them and include them in any winning coalition. Other electoral and legislative decision making alternatives are also available—for example, legislative cumulative voting—that are fair and legitimate, that preserve representational authenticity, and yet are more likely than current practices to promote just results.[11]

This attack on majoritarianism, the *sine qua non* of democracy, was and still remains highly controversial. Many scholars and policy makers simply reject her belief that "we need to put the idea of proportionality at the center of our conception of representation."[12]

My endorsement of cumulative voting is conditioned upon its separation from proportionality. I favor cumulative voting not for reasons of racial tribalism but for the advantages it gives to the individual voter. Cumulative voting responds to racial polarization and other structural barriers that routinely disadvantage African Americans by creating an environment in which the African American individual can succeed both as a candidate for elective office and, more importantly, as a citizen whose social and economic interests can be protected in the political process. Here, as in the case of all forms of limited separation—separate public schools, HBCUs, and cultural and economic integration—cumulative voting has merit because of its ability to create opportunities for the *individual*. Racial kinship is a distant second to individual opportunity; the latter is never to be sacrificed to the former.

Political Coalitions and Black PAC

Although cumulative voting can increase the ability of African Americans to elect candidates of their choice to office, it cannot resolve the voting power problem. Like racial redistricting, cumulative voting only facilitates the election of marginalized African American politicians, politicians who are always outnumbered and hence outvoted in their respective deliberative bodies. Guinier seems to have recognized this fact, which is why she added the kicker of proportionality to cumulative voting:

But while black legislative visibility is an important measure of electoral fairness, taken by itself it represents an anemic approach to political fairness and justice. A vision of fairness and justice must begin to imagine a full and effective voice for disadvantaged minorities, a voice that is accountable to self-identified community interests, a voice that persuades, and a voice that is included in and resonates throughout the political process. That voice will not be achieved by majoritarian means or by enforced separation into winner-take-all racial districts.[13]

But while Guinier believes that African American political power can only be built up by tearing down our traditional "majoritarian model of centralized, winner-take-all accountability and popular sovereignty,"[14] I believe it can be achieved through the less draconian measure of coalition building.

The strategy of forming cross-racial political coalitions is old and rather limited in its success. Jesse Jackson's Rainbow Coalition is a prime example. But cross-racial political coalitions look very different in the context of my overall strategy of limited separation. The probability of success of such coalitions is substantially increased when busing, racial preferences, and other racially explosive issues are taken out of the mix. As African Americans become more interested in quality education rather than integrated education, in revitalizing African American communities rather than escaping into unwelcoming white communities, and creating small businesses rather than demanding larger welfare checks or greater acceptance by white employers and fellow employees, the political base for the development of effective cross-racial coalitions will expand. It will not be unrealistic for African Americans to form political coalitions with white suburban parents to support school board candidates who favor greater local control over public schools. Nor will it be unreasonable for African Americans to work with the Chamber of Commerce for lower taxes and less government regulation over small businesses. Furthermore, as the race issue becomes less divisive, polarized voting may also become less likely. Whether or not race-conscious voting ever becomes a relic of the past, however, one thing is clear: meaningful cross-racial coalitions are impossible right now.

To buttress the bargaining power of African Americans in cross-racial political coalitions, the Black PAC is needed. The Black PAC would operate as other political action committees do and in conjunction with them. It would be similar to the Susan B. Anthony List, which funnels money to both Democratic and Republican candidates who support abortion rights and other women's interests, the Jewish federations that provide financial support to local and national politicians who take pro-Jewish stances, and GOPAC, an interlocking network of political action committees created by Newt Gingrich that raised money and refined a political ideology that sowed the seeds of the 1994 Republican congressional victory.[15] Financed in large part by African American businesses and wealthy individuals, the Black PAC would have local and national offices. It would provide African Americans with the financial wherewithal and structure to influence white candidates and office-holders at all levels.

Alongside influencing political spending, the Black PAC would also help to fashion a political ideology to help African Americans achieve their social and economic objectives. The principal political objective is to create a social and economic environment that nurtures the individual African American. Whatever the Black PAC may accomplish for African Americans as a group must be seen only as a means to help the individual. Whether conservative or liberal or centralist in content, African American ideology must place individual success above racial kinship—the individual must be placed before the group—as I have attempted to do in this book.

Epilogue

Limited separation should be treated *pari passu* with racial integration. That is the argument advanced in this book. So long as whites will not or cannot relinquish the cultural deference and socioeconomic privileges they hold over African Americans in our society, and so long as they continue to curtail or eliminate affirmative action and other means of sharing power, there will always be a need for limited separation. Otherwise, what else is left for African Americans to do? What hope do they have of achieving personal happiness and worldly success—individual dignity and empowerment—other than forging these for themselves?

It is not just angry average white males or rednecks who are unwilling to give up enough poker chips to allow integration to work better than it now does. White intellectuals and elites, driven by economic insecurity, years of frustration "playing the integration game," and age-old racism, also oppose meaningful attempts to promote racial integration. Lest we forget, it was two Berkeley professors who initiated the California anti-affirmative action campaign. Perhaps equally disheartening is the myriad of "decent" white folk who, through their silence, empower the Mark Furhmans in our society. In a very real sense, they are more thwarting of racial integration than the relatively few aggressive racists. Racial mixing, in short, simply cannot be nurtured in a society whose largeness of spirit diminishes with each passing decade.

Our political leaders, likewise, seem little interested in aggressively promoting racial integration. Some, no doubt, feel it is better to use our limited collective resources of time, money, energy, and moral fervor to tackle other national problems—AIDS, the budget deficit, environmental management—leaving racial integration for another time. Others, more sinisterly motivated, use racial division as a sword to hack for themselves a path to higher public office. And still others simply do not give a damn one way or another.

This hardening of racial attitudes should push African Americans to look to themselves rather than to whites for salvation. It should cause African Americans to face the cold reality that tells them they have never been and probably will never be equal partners in the integration enterprise. Slowly, this racial awakening is happening across black America now. Numerous studies show that middle-class African Americans feel marginalized in white institutions, even if they do not always show the rage and pain they feel around whites. Poor and working-class African Americans believe they have little or no access to the established avenues of worldly success in an integrated society.

If African Americans are not faking deep dissatisfaction with racial integration, if this well-intended but poorly executed civil rights strategy is really not working for the vast majority of them, one would expect that, regardless of socioeconomic class, African Americans would want to look for a different way to achieve racial equality. Indeed, many have been looking in the direction of total separation, which, in my judgment, is the wrong way to go. But this readiness to do something, this feeling that this may be put-up or shut-up time for African Americans, is a good sign.

Near the end of his life, the Reverend Martin Luther King, Jr., seemed to recognize the need to diversify our civil rights strategy. Overcoming the deepest of integrationist impulses, he came to accept racial separation in some form: "temporary separation as a way-station to a truly integrated society."[1] Had King lived long enough to follow through on this separatist strategy, he would undoubtedly have met strong opposition from some of the very same radical integrationists whom he had inspired. But to these well-meaning liberals (whites and African Americans) who fear any form of racial separation, he probably would have responded by referring them to his famous "Letter from Birmingham City Jail." Written in 1963 in answer to southern white religious leaders who criticized nonviolent demonstrations as "unwise and untimely," the text reads in part: "In the midst of blatant injustices inflicted upon the Negro, I have watched white churches stand on the sidelines and merely mouth pious irrelevancies and sanctimonious trivialities."[2] Asking African Americans to be patient with racial integration or attempting to shame whites into behaving more morally in the midst of blatant and persistent racial inequality amounts to nothing more than "pious irrelevancies and sanctimonious trivialities."

In writing this book, I (a moderate integrationist) have tried to steer clear of such self-indulgence. I have tried to fashion a civil rights policy that is both useful and universal. Limited separation—cultural and economic integration within a racial (or gender) group—is useful in that it will enable African Americans of all classes to succeed as individuals without white leadership or the burden of racial kinship. Limited separation is universal, not limited to African Americans. It is open to Asians and whites, women and men, so long as they can demonstrate the need for a supportive environment free of debilitating racism or, in the case of gender, sexism. Indeed, the idea of limited separation is similar to what has been successfully tried by prosperous ethnic groups—white and minority immigrants and, now, Native Americans—and by African Americans on a very limited scale and under far worse racial circumstances than exist today. Patterned in the specific ways described in this book, limited separation will not balkanize American society, as would total separation.

Although similar in concept to the American immigrant experience, limited separation is different in one important respect: casual subordination of other groups or individuals will not be allowed. Limited separation, in other words, seeks to serve and support individuals within the group without unnecessarily trammeling the interests of other individuals or groups. It draws no circles around African Americans or any other social group. The only circumstance under which race or gender could be used as a restrictive classification, thereby denying an individual an opportunity on account of his or her race or gender, is when race or gender is a bona fide selection qualification; in other words, reasonably necessary to the normal operation of the institution in question. We can look to contemporary civil rights case law involving religious, sex, and age discrimination to guide our application of this principle. But it is worth remembering that there would have to be a sizable number of people from other social groups *already* in the organization to successfully establish such a qualification.

Most importantly, limited separation tenders a form of self-help that is kinder and gentler than previous forms of self-help practiced by African Americans. Self-help founded on limited separation, with its emphasis on enlightened self-interest rather than altruism and its incorporation of the nonsubordination principle, may be more palatable to African Americans as well as whites than a form of self-help that embraces racial accommodation (à la Booker T. Washington) or racial subordination (internal or external), totalitarianism, and anti-white xenophobia (à la the Nation of Islam or the Black Panther Party). There is no nation-building agenda in the self-help concept limited separation embodies, nor is the individual sacrificed in the name of "the cause." Rather, the primary purpose of limited separation and its self-help concept is to give the individual, whether it be a young Thurgood Marshall or a young Clarence Thomas, an alternative path to dignity and empowerment. The secondary goal is to make *healthy*, two-way racial integration possible.

It is important to reiterate that there is little chance that limited separation will balkanize American society. Unlike total separation, limited separation does not endanger the idea of a shared Americanness. Limited separation embraces principles and values such as liberty, rational individualism, democratic institutions, and middle-class devotion to education and the work ethic—values that support the ideal of political and cultural unity in an ethnically diverse society. Likewise, limited separation rejects racism (black and white), Black Nationalism, ethnic nationalism, racial essentialism, racial mythmaking, and other belief systems that undermine unity. Limited separation, in short, broadens the American base without destroying it.

For these reasons I do not view limited separation merely as a "way-station" to racial integration, as would Martin Luther King. I envision it as that and more—namely, an alternative means to individual dignity and empowerment. For African Americans in particular, I see limited separation and racial integration (racial mixing) as two different strategies for entering mainstream society as first-class citizens. Those African Americans who cannot or will not swim in the unfriendly waters of racial integration, where racism patrols like a hungry shark, would have the alternative of a more dignified and more realistic approach to racial equality.

There is no doubt that the task of turning African American communities around is large and requires some outside assistance. But think of the number of inner-city young men and women this effort will pull into the social and economic mainstream. I see these challenges as opportunities rather than excuses for maintaining the status quo.

If the three civil rights strategies discussed in this book do not work individually or in combination, then Americans must face the unhappy prospect that the problem of equality in our society is without a real solution; that African Americans, other minorities, and women will have no choice but to live in quiet desperation or open confrontation. Even so, the quest for equality must and will continue. But I cannot be satisfied with the oft-stated refrain of the downtrodden that salvation is in the struggle itself. Let us instead hope to see African Americans empower themselves by starting their own poker game.

Notes

Index

Notes

I. Racial Integration

1. *Ottawa v. Tinnon,* 26 Kan. 1, 19 (1881).
2. Harrison Rainie, "Black and White in America," *U.S. News & World Report,* July 22, 1991, p. 18 (quoting Gunnar Myrdal).

1. Elementary and Secondary Education

1. 347 U.S. 483 (1954). This decision is commonly known as *Brown I,* while *Brown II* is *Brown v. Board of Education,* 349 U.S. 294 (1955), which ruled that *Brown I*'s school desegregation mandate must be executed "with all deliberate speed."

2. Robert Carter, "The Warren Court and Desegregation," *Michigan Law Rev.* 67 (1968): 54–72.

3. T. Harry Williams, Richard N. Current and Frank Freidel, *A History of the U.S. to 1877,* 3d ed. (New York: Alfred A. Knopf, 1969), p. 90. Arthur O. White, "The Black Leadership Class and Education in Antebellum Boston," *Journal of Negro Education* 42 (1973): 504–515. Carter J. Woodson, *The Education of the Negro Prior to 1861* (Washington, D.C.: Associated Publishers, 1919).

4. See White, "The Black Leadership Class and Education in Antebellum Boston," p. 509; S. Schultz, *The Culture Factory: Boston Public Schools, 1789–1860* (New York: Oxford University Press, 1973), pp. 159–161.

5. See Joan Davis Ratteray, "Independent Neighborhood Schools: A Framework for the Education of African Americans," *Journal of Negro Education* 61 (1992): 138; Woodson, *The Education of the Negro Prior to 1861,* p. 307. Dr. Woodson has spoken more broadly about the proper education of African Americans in *The Mis-Education of the Negro* (Nashville, Tenn: Winston-Derek, 1990, originally published in 1933). For a general discussion of the establishment of African

American schools during this period, see Woodson, *The Education of the Negro Prior to 1861;* Horace Mann Bond, *The Education of the Negro in the American Social Order* (New York: Octagon Books, 1966, originally published in 1934), pp. 367–390.

6. See Schultz, *The Cultural Factory,* pp. 159–161; Williams, Current, and Freidel, *A History of the U.S.,* p. 90.

7. See Roy L. Brooks, *Rethinking the American Race Problem* (Berkeley, Calif.: University of California Press, 1990), pp. 75–76.

8. 59 Mass. (5 Cush.) 198 (1850).

9. Id. pp. 201–204.

10. 163 U.S. 537 (1896).

11. The petitioner "was seven eighths Caucasian and one eighth African blood." This made him a person of "the colored race" for the purposes of the segregation laws of the day. See id. pp. 540–541, 551. For a discussion of our nation's racial classifications, see generally, F. James Davis, *Who Is Black: One Nation's Definition* (University Park, Penn.: Pennsylvania State University Press, 1991).

12. 163 U.S. at 550.

13. Id.

14. Walter G. Stephan, "Blacks and Brown: The Effects of School Desegregation on Black Students" (prepared for the United State Department of Education, National Institute of Education, 1983), p. 5.

15. See id. p. 3. See also Robert A. Margo, *Race and Schooling in the South, 1880–1950: An Economic History* (Chicago, Ill.: University of Chicago Press, 1990); James D. Anderson, *The Education of Blacks in the South, 1860–1935* (Chapel Hill, N.C.: University of North Carolina Press, 1988).

16. A report on the Kansas City schools can be found in a publication of the Harvard Project on School Desegregation, directed by Gary Orfield, cited as Alison Morantz, *Money, Choice and Equity in Kansas City: Major Investments with Modest Returns* (Cambridge, Mass.: Harvard University, April, 1994).

17. See W. E. B. Du Bois and Augustus Dill, *The Common School and the Negro American* (New York: Russell & Russell, 1969, originally published in 1911).

18. See Horace Mann Bond, *The Education of the Negro;* Horace Mann Bond, *Negro Education in Alabama: A Study in Cotton and Steel* (New York: Octagon Books, 1969, originally published in 1939).

19. See Gunnar Myrdal, *An American Dilemma: The Negro Problem and Modern Democracy* (New York: Harper & Brothers, 1944).

20. Robert A. Margo, *Race and Schooling in the South, 1880–1950: An Economic History* (Chicago, Ill.: University of Chicago Press, 1990), p. 56. "In the Deep South States of Louisiana and Mississippi, black teachers earned about 80 percent of what white teachers earned [in 1890]." Id. p. 54. See also Thurgood Marshall, "Teacher Salary Cases" in *The Negro Handbook 1946–1947,* ed. Florence Murray (New York: A. A. Wynn, 1947), pp. 40–50.

21. Stephan, *Blacks and Brown,* p. 3 (sources cited therein).

22. 98 F. Supp. 529 (1951).

23. Richard Kluger, *Simple Justice* (New York: Knopf, 1976), p. 332.

24. See *Alston v. School Board of City of Norfolk,* 112 F.2d 992 (1940), cert. den. 311 U.S. 693 (1940) (African American teachers cannot be arbitrarily paid less than white teachers for public services of the same kind and character); *Missouri ex rel. Gaines v. Canada,* 305 U.S. 337 (1938) (relying on *Plessy,* the Court held that an African American citizen of Missouri must be admitted to the state's all-white law school rather than be forced to attend an out-of-state law school); *Sweatt v. Painter,* 339 U.S. 629 (1950) (African American student ordered admitted to the all-white University of Texas Law School on ground that the state law school established for African Americans failed to offer equal educational opportunities); *McLaurin v. Oklahoma State Regents of Higher Education,* 339 U.S. 637 (1950) (state-imposed restrictions placed on African American graduate students attending an otherwise all-white university produced such inequalities as to offend the Equal Protection Clause).

25. The change in litigation strategy took effect at the trial level in *Briggs v. Elliott,* 98 F. Supp. 529 (1951), where the district court judge, J. Waites Waring, dismissed the case without prejudice to allow Thurgood Marshall to refile the case as an attack on the constitutionality of racial segregation rather than as a constitutional challenge based merely on equal facilities. See Richard Kluger, *Simple Justice,* p. 304. *Briggs* was one of four cases consolidated in *Brown v. Board of Education,* 347 U.S. 483 (1954). See *Briggs v. Elliott,* 347 U.S. 497 (1954). This strategy culminated with a NAACP victory in 1954 in *Brown.*

26. The Proclamation freed those slaves residing in states that had not rejected the Confederacy by January 1, 1863. Proclamation of January 1, 1863, No. 17, 12 Stat. 1268 (1863). See generally John Hope Franklin, *The Emancipation Proclamation* (Garden City, N.Y.: Doubleday, 1963).

27. *Brown v. Board of Education,* 347 U.S. 483, 494.

28. Id. p. 493, n.11.

29. For a more detailed discussion of the distinction between self-esteem and racial esteem, see J. R. Porter and R. E. Washington, "Minority Identity and Self-Esteem," *Annual Review of Sociology,* 19 (1993): 139–161.

30. 347 U.S. at 493.

31. Id. p. 493 n.10. This finding, however, is somewhat different from the previous finding in that it speaks in terms of educational opportunities rather than African American identity.

32. See id. p. 493 n.11.

33. See *Argument: The Oral Argument Before the Supreme Court in Brown v. Board of Education of Topeka, 1952–1955,* ed. Leon Friedman, Jr. (New York: Chelsea House Publishers, 1969), pp. xxxvii, 58.

34. William E. Cross, Jr., "Black Identity: Rediscovering The Distinction Between Personal Identity and Reference Group Orientation," in Margaret B. Spencer, Geraldine K. Brookins, and Walter R. Allen, eds., *Beginnings: The Social and Affective Development of Black Children* (Hillsdale, N.J.: Lawrence Erlbaum Associates, 1985), p. 162.

35. Kenneth B. Clark and Mamie K. Clark, "Racial Identification and Preference in Negro Children," in T. M. Newcomb and E. L. Hartley, eds., *Readings in Social Psychology*, 3d ed. (New York: Holt, Rinehart and Winston, 1958), pp. 602–604, 608–611, and Tables 1 and 5.

36. See *Brown*, 347 U.S. at 493–494, 493 n.11. See also Kenneth B. and Mamie K. Clark, "Segregation as a Factor in the Racial Identification of Negro Preschool Children: A Preliminary Report," *Journal of Experimental Education* 9 (1939): 161–163.

37. Clark and Clark, "Racial Identification and Preference in Negro Children," p. 610, Table 8.

38. Id. pp. 609, 610, 611, Table 6.

39. Id. pp. 603, 606, Table 3.

40. Id. p. 611.

41. Walter G. Stephan, "School Desegregation: Short-Term and Long-Term Effects," in Harry J. Knopke, Robert J. Norrell, and Ronald W. Rogers, eds., *Opening Doors: Perspectives on Race Relations in Contemporary America* (Tuscaloosa, Ala.: University of Alabama Press, 1991), p. 117.

42. F. H. Allport, et al., "The Effects of Segregation and the Consequences of Desegregation: A Social Science Statement," *Minnesota Law Review* 37 (1953): 429–440. For other scholarly support of the Clarks' theory see also R. E. Horowitz, "Racial Aspects of Self-Identification in Nursery School Children," *Journal of Psychology* 7 (1939): 91; K. Lewin, *Resolving Social Conflicts* (New York: Harper, 1948); H. Butts, "Skin Color Perception and Self-Esteem," *Journal of Negro Education* 32 (1963): 122.

43. Richard Kluger, *Simple Justice,* p. 415.

44. Id. p. 421.

45. Id.

46. *The Effects of Segregation and the Consequences of Desegregation: A Social Science Statement,* Appendix to Appellant's Brief in *Brown v. Board of Education,* October Term, 1952, p. 17.

47. See C. Jencks, *Inequality: A Reassessment of the Effects of Family and Schooling in America* (New York: Basic Books, 1972), pp. 97–98.

48. These statistics can be found in a publication of the Harvard Project on School Desegregation (directed by Gary Orfield) cited as Joseph Feldman, Edward Kirby, Susan E. Eaton, Alison Morantz, *Still Separate, Still Unequal: The Limits of Milliken II's Educational Compensation Remedies* (Cambridge, Mass.: Harvard University, April, 1994), p. 15. See also "Vital Signs: The State of African Americans in Higher Education," *The Journal of Blacks in Higher Education* (Spring 1994): 42; Brooks, *Rethinking the American Race Problem,* pp. 203–204; Elizabeth Gleick, "Segregation Anxiety," *Time,* April 24, 1995, p. 63.

49. Joy Keiko Asamen, "Afro-American Students and Academic Achievement," in Gordon LaVern Berry and Joy Keiko Asamen, eds., *Black Students: Psychosocial Issues and Academic Achievement* (Newbury Park, Calif.: Sage Publications, 1989), p. 12. See generally Jonathan Kozol, *Savage Inequalities: Children in American*

Schools (New York: Crown Publications, 1991). See Jacqueline Jordan Irvine, *Black Students and School Failure: Policies, Practices and Prescriptions* (New York: Greenwood Press, 1990), pp. 6–8.

50. *Missouri v. Jenkins,* 115 S. Ct. 2038, 2066 (1995) (Thomas J., concurring).

51. Alex M. Johnson, Jr., "Bid Whist, Tonk, and *United States v. Fordice:* Why Integrationism Fails African-Americans Again," *California Law Review* 81 (1993): 1409.

52. See generally Richard Delgado, "Enormous Anomaly? Left-Right Parallels in Recent Writing About Race," *Columbia Law Review* 91 (1991): 1547–1560.

53. Cross, "Black Identity," p. 156.

54. Id. p. 160.

55. Id. p. 155.

56. Id. p. 157.

57. Id.

58. Id. pp. 157–158.

59. Id. p. 157. See generally K. Lewin, *Resolving Social Conflicts* (New York, N.Y.: Harper, 1948); M. E. Goodman, *Race Awareness in Young Children* (New York, N.Y.: Collier Books, 1970); Harriette P. McAdoo, "The Development of Self-Concept and Race Attitudes in Black Children: A Longitudinal Study," in William E. Cross, Jr., ed., *The Third Conference on Empirical Research in Black Psychology,* (1977): p. 47.

60. Cross, "Black Identity," p. 162.

61. Excluded from this group were field studies that relied on case study and participant observation techniques and studies that used unscaled or informal questionnaires or interviews for gathering data. This type of work has proved of relatively minor importance in documenting negative African American identity from 1939 to 1967 and documenting the apparent change in African American identity from 1968 to the present. Sixty-three percent of the 161 studies were personal identity studies, all but one conducted in the post-1968 period. Id. p. 158.

62. Id. p. 160.

63. Id.

64. See Morris Rosenberg and Roberta E. Simmons, *Black and White Self-Esteem: The Urban School Child* (Washington, D.C.: American Sociological Association, 1972).

65. See Judith Porter, *Black Child, White Child: The Development of Racial Attitudes* (Cambridge, Mass.: Harvard University Press, 1971).

66. See McAdoo, "Development of Self-Concept and Race Attitudes in Black Children."

67. See S. J. Ward and J. Baum, "Self-Esteem and Racial Preference in Black Children," *American Journal of Orthopsychiatry* 42 (1972): 644, 647.

68. See A. Fouther-Austin, "Cross Geographical Study of Black Consciousness and Self-Concept Relative to Perceived Teacher Attitude and School Achievement," *Dissertation Abstracts International* 4650-A 38-OA (1978).

69. See B. D. Mobley, "Self-Concept and the Conceptualization of Ethnic Iden-

tity: The Black Experience," Ph.D dissertation on file at Purdue University, Microfilm N. 74–5017 (1973); H. Butts, "Skin Color Perception and Self-Esteem," *Journal of Negro Education* 32 (1963): 122, 128. See generally Cross, "Black Identity," pp. 161, 165–167.

70. See Cross, "Black Identity," p. 159, Table 9.1.

71. See W. Curtis Banks, "White Preference in Blacks: A Paradigm in Search of a Phenomenon," *Psychological Bulletin* 83 (1976): 1179–1186. Each of these studies dealt with children between the ages of 3–8, and the Clarks' study is the only pre-1954 study.

72. See H. Butts, "Skin Color Perception and Self-Esteem."

73. See Cross, "Black Identity," pp. 161, 169 (sources cited therein).

74. See generally id. pp. 24–25. For a detailed discussion, see Roy L. Brooks, "Understanding Black Self-Esteem Forty Years After Brown: Some Suggestions for the Supreme Court," *Temple Political & Civil Rights Law Review* 4 (1995): 217.

75. See, Cross, "Black Identity," p. 158, 159, Table 9.1; W. Banks, "White Preference in Blacks: A Paradigm in Search of a Phenomenon." Reviewing 32 RGO studies conducted before and after 1968, Banks also argues that 69% reported no racial preference and only 6% indicated a pattern of white preference both before and after 1968.

76. Stephan, *Blacks and Brown,* p. 31.

77. Rosenberg and Simmons, *Black and White Self-Esteem,* p. 25; J. G. Bachman, *Youth in Transition, Volume II: The Impact of Family Background and Intelligence in Tenth-Grade Boys* (Ann Arbor, Mich.: Institute for Social Research, University of Michigan, 1970), pp. 130, 265; G. J. Powell and M. Fuller, "Desegregation and Self-Concept" (paper presented at the 47th Annual Meeting of the American Orthopsychiatric Association, San Francisco, Calif., March 23–26, 1970).

78. See Stephan, *Blacks and Brown,* p. 31.

79. See J. L. Steitmatter, "School Desegregation and Identity Development," *Urban Education* 23 (1988): 280–293; E. G. Epps, "Future Directions for Desegregation Research," *Equity and Choice* 4 (1988): 18–20; R. Bowler, et al., "Racial Tension in a Multi-Ethnic High School and a Preventive Intervention" (paper presented at the American Psychological Association Convention in Washington, D.C., August 23–27, 1982).

80. Constance Johnson, "The Sad Ways Kids Look at Integration," *U.S. News & World Report,* May 23, 1994, p. 33.

81. Rosenberg and Simmons, *Black and White Self-Esteem,* p. 26.

82. Stephan, *Blacks and Brown,* p. 31.

83. Id.

84. See Michael Hughes and David H. Demo, "Self-Perception of Black Americans: Self-Esteem and Personal Efficacy," *American Journal of Sociology* 95 (1989): 132.

85. See Neal Kraus, "The Racial Context of Self-Esteem," *Social Psychology* 46 (1978): 98–107.

86. See generally Brooks, *Rethinking the American Race Problem,* pp. 76–79.

87. See Deborah J. Carter and Reginald Wilson, *Twelfth Annual Status Report on Minorities in Higher Education* (Washington, D.C.: American Council on Education, 1994), Table 1, pp. 44–45. See also Gerald David Jaynes and Robin M. Williams, *Common Destiny: Blacks and American Society* (Washington, D.C.: National Academy Press, 1989), p. 373.

88. See "Improving America's Schools Act of 1994," 103rd Congress 2d Sess., 140 *Congressional Record* S10163 (8/1/94), p. 10166.

89. Los Angeles Unified School District, *Dropouts 1992–1993: Senior High Schools;* Los Angeles Unified School District, *1993 Ethnic Percentages: Senior High Schools.*

90. "Improving America's Schools Act of 1994," 103rd Congress 2nd Sess., 140 *Congressional Record* S10163 (8/1/94), p. S10166.

91. Johnson, "The Sad Ways Kids Look at Integration," p. 35.

92. Martin Patchen, *Black-White Contact in Schools: Its Social and Academic Effects* (West Lafayette, Ind.: Purdue University Press, 1982), pp. 342–343.

93. Thomas Cook, "School Desegregation and Black Achievement" (paper prepared for the United States Department of Education, National Institute of Education 1984), p. 60.

94. Jaynes and Williams, *Common Destiny,* p. 348.

95. Christine Meldrum and Susan Eaton, *Resegregation in Norfolk, Virginia: Does Restoring Neighborhood Schools Work?,* The Harvard Project on School Desegregation (Cambridge, Mass.: Harvard University School of Education, May 1994), p. 48.

96. See David J. Armor, "Why Is Black Educational Achievement Rising?" *The Public Interest* (Summer 1992): 65–80.

97. See Patchen, *Black-White Contact in Schools,* pp. 33, 350.

98. See Meldrum and Eaton, *Resegregation in Norfolk, Virginia,* p. 48.

99. See Wightman and Muller, *An Analysis of Differential Validity and Differential Prediction for Black, Mexican American, Hispanic, and White Law School Students,* Report No. 90–103 (Washington, D.C.: Law School Admission Council Research Report, June 1990).

100. *Common Destiny,* pp. 17, 348, 350, 351.

101. "Improving America's Schools Act of 1994," 103rd Congress 2nd Sess., 140 *Congressional Record* S10163 (8/1/94).

102. Id. p. S10167.

103. Id. p. S10166.

104. Id. p. S10167.

105. Id.

106. *Milliken v. Bradley,* 433 U.S. 267, 288–289 (1977) (commonly referred to as *Milliken II*).

107. Id. p. 351.

108. Cook, *School Desegregation and Black Achievement,* p. 60.

109. See Brooks, *Rethinking the American Race Problem,* pp. 67–69, 80–81, 106–107, 109–116.

110. Id. p. 76. See also Irvine, *Black Students* (New York: Greenwood Press, 1990), p. 4. See generally Jennifer L. Hochschild, *Thirty Years After Brown* (1985) and *The New American Dilemma: Liberal Democracy and School Desegregation* (New Haven, Conn.: Yale University Press, 1984).

111. See Hochschild, *Thirty Years After Brown*, p. 5.

112. Brooks, *Rethinking the American Race Problem*, p. 77.

113. See Chen-Lin Kulik and James Kulik, "Effects of Ability Grouping on Secondary School Students: A Meta-Analysis of Evaluation Findings," *American Educational Research Journal* 19 (Fall 1982): 415–428.

114. Id. pp. 415–428.

115. See Irvine, *Black Students*, pp. 10, 16; Jaynes and Williams, *Common Destiny*, pp. 356, 357.

116. See Irvine, *Black Students*, p. 33.

117. Woodson, *The Mis-Education of the Negro*, p. 20.

118. See Marva Collins, *Marva Collins' Way* (Los Angeles, Calif.: J. P. Tarcher, 1982), p. 221.

119. Hochschild, *Thirty Years After Brown*, pp. 5, 6. See *San Diego Voice & Viewpoint*, January 11, 1996, p. A8.

120. See Irvine, *Black Students*, pp. 17, 18.

121. Brooks, *Rethinking the American Race Problem*, pp. 77–78. See Hochschild, *Thirty Years After Brown*, p. 12.

122. *Common Destiny*, p. 365.

123. Johnson, "The Sad Ways Kids Look at Integration," p. 35.

2. Higher Education

1. For a controversial discussion of this point by an African American college professor, see Shelby Steele, *The Content of Our Character: A New Vision of Race in America* (New York: St. Martin Press, 1990).

2. See "Vital Signs: The State of African Americans in Higher Education," *The Journal of Blacks in Higher Education* (Winter 1993–94): 31, 39 (relying on data from the Department of Education and the American Council on Education).

3. See Deborah Carter and Reginald Wilson, *12th Annual Status Report on Minorities in Higher Education* (Washington, D.C.: American Council on Education, 1993), pp. 44–45, Table 1. See also Roy L. Brooks, *Rethinking the American Race Problem* (Berkeley: University of California Press, 1990), p. 81; *A Common Destiny: Blacks and American Society*, eds. Gerald J. Jaynes and Robin M. Williams, Jr. (Washington, D.C.: National Academy Press, 1989), pp. 339–340.

4. See Carter and Wilson, *Minorities in Higher Education*, pp. 44–45.

5. Robert Bruce Slater, "The Growing Gender Gap in Black Higher Education," *The Journal of Blacks in Higher Education* (Spring 1994): 53.

6. Id. pp. 54–58.

7. Id. pp. 58, 59.

8. "Education Secretary Issues Final Policy Guidance on Minority Scholarships," *Civil Rights Monitor* (Winter 1994): 4–5.

9. See Brooks, *Rethinking the American Race Problem,* p. 99.

10. "Vital Signs," p. 38.

11. For a discussion of the minority scholarship issue, see "Guidance on Minority Scholarships."

12. See Brooks, *Rethinking the American Race Problem,* p. 100–103. See also Stanley Fish, "Affirmative Action and the SAT," *The Journal of Blacks in Higher Education* (Winter 1993–94): 83.

13. Theodore Cross, "Suppose There Was No Affirmative Action at the Most Prestigious Colleges and Graduate Schools," *The Journal of Blacks in Higher Education* (Spring 1994): 46.

14. Most of the studies on standardized tests are collected in Rita J. Simon and Mona J. E. Danner, "Developments Notes: Gender, Race, and the Predictive Value of the LSAT," *Journal of Legal Education* 40 (1990): 525, n.2. See especially Paul A. Mauger and Claire A. Kolmodin, "Long-Term Predictive Validity of the Scholastic Aptitude Test," *Journal of Educational Psychology* 67 (1975): 847 (discussing the SAT); Franklin R. Evans, "Recent Trends in Law School Validity Studies," in *Reports of LSAC Sponsored Research: Vol. IV, 1978–1983* (Princeton, N.J.: Law School Admissions Council, 1984), pp. 347, 358–360.

15. See Mauger and Kolmodin, "Scholastic Aptitude Test," p. 847; Evans, "Recent Trends," p. 359, 360; Donald E. Powers, "Long-Term Predictive and Construct Validity of Two Traditional Predictors of Law School Performance," *Journal of Educational Psychology* 74 (1982): 569.

16. See A. P. Johnson and M. A. Olsen, "Comparative Three-Year and One-Year Validities of the Law School Admission Test at Two Law Schools," in *Reports of LSAC Sponsored Research: Vol. 1, 1949–1969* (Princeton, N.J.: Law School Admission Council, 1976).

17. Powers, "Two Traditional Predictors of Law School Performance," p. 572.

18. Donald E. Powers, "Predicting Law School Grades for Minority and Nonminority Students: Beyond the First-Year Average," in *Reports of LSAC Sponsored Research: Vol. IV, 1978–1983* (Princeton, N.J.: Law School Admissions Council, 1984), p. 263. See also id. p. 264.

19. See Simon and Danner, "Gender, Race, and the Predictive Value of the LSAT," p. 525.

20. Fish, "Affirmative Action and the SAT," p. 83. See Brooks, *Rethinking the American Race Problem,* p. 37–38, regarding the percentages of whites and African Americans below the poverty line.

21. Brooks, *Rethinking the American Race Problem,* p. 39. See also Fish, "Affirmative Action and the SAT," p. 83. On the percentage of African Americans and whites families earning $12,000 or less, see Brooks at pp. 37–38.

22. Walter S. Mossberg, "Personal Technology," *Wall Street Journal,* October 26, 1995, p. B1.

23. "Vital Signs," p. 43. See also Fish, "Affirmative Action and the SAT," p. 83.

24. Mel Elfin, "Race on Campus," *U.S. News & World Report,* April 19, 1993, p.55; "Vital Signs," p. 43. See U.S. Department of Education, National Center for Education Statistics, *Persistence and Attainment in Postsecondary Education for Beginning AY 1980–90 Studies as of Spring 1992* (Washington, D.C.: Office of Educational Research and Improvement, NCES 94–477, November 1993). Shelby Steele reports a 72 to 76% dropout rate for African American students, and Charles Williams of the National Education Association says that the rate was 70% for a time even in the 1980s. See "The MacNeil-Lehrer Newshour," May 4, 1995; *Gannett News Service,* August 8, 1989.

25. Elfin, "Race on Campus," p. 55.

26. "Vital Signs," p. 17.

27. Robert B. Slater, "The Growing Gender Gap in Black Higher Education," *The Journal of Blacks in Higher Education* (Spring 1994): 55.

28. "Vital Signs," p. 39. HBCUs have severe funding problems. See *United States v. Fordice,* 112 S. Ct. 2727 (1992); Gil Kujovich, "Public Black Colleges: The Long History of Unequal Funding," *The Journal of Blacks in Higher Education* (Winter 1993–94): 82.

29. Brooks, *Rethinking the American Race Problem,* p. 99. See Slater, "Gender Gap," p. 57.

30. See "Why the Shortage of Black Professors?," *The Journal of Blacks in Higher Education* (Autumn 1993): 26.

31. Nathan McCall, *Makes Me Wanna Holler: A Young Black Man in America* (New York: Random House, 1994), p. 290.

32. Carter and Wilson, *Minorities in Higher Education,* p. 33. See Mary E. Levin and Joel R. Levin, "A Critical Examination of Academic Retention Programs for At-Risk Minority College Students," *Journal of College Student Development* 32 (July 1991): 325–330.

33. See Haynes Johnson, "Racism Still Smolders on Campus," *USA Today,* May 10, 1988; See Dinesh D'Souza, *Illiberal Education: The Politics of Race and Sex on Campus* (New York: Vintage Books, 1992), p. 125.

34. See Elfin, "Race on Campus," p. 53.

35. Michele Collison, "For Many Freshmen, Orientation Now Includes Efforts to Promote Racial Understanding," *Chronicle of Higher Education,* September 7, 1988, p. A-29.

36. Alvin P. Sanoff and Scott Minerbrook, "Students Talk About Race," *U.S. News & World Report,* April 19, 1993, p. 57; Ken Emerson, "Only Correct," *The New Republic,* February 18, 1991, p. 18; Jeff Rosen, "Hate Mail," *The New Republic,* February 18, 1991, p. 19; Elfin, "Race on Campus," p. 53. Each issue of *The Journal of Blacks in Higher Education* contains a record of the most recent racial incidents on college campus.

37. See Elfin, "Race on Campus," p. 55.

38. Christopher Shea, "Does Student Housing Encourage Racial Separation on Campuses?" *The Chronicle of Higher Education,* July 14, 1993, pp. A26–A27.

39. Sanoff and Minerbrook, "Students Talk About Race," p. 64.

40. Id. p. 63.

41. Id. p. 62.

42. Elfin, "Race on Campus," p. 55.

43. Id. p. 55. See also Sanoff and Minerbrook, "Students Talk About Race," p. 63.

44. Sanoff and Minerbrook, "Students Talk About Race," p. 62.

45. Id. p. 58, 64.

46. Thomas Sowell, *Inside American Education: The Decline, the Deception, the Dogmas* (New York: Free Press, 1993), p. 133.

47. Sanoff and Minerbrook, "Students Talk About Race," p. 64.

48. Id. p. 61.

3. Housing

1. Douglas S. Massey and Nancy A. Denton, *American Apartheid: Segregation and the Making of the Underclass* (Cambridge, Mass.: Harvard University Press, 1993), p. 19; Peter P. Swire, "The Persistent Problem of Lending Discrimination: A Law and Economics Analysis," *Texas Law Review* 73 (1995): 793–802.

2. Ira Berlin, *Slaves without Masters: The Free Negro in the Antebellum South* (New York: Pantheon Books, 1974), pp. 250–265. See Massey and Denton, *American Apartheid*, pp. 19, 25; Roy L. Brooks, *Rethinking the American Race Problem* (Berkeley: University of California Press, 1990), p. 71.

3. Massey and Denton, *American Apartheid*, p. 22.

4. Id. pp. 26, 29. See generally Nicholas Lemann, *The Promised Land: The Great Black Migration and How It Changed America* (New York: Alfred A. Knopf, 1991).

5. Massey and Denton, *American Apartheid*, pp. 29–30.

6. Stanley Lieberson, *Ethnic Patterns in American Cities* (New York: Free Press, 1963), p. 122.

7. Stanley Lieberson, *A Piece of the Pie: Blacks and White Immigrants Since 1880* (Berkeley: University of California Press, 1980), pp. 266, 288.

8. Massey and Denton, *American Apartheid*, p. 31.

9. Lieberson, *A Piece of the Pie*, pp. 266, 288.

10. Karl Taeuber and Alma Taeuber, *Negroes in Cities: Residential Segregation and Neighborhood Change* (Chicago: Aldine, 1965), pp. 39–41. See also Massey and Denton, *American Apartheid*, pp. 42–43.

11. Massey and Denton, *American Apartheid*, pp. 43–44.

12. Annematte Sorensen, Karl E. Taeuber, and Lesslie J. Hollingsworth, Jr., "Indexes of Racial Residential Segregation for 109 Cities in the United States, 1940 to 1970," *Sociological Focus* 8 (1975): 128–130.

13. James A. Kushner, "Causes of Residential Segregation—The Role of the Federal Government," in Robert G. Schwemm, ed., *The Fair Housing Act After Twenty Years: A Conference at Yale Law School, March 1988* (New Haven, Conn.: Yale Law School, 1989), p. 49.

14. Swire, "The Persistent Problem of Lending Discrimination," p. 794.

15. Id., quoting *Bradley v. School Bd.*, 338 F. Supp. 67, 217 (E.D. Va.), *rev'd* 462 F.2d 1058 (4th Cir. 1972), *aff'd by an equally divided court sub nom. School Bd. v. State Bd. of Educ.*, 412 U.S. 92 (1973) (per curiam).

16. Id. pp. 794–795, quoting *Zuch v. Hussey Co.*, 394 F. Supp. 1028, 1055 (E.D. Mich. 1975) (emphasis omitted) (quoting NAREB Code of Ethics), *aff'd sub nom. Zuch v. John H. Hussey Co.*, 547 F.2d 1168 (6th Cir. 1977).

17. Massey and Denton, *American Apartheid*, p. 74.

18. Douglas S. Massey and Nancy A. Denton, "Hypersegregation in U.S. Metropolitan Areas: Black and Hispanic Segregation Along Five Dimensions," *Demography* 26 (1989), p. 382. See also Massey and Denton, *American Apartheid*, p. 74.

19. Massey and Denton, *American Apartheid*, p. 124.

20. Douglas S. Massey, "American Apartheid: Segregation and the Making of the Underclass," *American Journal of Sociology* 96 (1990): 329–355.

21. Massey and Denton, *American Apartheid*, p. 119.

22. Id. pp. 331–333.

23. Id. p. 347.

24. See id. pp. 342–354. See also Douglas S. Massey, Andrew B. Gross, and Mitchell L. Eggers, "Segregation, the Concentration of Poverty, and the Life Chances of Individuals," *Social Science Research* 20 (1991): 415.

25. Massey and Denton, *American Apartheid*, pp. 134–135, 137.

26. Brooks, *Rethinking the American Race Problem*, p. 71.

27. Cornel West, *Race Matters* (Boston: Beacon Press, 1993), pp. 12–13. See also Kenneth Clark, *Dark Ghetto: Dilemmas of Social Power* (New York: Harper and Row, 1965), pp. 32–33.

28. See Thomas Sowell, *Race and Culture: A World View* (New York: Basic Books, 1994); George C. Galster and W. Mark Keeney, "Race, Residence, Discrimination, and Economic Opportunity: Modeling the Nexus of Urban Racial Phenomena," *Urban Affairs Quarterly* 24 (1988): 87. See also West, *Race Matters*, p. 11; William Ryan, *Blaming the Victim*, rev. ed. (New York: Vintage Books, 1976).

29. See Derrick A. Bell, *Race, Racism and American Law*, 3rd ed. (Boston, Mass.: Little, Brown, 1992), pp. 766–769. See also Gregory D. Squires, *Chicago, Ill.: Race, Class and Response to Urban Decline* (Philadelphia: Temple University Press, 1987); John Gehm, *Bringing It Home* (Chicago, Ill.: Chicago Review Press, 1984); Raymond J. Struyk and Marc Bendick, Jr., eds., *Housing Vouchers and the Poor: Lessons from a National Experiment* (Washington, D.C.: Urban Institute Press, 1981); Frances Fox Piven and Richard Cloward, "Desegregated Housing: Who Pays for the Reformer's Ideal?" *The New Republic*, December 17, 1966, pp. 17, 21; James Feron, "Councilmen in Yonkers Seek Relief," *New York Times*, August 31, 1988, p. B1.

30. See *Shannon v. U.S. Dept. of Housing and Urban Development*, 436 F.2d 809 (3d Cir. 1970); *Crow v. Brown*, 332 F.Supp. 382 (N.D. Ga. 1971); *Hicks v. Weaver*, 302 F.Supp. 619 (E.D. La. 1969); and *King v. Harris*, 464 F.Supp. 827 (E.D. N.Y. 1979).

31. Roy R. Silver, "Blacks on L.I. Kill Plan to House Poor Blacks," *New York Times*, July 24, 1970, p. 33.

32. See *Hills v. Gautreaux*, 425 U.S. 284 (1976).

33. 60 Minutes, "Alice Doesn't Live Here Anymore," CBS News transcript produced by Burrelle's Information Services (Livingston, N.J.) vol. 26, no. 14, December 19, 1993, p. 20. See James E. Rosenbaum, Susan J. Popkin, Julie E. Kaufman, and Jennifer Rusin, "Social Integration of Low-Income Black Adults in Middle-Class White Suburbs," *Social Problems* 38 (1991): 449, 449–450.

34. "Alice Doesn't Live Here Anymore," pp. 17, 20.

35. Rosenbaum, et al., "Social Integration," p. 453.

36. Id., p. 451.

37. Id., pp. 452, 454–455.

38. Id., pp. 455–456.

39. Id., p. 456. See also James E. Rosenbaum, Len Rubinowitz, and Marilyn Kulieke, "The Social Integration of Low-Income Black Children into White Suburbs," *Journal of Negro Education* 56 (1987): 35.

40. Rosenbaum, et al., "Social Integration," pp. 451, 459.

41. "Alice Doesn't Live Here Anymore," p. 21.

42. Juliet Saltman, "Maintaining Racially Diverse Neighborhoods," *Urban Affairs Quarterly* 26 (1991): 416, 418, 430–433.

43. "Alice Doesn't Live Here Anymore," pp. 18–19. See also William Sampson, "Race and Housing Satisfaction in the City," unpublished paper, Department of Sociology, Northwestern University (1989).

44. "Alice Doesn't Live Here Anymore," pp. 18–20.

45. Id. p. 20.

46. Massey and Denton, *American Apartheid*, p. 225.

47. William Julius Wilson, *The Truly Disadvantaged: The Inner City, the Underclass, and Public Policy* (Chicago: University of Chicago Press, 1987), pp. 7, 29–62, 143–147, 160.

48. See Brooks, *Rethinking the American Race Problem*, pp. 123–124.

49. Douglas A. Massey and Nancy A. Denton, "Trends in the Residential Segregation of Blacks, Hispanics, and Asians: 1970–1980," *American Sociological Review* 52 (1987): 802, 819. Massey's research is collected in Massey, "American Apartheid," pp. 330–331.

50. George C. Galster, "Black Suburbanization: Has It Changed the Relative Location of the Races," *Urban Affairs Quarterly*, 26 (1991): 621, 622.

51. Douglas S. Massey and Mitchell L. Eggers, "The Ecology of Inequality: Minorities and the Concentration of Poverty, 1970–1980," *American Journal of Sociology* 95 (1990): 1153, 1171.

52. West, *Race Matters*, p. 5 (quoting musician George Clinton).

53. Massey and Denton, *American Apartheid*, p. 213.

54. Martin E. Sloane, "Causes of Residential Segregation: Other Views," in Robert G. Schwemm, ed., *The Fair Housing Act After Twenty Years: A Conference at Yale Law School* (New Haven, Conn.: Yale Law School, 1989), p. 55.

55. See Brooks, *Rethinking the American Race Problem*, pp. 72–74. See also, *Adarand Constructors, Inc. v. Pena*, 115 S. Ct. 2097, 2135 n.5 (1995) (Justice Gins-

burg, with whom Justice Breyer joins, dissenting); Gerald D. Jaynes and Robin M. Williams, Jr., eds., *A Common Destiny: Blacks and American Society* (Washington, D.C.: National Academy Press, 1989), p. 50.

56. See generally James A. Kushner, "Causes of Residential Segregation: The Role of the Government," Robert G. Schwemm, ed., *The Fair Housing Act After Twenty Years: A Conference at Yale Law School* (New Haven, Conn.: Yale Law School, 1989), pp. 48–54.

57. "HUD to Settle Discrimination Suits," *Time,* March 14, 1994, p. 21.

58. See Swire, "The Persistent Problem of Lending Discrimination," pp. 806–814.

59. Alicia H. Munnel, et. al., *Mortgage Lending in Boston: Interpreting HMDA Data 2* (Federal Reserve Bank of Boston Working Paper no. 92–7, October, 1992), p. 44 n.2.

60. A partial listing of pertinent federal statutes includes: Real Estate Settlement Procedures Act, Truth-in-Lending Act, Equal Credit Opportunity Act, Fair Credit Reporting Act, Fair Housing Act, Home Mortgage Disclosure Act, and Community Reinvestment Act.

61. 15 U.S.C. § 1601.

62. 12 U.S.C. § 2801.

63. 42 U.S.C. § 3601.

64. 12 U.S.C. § 2901.

65. These regulations are found at 12 C.F.R. § 202.1-.14. Official interpretations of Regulation B are found in Supplement 1 to 12 C.F.R. § 202.

66. 12 C.F.R. § 202.4.

67. 12 C.F.R. § 202.2(m).

68. 12 C.F.R. § 202.2(1).

69. See Brooks, *Rethinking the American Race Problem,* pp. 54–56, for a more detailed discussion of the "effects tests."

70. 12 C.F.R. § 202.6(a)n.2. See also Swire, "The Persistent Problem of Lending Discrimination," pp. 803–804.

71. See 15 U.S.C. § 1691e(a),(b),(h).

72. Paul Barron, *Federal Regulation of Real Estate and Mortgage Lending,* 3rd ed. (Boston: Warren, Gorham & Lambert, 1992) § 11.01[1] n.6.

73. See 42 U.S.C. §§ 3601–3606.

74. See 42 U.S.C. § 3606.

75. See 42 U.S.C. §§ 3612, 3613, 3614.

76. 12 U.S.C. § 2901(b).

77. See Paul Scheiber, "Community Reinvestment Act Update," *Banking Law Journal* 110 (1993): 62; Swire, "The Persistent Problem of Lending Discrimination," p. 805; A. Brooke Overby, "The Community Reinvestment Act Reconsidered," *University of Pennsylvania Law Review* 143 (1995): 1453–1455.

78. 12 U.S.C. § 2901.

79. 12 U.S.C. § 2803(b).

80. 12 U.S.C. § 2901(a).

81. See Robert G. Boehmer, "Mortgage Discrimination: Paperwork and Prohibitions Prove Insufficient—Is It Time for Simplification and Incentives?" *Hofstra Law Review* 21 (1993): 624.

82. Comptroller of the Currency, "Community Reinvestment Act," *Banking Bulletin*, August 10, 1992, pp. 92–93.

83. Kenneth Bacon, "Under Strong Pressure, Banks Expand Loans for Inner-City Homes," *Wall Street Journal*, February 23, 1994, p. A1.

84. Jonathan R. Macey and Geoffrey P. Miller, "The Community Reinvestment Act: An Economic Analysis," *Virginia Law Review* 79 (1993): 333–334.

85. Boehmer, "Mortgage Discrimination," p. 627.

86. Comptroller of the Currency, "Guide to Fair Mortgage Lending," *Banking Bulletin*, March 31, 1992.

87. Id.

88. Munnell, et al., *Mortgage Lending in Boston*, p. 44.

89. *Home Mortgage Lending and Equal Treatment: A Guide for Financial Institutions* (Washington, D.C.: Federal Financial Institutions Examination Council, 1991), p. 13.

90. Id. p. 15.

4. Employment

1. Section 703(a), 42 U.S.C. § 2000e-2(a).

2. 110 Cong. Rec. 13088 (1964). For a detailed discussion of the history of Title VII see Francis J. Vaas, "Title VII: Legislative History," *Boston College Industrial and Commercial Law Journal* 7 (1966): 431–458; Charles and Barbara Whalen, *The Longest Debate: A Legislative History of the 1964 Civil Rights Act* (Washington, D.C.: Seven Locks Press, 1985).

3. Robert Belton, "The Unfinished Agenda of the Civil Rights Act of 1991," *Rutgers Law Review* 45 (1993): 921; Julia C. Lamber, "And Promises to Keep: The Future in Employment Discrimination," *Indiana Law Journal* 68 (1993): 861–862. For a detailed analysis of the 1991 amendment see CCH Business Law Editors, *Civil Rights Act of 1991: Law and Explanation* (Chicago, Ill.: Commerce Clearing House, 1991). See *Officers for Justice v. Civil Service Commission,* 979 F.2d 721 (9th Cir. 1992).

4. Paul R. Krugman, "The Painful Cost of Workplace Discrimination," *U.S. News & World Report,* November 4, 1991, p. 63.

5. See U.S. Bureau of the Census, *Current Population Reports: Consumer Income,* Series P-60, n. 37 (Washington, D.C.: U.S. Government Printing Office, 1962); U.S. Bureau of the Census, *Current Population Reports: Income in 1965 of Families and Persons in the United States,* Series P-60, n. 51 (Washington, D.C.: U.S. Government Printing Office, 1967); U.S. Bureau of the Census, *Current Population Reports: Income in 1970 of Families and Persons in the United States,* Series P-60, n. 80 (Washington, D.C.: U.S. Government Printing Office, 1971); U.S. Bureau of the Census, *Current Population Reports: Money Income in 1975 of Families*

and Persons in the United States, Series P-60, n. 105 (Washington, D.C.: U.S. Government Printing Office, 1977); *A Common Destiny: Blacks and American Society,* eds. Gerald J. Jayes and Robin M. Williams, Jr. (Washington, D.C.: National Academy Press, 1989), pp. 28, 269–328.

6. See U.S. Equal Employment Opportunity Commission, *Indicators of Equal Employment Opportunity: Status and Trends* (Washington, D.C.: Government Printing Office, 1993).

7. Id.

8. See id. at pp. 14, 15. See also Andrew Hacker, *Two Nations: Black and White, Separate, Hostile, Unequal* (New York: Ballantine Books, 1992), p. 111.

9. James P. Smith and Finis R. Welch, *Closing the Gap: Forty Years of Economic Progress for Blacks* (Santa Monica, Calif.: Rand Corporation, 1986), p. 23, emphasis added. See id for figures taken from the Rand Corporation study. See also Walter L. Updegrave, "Personal Finance: Race and Money," *Money,* December 1989, p. 152; Brett Pulley and Jeff Bailey, "Pool of Qualified Blacks Expands, But Very Few Sit on Corporate Boards," *Wall Street Journal,* June 28, 1994, p. B1.

10. See Reynolds Farley and Walter R. Allen, *The Color Line and the Quality of Life in America* (New York: Russell Sage Foundation, 187); *A Common Destiny,* pp. 28, 269–328; Kathryn M. Neckerman and Joleen Kirschenman, "Hiring Strategies, Racial Bias, and Inner-City Workers," *Social Problems* 38 (1991): 433; Muriel L. Whetstone, "The Story Behind the Explosive Statistics: Why Blacks Are Losing Ground in the Workforce," *Ebony,* December 1993, p. 102; Joe R. Feagin and Melvin P. Sikes, *Living with Racism: The Black Middle-Class Experience* (Boston: Beacon Press, 1994); Krugman, "The Painful Cost of Workplace Discrimination," p. 63. Several studies are collected in Jerry Thomas and Matthew S. Scott, "In the News: Studies Show Widespread Bias Against Blacks," *Black Enterprise,* August 1991, p. 11.

11. Neckerman and Kirschenman, "Racial Bias," pp. 433–444.

12. Barbara Becnel, "Minority Lawyers: Some Firms Fear Client Objections," *Los Angeles Daily Journal,* May 11, 1987.

13. Feagin and Sikes, *Living with Racism,* p. 135.

14. This point comes across in numerous interviews with Asian and Hispanic businesspersons. See Jonathan Kaufman, "Help Wanted: Immigrants' Businesses Often Refuse to Hire Blacks in Inner City," *Wall Street Journal,* June 6, 1995, p. A1.

15. Feagin and Sikes, *Living with Racism,* p. 137.

16. Ellis Cose, *The Rage of a Privileged Class: Why Are Middle-Class Blacks Angry? Why Should America Care?* (New York: Harper Collins, 1993).

17. Ellis Cose, "Rage of the Privileged," *Newsweek,* November 15, 1993, pp. 53–63. For a more detailed discussion, see Cose, *The Rage of a Privileged Class,* pp. 53–72.

18. Much of the cost arises from African Americans being in positions that do not make full use of their talents. Andrew F. Brimmer, "The Economic Cost of Discrimination," *Black Enterprise,* November 1993, p. 27; Andrew F. Brimmer, "The Economic Cost of Discrimination Against Black Americans," in *Economic Perspec-*

tives on Affirmative Action, Margaret C. Simons, ed. (Washington, D.C.: Joint Center for Political and Economic Studies, 1995), pp. 11–17.

19. 29 C.F.R. §1608.1(c) (1979).

20. See Owen Fiss, "A Theory of Fair Employment Law," *University of Chicago Law Review* 38 (1971): 237–240.

21. George Schatzki, "United Steelworkers of America v. Weber: An Exercise in Understandable Indecision," *Washington Law Review* 56 (1980): 56–57.

22. Exec. Order No. 10925, 3 C.F.R. § 448 (1959–63 Compilation). See *Contractors Ass'n of Eastern Pa. v. Secretary of Labor,* 442 F.2d 159, 170 (3d Cir.), *cert. denied,* 404 U.S. 954 (1971). Note that 20 years earlier President Roosevelt had created the Fair Employment Practice Committee and authorized it to receive and investigate complaints of discrimination by federal employees, participants in vocational and training programs administered by federal agencies, and employees of federal defense contractors. Executive Order No. 8802, June 25, 1941. The Committee was also authorized to take "appropriate steps" to redress valid grievances, but that term did not—and, prior to *Brown v. Board of Education,* 347 U.S. 483 (1954), could not—encompass affirmative action as the concept is understood today.

23. See *Lichter v. United States,* 334 U.S. 742, 785 (1948); *Farkas v. Texas Instrument, Inc.,* 375 F.2d 629, 632 (5th Cir.), *cert. denied,* 389 U.S. 977 (1967); *Farmer v. Philadelphia Elec. Co.,* 329 F.2d 3, 8 (3d Cir. 1964). See also 42 Op. Att'y Gen. 97 (Sept. 6, 1961).

24. See *Braden v. University of Pittsburgh,* 343 F. Supp. 836 (W.D. Pa. 1972), *remanded on other grounds,* 477 F.2d 1 (3d Cir. 1973); *Legal Aid Society of Alameda County v. Brennan,* 381 F. Supp. 125 (N.D. Cal. 1974).

25. 347 U.S. 483 (1954).

26. Jack Bass, *Unlikely Heroes* (New York: Simon and Schuster, 1981), pp. 17–18. *Swann v. Charlotte-Mecklenburg Bd. of Educ.,* 402 U.S. 1 (1971); *McDaniel v. Barresi,* 402 U.S. 39 (1971).

27. 3 C.F.R. § 339 (1964–65 Compilation), *reprinted following* 42 U.S.C. § 2000e, at 1232, *amended by* Exec. Order No. 12086, 43 Fed. Reg. 196, 46501 (Oct. 10, 1978). Section 403(a) of Executive Order 11246 states that the executive order supersedes Executive Order 10925 and several other earlier executive orders dealing with discrimination.

28. 42 U.S.C. § 2000e-5(g).

29. See § 501 of the Rehabilitation Act of 1973, 29 U.S.C. § 791; *Overton v. Reilly,* 977 F.2d 1190 (7th Cir. 1992); *Personnel Administrator v. Feeney,* 442 U.S. 256 (1979).

30. 3 C.F.R. §340 (1965), *reprinted as amended in* 42 U.S.C. § 2000e, at p. 1233.

31. See *Legal Aid Society of Alameda County v. Brennan,* 381 F. Supp. 125 (N.D. Cal. 1974).

32. See 41 C.F.R. §§ 60–2.11, 60–2.13, 60–2.14.

33. 41 C.F.R. § 60–211. See generally Roy L. Brooks, "The Affirmative Action Issue: Law, Policy, and Morality," *Connecticut Law Review* 22 (1990): 335–336.

34. For examples of voluntary affirmative action programs see *Local No. 93, Int'l Ass'n of Firefighters v. City of Cleveland*, 478 U.S. 501 (1986); *Johnson v. Transportation Agency*, 480 U.S. 616 (1987); *United Steelworkers of America v. Weber*, 443 U.S. 193 (1979); *City of Richmond v. J.A. Croson Co.*, 488 U.S. 469 (1989). For examples of involuntary affirmative action programs see *Local 28 of Sheet Metal Workers' Int'l Ass'n v. EEOC*, 478 U.S. 421 (1986); *United States v. Paradise*, 480 U.S. 149 (1987); *Adarand Constructors, Inc. v. Pena*, 115 S. Ct. 2097 (1995). See generally Brooks, "The Affirmative Action Issue," pp. 334–348.

35. See Mary Thorton, "Affirmative Action Found to Diversify Work Force," *Washington Post*, June 20, 1983, p. A3. See also Robert Pear, "Study Says Affirmative Rule Expands Hiring of Minorities," *New York Times*, June 19, 1983, p. A16.

36. See Jonathan S. Leonard, "The Impact of Affirmative Action on Employment," *Journal of Labor Economics* 2 (October 1984): 439; Jonathan S. Leonard, "What Was Affirmative Action?" in *Selected Affirmative Action Topics in Employment and Business Set-Asides: A Consultation/Hearing of the United States Commission on Civil Rights, March 6–7, 1985* Vol. 1: 439–463 (Washington, D.C.: U.S. Commission on Civil Rights, 1985); Jonathan S. Leonard, "The Effectiveness of Equal Employment Law and Affirmative Action Regulation," *Research in Labor Economics* 8 (1986): 319.

37. Leonard, "The Impact of Affirmative Action in Employment," pp. 451, 440.

38. See Orley Ashenfelter and James Heckman, "Measuring the Effect of an Antidiscrimination Program," in Orley Ashenfelter and James Blum, eds., *Evaluating the Labor Market Effects of Social Programs* (Princeton, N.J.: Princeton University, 1976), pp. 46–84.

39. Leonard, "The Impact of Affirmative Action on Employment," p. 451.

40. Id. at p. 459. See John J. Donohue III and James Heckman, "Continuous Versus Episodic Change: The Impact of Civil Rights Policy on the Economic Status of Blacks," *Journal of Economic Literature* 29 (1991): 1632.

41. Donohue and Heckman, "Continuous Versus Episodic Change," p. 1632.

42. Smith and Welch, *Closing the Gap*, pp. xxi, 89.

43. See Smith & Welch, *Closing the Gap*, p. 89; Donohue and Heckman, "Continuous Versus Episodic Change," p. 1632.

44. James P. Smith and Finis R. Welch, "Affirmative Action and Labor Markets," *Journal of Labor Economics* 2 (April 1984): 290, 298.

45. Carl C. Monk, *Memorandum 94–14 re: AALS Statistical Report on Full-Time Law School Faculty* (Washington, D.C.: Association of American Law Schools, February 28, 1994), Table 3.

46. See Smith and Welch, *Closing the Gap*, at p. 89.

47. Dave M. O'Neill and June O'Neill, "Affirmative Action in the Labor Market," *Annals of the American Academy* 523 (September 1992), p. 95.

48. O'Neill & O'Neill, "Affirmative Action in the Labor Market," p. 95. See also, Smith and Welch, *Closing the Gap*, p. 89.

49. See Smith and Welch, *Closing the Gap*, p.95.

50. Daniel Farber, "The Outmoded Debate Over Affirmative Action: Some Uncomfortable Reflections on Critical Race Theory," *California Law Review* 82 (1994):

923, quoting James Smith, "Affirmative Action and the Racial Wage Gap," *American Economic Review* 83 (1993): 84.

51. Farber, "The Outmoded Debate Over Affirmative Action," p. 924. See also id. at 922–924.

52. O'Neill and O'Neill, "Affirmative Action in the Labor Market," p. 101.

53. Smith and Welch, *Closing the Gap*, p. 89 n.14.

54. See Derrick A. Bell, *And We Are Not Saved: The Elusive Quest for Racial Justice* (New York: Basic Books, 1987), p. 154; Richard Delgado, "Affirmative Action as a Majoritarian Device: Or, Do You Really Want to Be a Role Model?" *Michigan Law Review* 89 (1991): 1226.

55. Harry T. Edwards, "Personal Reflections on 30 Years of Legal Education for Minority Students," *The University of Michigan Law School, Law Quadrangle Notes* (Summer 1994), p. 42.

56. Derrick A. Bell, "*Bakke,* Minority Admissions and the Usual Price of Racial Remedies," *California Law Review* 67 (1979): 8.

57. Derrick A. Bell, "Xerces and the Affirmative Action Mystique," *George Washington Law Review* 57 (1989): 1598.

58. Id. at p. 1601.

59. Delgado, "Affirmative Action as a Majoritarian Device," p. 1225.

60. Id. at pp. 1225, 1226 n.20.

61. Id. at pp. 1225–1226.

62. Id. at pp. 1226–1227. See also id. at p. 1230.

63. Id. at p. 1227.

64. Stephen L. Carter, *Reflections of an Affirmative Action Baby* (New York: Basic Books, 1991), p. 71.

65. Id. at pp. 32, 59.

66. Id. at p. 33.

67. For a more in-depth discussion of "best black syndrome" see id. at pp. 47–69.

68. Thomas Sowell, *Civil Rights: Rhetoric or Reality?* (New York: William Morrow, 1984), p. 110. (emphasis in original text)

69. Id. at pp. 50–51.

70. Id. at p. 90.

71. Shelby Steele, *The Content of Our Character: A New Vision of Race in America* (New York: St. Martin's Press, 1990), pp. 116.

72. Id. at p. 118.

73. Id. at p. 119.

5. Voting

1. *Yick Wo v. Hopkins,* 118 U.S. 356, 370 (1886).

2. Codified at 42 U.S.C. § 1973.

3. Abigail Thernstrom, *Whose Votes Count? Affirmative Action and Minority Voting Rights* (Cambridge, Mass.: Harvard University Press, 1987), p. 1.

4. Joint Center for Political and Economic Studies, *Joint Center for Political*

and Economic Studies Annual Report 1990 (Washington, D.C.: Joint Center for Political and Economic Studies Press, 1990), p. 5. Joint Center for Political and Economic Studies, *Black Elected Officials, A National Roster 1990* (Washington, D.C.: Joint Center for Political and Economic Studies Press, 1991), p. 9.

5. *Giles v. Harris*, 189 U.S. 475, 488 (1903).

6. See generally U.S. Commission on Civil Rights, *The Voting Rights Act: Unfulfilled Goals* (Washington, D.C.: U.S. Government Printing Office, 1981).

7. U.S. Commission on Civil Rights, *The Voting Rights Act: The First Months* (Washington, D.C.: U.S. Government Printing Office, 1965), pp. 25, 26 n.6.

8. *Gaston County, N.C. v. U.S.*, 395 U.S. 285, 295, 297 (1969).

9. *The Voting Rights Act: The First Months*, p. 35.

10. *Toney v. White*, 476 F.2d 203, 206 (5th Cir. 1973).

11. Id.

12. Id. p. 207.

13. Id. pp. 208, 209.

14. U.S. Commission on Civil Rights, *The Voting Rights Act: Ten Years After* (Washington, D.C.: U.S. Government Printing Office, 1975), pp. 72–75.

15. Id. pp. 75–77.

16. Id. pp. 76–78.

17. Id. pp. 78, 80–83.

18. Id. pp. 87–90.

19. Id. pp. 93–95.

20. Id. pp. 98–99.

21. Id. pp. 126–128.

22. Id. pp. 174–201.

23. Id. pp. 192–193.

24. Id. pp. 193–199.

25. *The Voting Rights Act: Unfulfilled Goals*, pp. 35–36.

26. *U.S. v. St. Landry Parish*, 601 F.2d 859, 861, 866 (5th Cir. 1979).

27. *Smith v. Meese*, 821 F.2d 1484, 1486–1488 (11th Cir. 1987).

28. *Harris v. Siegelman*, 695 F. Supp. 517, 522–527 (M.D. Ala., N.D. 1988).

29. *Mississippi State Chapter, Operation Push, Inc. v. Mabus*, 932 F.2d 400 (5th Cir. 1991).

30. *Robinson v. Alabama State Department of Education*, 652 F. Supp. 484, 485–486 (M.D. Ala., N.D. 1987).

31. *Ashe v. Board of Elections in the City of New York*, 124 F.R.D. 45, 46 (E.D. N.Y. 1989).

32. *Marks v. Stinson*, 1994 WL 146113 (E.D. Pa.), pp. 30, 34.

33. Id. pp. 30–36.

34. *Minority Vote Dilution* Chandler Davidson, ed. (Washington, D.C.: Howard University Press, 1984), p. 4.

35. Frank R. Parker, "Racial Gerrymandering and Legislative Reapportionment," in Chandler Davidson, ed., *Minority Vote Dilution* (Washington, D.C.: Howard University Press, 1984), pp. 87, 89.

36. Davidson, *Minority Vote Dilution,* pp. 1, 5.

37. Id. at pp. 1–2, 6.

38. Chandler Davidson, *Biracial Politics: Conflict and Coalition in the Metropolitan South* (Baton Rouge: Louisiana State University Press, 1972), pp. 65–66.

39. Davidson, *Minority Vote Dilution,* p. 6.

40. Id. at pp. 6–7.

41. Id.

42. Id. at pp. 7–8.

43. Parker, *Racial Gerrymandering,* pp. 85–96.

44. Id. at p. 89.

45. Id. at p. 92.

46. Id. at p. 96.

47. Id.

48. Andrew Hacker, *Two Nations: Black and White, Separate, Hostile, Unequal* (New York: Ballantine Books, 1992), p. 211.

49. Laughlin McDonald, "The Quiet Revolution in Minority Voting Rights," *Vanderbilt Law Review* 42 (1989): 1277.

50. Id.

51. Id.

52. Id. pp. 1277–1278.

53. Id.

54. Id.

55. Margaret Edds, "Southern Odyssey: Two Decades of Racial Evolution," in Karen McGill Arrington and William L. Taylor, eds., *Voting Rights in America: Continuing the Quest for Full Participation,* (Washington, D.C.: Leadership Conference Education Fund and the Joint Center for Political and Economic Studies, 1992), pp. 121, 122.

56. Id. at p. 122.

57. Id. at p. 121. See also id. at p. 117.

58. See Keith Reeves, *Voting Hopes or Fears? White Voters, Black Candidates and Racial Politics in America* (New York: Oxford University Press, forthcoming) (responding to Abigail Thernstrom and others who minimize the prevalence of bloc voting by whites).

59. Davidson, *Minority Vote Dilution,* p. 14.

60. Id. at p. 15.

61. Derrick Bell, *Race, Racism and American Law,* 3rd ed. (Boston: Little, Brown, 1992), p. 213.

62. Armand Derfner, "Vote Dilution and the Voting Rights Act Amendments of 1982," in Chandler Davidson, ed., *Minority Vote Dilution* (Washington, D.C.: Howard University Press, 1984), p. 149. See 42 U.S.C. § 1973c.

63. Armand Derfner, "Development of the Franchise: 1957–1980," in McGill Arrington and Taylor, eds., *Voting Rights in America: Continuing the Quest for Full Participation,* p. 94.

64. *Allen v. State Board of Elections,* 393 U.S. 544, 565 (1969).

65. Davidson, *Minority Vote Dilution*, p. 16.

66. 425 U.S. 130 (1976).

67. 112 S. Ct. 820 (1992).

68. Id. at 830.

69. 412 U.S. 755 (1973).

70. Id. at 766.

71. 485 F.2d 1297 (1973).

72. Id. p. 1305.

73. Id.

74. 446 U.S. 55 (1980).

75. Id. at pp. 65, 66.

76. Id. at pp. 60–61.

77. Davidson, *Minority Vote Dilution*, p. 17.

78. Lani Guinier, "Development of the Franchise: 1982 Voting Rights Amendments," in McGill Arrington and Taylor, eds., *Voting Rights in America: Continuing the Quest for Full Participation*, p. 106.

79. G. Hunter Bates, "Reapportionment and the Dilution of Minority Voting Strength: Growe v. Emison, 113 S. Ct. 1075 (1993), and Vionovich v. Quilter, 133 S. Ct. 1149 (1993)," *Harvard Journal of Law and Public Policy* 16 (1993): 822.

80. *Thornburg v. Gingles*, 478 U.S. 30 (1986).

81. Id. at pp. 48–49.

82. Bell, *Race, Racism and American Law*, p. 243.

83. Allan J. Lichtman and J. Gerald Hebert, "High Court Decision on Voting Act Helps to Remove Minority Barriers," *The National Law Journal*, November 10, 1986, p. 24.

84. Id.

85. *Houston Lawyers' Association v. Attorney General of Texas*, 111 S. Ct. 2376 (1991).

86. *Clark v. Roemer*, 111 S. Ct. 2096 (1991).

87. *Whitcomb v. Chavis*, 403 U.S. 124, 142 (1973).

88. Id. at p. 143.

89. Id. at p. 144.

90. See Bell, *Race, Racism and American Law*, p. 234–235.

91. Id. at p. 244, citing James U. Blacksher and Larry T. Menefee, "From Reynolds v. Sims to City of Mobile v. Bolden: Have the White Suburbs Commandeered the Fifteenth Amendment?" *Hastings Law Journal* 34 (1982): 1–64.

92. 113 S. Ct. 2816 (1993).

93. See *Miller v. Johnson*, 115 S. Ct. 2475 (1995) (holding that the strict scrutiny test applies to majority-black redistricting); *United States v. Hays*, 115 S. Ct. 2431 (1995) (holding that voters who do not live in a majority-black district lack standing to challenge it).

94. T. Alexander Aleinikoff and Samuel Issacharoff, "Race and Redistricting: Drawing Constitutional Lines After Shaw v. Reno," *Michigan Law Review* 92 (1993): 590.

95. *Shaw,* 113 S. Ct. at pp. 2819–2820.

96. Id. at p. 2828.

97. Id. at p. 2827.

98. Id.

99. Lani Guinier, "What Color Is Your Gerrymander?" *Washington Post,* March 27, 1994, p. C3.

100. Id.

101. Id.

102. Davidson, *Biracial Politics,* p. 5.

6. Why Racial Integration Has Failed

1. See Roy L. Brooks, *Rethinking the American Race Problem* (Berkeley: University of California Press, 1990).

2. Peter Applebome, "John Hope Franklin, the Last Integrationist," *New York Times Magazine,* April 23, 1995, p. 34.

3. See Amy Stevens, "Somber Reunion for Harvard Law's Class of '85," *Wall Street Journal,* May 8, 1995, p. B1.

4. John Edgar Wideman, *Fatheralong: A Meditation on Fathers and Sons, Race and Society* (New York: Pantheon Books, 1994), p. xxiv.

5. For a detailed discussion of these points, see Brooks, *Rethinking.*

6. Joe R. Feagin and Hernan Vera, *White Racism: The Basics* (New York: Routledge, 1995), p. x.

7. Wideman, *Fatheralong,* pp. 68–69.

8. Feagin and Vera, *White Racism,* pp. ix–x and 7.

9. See Roy L. Brooks and Mary Jo Newborn, "Critical Race Theory and Classical-Liberal Civil Rights Scholarship: A Distinction Without a Difference?" *California Law Review* 82 (1994): 798–799.

10. For further discussion of this point and an argument in defense of the continued use of the concept, see Robert Miles, *Racism* (New York: Routledge, 1989).

11. See generally Alphonso Pinkney, *The Myth of Black Progress* (New York: Cambridge University Press, 1984); Ellis Cose, *The Rage of a Privileged Class* (New York: Harper Collins, 1993); Joe R. Feagin and Melvin P. Sikes, *Living with Racism: The Black Middle-Class Experience* (Boston: Beacon Press, 1994).

12. Cose, *The Rage of a Privileged Class,* pp. 38, 39, 44, 85.

13. Id. p. 22.

14. Id. pp. 48–49.

15. Id. pp. 43, 16.

16. Bob Blauner, *Black Lives, White Lives* (Berkeley: University of California Press, 1989), p. 287.

17. Joe R. Feagin, "The Continuing Significance of Race: Antiblack Discrimination in Public Places," *American Sociological Review* 56 (1991): 107.

18. Cose, *The Rage of a Privileged Class,* p. 58.

19. Feagin, "The Continuing Significance of Race," p. 108.

20. Id. p. 41.

21. Id. p. 64.

22. Id. p. 61.

23. Id. p. 46.

24. Feagin, *The Continuing Significance of Race,* p. 107.

25. Id. p. 108.

26. Joe R. Feagin and Melvin P. Sikes, *Living with Racism: The Black Middle-Class Experience* (Boston: Beacon Press, 1994).

27. Feagin, "The Continuing Significance of Race," p. 103.

28. Id. p. 104.

29. Id. p. 109.

30. Id. pp. 102, 104, 111. Carol Brooks Gardner, "Passing By: Street Remarks, Address Rights, and the Urban Female," *Sociological Inquiry* 50 (1980): 328.

31. Feagin, "The Continuing Significance of Race," p. 111.

32. Id. p. 112.

33. Id. p. 110.

34. Id. pp. 110, 113. See also David C. Perry and Paula C. Sornoff, *Politics at the Street Level: The Select Case of Police Administration and the Community* (Beverly Hills, Calif.: Sage Publications, 1973).

35. Feagin, "The Continuing Significance of Race," pp. 104, 106, 108.

36. Id. p. 106.

37. Id. pp. 106, 110.

38. Id. p. 105.

39. Feagin and Vera, *White Racism,* pp. 163–194.

40. For further discussion of economic analysis and discrimination, see Roy L. Brooks, Gilbert Paul Carrasco, and Gordon A. Martin, Jr., *Civil Rights Litigation: Cases and Perspectives* (Durham, North Carolina: Carolina Academic Press, 1995), pp. 346–351; Richard Epstein, *Forbidden Grounds: The Case Against Employment Discrimination Laws* (Cambridge: Harvard University Press, 1992); Peter P. Swire, "The Persistent Problem of Lending Discrimination: A Law and Economics Analysis," *Texas Law Review* 73 (1995): 787–869.

41. See Derrick Bell, *Faces at the Bottom of the Well* (New York: Basic Books, 1992); Richard Delgado, *The Rodrigo Chronicles: Conversations About America and Race* (New York: New York University Press, 1995).

II. Total Separation

1. 347 U.S. 483 (1954).

2. The Solicitor General of the United States has suggested that a growing number of African Americans are turning away from the ideal of racial integration. See Drew S. Days III, "Brown Blues: Rethinking the Integrative Ideal," *William & Mary Law Review* 34 (1992): 53.

3. *The End of White World Supremacy: Four Speeches by Malcolm X,* Benjamin

Goodman, ed. (New York: Merlin House, 1971), p. 75.

4. Alexis de Tocqueville, *Democracy in America,* trans. Henry Reeve, ed. Francis Bowen (Cambridge, Sever & Francis, 1862), vol. 1, pp. 458–459.

5. Thomas Jefferson, "Notes of the State of Virginia (1781–82)" in *Writings* (New York: Library of America, 1984), p. 264.

6. See Chapter 7.

7. Norman L. Crockett, *The Black Towns* (Lawrence, Kan.: The Regents Press of Kansas, 1979), p. 1.

7. Booker T. Washington and W. E. B. Du Bois

1. "Nothing ever comes to one, that is worth having, except as a result of hard work." Booker T. Washington, *Up from Slavery* (New York: Bantam Books, 1963), pp. 132–133. See also id. at pp. 1–43; Samuel R. Spencer, Jr., *Booker T. Washington: And the Negro's Place in American Life* (Boston: Little, Brown, 1955), pp. 108–124.

2. See Elliot M. Rudwick, *W. E. B. Du Bois, Propagandist of the Negro Protest* (New York: Atheneum, 1969), p. 62. As we shall see later on in this chapter, W. E. B. Du Bois believed higher education was the vehicle by which African Americans would reach equality. Marcus Garvey also focused on higher education in his separatist movement. He declared that in modern society, western civilization and its culture were the hallmark of education and that African Americans must emulate Europeans in their education.

3. He writes: "How many times I wished . . . that by some power of magic I might remove the great bulk of these people into the country districts and plant them upon the soil . . . where all nations and races that have ever succeeded have gotten their start . . ." Washington, *Up from Slavery,* p. 63.

4. Id. p. 155.

5. *Booker T. Washington in Perspective,* ed. Raymond W. Smock (Jackson, Miss.: University Press of Mississippi, 1988), p. 77. The Tuskegee Institute brought Washington much acclaim. He became such an influential force that eventually Tuskegee graduates participated in governmental programs in Africa. Id. at pp. 68–69. See also Elliot M. Rudwick, *Voice of the Black Protest Movement* (Urbana, Ill.: University of Illinois Press, 1982) pp. 62–63.

6. Washington, *Up from Slavery,* p. 146.

7. *Booker T. Washington,* ed. Emma Lou Thornbrough (Englewood Cliffs, N.J.: Prentice-Hall, 1969), p. 59. See Spencer, *Booker T. Washington,* pp. 94–95.

8. Washington, *Up from Slavery,* p. 156.

9. Smock, *Booker T. Washington in Perspective,* p. 102.

10. Washington, *Up from Slavery,* p. 25.

11. Smock, *Booker T. Washington in Perspective,* p. 166.

12. For a thorough discussion of W. E. B. Du Bois's early life, see David Levering Lewis, *W. E. B. Du Bois, Biography of a Race, 1868–1919* (New York: Henry Holt, 1993).

13. "He was a leader who sometimes chafed under his role as a political messiah,

a poet who had been drafted into a social movement with which he was often at odds. Du Bois could not be the charismatic leader or the mesmerizing orator of the Douglass tradition." Manning Marable, *W. E. B. Du Bois: Black Radical Democrat* (Boston: Twayne Publishers, 1986), p. 98.

14. Myrtle G. Glascoe, *The Educational Thought of William Edward Burghardt DuBois: An Evolutionary Perspective* (Ann Arbor, Mich.: University Microfilms International, 1980), p. 63. Du Bois has received much criticism because he laid out no actual strategy for black empowerment. See id.

15. See Glascoe, *The Educational Thought of W. E. B. Du Bois*, p. 79. See also Richard Kluger, *Simple Justice* (New York: Alfred A. Knopf, 1976), p. 94. Recall that Washington viewed economic self-sufficiency as the path to equality.

16. *W. E. B. Du Bois Speaks: Speeches and Addresses 1890–1919*, ed. Philip S. Foner (New York: Pathfinder Press, 1970), p. 47. See also Rudwick, *W. E. B. Du Bois*, pp. 96–97.

17. W. E. B. Du Bois, *Dusk of Dawn: An Essay Toward an Autobiography of a Race Concept* (New York: Harcourt, Brace & World, 1968), p. 180. The first quote is on p. 305.

18. Id.

19. *W. E. B. Du Bois Speaks: Speeches and Addresses 1920–1963*, p. 84.

20. Id. at 85.

21. Id.

8. Marcus Garvey

1. *Marcus Garvey and the Vision of Africa*, ed. John H. Clarke (New York: Random House, 1974), p. 378. While this section focuses primarily on Garvey's impact on African Americans, it is important to note that the movement was international in scope. Garvey was not the first to introduce a separation theory. Strong "back to Africa" movements were formulated during the eighteenth and nineteenth centuries; after the Civil War one was led by Bishop Henry McNeal Turner. Id., pp. xv, 1. Garvey's papers are collected in a 7-volume set, *The Marcus Garvey and Universal Negro Improvement Association Papers*, ed. Robert A. Hill (Berkeley: University of California Press, 1983–1986, 1989, 1990).

2. Tony Martin, *Marcus Garvey, Hero: A First Biography* (Dover, Mass.: Majority Press, 1983), pp. 11, 15–20. As a young child, Garvey lived with and attended school with white children, but during adolescence the African West Indian and white children were separated. For further details on Garvey's earlier years, see id.; Rupert Lewis, *Marcus Garvey, Anti-Colonial Champion* (Trenton, N.J.: Africa World Press, 1988); *Marcus Garvey—Great Lives Observed*, ed. E. David Cronon (Englewood Cliffs, N.J.: Prentice-Hall, 1973).

3. Martin, *Marcus Garvey, Hero*, pp. 31–32; *Marcus Garvey—Great Lives Observed*, pp. 20–24. The UNIA's motto was: "One God! One Aim! One Destiny!"

Lewis Nembhard, *Trials and Triumphs of Marcus Garvey* (Millwood, N.Y.: Kraus Reprint Co., 1978), p. 15.

4. Judith Stein, *The World of Marcus Garvey: Race and Class in Modern Society* (Baton Rouge: Louisiana State University Press, 1986), p. 31.

5. Id. pp. 31–32.

6. Id. p. 34.

7. Id. pp. 34, 37. See Martin, *Marcus Garvey, Hero*, pp. 34–37.

8. *Black Leaders of the Twentieth Century*, eds. John Franklin and August Meier (Urbana, Ill.: University of Illinois Press, 1982), p. 112.

9. Id. pp. 112, 113.

10. Clarke, *Marcus Garvey and the Vision of Africa*, p. 9. See also *Marcus Garvey—Great Lives Observed*, p. 10.

11. Tony Sewell, *Garvey's Children: The Legacy of Marcus Garvey* (London: Macmillan Caribbean, 1990), p. 30.

12. *Marcus Garvey and the Vision of Africa*, pp. 378–381.

13. Id. pp. 345–346.

14. See *The Marcus Garvey and Universal Negro Improvement Association Papers*, Vol. I, pp. l–li.

15. *Marcus Garvey and the Vision of Africa*, p. 85.

16. Id. pp. 84–87. *Marcus Garvey—Life and Lessons: A Centennial Companion to the Marcus Garvey and Universal Negro Improvement Association Papers*, ed. Robert A. Hill (Berkeley: University of California Press, 1987), p. xxvi.

17. Martin, *Marcus Garvey, Hero*, pp. 48–54; Marcus Garvey, *Message to the People, The Course of African Philosophy*, ed. Tony Martin (Dover, Mass.: Majority Press, 1986) p. xvi.

18. Tony Martin, *Race First: The Ideological and Organizational Struggles of Marcus Garvey and the Universal Negro Improvement Association* (Westport, Conn: Greenwood Press, 1976), pp. 31–32.

19. Id. p. 113.

20. *Black Leaders of the Twentieth Century*, p. 119.

21. *Marcus Garvey and the Vision of Africa*, p. 59.

22. Id. p. 8.

23. *Black Leaders of the Twentieth Century*, pp. 119–120.

24. *Marcus Garvey—Great Lives Observed*, p. 9.

25. *The Marcus Garvey and Universal Negro Improvement Association Papers*, vol. 5, p. 521. See also id. vol. 4, pp. 652–653. Garvey established a technical secondary school, called Liberty University, which stressed the educational philosophy of Booker T. Washington. The school was plagued by mismanagement and lack of funds. See id. vol. 6, pp. xli, 439–440 n.1, 570.

26. *Marcus Garvey—Great Lives Observed*, p. 40. See id. pp. 40–41; Martin, *Race First*, p. 30; Martin, *Marcus Garvey, Hero*, pp. 48–54.

27. *Black Leaders of the Twentieth Century*, pp. 131–132. See also id. pp. 129–130.

28. *Marcus Garvey and the Vision of Africa*, pp. 104, 112, 396.

29. Id. p. 104.

30. Philip Sterling, *The Question of Color: Marcus Garvey, Malcolm X* (New York: Scholastic Book Services, 1973), p. 9.

31. *Black Leaders of the Twentieth Century,* pp. 132–133.

32. Id. pp. 126–127.

33. Id. p. 127.

34. Sewell, *Garvey's Children,* pp. 48–49.

35. *Marcus Garvey and the Vision of Africa,* p. 111.

36. *Black Leaders of the Twentieth Century,* p. 127.

37. Martin, *Marcus Garvey, Hero,* pp. 85–99.

38. *The Marcus Garvey and United Negro Improvement Association Papers,* vol. 6, p. 217.

39. Martin, *Marcus Garvey, Hero,* p. 306.

40. Sewell, *Garvey's Children,* p. 44.

41. Id. p. 45; *Marcus Garvey—Great Lives Observed,* pp. 97–101.

42. See *The Marcus Garvey and United Negro Improvement Association Papers,* vol. 6, p. 433 (Deposition of George Weston, President General of UNIA).

43. Id. vol. 6, pp. xxxvi, 90, 129, 146, 313; id. vol. 7, pp. lxvii, lxxxix. See Sterling, *The Question of Color,* pp. 45–47, 49.

44. See *The Marcus Garvey and United Negro Improvement Association Papers,* vol. 4, pp. 753–754; Horace Campbell, "Garveyism, Pan-Africanism and African Liberation in the Twentieth Century," in Rupert Lewis and Patrick Bryan, eds., *Garvey: His Work and Impact* (Trenton, N.J.: Africa World Press, 1991), p. 174.

9. The Nation of Islam

1. Clifton E. Marsh, *From Black Muslims to Muslims: The Transition from Separatism to Islam, 1930–1980* (Metuchen, N.J.: Scare Crow Press, 1984), p. 51.

2. Id. pp. 51–52.

3. C. Eric Lincoln, *The Black Muslims in America* (Boston: Beacon Press, 1961); Marsh, *From Black Muslims to Muslims,* p. 53.

4. Morroe Berger, "The Black Muslims," *Horizon* (Winter 1964): 56.

5. Marsh, *From Black Muslims to Muslims,* p. 51. Historians believe Fard was originally affiliated with the Prophet Noble Drew Ali, the leader of the Moorish Science Temple of America, defunct by Fard's time. Berger, "The Black Muslims," p. 56. See also Lincoln, *Black Muslims,* pp. 52–57.

6. Berger, "The Black Muslims," p. 66.

7. Lincoln, *Black Muslims,* pp. 13–15.

8. Berger, "The Black Muslims," p. 56. The major faction of the Nation of Islam followed Elijah Muhammad to Chicago's Temple 2. Another faction, Muslims loyal to the United States Constitution, dissolved, and Muhammad absorbed it. Elijah Muhammad ruled his organization with absolute authority. Although he appointed a hierarchy of administrators in all of the temples, the temples were not autonomous; every order had to be cleared through him.

9. Marsh, *From Black Muslims to Muslims,* pp. 60–61.

10. Lincoln, *Black Muslims,* pp. 116–120.

11. Berger, "The Black Muslims," p. 52.

12. Elijah Muhammad, *Message to the Blackman in America* (Chicago, Ill.: Mu-

hammad Mosque of Islam No. 2, 1965), pp. 32–43; Lincoln, *Black Muslims,* p. 110.

13. Berger, "The Black Muslims," pp. 60–61; Louis E. Lomax, *When the Word is Given* (Westport, Conn.: Greenwood Press, 1963), p. 48. As 1960 approached Armageddon drew closer, but Muhammad refused to disclose to his followers the precise date on which it would occur. Id. at pp. 27, 48.

14. Berger, "The Black Muslims," p. 61.

15. Marsh, *From Black Muslims to Muslims,* p. 55.

16. Id. p. 63.

17. Lomax, *When the Word Is Given,* pp. 23–26, 105–107, 134–137.

18. Elijah Muhammad, "Separation of the So-called Negroes from Their Slave-masters' Children Is a Must," in John H. Bracey, Jr. et al., eds., *Black Nationalism in America* (New York: Bobbs-Merrill, 1970), p. 408.

19. Malcolm X, "Minister Malcolm X Enunciates the Muslim Program," id. p. 413. Malcolm X continues: "How can [integrationist African Americans] expect the white man to accept us into his social unit, political unit, or economic unit when we are not yet in unity (as a unit) among our own kind." Id.

20. Lincoln, *Black Muslims,* p. 102.

21. Eugene V. Wolfenstein, *The Victims of Democracy: Malcolm X and the Black Revolution* (Berkeley: University of California Press, 1981), p. 245.

22. Id.

23. C. Eric Lincoln, *My Face is Black* (Boston: Beacon Press, 1964), p. 85.

24. C. Eric Lincoln, *Sounds of the Struggle: Persons and Perspectives in Civil Rights* (New York: William Morrow, 1967), p. 44.

25. Lincoln, *Black Muslims,* pp. 83–86, 109–110; Lincoln, *Sounds,* p. 47.

26. Lincoln, *Black Muslims,* pp. 84–85; Marsh, *From Black Muslims to Muslims,* p. 60.

27. Marsh, *From Black Muslims to Muslims,* p. 60.

28. Id. p. 62.

29. For a detailed discussion of Malcolm X and his life, see generally Malcolm X, *Autobiography of Malcolm X* (New York: Grove Press, 1964).

30. Marsh, *From Black Muslims to Muslims,* pp. 74, 76.

31. Lincoln, *Black Muslims,* p. 107.

32. Lomax, *When the Word Is Given,* pp. 55–58.

33. Black Muslims criticize black leaders who advocate integration and assimilation. They argue that upward mobility for African Americans in the United States is hindered by both institutional racism and economic inequality. Elijah Muhammad teaches that the solution to this hindrance is not integration but complete withdrawal. Black Muslims do not rally behind the civil rights movement because they believe that America's apparent acceptance of it is false; giving African Americans their civil rights is against the very nature and will of the white race. Black Muslims teach that only the "So-Called Negro" leaders want to integrate, not the black masses.

34. Marsh, *From Black Muslims to Muslims,* pp. 62–63; Elijah Muhammad, "What Do Muslims Want," in *Black Nationalism in America,* p. 404.

35. As one Nation minister told his congregation, "the white man's time is up,

and he knows it. He has no friends anywhere. He now hopes that by integrating with the rising Black Man, he can avoid paying for the long list of crimes he has perpetrated against humanity." Lincoln, *Black Muslims,* pp. 124–125.

36. Lomax, *When the Word Is Given,* p. 150; Elijah Muhammad, "What Do Muslims Want," p. 404.

37. Lincoln, *Sounds,* p. 58; Malcolm X, "Minister Malcolm X," pp. 419–420.

38. Marsh, *From Black Muslims to Muslims,* p. 57.

39. Id. p. 64.

40. Id. pp. 58–59. See also id. pp. 59–60; Lincoln, *Black Muslims,* p. 95.

41. Harold R. Isaacs, "Integration and the Negro Mood," *Commentary* (December 1962), p. 490. Actual statistics are unavailable because the Black Muslims did not release such information to the public.

42. M. S. Handler, "James Baldwin Rejects Despair Despite Race 'Drift and Danger,'" *New York Times,* June 3, 1963, p. 19.

43. Herbert Krosney, "America's Black Supremacists," *The Nation,* May 6, 1961, p. 390.

44. See generally Malcolm X, *Autobiography.*

45. Id. pp. 374–377. For further discussion see Shawna Maglangbayan, *Garvey, Lumumba, and Malcolm: Black National-Separatists* (Chicago: Third World Press, 1972).

46. See William A. Henry III, "Cover Stories: Pride and Prejudice," *Time,* February 28, 1994: 20–27; Adolph Reed, Jr., "False Prophet-I: The Rise of Louis Farrakhan," *The Nation,* January 21, 1991: 37, 51–56; "Predicting Disaster for Racist America, Louis Farrakhan Envisions an African Homeland for U.S. Blacks," *People Weekly,* September 17, 1990: 111–116; Juan Williams, "Black Separatist Farrakhan Widening Support," *The Washington Post,* March 4, 1985, p. A1. See generally Marsh, *From Black Muslims to Muslims.*

47. Lincoln, *My Face,* p. 87.

48. Id.

49. Wolfenstein, *The Victims of Democracy,* p. 246.

50. Id. p. 271.

51. Id. pp. 272–284. See also James Baldwin, *The Fire Next Time* (New York: Dial Press, 1963), p. 141.

52. Wolfenstein, *The Victims of Democracy,* p. 246; Berger, "The Black Muslims," p. 64.

10. Emigration

1. See Larry Minear and Thomas G. Weiss, "Liberia Sinks into Shambles," *The San Diego Union-Tribune,* December 11, 1994, p. A-39. One of the most interesting historical studies of the efforts to colonize Liberia is P. J. Staudenraus, *The African Colonization Movement, 1816–1865* (New York: Columbia University Press, 1961). See also Charles H. Huberich, *The Political and Legislative History of Liberia,* 2 vols. (New York: Central Book, 1947). His work brings together some of the most

significant documents of the pre-1847 period and contains interesting biographical sketches of the pioneers. The presentation in this chapter also greatly benefited from a paper written by a former student, attorney Sharon D. Ramirez, hereinafter cited as Sharon D. Ramirez, "Racial Separation: A Study of Liberia and the Commonwealth of Puerto Rico," Student Research Paper, University of Minnesota Law School, April 22, 1991.

2. See Ramirez, "Racial Separation," p. 9 n.3; see also, Francis A. J. Utting, *The Story of Sierra Leone* (New York: Book for Library Press, 1971), pp. 31–35.

3. See James L. Sibley, *Liberia—Old and New* (London: James Clarke, 1929), p. 5; Joseph E. Holloway, *Liberia Diplomacy in Africa: A Study of Inter-African Relations* (Washington, D.C.: University Press of America, 1981), p. xii.

4. Ramirez, "Racial Separation," p. 10; Tom W. Shick, *Behold the Promised Land: A History of Afro-American Settler Society in Nineteenth-Century Liberia* (Baltimore: The Johns Hopkins University Press, 1980), p. 13.

5. Staudenraus, *The African Colonization Movement,* pp. 19–22; J. Gus Liebenow, *Liberia: The Evolution of Privilege* (Ithaca: Cornell University Press, 1969), p. 17.

6. Shick, *Behold the Promised Land,* p. 14.

7. Id.

8. Id.

9. Ramirez, "Racial Separation," p. 12. See Samuel E. Morison, *"Old Bruin": Commodore Mathew C. Perry* (Boston: Little, Brown, 1967).

10. Ramirez, "Racial Separation," p. 12. See Amos J. Beyan, *The American Colonization Society and the Creation of the Liberian State: A Historical Perspective* (Lanham: University Press of America, 1991), pp. 64–66. See generally Jehudi Ashmun, *History of the American Colony in Liberia, from December 1821 to 1823* (Washington, D.C.: Way and Gideon, 1826); Ralph R. Gurley, *Life of Jehudi Ashmun, Late Colonial Agent in Liberia* (Washington, D.C.: James C. Dunn, 1835); William Innes, *Liberia* (Edinburgh, Scotland: Waugh and Innes, 1831); Archibald Alexander, *A History of Colonization on the Western Coast of Africa* (Philadelphia: W. S. Martien, 1846).

11. Ramirez, "Racial Separation," p. 13 n.15.

12. See Shick, *Behold the Promised Land,* pp. 122–134.

13. Ramirez, "Racial Separation," p. 14. Listings of emigrants by name, occupation, origin, and other data are contained in Tom W. Shick, *Emigrants to Liberia—1820 to 1843: An Alphabetical Listing* (Newark: Liberian Studies Association in America, 1971).

14. Staudenraus, *African Colonization,* p. 32; Ramirez, "Racial Separation," p. 15.

15. Shick, *Behold the Promised Land,* p. 3.

16. Ramirez, "Racial Separation," p. 15 n.19.

17. Id. p. 15 n.20, citing Staudenraus, *African Colonization,* p. 109.

18. Id.

19. Id., pp. 16–17. For an analysis of the distinctions between Americo-Liberians and others, see James Martin, "How to Build a Nation: Liberian Ideas About

National Integration in the Later Nineteenth Century," *Liberian Studies Journal* 2 (1969): 15–42.

20. Id. p. 16, citing Dwight N. Seyfert, "The Origins of Privilege: Liberian Merchants, 1822–1847," *Liberian Studies Journal* 6 (1975): 109–128.

21. World Bank, *World Development Report, 1985* (New York: Oxford University Press, 1985).

22. Ramirez, "Racial Separation," pp. 17–18, citing Elliott Berg Associates, *Final Report: The Liberian Crisis and an Appropriate U.S. Response* (Washington: U.S. AID, February 1982), p. 4.

23. *World Development Report*, p. 210, table 19.

24. Ramirez, "Racial Separation," p. 19, citing Robert W. Clower, George Dalton, Mitchell Harwitz, A. A. Walters, et al., *Growth without Development: An Economic Survey of Liberia* (Evanston: Northwestern University Press, 1966).

25. Ramirez, "Racial Separation," p. 23 n.28, citing Kenneth B. Noble, "Liberian President Captured by Rebels in a Fierce Gunfight," *The New York Times,* September 10, 1990, p. A1.

26. See id. p. 22.

27. See id. p. 23.

28. Id. at pp. 23–24.

29. Bradley Martin and Jane Whitmore, "Treasure for Pleasure," *Newsweek,* February 13, 1989, p. 39.

30. Id.

31. Otto Friedrich, "To the Last Man," *Time,* August 20, 1990, pp. 51–52.

32. Bill Berkeley, "Doe Our Dear," *The New Republic,* March 19, 1990, p. 19.

33. Denis Johnson, "The Civil War in Hell," *Esquire,* December 1990, p. 45.

34. Ramirez, "Racial Separation," p. 25.

35. Johnson, "The Civil War in Hell," p. 44

36. Ramirez, "Racial Separation," p. 26; John Bierman and George Ola Davis, "Senseless Slaughter," *Maclean's,* September 24, 1990, p. 30.

37. Ramirez, "Racial Separation," p. 26, citing "Aid Arrives Slowly," *Africa News,* November 12, 1990.

38. Id.

39. See Minear and Weiss, "Liberia Sinks into Shambles," p. 39.

40. Id.

41. Marguerite Michaels, "In the Land of Blood and Tears," *Time,* October 29, 1990, pp. 62–63. Shick reports that in 1927 the Liberian government gave "Henry Firestone control over a vast area of the interior for the development of a rubber plantation." Shick, *Behold the Promised Land,* p. 142.

11. Black Towns

1. See Arthur Cromwell, Jr., *The Black Frontier* (Lincoln: University of Nebraska Television, 1970), p. 75. This book was written in conjunction with a television series of the same title.

2. James L. Sibley, *Liberia—Old and New* (London: James Clarke, 1929), p. 5.

3. Norman L. Crockett, *The Black Towns* (Lawrence: The Regents Press of Kansas, 1979), p. xiii.

4. Id. p. xii.

5. Id. p. 40.

6. Kenneth Marvin Hamilton, *Black Towns and Profit: Promotion and Development in the Trans-Appalachian West* (Urbana: University of Illinois Press, 1991), p. 1.

7. Charles Allen Humphrey, *Socio-Economic Study of Six All-Black Towns in Oklahoma* (Ann Arbor: University Microfilms No. 74–8049, 1974), p. 88.

8. Crockett, *The Black Towns*, pp. 39–40.

9. Cromwell, *The Black Frontier*, p. 75.

10. Hamilton, *Black Towns and Profit*, p. 5.

11. Id.

12. Id.

13. Cromwell, *The Black Frontier*, pp. 77–78.

14. Id. p. 78.

15. Crockett, *The Black Towns*, pp. 2 and 6.

16. Id. p. 2.

17. Id.

18. Id. p. 6. See also Hamilton, *Black Towns and Profit*, pp. 10–12.

19. Crockett, *The Black Towns*, p. 8.

20. Id.

21. Hamilton, *Black Towns and Profit*, p. 25.

22. Id.

23. Crockett, *The Black Towns*, pp. 176–177; Cromwell, *The Black Frontier*, pp. 82, 85.

24. Hamilton, *Black Towns and Profit*, p. 43.

25. Crockett, *The Black Towns*, p. 9.

26. Id.

27. Id. p. 11.

28. Id.

29. Hamilton, *Black Towns and Profit*, p. 48.

30. Crockett, *The Black Town*, p. 12.

31. Id. p. 14.

32. Id. p. 15.

33. Id.

34. Id.

35. Hamilton, *Black Towns and Profit*, p. 52.

36. Id.

37. Id. p. 55. See also id. p. 54.

38. Crockett, *The Black Towns*, pp. 95–97.

39. Id. p. 97.

40. Hamilton, *Black Towns and Profit*, p. 58.

41. Id. p. 84.

42. Crockett, *The Black Towns,* pp. 152, 160, 161, 162, 164, 177, 179.

43. Hamilton, *Black Towns and Profits,* p. 84.

44. Id. p. 99.

45. Id. See also Crockett, *The Black Towns,* p. 20.

46. Crockett, *The Black Towns,* p. 22.

47. Id. p. 23.

48. Id. p. 26.

49. Hamilton, *Black Towns and Profits,* p. 100.

50. Id. p. 104.

51. Id. p. 112.

52. Id. at pp. 113–114; Crockett, *The Black Towns,* p. 178.

53. Crockett, *The Black Towns,* pp. 28, 29.

54. Id. pp. 26–27, citing the *Clearview Patriarch,* May 5, 1911, a local newspaper financed by Thompson.

55. Id. p. 33.

56. Id. pp. 33, 34.

57. Id. p. 179.

58. Id. pp. 35–36.

59. Id. pp. 39, 40.

60. Hamilton, *Black Towns and Profits,* p. 120.

61. Id. pp. 122, 123.

62. Id. p. 127. See also id. p. 126.

63. Id. p. 127.

64. Id.

65. Id. p. 133.

66. Id.

67. Crockett, *The Black Towns,* pp. 180, 181.

68. Id. p. 181.

69. Hamilton, *Black Towns and Profits,* pp. 138–139.

70. Id. pp. 139–140.

71. Id. pp. 140, 141.

72. Id. p. 143. See also id. p. 141.

73. Id. pp. 143–144.

74. Id. p. 145.

75. Id. p. 146.

76. Id.

77. Crockett, *The Black Towns,* p. 166.

78. Id. p. 167.

79. Id.

80. Id. p. 164.

81. Id. p. 165.

12. Intra-Racial Conflicts and Racial Romanticism

1. See Jane Mayer and Jill Abramson, *Strange Justice: The Selling of Clarence Thomas* (New York: Houghton Mifflin, 1994). There has never been a woman executive director of the NAACP, Urban League, or any other major civil rights organization.

2. See Roy L. Brooks, *Rethinking the American Race Problem* (Berkeley: University of California Press, 1990).

3. During the 1940s and 1950s, intra-racial discrimination among African Americans in California "had a lot more to do with how long ago your family had escaped from the South than it did with color differentiations." Bonnie Allen, "It Ain't Easy Being Pinky," *Essence*, July 1982, p. 128.

4. Gunnar Myrdal, *An American Dilemma* (New York: Harper & Brothers, 1944), p. 697.

5. Paul R. Spickard, *Mixed Blood: Intermarriage and Ethnic Identity in Twentieth Century America* (Madison: University of Wisconsin Press, 1989), p. 323.

6. Amy Jacques Garvey, *The Philosophy and Opinions of Marcus Garvey*, 2 vols. (Denver: The Majority Press, 1986), p. 16.

7. R. Z. Sheppard, "The Great Enunciator," *Time*, November 15, 1993, p. 98.

8. See Chapter 10. For a detailed critical analysis of the distinctions between Americo-Liberians and others *see* Jane Martin, "How to Build a Nation: Liberian Ideas about National Integration in the Later Nineteenth Century," *Liberian Studies Journal* 2 (1969): 15–42.

9. Crockett, Norman L., *The Black Towns* (Lawrence: The Regents Press of Kansas, 1979), p. 69.

10. Id.

11. Id.

12. Id., p. 71.

13. Id.

14. Id.

15. Spickard, *Mixed Blood,* p. 323.

16. Alexis De Veaux, "Loving the Dark in Me," *Essence,* July 1982, p. 125.

17. See also Brooks, *Rethinking the American Race Problem,* p. 193, n.63, citing EEOC Decision No. 72-0454 (September 15, 1971) (an unpublished EEOC decision where reasonable cause was found in an employment discrimination case in which a light-skinned African American was selected over a dark-skinned African American with more Negroid features).

18. *Casteneda v. Partida,* 430 U.S. 482, 504 (1977) (Marshall, J., concurring).

19. Christina Hoff Sommers, *Who Stole Feminism: How Women Have Betrayed Women* (New York: Simon & Schuster, 1994), p. 74.

20. Id. at p. 75 (emphasis in original) (quoting Susan Haack).

III. Limited Separation

1. *Wall Street Journal,* May 18, 1995, p. 1, col. 2 (citing the Southern Education Foundation).

2. 112 S. Ct. 2727 (1992).

13. The Case for a Policy of Limited Separation

1. §703(e)(1), 42 U.S.C. § 2000e-2(e).

2. See *Western Air Lines, Inc. v. Criswell,* 472 U.S. 400 (1985); *International Union, UAW v. Johnson Controls, Inc.,* 111 S.Ct. 1196 (1991).

3. 29 U.S.C § 623(f)(1).

4. Joe R. Feagin and Clairece Booker Feagin, *Racial and Ethnic Relations* (Englewood, N.J.: Prentice Hall, 1993), p. 166.

5. Race is a suspect classification. See *McDonald v. Board of Election Comm'rs,* 394 U.S. 802, 807 (1969); *Bolling v. Sharpe,* 347 U.S. 497, 499; see also Polyvios G. Polyvios, *The Equal Protection of the Laws* (London: Duckworth, 1980), pp. 238–240, 311–314 (characterizing race as a suspect classification deserving of strict scrutiny); "Developments in the Law—Equal Protection," *Harvard Law Review* 82 (1969): 1087–1091 (characterizing race as a suspect classification and discussing the Court's rejection of the "color-blind" interpretation of the Equal Protection Clause). Courts often find invidious discrimination present when fundamental personal interests are violated. See *Reynolds v. Sims,* 377 U.S. 533, 561 (1964). Fundamental personal interests include the right to procreate, *Skinner v. Oklahoma,* 316 U.S. 535, 541 (1942), the right to vote, *Reynolds,* 377 U.S. at 561–562, and the right to engage in interstate travel, *Shapiro v. Thompson,* 394 U.S. 618, 629–631 (1969), overruled on other grounds by *Edelman v. Jordan,* 415 U.S. 651 (1974). For cases applying the strict scrutiny test to claims based on the Equal Protection Clause of the Fourteenth Amendment, see *City of Richmond v. J.A. Croson Co.,* 488 U.S. 469, 493–494 (1989); *United States v. Paradise,* 480 U.S. 149, 166 & n.17 (1987). For an example applying the test to a claim based on the equal protection component of the Fifth Amendment's Due Process Clause, see *Local 28 of the Sheet Metal Workers' Int'l Ass'n v. EEOC,* 478 U.S. 421, 479–480 (1986).

6. Gerald Gunther, "The Supreme Court, 1971 Term—Foreword: In Search of Evolving Doctrine on a Changing Court: A Model for a Newer Equal Protection," *Harvard Law Review* 86 (1972): 8.

7. Roy L. Brooks, *Rethinking the American Race Problem* (Berkeley: University of California Press, 1990), p. 52. See also *Wygant v. Jackson Bd. of Educ.,* 476 U.S. 267, 273–274 (1986) (plurality opinion) (discussing this test); *Palmore v. Sidoti,* 466 U.S. 429, 432–433 (1984) (same).

8. *United States v. Paradise,* 480 U.S. 149, 196 (1987) (O'Connor, J., dissenting) (quoting *Wygant v. Jackson Bd. of Educ.,* 476 U.S. 267, 273 (1986)).

9. *Fullilove v. Klutznick,* 448 U.S. 448, 522–523 (1980) (Stewart, J., dissenting) (quoting *Plessy v. Ferguson,* 163 U.S. 537, 558 (1896) (Harlan, J., dissenting), overruled by *Brown v. Board of Educ.,* 347 U.S. 483 (1954)) (alteration in original).

10. Id. at 526.

11. *City of Richmond v. J. A. Croson, Co.,* 488 U.S. 469, 520–521 (1989) (Scalia, J., concurring in the judgment) (quoting Alexander Bickel, *The Morality of Consent* [New Haven, Conn.: Yale University Press, 1975]), p. 133.

12. *Plessy v. Ferguson,* 163 U.S. 537, 558 (1896) (Harlan, J. dissenting).

13. Eric Foner, *Reconstruction: America's Unfinished Revolution, 1863–1877* (New York: Harper & Row, 1988), pp. 256–257.

14. Eric Schnapper, "Affirmative Action and the Legislative History of the Fourteenth Amendment," *Virginia Law Review* 71 (1985): 784–785 (footnotes omitted). For further discussion of the Freedmen's Bureau Act, see *Encyclopedia of Black America,* W. Augustus Low and Virgil A. Clift, eds. (New York: Da Capo Press, 1981), pp. 72–77.

15. Early cases supporting the color-blind principle include *Bush v. Kentucky,* 107 U.S. 110 (1882); *Gibson v. Mississippi,* 162 U.S. 565 (1896); *Carter v. Texas,* 177 U.S. 442 (1900); *Buchanan v. Warley,* 245 U.S. 60 (1917). But the color-blind principle appears to have been a minority position, as the ensuing discussion indicates.

16. 109 U.S. 303 (1880).

17. Id. p. 308.

18. 103 U.S. 370 (1880).

19. Id. p. 397.

20. 118 U.S. 356 (1886).

21. Id. pp. 373–374.

22. 163 U.S. 537 (1896).

23. Id. p. 543.

24. Id. p. 551.

25. See Alexander T. Aleinikoff, "Re-reading Justice Harlan's Dissent in Plessy v. Ferguson: Freedom, Antiracism, and Citizenship," *University of Illinois Law Review* 1992 (1992): 961–977.

26. 170 U.S. 213 (1898).

27. Id. p. 225.

28. 175 U.S. 528 (1899).

29. Id. p. 545.

30. 192 U.S. 226 (1904).

31. Id. p. 230.

32. 273 U.S. 536 (1927).

33. Id. p. 541.

34. 286 U.S. 73 (1932).

35. Id. p. 89.

36. 330 U.S. 552 (1947).

37. Id. p. 556.

38. 339 U.S. 637 (1950).

39. Id. p. 641.

40. 339 U.S. 629 (1950).

41. Id. pp. 634–635.

42. Id.

43. 347 U.S. 483 (1954).

44. Id. p. 494 (emphasis added). See also the discussion of *Brown* in Chapter 1.

45. 347 U.S. 497 (1954).

46. Id. p. 500.

47. 373 U.S. 683 (1963).

48. Id. p. 687.

49. 375 U.S. 399 (1964).

50. Id. p. 403.

51. 388 U.S. 1 (1967).

52. Id. p. 11.

53. 430 U.S. 144 (1977).

54. 401 U.S. 1 (1971).

55. 430 U.S. 144 (1977).

56. Id. p. 165.

57. 438 U.S. 265 (1978).

58. Id. pp. 320, 414. Pertinent sections of the Civil Rights Act are found at 42 U.S.C. §§ 2000d-2000d-4.

59. Id. p. 336.

60. 458 U.S. 718 (1982).

61. Id. p. 728.

62. 488 U.S. 469 (1989).

63. Id. p. 493.

64. Id. p. 494.

65. See *Adarand Constructors, Inc. v. Pena,* 115 S. Ct. 2097 (1995); *Miller v. Johnson,* 115 S.Ct. 2475 (1995).

14. Elementary and Secondary Education

1. Carter G. Woodson, *The Mis-Education of the Negro* (Nashville, Tenn.: Winston-Derek Publishers, 1990, originally published in 1933), p. 20.

2. See Thomas H. Jones, *Introduction to School Finance: Technique and Social Policy* (New York: Macmillan, 1985), pp. 16–17, Tables 1–6; Christopher F. Edley, Jr., "Introduction: Lawyers and Education Reform," *Harvard Journal on Legislation* 28 (1991): 299; Blaise A. Scinto, "Talents Which Nature Has Liberally Sown: Promoting Fiscal Equality in Virginia's Public Education System," *Journal of Law & Politics* 9 (1993): 752–753; John C. Reitz, "Public School Financing in the United States: More on the Dark Side of Intermediate Structures," *Brigham Young University Law Review* (1993): 625–626.

3. 411 U.S. 1 (1973).

4. See *Shofstall v. Hollins,* 110 Ariz. 88 (1973); *Knowles v. State Board of Education,* 219 Kan. 271 (1976); *Milliken v. Green,* 212 N.W.2d 711 (Mich. 1973); *Thompson v. Engelking,* 537 P.2d 635 (Ida. 1975); *Kukor v. Grover,* 436 N.W.2d 568 (Wis. 1989); *Olson v. State of Oregon,* 554 P.2d 139 (Ore. 1976); *People ex rel. Jones v. Adams,* 40 Ill. App. 3d 189 (1976); *Danson v. Casey,* 399 A.2d 360 (Pa. 1979); *Board of Education of the City School District of the City of Cincinnati v. Walters,* 390 N.E.2d 813 (Ohio 1979); *McDaniel v. Thomas,* 285 S.E.2d (Ga. 1981); *Lujan*

v. Colorado State Board of Education, 649 P.2d 1005 (Colo. 1982); *Board of Education, Levittown Union Free School District v. Nyquist,* 439 N.E.2d 359 (N.Y. 1982); *Hornbeck v. Somerset County Board of Education,* 458 A.2d 758 (Md. 1983); *Fair School Finance Council of Oklahoma, Inc. v. State of Oklahoma,* 746 P.2d 1135 (Okla. 1987); and *Richland County v. Campbell,* 364 S.E.2d 470 (S.C. 1988).

5. See *Dupree v. Alma School District No. 30 of Crawford County,* 279 Ark. 340 (1983); *Serrano v. Priest,* 18 Cal. 3d 728 (1976), cert. denied, 432 U.S. 907 (1977); *Horton v. Meskill,* 172 Conn. 615 (1977); *Rose v. Council for Better Educ., Inc.,* 790 S.W.2d 186 (Ky. 1989); *Helena Elementary School District v. State of Montana,* 236 Mont. 44 (1989); *Abbott v. Burke,* 119 N.J. 287 (1990); *Robinson v. Cahill,* 62 N.J. 473 (1973); *Edgewood Independent School District v. Kirby,* 777 S.W.2d 391 (Tex. 1989); *Seattle School District v. State,* 90 Wash. 2d 476 (1978); *Pauley v. Kelly,* 255 S.E.2d 859 (W. Va. 1979); *Washakie County School District Number One v. Herschler,* 606 P.2d 310 (Wyo. 1980).

6. See *McDuffy v. Secretary of the Executive Office of Education,* 415 Mass. 545, 619 n.92.

7. G. Alfred Hess, Jr., et al., *Overcoming the Inequities in Illinois School Finance: An Analysis of Options Toward Equity* (Chicago, Ill.: EdEquity Coalition, 1991), pp. 3–4. See Carol Ascher, *Efficiency, Equity, and Local Control—School Finance in Texas* (New York: Columbia University/ERIC Clearinghouse on Urban Education, 1993), p. 4.

8. *Overcoming the Inequalities,* p. 4.

9. Jonathan Kozol, *Savage Inequalities: Children in American Schools* (New York: Crown, 1991), p. 209.

10. David Van Biema, "The Great Tax Switch," *Time,* March 28, 1994, p. 31.

11. Alison Morantz, *Money, Choice and Equity in Kansas City: Major Investments with Modest Returns,* The Harvard Project on School Desegregation (Cambridge, Mass.: Harvard University, 1994), p. i. See also Joseph Feldman et al., *Still Separate, Still Unequal: The Limits of Milliken II's Educational Compensation Remedies,* The Harvard Project on School Desegregation, loc cit.

12. See Morantz, *Money, Choice and Equity,* p. 3.

13. Id. at unnumbered foreword.

14. Robert L. Crain, Rita E. Mahard, and Ruth E. Narot, *Making Desegregation Work: How Schools Create Social Climates* (Cambridge, Mass.: Ballinger, 1982), pp. 210, 213, 217.

15. Id. at 138, 139, 141.

16. Id. at 172.

17. Id. pp. 97, 99, 105, 108.

18. Carol Ascher, *Student Alienation, Student Behavior and the Urban Schools,* ERIC/CUE Urban Diversity Series (New York: Teachers College Press, Columbia University, 1982), p. 29.

19. R. H. Wiegel, Patricia L. Wiser, and Stuart W. Cook, "The Impact of Cooperative Learning Experience on Cross-Ethnic Relations and Attitudes," *Journal of Social Issues* 31 (1975): 219–244.

20. Walter G. Stephan, "Blacks and Brown: The Effects of School Desegregation on Black Students" (prepared for the United States Department of Education, National Institute of Education, 1983), p. 35.

21. Dr. Benjamin E. Mays, "Comment: Atlanta—Living with Brown Twenty Years Later," *Black Law Journal* 3 (1974): 191–192.

22. W. E. B. Du Bois, "Does the Negro Need Separate Schools?" *Journal of Negro Education* 4 (1935): 335.

23. Id. p. 331.

24. Derrick Bell, "The Case for a Separate Black School System," in Willy DeMarcell Smith and Eva Wells Chunn, eds., *Black Education: A Quest for Equity and Excellence* (New Brunswick, N.J.: Transaction Publishers, 1989), p. 143.

25. See *Milliken v. Bradely,* 433 U.S. 267 (1977); *Liddell v. Caldell,* 546 F.2d 768 (8th Cir. 1976), remanded sub nom *Liddell v. Board of Education of the City of St. Louis, Mo.,* 469 F. Supp. 1304 (E.D. Mo. 1979). See also Bill Lann Lee, "A Right to an Integrated Education: A Survey," *The Urban Lawyer* 14 (Summer 1982): 429.

26. Robert L. Carter, "A Reassessment of *Brown v. Board,*" in Derrick Bell, ed., *Shades of Brown: New Perspectives on School Desegregation,* (New York: Teachers College Press, Columbia University, 1980), pp. 27, 28.

27. See Judith H. Dobrzynski, "How to Succeed? Go to Wellesley: Its Graduates Scoff at the Glass Ceilings," *New York Times,* October 29, 1995, sect. 3, p. 1.

28. Deborah M. Wilkinson, "Black Independent Schools: Reality of Alternative Education," *Integrated Education* 21 (1984): 219.

29. E. R. Shipp, "A Better Chance," *The San Diego Union-Tribune,* May 15, 1994, p. G4.

30. Steve Stecklow, "Born Again: Evangelical Schools Reinvent Themselves by Stressing Academics," *Wall Street Journal,* May 12, 1994, p. A6.

31. See Shipp, "A Better Chance," p. G4.

32. See Stecklow, "Born Again," p. A1. Apparently the test was given at the end of the academic year. Scores for other grades were not reported.

33. Walter Williams, "A Bleak Vision of Blacks in America," *Wall Street Journal,* November 7, 1994, p. A14.

34. Id.

35. See Wilkinson, "Black Independent Schools," p. 221.

36. Sam Allis, "The Bus Doesn't Stop Here," *Time,* December 17, 1990, p. 102.

37. See Wilkinson, "Black Independent Schools," pp. 221, 223.

38. See Joan Davis Ratteray, "Independent Neighborhood Schools: A Framework for the Education of African Americans," *Journal of Negro Education* 61 (1992): 138–147; Donald Leake and Brenda Leake, "African-American Immersion Schools in Milwaukee: A View from the Inside," *Phi Delta Kappan* (June 1992): 785.

39. *New York Globe,* reprinted in Martin Dann, ed., *The Black Press, 1827–1890. The Quest for National Identity* (New York: Putnam, 1971), pp. 103–104. For further discussion see Robert C. Maynard, "Black Nationalism and Community Schools," in Henry M. Levin, ed., *Community Control of Schools* (Washington, D.C.: Brookings Institute, 1970), p. 100; Leonard J. Fein, *The Ecology of the Public Schools* (New York: Pegasus, 1971), pp. 19, 20, 22, 39, 40.

40. Mary Eleanor Rhodes Hoover, "The Nairobi Day School: An African American Independent School, 1966–1984," *Journal of Negro Education* 61 (1992): 203; Charles D. Moody and Christella D. Moody, "Elements of Effective Black Schools," in *Black Education: A Quest for Equity and Excellence,* p. 178; Ray Cross, "What Makes an Effective Principal?" *Principal* 22 (Mar. 1981): 22.

41. See Moody, "Elements of Effective Black Schools," p. 179.

42. See Wilkinson, "Black Independent Schools," pp. 221, 223; Kenneth W. Haskins, "A Black Perspective on Community Control," *Inequality in Education* 14 (November 1973): 25; Gary Putka, "Back to Basics: Education Reformers Have New Respect for Catholic Schools," *Wall Street Journal,* March 28, 1991, p. A1.

43. Jonathan Kozol, *Free Schools* (Boston: Houghton Mifflin, 1972), p. 33. See Richard Louv, "Hope in Hell's Classroom," *The New York Times Magazine,* November 25, 1990, pp. 30–33.

44. See Louis L. Knowles and Kenneth Prewitt, *Institutional Racism in America* (Englewood Cliffs, N.J.: Prentice Hall, 1969), pp. 42, 43.

45. Roy L. Brooks, *Rethinking The American Race Problem* (Berkeley: University of California Press, 1990), pp. 143–144.

46. H. Aaron, *Day School EPA* (East Palo Alto, Calif.: MEE Bookstore, 1970), p. 42.

47. G. Wilks, "Nairobi Day School" in Hoover, M., Daloney, N., and Lewis, S., eds., *Successful Black and Minority Schools: Classic Models* (San Francisco: Julian Richardson and Associates, 1990), p. 27. See also Mary Eleanor Rhodes Hoover, "The Nairobi Day School," pp. 203, 204, 206.

48. Albert Shanker, "Where We Stand: America, the Multicultural," *The New York Times,* Feb. 17, 1991, Week in Review (sect. E), p. 7; Terry Tang, "The African American Academy—Separatisms for Success—An Afrocentric Focus in New Seattle Pilot Program," *Seattle Times,* March 17, 1991, sect. A, p. 21.

49. See William Julius Wilson, *The Truly Disadvantaged: The Inner City, The Underclass, and Public Policy* (Chicago: University of Chicago Press, 1987); Carol Ascher, "School Programs for African American Male Students," *Trends and Issues* 15 (1991): 3; John Kasarda, "Caught in the Web of Change," *Society* 21 (1983): 41; John Kain, "Housing Segregation, Negro Employment, and Metropolitan Decentralization," *The Quarterly Journal of Economics* 82 (1968): 175.

50. For a criticism of the exodus theory, see Douglas Massey and Mitchell Eggers, "The Ecology of Inequality: Minorities and the Concentration of Poverty," *American Journal of Sociology* 5 (1990): 1153–1188. For a response, see Brooks, "The Ecology of Inequality: The Rise of The African American Underclass," *Harvard Blackletter Journal* 8 (1991): pp. 1–15.

51. Ascher, "School Programs for African American Male Students," pp. 4, 5; Brooks, *Rethinking the American Race Problem,* p. 107; "Vital Signs: The State of African Americans in Higher Education," *The Journal of Blacks in Higher Education* (Winter 1993/1994): 38.

52. John Paul Newport, Jr., "Steps to Help the Urban Black Man," *Fortune,* December 18, 1989, p. 168.

53. Ascher, "School Programs for African American Male Students," p. 5.

54. James Comer and Alvin Poussaint, *Black Child Care* (New York: Simon and Schuster, 1975), p. 21.

55. Barbara Kantrowitz, Karen Springen, Lydia Denworth, and Pat Wingert, "Can the Boys Be Saved?" *Newsweek,* October 15, 1990, p. 67. See also "Vital Signs," p. 38.

56. Ethelbert W. Haskins, *The Crisis in Afro-American Leadership* (Buffalo, N.Y.: Prometheus Books, 1988), p. 16.

57. Newport, "Steps to Help the Urban Black Man," p. 168. See generally Jawanza Kunjufu, *Countering the Conspiracy to Destroy Black Boys* (Chicago, Ill.: Afro-American Publishing Company, 1983); D. N. Lloyd, "Prediction of School Failure from Third Grade Data," *Educational and Psychological Measurement* 38 (1978): 1193–1200; James P. Comer, "Educating Poor Minority Children," *Scientific American* (Nov. 1988): 42–49; Robert Staples, *Black Masculinity: The Black Male's Role in American Society* (San Francisco: Black Scholars Press, 1982), p. 22.

58. Ascher, "School Programs for African American Male Students," p. 11.

59. See id. p. 12.

60. See id. p. 13.

15. Higher Education

1. Eulius Simien, "The Law School Admission Test as a Barrier to Almost Twenty Years of Affirmative Action," *Thurgood Marshall Law Review,* 12 (1987): 359–393. Gil Kujovich, "Public Black Colleges: The Long History of Unequal Funding," *The Journal of Blacks in Higher Education* (Winter 1993–94): 73, 74.

2. Id. p. 78.

3. Id. pp. 76, 77, 80–82.

4. *United States v. Fordice,* 112 S. Ct. 2727, 2746 (1992).

5. See Susan T. Hill, *The Traditionally Black Institutions of Higher Education, 1960 to 1982* (Washington, D.C.: The National Center for Education Statistics, 1985), pp. xiv–xv.

6. Jean L. Preer, *Lawyers v. Educators: Black Colleges and Desegregation in Public Higher Education* (Westport, Conn.: Greenwood Press, 1982), p. 2.

7. Carnegie Commission on Higher Education, *From Isolation to Mainstream: Problems of the Colleges Founded for Negroes* (New York: McGraw-Hill, 1971), p. 11.

8. Walter Allen, Jr., "Black Colleges v. White Colleges: The Fork in the Road for Black Students," *Change* (May/June 1987), p.28.

9. Ronald R. Edmonds and Charles V. Willie, eds., *Black Colleges in America: Challenge, Development, Survival* (New York: Teachers College Press, 1978), pp. 19–50.

10. Daniel C. Thompson, *Private Black Colleges at the Crossroads* (Westport, Conn.: Greenwood Press, 1973), pp. 180–194.

11. Edmonds and Willie, *Black Colleges in America,* at 235–260.

12. Antoine Garibaldi, ed., *Black Colleges and Universities: Challenges for the Future* (New York: Praeger, 1984), pp. 26–47.

13. *Fordice,* 112 S. Ct. at 2746.

14. See Chapter 2; Garibaldi, *Black Colleges and Universities,* pp. 3–9.

15. U.S. Commission on Civil Rights, *The Black/White Colleges: Dismantling the Dual System of Higher Education* (Washington, D.C.: U.S. Commission on Civil Rights Clearinghouse Publication 66, April 1988) p. 44. See William B. Harvey and Lea E. Williams, "Historically Black Colleges: Models for Increasing Minority Representation," *Education and Urban Society,* 21-3 (May 1989): 328–330.

16. Cultural Integration within the Community

1. See Marshall Sklare, *America's Jews* (New York: Random House, 1971), pp. 105–107; Abraham Cronbach, "Jewish Pioneering in American Social Welfare," in Jacob R. Marcus, ed., *Critical Studies in American Jewish History: Selected Articles from American Jewish Archives,* vol. 1 (Cincinnati: American Jewish Archives, 1971): 217–243; Nathan Glazer and Daniel Patrick Moynihan, *Beyond the Melting Pot: The Negroes, Puerto Ricans, Jews, Italians, and Irish of New York City* (Cambridge, Mass.: MIT Press, 1970), pp. 140–141; James Yaffe, *The American Jews* (New York: Random House, 1968), pp. 12, 13; Milton M. Gordon, *Assimilation in American Life: The Role of Race, Religion, and National Origins* (New York: Oxford University Press, 1964), pp. 140–141.

2. See Sklare, *America's Jews,* p. 107.

3. Richard Fiol, "Experiences of Chinese and Italian Americans Living Under a Regime of Racial Separation" (Research Paper, University of San Diego School of Law, 1991), pp. 15–18. See also Joe R. Feagin and Clairece B. Feagin, *Racial and Ethnic Relations,* 4th ed. (Englewood Cliffs, N.J.: Prentice Hall, 1993), p. 118.

4. Cathy Booth, "The Capital of Latin America: Miami," *Time,* Fall 1993, Special Issue, p. 84. See also Feagin and Feagin, *Racial and Ethnic Relations,* p. 322.

5. Gilbert Ware, *William Hastie: Grace Under Pressure* (New York: Oxford University Press, 1984), p. 16.

6. See Thomas Sowell, *Race and Culture: A World View* (New York: Basic Books, 1994); Thomas Sowell, *Civil Rights: Rhetoric or Reality?* (New York: William Morrow, 1984); Thomas Sowell, *The Economics and Politics of Race: An International Perspective* (New York: William Morrow, 1983).

7. Richard Neely, *Tragedies of Our Own Making: How Private Choices Have Created Public Bankruptcy* (Urbana, Ill.: University of Illinois Press, 1994).

8. See Sowell, *Race and Culture;* Sowell, *The Economics and Politics of Race.*

9. See Shelby Steele, *The Content of Our Character: A New Vision of Race in America* (New York: St. Martin's Press, 1990), pp.24–25, 28–30, 45–47, 49–53, 55, 139, 167, 170.

10. See Stanley M. Elkins, *Slavery: A Problem in American Institutional and Intellectual Life* (Chicago, Ill.: University of Chicago Press, 1959), pp. 89–98.

11. See Charles E. Bicknell, *Black Culture in America: An Educator's Perspective* (Albuquerque, N.M.: Horizon Communications, 1987); Lawrence W. Levine, *Black*

Culture and Black Consciousness (New York: Encyclopedia Americana/CBS News Audio Resource Library, 1977).

12. See C. Vann Woodward, *Origins of the New South* (Baton Rouge, La.: Louisiana State University Press, 1951).

13. See Nechal Sobel, *The World They Made Together: Black and White Values in Eighteenth-Century Virginia* (Princeton, N.J.: Princeton University Press, 1987), pp. 64–67, 165–167, 226–229.

14. See Richard Schaefer, *Sociology,* 3d ed. (New York: McGraw-Hill, 1989), pp. 63–83, 86, 182, 202, 609.

15. For further discussion of the African American underclass, see Bill E. Lawson, ed., *The Underclass Question* (Philadelphia: Temple University Press, 1992); William Julius Wilson, *The Truly Disadvantaged: The Inner City, The Underclass, and Public Policy* (Chicago: University of Chicago Press, 1987); Roy L. Brooks, *Rethinking the American Race Problem* (Berkeley: University of California Press, 1990), pp. 106–130.

16. See John Hope Franklin, *From Slavery to Freedom: A History of American Negroes* (New York: A. A. Knopf, 1947), pp. 200–201; Philip S. Foner and Josephine F. Pacheco, *Three Who Dared: Prudence Crandall, Margaret Douglass, Myrtilla Miner: Champions of Antebellum Black Education* (Westport, Conn.: Greenwood Press, 1984), pp. xiv–xv; Carter G. Woodson, *Education of the Negro Prior to 1861* (New York: Arno Press, 1968), pp. 24–29; see Ronald K. Goodenow and Arthur O. White, eds., *Education and the Rise of the New South* (Boston: G. K. Hall, 1981); Thomas L. Webber, *Deep Like the Rivers: Education in the Slave Quarter Community, 1831–1865* (New York: Norton, 1978).

17. Peter Reuter, Robert MacCoun, and Patrick Murphy, *Money from Crime: A Study of the Economics of Drug Dealing in Washington, D.C.* (Santa Monica, Calif.: RAND, Drug Policy Research Center, 1990), p. xi.

18. Id. p. x.

19. Bruce Johnson, Terry Williams, Kojo Dei, and Harry Sanabria, "Drug Abuse in the Inner City: Impact on Hard-Drug Users and the Community," in Michael Tonry and James Wilson, eds., *Drugs and Crime* (Chicago: University of Chicago Press, 1990), p. 9.

20. Id. (emphasis added).

21. Reuter, et al., *Money from Crime,* p. xi.

22. Brooks, *Rethinking the American Race Problem,* p. 145.

23. Leon Lewis, "About Men: In On the Game," *New York Times Magazine,* February 3, 1985, p. 70.

24. Ralph Ellison, *Invisible Man* (New York: Random House, 1952).

25. See Gilbert Osofsky, ed., *Puttin' on Ole Massa* (New York: Harper & Row, 1969).

26. James Comer and Alvin Poussaint, *Black Child Care: How to Bring Up a Black Child in America—A Guide to Emotional and Psychological Development* (New York: Simon and Schuster, 1975).

27. Id. pp. 19–21, 22–23.

28. Langston Hughes, "Mother to Son," *The Weary Blues* (New York: A. A. Knopf, 1926), p. 107.

29. On the social role of the African American church, see William L. Banks, *The Black Church in the U.S.: Its Origin, Growth, Contributions, and Outlook* (Chicago: Moody Press, 1972); E. Franklin Frazier, *The Negro Church in America* (Liverpool, U.K.: Liverpool University Press, 1964); Hart M. Nelson and Anne Kusener Nelson, *Black Church in the Sixties* (Lexington, Kentucky: University Press of Kentucky, 1975); James H. Cone, *For My People: Black Theology and the Black Church* (Maryknoll, N.Y.: Orbis Books, 1984); Albert B. Cleage, *Black Christian Nationalism: New Directions for the Black Church* (New York: William Morrow, 1972); W. D. Weatherford, *American Churches and the Negro: An Historical Study from Early Slave Days to the Present* (Boston: Christopher Publishing House, 1957).

30. Steele, *The Content of Our Character*, pp. 108–109.

31. See Roy Brooks, "Re-packaging Noblesse Oblige," *American Visions* (June 1987): 12.

17. Economic Integration within the Community

1. Marlene Kleinman, "Slaves and Tailors: A Comparison of the African American and Jewish Experiences in America" (Research Paper, University of Minnesota Law School, April 22, 1991), p. 18. See also, Israel Rubinow, "The Economic Condition of Jews in Russia," *Bulletin of the Bureau of Labor* 72 (Washington, D.C.: Government Printing Office, 1907), pp. 487–583.

2. Kleinman, "Slaves and Tailors," p. 20 (sources cited therein). See also Stephen Birmingham, *"Our Crowd" The Great Jewish Families of New York* (New York: Harper & Row, 1967), pp. 99–167.

3. Joe R. Feagin and Clairece R. Feagin, *Racial and Ethnic Relations*, 4th ed. (Englewood Cliffs, N.J.: Prentice Hall, 1993), p. 155. See also Henry L. Feingold, *Zion in America: The Jewish Experience from Colonial Times to the Present* (New York: Twayne, 1974), p. 12.

4. Moses Rischin, *The Promised City: New York's Jews, 1870–1914* (Cambridge, Mass.: Harvard University Press, 1962), p. 59.

5. See generally Feagin and Feagin, *Racial and Ethnic Relations*, pp. 100–111; Michael Walsh, "The Shadow of the Law: For Illegal Aliens, Life in a New Land Is Mostly One of Poverty, Anxiety and Loneliness," *Time*, Special Issue, Fall 1993, p. 17.

6. See Feagin and Feagin, *Racial and Ethnic Relations*, p. 127.

7. Id. at 129.

8. James Walsh, "The Perils of Success: Asians Have Become Exemplary Immigrants, But at a Price," *Time*, Special Issue, Fall 1993, p. 55.

9. See Ivan H. Light, *Ethnic Enterprise in America: Business and Welfare Among Chinese, Japanese, and Blacks* (Berkeley: University of California Press, 1972), p. 89.

10. Id., p. 24–26.

11. See Feagin and Feagin, *Racial and Ethnic Relations*, pp. 322–323.

12. Dirk Johnson, "Economies Come to Life on Indian Reservations," *New York Times*, July 3, 1994, p. 1 (citing data from the Census Bureau and the National Indian Policy Center).

13. Id.

14. Feagin and Feagin, *Racial and Ethnic Relations*, at pp. 196–197, citing James Cook, "Help Wanted—Work, Not Handouts," *Forbes*, May 4, 1987: 68–71.

15. See id. at pp. 269–272. See also *Garcia v. Spun Steak Co.*, 998 F.2d 1480 (9th Cir. 1993); Juan F. Perea, "English Only Rules and the Right to Speak One's Primary Language in the Workplace," *University of Michigan Journal of Law Reform* 23 (1990): 265.

16. Remarks of Bonnie Erbe, host of "To the Contrary," transcript #406, May 5, 1995, p. 12.

17. Carol Hymowitz, "World's Poorest Women Advance by Entrepreneurship," *Wall Street Journal*, September 5, 1995, p. B1.

18. Roy L. Brooks, "Small Business Financing Alternatives Under the Securities Act of 1933," *U.C. Davis Law Review* 13 (1980): 544.

19. 13 C.F.R. §§121.402(a) & 121.407.

20. 13 C.F.R. §121.601.

21. See John Sibley Butler, *Entrepreneurship and Self-Help Among Black Americans: A Reconsideration of Race and Economics* (Albany, N.Y.: State University of New York Press, 1991), p. 294; John Sibley Butler, "For Black Prosperity: The Need for Black Business," *Current*, January 1991, pp. 10, 12.

22. Timothy Bates, *Banking on Black Enterprise: The Potential of Emerging Firms for Revitalizing Urban Economies* (Washington, D.C.: Joint Center for Political and Economic Studies, 1993), pp. 6–7.

23. *State of Small Business: A Report of the President Transmitted to the Congress* (Washington, D.C.: U.S. Government Printing Office, 1991), p. xvii. The United States experienced a "bottom-up small business entrepreneurial revolution" in the early 1980s. Ninety percent of the 7 million new jobs created between 1983 and 1985 were created by small companies. Butler, *Entrepreneurship and Self-Help*, p. 294.

24. *The State of Small Business: A Report of the President Transmitted to the Congress* (Washington, D.C.: U.S. Government Printing Office, 1990), p. 21.

25. Bates, *Banking on Black Enterprise*, p. 5.

26. Gregory A. Patterson, "A Delicate Balance," *Wall Street Journal*, April 3, 1992, p. R5.

27. Thomas Petzinger, Jr., "The Front Lines: Lewis Roland's Knack for Finding Truckers Keeps Firm Rolling," *Wall Street Journal*, December 1, 1995, p. B1.

28. Bates, *Banking on Black Enterprise*, pp. xvii–xviii.

29. Richard Gordon Hatcher, "Towards a Black Common Market: The Minority Economic Community," *Valparaiso Law Review* 24 (1990): 397–398.

30. Frank A. Fratoe, "Sociological Analysis of Minority Business," *Review of Black Political Economy* (Fall 1986): 14. See also Lorenzo Brown, "Why Should Black-Owned Businesses Hire Predominately Black Labor Forces?" *Review of Black Political Economy* (Fall 1986): 113.

31. Id. at p. 13.

32. Butler, *Entrepreneurship and Self-Help,* pp. 310–311.

33. Lloyd Gite, "The New Agenda of the Black Church: Economic Development for Black America," *Black Enterprise,* December 1993, p. 56.

34. George Fraser, "Tapping into the Power of Networking," *Black Enterprise,* July 1994, p. 68.

35. Gite, "The New Agenda of the Black Church," pp. 57–58.

36. "The B.E. 100's Industrial/Service Companies," *Black Enterprise,* June 1994, p. 87.

37. Elizabeth Lesly and Maria Mallory, "Inside the Black Business Network," *Business Week,* November 29, 1993, pp. 69, 71.

38. Brenda Dalglish, "Are They Worth It?" *Maclean's,* May 9, 1994, p. 37.

39. Lesly and Mallory, "Inside the Black Business Network," pp. 70, 72.

40. Carolyn M. Brown, "How to Start an Investment Club," *Black Enterprise,* April 1993, pp. 48–50.

41. Fraser, "Tapping into the Power of Networking," p. 67.

42. Id.

43. Adrienne S. Harris, "Hot Kidpreneur Programs That Are Making a Difference," *Black Enterprise,* February 1994, p. 178.

44. Id at p. 179.

45. Id.

46. Philip H. Mann, "Nontraditional Business Education For Black Entrepreneurs: Observations from a Successful Program," *Journal of Small Business Management* (April 1990): 33.

47. Wiley M. Woodard, "Help Wanted," *Black Enterprise,* February 1992, p. 220.

48. Id.

49. Henry Louis Gates, Jr., *Colored People: A Memoir* (New York: A. A. Knopf, 1994).

50. The histories of Greenwood and Durham are told in a handful of excellent books, most notably, John Sibley Butler, *Entrepreneurship and Self-Help Among Black Americans* (Albany, N.Y.: State University of New York Press, 1991); Scott Ellsworth, *Death in a Promised Land: The Tulsa Race Riot of 1921* (Baton Rouge, La.: Louisiana State University Press, 1982); Jimmie Lewis Franklin, *The Blacks in Oklahoma* (Norman, Ok.: University of Oklahoma Press, 1980); R. Halliburton Jr., *The Tulsa Race War of 1921* (San Francisco, Calif.: R and E Research Associates, 1975); William Kenneth Boyd, *The Story of Durham, City of the New South* (Durham, N.C.: Duke University Press, 1925).

51. Ellsworth, *Death in a Promised Land,* p. 1.

52. Id. at pp. 115–117.

53. Butler, *Entrepreneurship and Self-Help Among Black Americans,* pp. 206, 209.

54. Id. at p. 209.

55. Ellsworth, *Death in a Promised Land,* pp. 15–16.

56. Id.

57. Butler, *Entrepreneurship and Self-Help Among Black Americans,* p. 221, quoting Walter White, "The Eruption of Tulsa," *The Nation,* June 29, 1921, p. 909.

58. Halliburton, *The Tulsa Race War*, p. vii; Ellsworth, *Death in a Promised Land*, p. 32.

59. Butler, *Entrepreneurship and Self-Help Among Black Americans*, pp. 210, 211; Franklin, *The Blacks in Oklahoma*, p. 32.

60. Butler, *Entrepreneurship and Self-Help Among Black Americans*, p. 211.

61. Id. at p. 213; Ellsworth, *Death in a Promised Land*, p. 55.

62. Butler, *Entrepreneurship and Self-Help Among Black Americans*, p. 222.

63. Id. pp. 223–224.

64. See generally Ellsworth, *Death in a Promised Land*, pp. 109–110.

65. Butler, *Entrepreneurship and Self-Help Among Black Americans*, p. 166, citing William Kenneth Boyd, *The Story of Durham* (Durham, N.C.: Duke University Press, 1927), p. 277.

66. Id. at pp. 169–170.

67. Id. at pp. 172–173, citing Thomas H. Houck, "A Newspaper History of Race Relations in Durham, North Carolina: 1910–1940" (Masters Thesis: Duke University, 1941), pp. 30–33.

68. Id. at p. 175.

69. Id. at p. 171.

70. Id. at p. 189.

71. Walter B. Weare, *Black Business in the New South: A Social History of the North Carolina Mutual Life Insurance Company* (Urbana, Ill.: University of Illinois Press, 1973), pp. 4–5.

72. Butler, *Entrepreneurship and Self-Help Among Black Americans*, p. 190.

73. Weare, *Black Business*, p. 180.

18. Political Power

1. 115 S.Ct. 2475 (1995) (applying the strict scrutiny test to racial redistricting).

2. See *John Dillard v. Chilton County Commission*, 699 F.Supp. 870 (M.D. Ala., N.D. 1988).

3. Clint Bolick, "Clinton's Quota Queen," *The Wall Street Journal*, April 30, 1993, p. A10.

4. "A Civil Rights Struggle Ahead," *New York Times*, May 23, 1993, p. 14, col. 1.

5. Neil A. Lewis, "Clinton Faces a Battle Over Civil Rights Nominee," *New York Times*, May 21, 1993, p. B9, col. 3.

6. Id.

7. "A Civil Rights Struggle Ahead," *New York Times*, May 23, 1993, p. 14.

8. See Clint Bolick, "The Legal Philosophy That Produced Lani Guinier," *Wall Street Journal*, June 2, 1993, p. A15. Guinier tells her story in *The Tyranny of the Majority: Fundamental Fairness in Representative Democracy* (New York: Free Press, 1994).

9. See Michael Putzel, "Rights Pick Withdrawn: Clinton Said He Lacked Data on Guinier," *Boston Globe,* June 4, 1993, p. 1.

10. See Lani Guinier, "Keeping the Faith: Black Voters in the Post-Reagan Era," *Harvard Civil Rights-Civil Liberties Law Review* 24 (Spring 1989): 393; Lani Guinier, "The Triumph of Tokenism: The Voting Rights Act and the Theory of Black Electoral Success," *Michigan Law Review* 89 (1991): 1077; Lani Guinier, "The Representation of Minority Interests: The Question of Single Member Districts," *Cardozo Law Review* 14 (1993): 1135.

11. Lani Guinier, "Second Proms and Second Primaries: The Limits of Majority Rule," *Boston Review,* Sept./Oct. 1992, p. 34.

12. Id.

13. Id.

14. Id.

15. See Stephen Engelberg and Katharine Q. Seelye, "Gingrich: Man in Spotlight and Organization in Shadow," *New York Times,* December 18, 1994, § 1, p. 1; Rick Wartzman, "Power of the Purse: Women Are Becoming Big Spenders in Politics and on Social Causes," *Wall Street Journal,* October 17, 1994, p. 1.

Epilogue

1. Christopher Lasch, *The True and Only Heaven* (New York: W. W. Norton & Company, Inc., 1991), p. 403.

2. Martin Luther King Jr., "Letter from a Birmingham Jail," in *Afro-American History: Primary Sources,* Thomas R. Frazier, ed. (New York: Harcourt, Brace & World, Inc. 1970), p. 402.

Index

Academic achievement. *See* Scholastic achievement

Affirmative action, 73; Clinton administration, 35; colleges and universities, 35, 44–45, 235–239; criticism, 80–83; employment, 73–83; first mandate for, 74–75; higher education, 212–213; Public Interest Affirmative Action, 235–239, 240; Reagan administration, 77; voluntary programs, 76, 78–79, 306; women, 35, 79, 80, 82, 236

Affirmative duties, doctrine of, 75

African American history: "Black towns," 122–123, 168–183, 186; Colonial America, 5–6, 157–159; Du Bois, W. E. B., 119, 120, 125, 128–131, 139–140, 186, 222, 273; Farrakhan, Louis, 121, 153–155; Garvey, Marcus, 119–120, 121, 132–142, 146, 186, 200; Liberia, 121–122, 123, 137, 139, 140, 156–167, 186; Malcolm X, 117–118, 120–121, 148–155, 187, 200; miscegenation, 157–158, 211; Muhammad, Elijah, 120, 121, 143–155, 316, 317; Nation of Islam, 120–121, 143–155; post-Civil War, 11, 159–160, 168, 170, 206–207; Washington, Booker T., 119, 125–128, 130–131, 174, 175, 176, 180; World War I, 133–135, 137. *See also* Employment; Migration, domestic; Separatism

African Americans: class differences, 250; color-blind legal principle, 204–213, 243; color discrimination among, 157–158, 185–188, 323; cultural integration, 189, 247–257; income, 35–36, 71–72, 79; intraracial conflicts, 185–188, 323; lawyers, 109–110, 111; miscegenation, 157–158, 211; mulattos, 157–158; nihilism, 54; personal identity (PI) studies, 18–21; poverty, 51–54; progress in last 30 years, 1–2, 17, 105–123; racial romanticism, 123, 141, 188, 190; reference group orientation (RGO) studies, 18–21, 294; role models, 34, 81, 82, 231–232, 264; self-help, 256, 263–269, 284–285; socioeconomic status, 2, 26, 31, 38, 71–72; survival tactics, 253–255; underclass, 105, 250; values, 251–257; work ethic, 251–253, 313. *See also* Class segregation; Colleges and universities; Elementary education; Employment; High schools; Housing; Political power; Private schools; Public schools; Racial pride; Racial segregation; Self-esteem; Voter registration; Voting; Women

African American schools, 221–225; curriculum, 218–219, 228–229; parental involvement, 225–229; principal, 226–227; students, 229–234; teachers, 227–228

African Methodist Episcopal Church, 224, 265–266

African Orthodox Church, 136–137

Agrarian economy, 126, 169–183

Alabama: poverty, 95–96; thwarting the right to vote, 86–90

Aleinikoff, Alexander, 208

Allensworth, Allen, 181–182

Allensworth (CA), 181–183

Allport, F. H., 15

American Colonization Society (ACS), 157–159

Americo-Liberians, 121, 158–159, 186, 323

Anderson v. Martin, 211